NO
FO
ANNUAL 1992-93

EDITED BY BRUCE SMITH

HEADLINE

First published in 1992
by HEADLINE BOOK PUBLISHING PLC

10 9 8 7 6 5 4 3 2 1

Cover photograph: Mike Floate

Gary Blackson of Redbridge Forest dribbles away from trouble in the form of
Colchester United's Steve McGavin during a GM Vauxhall Conference match.

ISBN 0-7472-4033-7

Typeset by Bruce Smith Books Ltd using Quark XPress 3.

Printed and bound in Great Britain by HarperCollins Manufacturing, Glasgow

HEADLINE BOOK PUBLISHING PLC
Headline House
79 Great Titchfield Street
London
W1P 7FN

CONTENTS

Editorial

A moment of madness, a rush of blood, a moment of genius or perhaps a stroke of luck. On such things a season's ambition can be realised or die a forgotten death. The purists will say that such moments of fate even themselves out during the course of a season and for the most part they are right, but occasionally a season throws up a couple of off-beat turning points which are a little out of the ordinary. The double triumph of Colchester United certainly provided two such moments and they fell to the feet and head of goalkeeper Scott Barrett, an ever-present for the U's and my own choice as player of the season. Not content to contribute no fewer than 20 clean sheets in the Essex side's league campaign, he contrived to score a 90th-minute winner at deadly rivals Wycombe when a 1-1 draw looked certain. Those extra two points made the difference when the final whistle blew on the season. With the seconds ticking away at Layer Road, United found themselves trailing 1-2 to Kingstonian in the first round of the Trophy. With a corner awarded for the home side, Barrett raced upfield to head on for Tony English to bundle over the line to equalise and the rest is, as they say, history.

Those two moments highlight a season of high tension both on and off the field. Vauxhall Motors – hardly the most fashionable of sides – ended the 1990-91 season winning promotion to Diadora Division One for the first time in their history. Yet as the players reported back for pre-season training, the parent company decided to fold the football club to make way for a new astro-based sports club. How ironic that before the year was out GM would be the first ever sponsors of a national FA competition – £30,000 being ploughed into the FA Vauxhall Challenge Trophy.

Motors were not the only club to strike out as the season unfolded and more are likely to follow. However, several famous old names are on the way back including South Liverpool and Romford – the latter holding fond memories for me personally. But while some clubs fold, others are devoured and Dagenham FC followed in the path of Leytonstone, Ilford and Walthamstow Avenue when the inevitable became reality on 1 July with the amalgamation of Redbridge Forest and Dagenham to form Dagenham and Redbridge FC. The new club is playing in the Conference, but how long will it be until Dagenham fades into obscurity?

But from mergers new vibrant football life can be born. In no case is this better illustrated than with Wingate-Finchley FC. Wingate, without a home for over ten years, found one at Summers Lane with a Finchley club faced with bankruptcy. The result is a marvellous ground complete with computerised watering systems and a club house and player facilities the envy of many League clubs. Despite an obscene bank balance, the club remains loyal to its principles and remains totally amateur. A trip to North London for a South Midlands League game is not to be missed.

Without doubt, though, the main talking point of the season has been the decision of the FA of Wales to introduce its own national league which has forced many of our major Non-League clubs to move or face certain extinction. The aspects of this are discussed later, but the close season has seen the Non-League game go through its biggest upheaval since the introduction of the Conference and the establishment of the Pyramid of Football.

The FA of Wales also found themselves in controversy over their handling of matters in the Manweb Cymru Alliance. Welshpool completed their season as champions with 67 points, having led the table all season and suffering just three defeats in the process. However, it transpired that they had fielded an ineligible player in each of their 30 games and were docked three points per game in which the player appeared – a total of 66 points leaving the club on just one point! Their subsequent appeal was turned down and Caersws won three of their last six games to take the title!

On the playing side, Woking and Stalybridge both went one better than their respective runners-up spots in the Diadora and HFS Loans Leagues last season by some distance. Both look likely to make impacts in the Conference. Bromsgrove Rovers put in a late burst to take the Beazer Homes League title when VS Rugby and Dover looked the more likely.

For the second season in succession, the FA Trophy final was totally eclipsed by its lesser cousin, the FA Vase. Wimborne and Guiseley produced a real treat that would have graced the FA Cup final. What a pity that this final, which produced some of the best games Wembley has seen in recent years, stays off the TV screens. Perhaps Sky Sports or Channel 4 can rectify that soon.

Once again, the FA Cup threw up some fascinating games and created new heroes around the country. For sheer excitement there cannot have been a better match than Farnborough v Torquay. The £200,000 Town collected from their Cup run will help provide much-needed refurbishment at Cherrywood Road.

From death comes life and Aldershot Town begin their climb up the Pyramid of Football as a Diadora League Division Three club. The system will allow them to return from whence they came should they have the desire. The inclusion of Wycombe in the Football League as Aldershot FC's replacement is a non-starter as it will be for any clubs with ambitions at the expense of another. Football will have us believe that these are hard times. What sums are available must go as far as possible – a newer, streamlined Football League is inevitable. Natural wastage is the obvious route. How ironic that the money currently being poured in to the game by TV cannot be funnelled to help those who play the game.

Screaming in the Valleys

There are of course two sides to any argument, but the FA of Wales have shown in their attitude to many of their affiliated clubs that they have little regard to their personal views on the matter and indeed those of their supporters. While the underlying reasons behind their need to create a national league are sound and in principle highly commendable, their rules of combat in applying them have been double-handed. A League of Wales can be nothing if it does not contain Cardiff, Swansea and Wrexham – and it will not contain Merthyr Tydfil for the next five years at least, and not at all if they obtain English Football League status. But while the rules have been made for the uppercrust clubs, those below in the Beazer and HFS Loans League have been forced to leave their ancestral homes to relocate in an English county or to buckle down and toe the country line.

Thus, for the 1992-93 season, we will see no more the likes of Rhyl or Newtown while clubs such as Newport, Barry and Colwyn Bay will be playing from their new, adopted homes of Gloucester City, Worcester City and Northwich Victoria.

And what of their fans? Have national considerations deprived them of a higher grade of football or has the clubs' selfishness deprived them of a home town football team? Perhaps both. Then again, won't the followers of Welsh football now see a higher grade of football? Perhaps, if the clubs will be able to keep their quality players. I doubt this will happen and so there will be losers all round.

But why a League of Wales in the first place? There are several reasons: to provide a national identity (after all England, Scotland and Ireland have their own leagues), to give Wales three teams in Europe (European Cup, Cup-Winners' Cup and UEFA Cup) and to aid the long-term development of Welsh football. The FA of Wales has also found itself under other pressure, in particular from FIFA, where the emerging African nations have been extremely vociferous in claiming that Britain should be allowed only one entry in international competitions (this is also a reason why no British team is entered in the Olympic soccer tournament). When this particular item was last on FIFA's agenda it was only just defeated and four European countries also voted with the Africans and South Americans.

However, over the past year FIFA have also made a rod for their own backs and set the FA of Wales a very clear precedent. Wales has its own identity every bit as much as San Marino, Faroe Islands, Liechtenstein and the various new members of UEFA from the old Soviet Union such as Lithuania and Latvia, just as the republics from Yugoslavia and Czechoslovakia will surely follow.

There has been much talking and negotiating among the clubs concerned during the past 12 months. The most outspoken of the clubs have, to their great credit, stood by their initial outrage. Colwyn Bay, Caernarfon, Barry and Newport have all moved to new homes in English counties to enable them to carry on. Alan Banks of Colwyn Bay said from the off that the club would rather fold than enter into a League of Wales. The club's poll of its supporters came out 317 to seven in favour of such a stand. Things were equally decisive at Caernarfon where a poll came down 96 percent in favour of staying put. At Newport the voting went 369 to four in favour of the Pyramid and at Barry there was a full 100 percent support behind the club. The problem is that these are the views of the supporters – which count for nothing.

But the clubs are not just being bloody-minded about the whole affair – they wish to maintain standards which will undoubtedly fall with such a move. It is the standard of soccer that attracts the standard of player and ambitious players are unlikely to move into a dead-end league. There are also the communication problems within Wales, which make journeys into massive treks. Colwyn Bay were drawn against Briton Ferry in the Welsh Cup last season and faced a six-hour journey each way at a cost to the club of some £600.

Some ground was made when the Welsh Football League clubs realised that their futures were in the melting pot. Should Wrexham finish bottom of the League, they would be faced not with relegation into the GMVC but into the League of

Wales and obscurity. Merthyr's campaigning has done some good and again the FA of Wales have bent the rules for one of their more prominent clubs, allowing them five years' grace to either gain promotion to the Football League or move into the League of Wales at the end of the period.

There have been casualties. Rhyl have said publicly that they could not sustain a team in the League of Wales, but they have resigned from the HFS Loans League to join it and braced themselves for a mass exodus of players. Bangor and Newtown have also followed suit.

The FA of Wales say that they have to exercise control over their leading clubs, but all they have done is to use oppression. There has been clear discrimination against Non-League football, as the three League clubs have not been forced into leaving the Pyramid, while Merthyr, on the fringes of the Football League, have been given the opportunity to make themselves safe. No one argues against the principles behind a League of Wales – but very clearly it has all boiled down to being one rule for the rich...

The Pyramid of Football

In a perfect world the Pyramid would not need explaining. A club would simply move up and down the regional arms of the tree-like structure and, like water, find its own level as its playing resources dictated. However, it is not a perfect world and there remains a great deal of confusion about the mechanics of it all. What follows is a summary of the system as it works now.

About Promotion

A club will only be promoted to a higher division if it has a ground and facilities that are acceptable to the division which the club is proposing to join. If this is not the case, then the club will probably not be promoted even though it may have won all its games and not conceded a goal all season. Like it or not, that is generally the way it is. But clubs should not complain because these facts are normally spelled out in league rules. Now, this contentious rule – which I believe is the correct one – is sometimes bent if a club can convince the league that work required to make the grade will be in place for the start of the following season. If the champion club cannot achieve, or does not want, promotion then the invitation may be extended to another club, generally the runners-up, but not always.

The Conference champion club is invited to join the Football League Third Division. It is unlikely that the winners would ever wish to decline such an invitation, but if they did the invitation would not – unless the Football League was looking to expand its numbers – be extended to a second or third placed club.

A club coming down into the GMVC must notify the Conference of its intention to play in the Conference before the AGM. There has not been relegation from the Football League for the past two seasons, though it is due to commence again at the end of the 1992-93 season.

Below the GMVC, the Pyramid branches into three distinct chains. These are headed by the Northern Premier League, the Southern League and the Isthmian

League. These are the correct names of the leagues as each is a limited company. However, they are more commonly known by their sponsors' names which are currently HFS Loans, Beazer Homes and Diadora respectively.

The rules of the Conference allow for a maximum of three clubs to be relegated to these three arms. In the past two seasons, no club has been relegated from the Football League and thus only two clubs have been relegated to the lower divisions. This can, and often does, have a knock-on effect right down the leagues.

A club may also escape relegation if a side capable of being promoted does not meet the criteria for grounds and facilities as outlined. This again applies all the way down the Pyramid and is one of the reasons why confirmation of promotion and relegation may not take place until two or three weeks after the end of the season.

Clubs being relegated from one league to another are normally relegated to the league from whence they came. This solves the dilemma of whether a club in the south is relegated from the Conference to either the Southern or Isthmian Leagues.

But there can be another spanner in the works here. Everything is fine so long as the bottom three clubs are ultimately dropping into the Premier Divisions of the Northern, Southern and Isthmian. But what if the bottom three clubs all come from the North? They cannot be shifted into either the Southern or Isthmian and so they can only go into the Northern Premier League. Once again, this has a knock-on effect such that clubs lower down the Pyramid may not be promoted to allow for it.

However, such drastic action may not happen because, in such a circumstance, the Joint Management Committee (made up of members of the Conference, Northern Premier, Southern and Isthmian Leagues) would almost certainly endeavour to shift clubs from one league to another.

For example, a club based in Derbyshire and playing in the Northern Premier League may be asked/compelled to play in the Southern League for the new season. A similar movement may take place between the Southern and Isthmian Leagues should relegation prove problematic.

Clearer – Just!

Below the Premier Divisions of the three major regional leagues things remain a little clearer, for a while. Firstly, promotion and relegation between the regional leagues' divisions is relatively straightforward, but again subject to ground grading.

Two clubs are transferred between the Premier and First Divisions of the NPL in normal circumstances three clubs are transferred between the Premier Division and between Divisions One, Two and Three of the Isthmian. The champions and runners-up in the Southern League's Southern and Midlands divisions are promoted and the bottom four in the Southern League's Premier are relegated.

These relegated clubs will go into the appropriate regional division. If a club is geographically located such that it must go into the Midlands Division, for example, then it would be switched from the Midlands to the Southern Division.

From this point on there is no automatic promotion to the Southern and Isthmian Leagues. Leagues apply to be affiliated to a particular arm of the Pyramid which is normally defined by their geographical position. Feeder leagues to the Isthmian League include the South Midlands, Combined Counties, Essex and London

Spartan Leagues. Clubs in these leagues – which are still classed as senior leagues – may apply to join the Isthmian League.

As two clubs only are relegated from the Isthmian League, only two of four clubs have a chance of being successful. The expectant clubs have to present their case and, of course, have the correct facilities, etc.

This set-up is mirrored for the Northern Premier and Southern Leagues. Which clubs – if any – get promoted is decided by the League. It may be that only one or perhaps none are accepted and, as such, the relegated clubs are reprieved.

Continuing the Isthmian scenario, there now comes a series of additional leagues which are not normally classified as Senior. These are the Herts County, Chiltonian, Middlesex and Surrey and clubs in these can apply to join their appropriate feeder leagues. For example, a Herts County League club might apply to join the South Midlands and a Chiltonian the Combined Counties League. The rules of acceptance are the same.

The Northern Premier League has a slightly more balanced set-up in that there is automatic promotion (grounds permitting) into the First Division from the North West Counties, Northern Counties East and Northern Leagues for one club, with three coming down from the First Division. The Northern League arm of the Pyramid only came into operation this season and again there is automatic promotion for Northern Alliance and Vaux Wearside League clubs that feed into it.

The application and acceptance criteria apply to the other two leagues.

Of course, not all leagues are in the system but several – such as the Leicestershire Senior League – are looking to join as soon as possible. The Pyramid is not as clear-cut as one might have first thought and it is perhaps not surprising that there is a good deal of confusion.

Acknowledgments

As with the first edition of this Annual there are many to thank for their help. None more so than **Phil Heady** whose contribution has been considerable. The club and league histories and club positions are entirely his doing and are, I believe, a major contribution to the completed product. Phil also helped research appearance details. Thank you to those club secretaries and programme editors who helped him!

Considerable thanks are also due to the various league secretaries and publicity officers and agencies for sending bulletins and information on request, in particular to Peter Hunter and Scott and Jones (GMVC), Alan Turvey and Nick Robinson (Diadora), Dennis Strudwick (BHL) and Duncan Bayley (HFS). Thanks also to Phil Bradley for the HFS Loans report and his input to HFS Loans section and also to Jon Weaver for Beazer Homes League information and to Ian Marshall my Editor at Headline.

They are last in this list but probably should be top – Steve Clark and Sue Ball at the FA Competitions Department who go out of their way to be helpful. I hope that the FA and the clubs they handle know how lucky they are.

Bruce Smith, PO Box 382, St Albans, Herts, AL2 3JD.

About Your Playfair

A lot of hard thought went into the contents of this Annual and the format of the information contained within. As a small pocket-sized book it has been designed to be an aid to the Non-League supporter on the move and, as such, much of its contents are fairly contemporary in nature. But, as an adjunct to that, we also felt it necessary to provide some historical background that would be informative, innovative and be capable of settling some of those odd, but quite friendly, arguments that raise their heads on the terraces from time to time.

Your Playfair is divided into three quite distinct sections for ease of reference. Each of these is described briefly below, along with the conventions used.

FA Competitions

This section provides full match details for all the FA competitions. This includes: FA Cup, FA Trophy, FA Vase, FA Sunday Cup and the England Semi-Pro International scene. In most instances, match results and attendances are given, with scorers for the final stages of the competition. The FA Cup is covered until the Non-League interest is exhausted.

Where replay details are listed, unless otherwise specified, the replay took place at the home of the team who were originally drawn away.

Final line-ups and scorer details are provided for previous Trophy and Vase finals along with all England Semi-Pro matches.

Club Guide

The club guide is arranged by league and overall the same format is adhered to throughout. For the GMVC and all Premier Division clubs in the three feeder leagues, a brief club history is provided along with a complete five-year playing record. Thus you can see instantly how consistent a team has been in recent years.

For the Conference sides, league appearances, substitutions and goalscorers are listed along with the clubs' major achievements past and present.

In addition to acrostic results grids for all the leagues in the main Pyramid section, attendance grids are given for the GMVC and Premier Division games of the three feeders.

GM Vauxhall Conference

This section provides full details on the 1991-92 GMVC campaign. In addition to listing scorers it also provides full attendance grids. Each club is allocated a page and league appearance, substitute and goalscoring details are also listed, including those for the promoted and relegated sides. Club histories by necessity are brief. The five-year playing records provide a useful indication of recent club form and the notations used are listed below.

Beazer, Diadora, HFS Homes Leagues

Each of the three main feeders into the Conference are given similar treatment. However, club histories and five-year playing records are limited to those clubs participating in the Premier Division of each league.

11

League Tables

The third and final section of your Playfair contains final tables from all the major regional leagues that in general supply clubs to the Beazer, Diadora and HFS Loans Leagues. There are a few exceptions to this and these tables are listed under a separate heading.

Notations Used

Five-year playing record: P, matches played; W, matches won; D, matches drawn; F, goals for; A, goals against; Pts, points; Psn, final league position; Cup, round reached in FA Cup (Pr, preliminary round; q, qualifying round); FAT, round reached in FA Trophy (Pr, preliminary round; q, qualifying round). If a club competed in the FA Vase the details appear in brackets and with a V.

Leagues: CONF, GM Vauxhall Conference; VLP, Vauxhall League Premier Division; VL1, Vauxhall League First Division; VL2S, Vauxhall League Division Two South; VL2N, Vauxhall League Division Two North; DLP, Diadora League Premier Division; DL1, Diadora League First Division; HFSP, HFS Loans Premier Division; HFS1, HFS Loans First Division; NPLP, Northern Premier League Premier Division; NLP1, Northern Premier League First Division; BHLP, Beazer Homes League Premier Division; BHLM, Beazer Homes League Midland Division; BHLS, Beazer Homes League Southern Division; NCEP, Northern Counties East League Premier Division; NWC1, North West Counties League First Division; NL1, Northern League First Division; WSX, Wessex League; MC, Midland Combination.

Ground: Where capacities are given the value in brackets is the seating capacity. With respect to records the following abbreviations are used: f.o., floodlight opening; g.o., ground opening.

Miscellaneous: na, not available; tba, to be announced.

Disclaimer

In a book of this type it is inevitable that some errors will creep in. Non-League football also suffers heavily with movement of managers, players, etc during the close season. While every effort has been made to ensure that the details given in this annual are correct at the time of going to press, neither the editor nor the publishers can accept any responsibilities for errors within.

FA CUP 1991-92

Fabulous Farnborough!

It was another classic year for the FA Cup minnow. Rarely in recent years have the Non-League fraternity thrown up successive campaigns of glory, so I was expecting a quiet time. Not so thanks to the outstanding exploits of Ted Pearce's Farnborough and another wonderful Woking performance. Then there were Kettering, Emley and little Lincoln United of the Central Midlands League.

Woking – a name to make every WBA supporter cringe – reached the third round for the second successive season and gave opponents Hereford the fright of their lives across their two games. Perhaps the best thing that can be said about the. West Country side was that they gave a professional performance in the two games, but it was the Cardinals who played the football and would have reached the fourth round again had a god smiled on them for even the briefest of moments.

In the first round proper, the meeting of Kettering and Wycombe provided two classic games in an electric atmosphere, first at Rockingham Road and then at Adams Park. It was no surprise when the Poppies won at Maidstone in the next, but they bowed out gracefully at Blackburn in the third.

Hayes and Crawley fought out their own local encounter before the Sussex side travelled to Brighton and completed their run £50,000 to the good. Double champions Colchester, in hindsight, may have been helped by their first round exit at Exeter, and they go into the record books as the first Non-League club to be knocked out of the FA Cup on penalties.

While the glamour of the FA Cup makes it possible for Non-League clubs to be thrown a financial lifeline, just stumping up the cash to pay for the entry in the first place can be a bit of a problem. Thus it was for Lincoln United of the Central Midlands League. Secretary Keith Weaver takes up the story: "We were discussing which cups to enter, we hadn't entered the FA Cup for a while and the £75 entry fee was causing a problem and so four committee members dug into their own pockets to provide the £125 to enter the FA Cup and Vase." United's run included a 3-1 home win over HFS side Gainsborough Trinity, followed by a 2-0 win over Oakham United. In the next round, Lincoln disposed of Frickley Athletic 3-2, after a 0-0 draw, before beating Leek Town 2-0. The dream ended in the first round proper of the competition with a 6-0 drubbing at Huddersfield.

But the 1991-92 Cup run was that of Farnborough Town, a club managed since 1970 by Ted Pearce, when at the age of 28 he also played at the local recreation ground. The changing rooms of Upton Park are a long way from the huddle of players behind the nets two decades ago. But Boro' didn't just give West Ham a game, "they frightened the life out of them" to rephrase Hammers boss Billy Bonds and came within a whisker of beating them in both games. Indeed, it needed an 89th-minute goal in the replay to separate the two sides.

Clubs Exempt to the Fourth Qualifying Round – 1991-92

Atherstone United	Farnborough Town	Sutton United
Altrincham	Halesowen Town	Telford United
Aylesbury United	Hayes	Welling United
Barrow	Leek Town	Whitley Bay
Bishop Auckland	Merthyr Tydfil	Witton Albion
Chorley	Runcorn	Yeovil Town
Colchester United	Stafford Rangers	

Non-League Clubs Exempt to First Round Proper – 1991-92

Trophy Finalists 90-91:	Kidderminster Harriers	Wycombe Wanderers
Most appropriate:	Woking	

Preliminary Round – 31 August 1991

Home		Away	Res	Att.	Replay	
Alnwick Town	v	Chester-le-Street	4-3	85		
Arlesey Town	v	Clapton	0-1	55		
Armthorpe Welfare	v	Vauxhall GM	1-1	47	2-1†	28
Arnold Town	v	Belper Town	0-2	222	*(at Belper)*	
Ashington	v	Crook Town	3-1	58		
Ashton United	v	Rhyl	0-0	320	0-1	435
Aveley	v	Felixstowe Town	2-0	95		
Banbury United	v	Stratford Town	4-1	226		
Barkingside	v	Baldock Town	1-1	45	0-5	215
Barry Town	v	Ton Pentre	3-1	381		
Barton Rovers	v	Bourne Town	3-4	138		
Basildon United	v	Brimsdown Rvrs	0-1†	51		
Beckenham Town	v	Wingate & Fin	1-0	43		
Bideford	v	Falmouth Town	2-3	185		
Blackpool (wren) Rovers	v	Thackley	3-2	97		
Boston	v	Harrogate Town	2-3	65		
Bournemouth	v	Abingdon Town	1-2	92		
Bracknell Town	v	Portfield	2-2	50	1-2†	114
Braintree Town	v	Bury Town	2-1	275		
Brandon United	v	Shotton Comrades	7-1	103		
Bridgend Town	v	Chippenham Town	2-0	55		
Bridlington Town	v	Evenwood Town	5-1	225		
Buckingham Town	v	Abingdon United	1-0	137		
Burnham	v	Feltham & HB	1-1	95	4-0	150
					(at Windsor & Eton)	
Burscough	v	Leyland DAF			*walkover for Burscough*	
Calne Town	v	Westbury United	1-2	105		
Canterbury City	v	Arundel	1-0	61		
Canvey Island	v	Harwich & Park'n	0-2	130		
Chalfont St Peter	v	Flackwell Heath	2-0	60		
Chard Town	v	Witney Town	1-2	149		
Chatham Town	v	Steyning Town	1-3	77		

Home		Away	Res	Att.	Replay	
Chertsey Town	v	Worthing	2-2	143	1-4	215
Cheshunt	v	Tilbury	0-3	52		
Chichester City	v	Chipstead	1-3	215		
Clandown	v	Ilfracombe Town	1-3	24		
Clitheroe	v	Langley Park	4-4	90	1-1†	180
(replay at Clitheroe)					0-1	113
Collier Row	v	Saffron Walden Town	2-2	95	3-2	125
Consett	v	Willington	5-0	120		
Corinthian	v	Merstham	6-0	44		
Cove	v	Slade Green	2-1	74		
Croydon	v	Darenth Heathside	3-0	66	*(at Darenth H.)*	
Cwmbran Town	v	Paulton Rovers	1-0	78		
Darlington CB	v	Horden CW	3-2	31		
Darwen	v	Hebburn	1-1	96	1-2	—
Dawlish Town	v	Maesteg Park	1-2	84		
Desborough Town	v	Vauxhall Motors		*(Vauxhall Motors withdrew)*		
Dudley Town	v	Lincoln United	1-4	143		
Dulwich Hamlet	v	Harefield United	2-1	107		
Durham City	v	South Bank	4-0	82		
East Thurrock Utd	v	Royston Town	1-0	123		
Eastwood Town	v	Farsley Celtic	2-4	179		
Edgware Town	v	Southall	4-0	138		
Egham Town	v	Wembley	0-1	76		
Epsom & Ewell	v	Walton & Hers	1-5	143		
Esh Winning	v	Netherfield	1-3	55		
Evesham United	v	Rothwell Town	3-1	153		
Fareham Town	v	Thatcham Town	1-5	112		
Faversham Town	v	Eastbourne Town	0-0	150	3-0	214
(Replay at Eastbourne United)						
Ford United	v	Hornchurch	2-1	63		
Frome Town	v	Exmouth Town	3-1	87		
Garforth Town	v	Whickham	4-1	92		
Glastonbury	v	Keynsham Town	1-0	80		
Gosport Borough	v	Clevedon Town	1-3	158		
Grantham Town	v	Ilkeston Town	1-5	1402		
Great Harwood Tn	v	Eccleshill United	6-0	111		
Halstead Town	v	Hoddesdon Town	3-2	120		
Hampton	v	Haywards Heath T	3-0	143		
Haringey Borough	v	Watton United	5-0	35		
Harworth CI	v	Maltby MW	2-1	90		
Hednesford Town	v	Northampton Spencer	1-1	470	1-1	146
					1-0	771
Hertford Town	v	Northwood	3-2	82		
Highgate United	v	Chasetown	0-3	45		
Hinckley	v	Bridgnorth Town	2-4	90		
Hinckley Town	v	Boldmere St Mic's	3-1	153		
Hitchin Town	v	Tiptree United	1-1	343	0-1	143

15

Home		Away	Res	Att.	Replay	
Holbeach United	v	Hinckley Athletic	2-3	56		
Horsham	v	Hungerford Town	2-1	115		
Horsham YMCA	v	Erith & Belvedere	1-2	58		
Hythe Town	v	Croydon Athletic	4-4	253	1-2	91
Irlam Town	v	Curzon Ashton	0-0	30	1-4	152
Irthlingboro Diamonds	v	Wednesfield	2-2	72	3-3	140
					1-2	174
King's Lynn	v	Haverhill Rovers	5-2	411		
Knowsley United	v	Atherton LR	5-1	67		
Lancaster City	v	Winsford United	1-5	139		
Lancing	v	Wick	4-1	139		
Langney Sports	v	Southwick	0-1	179		
Leatherhead	v	Corinthian Casuals	3-1	130		
Leighton Town	v	Kingsbury Town	3-2	120		
Letchworth GC	v	Potton United	1-1	99	0-2	155
Lewes	v	Three Bridges	4-3	104		
Leyton Wingate	v	Eynesbury Rovers	6-0	107		
Liversedge	v	Maine Road	3-1	108		
Malvern Town	v	Halesowen Har's	3-2	66		
March Town United	v	Histon	1-1	175	1-2†	128
Melksham Town	v	Welton Rovers	1-1	80	2-1	170
Metropolitan Police	v	Hastings Town	2-4	72		
Mirrlees Blackstone	v	Great Yarmouth Town	2-1	80		
Molesey	v	Ringmer	3-0	25		
Newbury Town	v	Horndean	1-0	78		
Newcastle Town	v	Ossett Albion	2-0	142		
Newmarket Town	v	Biggleswade Town	1-1	103	2-2†	186
					0-1	271
Newtown	v	Glossop	4-2	176		
Oakwood	v	Havant Town	0-3	50		
Oldbury United	v	Blakenall	1-2	70		
Ossett Town	v	North Ferriby Utd	2-0	185		
Penrith	v	Ferryhill Athletic	1-0	103		
Prescot AFC	v	Chadderton	3-2	94		
Prudhoe East End	v	Bedlington Ter.	0-2	55		
Purfleet	v	Gorleston	3-1	79		
Radcliffe Borough	v	Nantwich Town	0-1	129		
Radstock Town	v	Devizes Town	0-2	65		
Rainham Town	v	Lowestoft Town	0-1	179		
(at Lowestoft Town)						
RC Warwick	v	Rushall Olympic	2-1	150		
Rocester	v	Oakham United	1-3	125		
Rossendale United	v	Heanor Town	2-4	220		
Rushden Town	v	Friar Lane OB	3-2	222		
St Blazey	v	Minehead	0-3	97		
St Helens Town	v	Borrowash Vic.	1-3	90		
Salford City	v	Warrington Town	0-0	115	0-1	194

Home		Away	Res	Att.	Replay	
Sandwell Borough	v	Alfreton Town	1-2	45		
Seaham Red Star	v	Peterlee Newtown	3-2	70		
Selsey	v	Malden Vale	2-1	105		
Sheffield	v	Congleton Town	2-0	67		
Sholing Sports	v	Maidenhead United	0-6	127		
Shoreham	v	Sheppey United	0-3	65		
Shortwood United	v	Weston-Super-Mare	3-0	156		
Solihull Borough	v	Spalding United	1-0	99		
Spennymoor United	v	Easington Colliery	1-0	116		
Stamford Town	v	Paget Rangers	2-1	130		
Stockton	v	Billingham Town	2-4	47		
Stourbridge	v	Long Buckby	1-0	446		
Sudbury Town	v	Barking	2-2	425	2-2†	202
					2-1	591
Tamworth	v	Lye Town	2-2	778	3-1	379
Thame United	v	Eastleigh	1-1	156	2-0	156
Tooting & Mitcham	v	Redhill	2-0	178		
Torrington	v	Barnstaple Town	3-1	250		
Totton AFC	v	Lymington AFC	2-2	126	2-3	119
Tring Town	v	Hemel Hempstead	0-3	70		
Tunbridge Wells	v	Burgess Hill Town	0-2	131		
Walsall Wood	v	Raunds Town	1-1	97	1-3	122
Waltham Abbey	v	Stevenage Boro'	0-1	219		
Walthamstow Pen	v	Langford	3-2	59		
Ware	v	Milton Keynes B	5-1	149		
Washington	v	Shildon	1-3	100		
(at Shildon)						
West Auckland Tn	v	Denaby United	3-5†	90		
Whitstable Town	v	Eastbourne United	0-1	204		
Whyteleafe	v	Ashford Town	2-0	131		
Willenhall Town	v	Wellingborough T	6-1	110		
Wisbech Town	v	Burnham R'blers	4-3	316		
Witham Town	v	Welwyn Garden C	3-1	102		
Wolverton	v	Uxbridge	1-0	93		
Worksop Town	v	Brigg Town	3-1	118		
Yate Town	v	Bristol Manor Frm	4-1	241		
Yeading	v	Rayners Lane	8-0	101		

First Qualifying Round – 14 September 1991

Home		Away	Res	Att.	Replay	
Alfreton Town	v	Hinckley Athletic	1-0	199		
Alnwick Town	v	Brandon United	1-1	135	1-0	182
Annfield Plain	v	North Shields	0-4	198		
APV Peterborough	v	Alvechurch	0-0	47	0-2	181
Ashington	v	Consett	0-4	106		
Aveley	v	Heybridge Swifts	0-2	102		

Home		Away	Res	Att.	Replay	
Banbury United	v	Hednesford Town	2-1	258		
Banstead Athletic	v	Wokingham Town	1-2	121		
Bedworth United	v	Bromsgrove Rovers	0-2	264		
Berkhamsted Town	v	Harrow Borough	3-2	131		
Biggleswade Town	v	Brimsdown Rovers	1-2†	74		
Bishops Stortford	v	Mirrless Blackstone	1-1	242	0-2	204
Blakenall	v	Boston United	1-2	498		
Bootle	v	Newcastle Town	2-1	50		
Borrowash Victoria	v	Belper Town	2-0	173		
Bourne Town	v	Braintree Town	0-3	258		
Bridgend Town	v	Cheltenham Town	3-3	110	0-5	480
Bridgnorth Town	v	Matlock Town	1-2	150		
Bridlington Town	v	Blyth Spartans	3-2	316		
Brockenhurst	v	Dorchester Town	1-2	230		
Buxton	v	Burscough	4-2	355		
Caernarfon Town	v	Colwyn Bay	1-1	342	1-2	795
Camberley Town	v	Marlow	1-3	92		
Chalfont St Peter	v	Nuneaton Borough	0-4	250		
Chasetown	v	Bilston Town	0-0	114	1-0	107
Chesham United	v	Wolverton	2-0	564		
Clacton Town	v	Billericay Town	2-1	230		
Clapton	v	Chelmsford City	1-5	195		
Cleator Moor Celtic	v	Gretna	0-7	142		
Clevedon Town	v	Witney Town	2-2	140	0-1	176
Corby Town	v	Hemel Hempstead	1-0	287		
Corinthian	v	Erith & Belvedere	1-3	109		
Cove	v	Burgess Hill Town	1-1	74	0-4	164
Curzon Ashton	v	Bangor City	1-1	121	2-1	305
Darlington CB	v	Murton	1-3	66		
Dartford	v	Ware	5-1	631		
Denaby United	v	Harrogate RA	1-0	123		
Desborough Town	v	Rushden Town	2-4	200		
Dover Athletic	v	Chipstead	6-0	809		
Dulwich Hamlet	v	Burnham	1-0	138		
Dunston FB	v	Guisborough Town	1-0	140		
Durham City	v	Tow Law Town	1-0	100		
East Thurrock Utd	v	Grays Athletic	1-1	457	1-2	503
Eastbourne United	v	Lewes	1-4	107		
Eastwood Hanley	v	Northwich Victoria	2-1	321		
Enfield	v	Walthamstow Pennant	4-0	412		
Evesham United	v	Malvern Town	2-4	328		
Falmouth Town	v	Minehead	2-0	393		
Farsley Celtic	v	Emley	0-1	425		
Faversham Town	v	Carshalton Athletic	3-2	208		
Fisher Athletic	v	Beckenham Town	4-0	203		
Fleetwood Town	v	Blackpool (wren) Rovers	3-2	298		
Flixton	v	Mossley	1-1	174	1-2	376

18

Home		Away	Res	Att.	Replay	
Ford United	v	Wivenhoe Town	3-1	98		
Glastonbury	v	Trowbridge Town	0-4	381		
Gloucester City	v	Shortwood United	4-1	744		
Goole Town	v	Oakham United	0-1	231		
Gravesend & N'thf't	v	Canterbury City	2-1	336		
Hailsham Town	v	Sheppey United	1-1	146	1-4	182
Halstead Town	v	Baldock Town	2-3	240		
Harlow Town	v	Leyton Wingate	4-1	61	*(at Ware)*	
Harrogate Town	v	Frickley Athletic	2-2	358	3-3	429
(Replay at Harrogate Town)					2-3	382
Harwich & Parkes	v	Potton United	2-1	280		
Harworth CI	v	Droylsden	0-1	200		
Heanor Town	v	Armthorpe Welfare	0-2	167		
Herne Bay	v	Kingstonian	0-2	301		
Hertford Town	v	Staines Town	2-0	112		
Hinckley Town	v	Leicester United	2-0	238		
Horsham	v	Buckingham Town	1-0	225		
Horwich RMI	v	Ilkeston Town	1-0	161		
King's Lynn	v	Cambridge City	3-3	816	2-1†	369
Knowsley United	v	Sheffield	2-0	106		
Lancing	v	Hampton	1-3	135		
Leatherhead	v	Dorking	1-2	370		
Lincoln United	v	Gainsborough Trinity	3-1	319		
Lowestoft Town	v	Boreham Wood	2-1	214		
Lymington AFC	v	Bashley	2-4	433		
Maesteg Park	v	Frome Town	4-0	54		
Mangotsfield Utd	v	Cwmbran Town	4-2	171		
Marine	v	Liversedge	4-0	220		
Molesey	v	Crawley Town	1-5	154		
Moor Green	v	Tamworth	0-3	757		
Morecambe	v	Great Harwood Town	1-0	402		
Netherfield	v	Billingham Synthonia	3-2	130		
Newcastle Blue Star	v	Hebburn	5-1	169		
Newport (IoW)	v	Maidenhead United	0-3	443		
Northallerton Town	v	Langley Park	1-0	71		
Norton & Stockton	v	Guiseley	0-4	89		
Ossett Town	v	Southport	0-1	270		
Pagham	v	Basingstoke Town	1-3	210		
Peacehaven & Tels	v	Hastings Town	2-1	355		
Penrith	v	Billingham Town	4-2	121		
Poole Town	v	Westbury United	3-1	169		
Portfield	v	Havant Town	1-2	160		
Prescot AFC	v	Accrington Stanley	0-5	300		
Purfleet	v	Collier Row	2-2	86	1-0	164
Raunds Town	v	Gresley Rovers	1-1	162	0-2	644
Redbridge Forest	v	Haringey Borough	5-0	244		
Redditch United	v	Edgware Town	5-1	182		

19

Home		Away	Res	Att.	Replay	
Rhyl	v	Newtown	1-0	317		
Romsey Town	v	Newbury Town	2-1	120		
St Austell	v	Liskeard Athletic	2-3	122		
Saltash United	v	Ilfracombe Town	6-0	143		
Seaham Red Star	v	Shildon	3-0	70	1-2	126
(Match ordered replayed – Seaham fielded ineligible player)						
Selsey	v	Andover	2-1	112		
Shepshed Albion	v	Stourbridge	2-0	291		
Skelmersdale United	v	Macclesfield Town	0-4	417		
Slough Town	v	Croydon	2-2	524	3-0	246
Solihull Borough	v	Wednesfield	3-0	209		
Southwick	v	Sittingbourne	1-3	111		
Spennymoor United	v	Bedlington Terriers	0-1	154		
Stalybridge Celtic	v	Worksop Town	4-0	403		
Stevenage Borough	v	Sutton Coldfield Town	0-2	464		
Steyning Town	v	Bognor Regis Town	0-1	197		
Stowmarket Town	v	Hendon	1-4	180		
Stroud	v	Bath City	1-3	272		
Sudbury Town	v	Histon	1-0	504		
Swanage & Herston	v	Waterlooville	1-1	118	0-2	151
Taunton Town	v	Devizes Town	2-0	237		
Thame	v	Abingdon Town	2-0	335		
Thatcham Town	v	Salisbury	1-1	321	0-3	221
Thetford Town	v	St Albans City	0-2	131		
Tilbury	v	Leighton Town	1-1	63	0-1	380
Tiptree United	v	Dagenham	1-0	163		
Tonbridge	v	Croydon Athletic	2-1	352		
Tooting & Mitcham	v	Margate	2-1	255		
Torrington	v	Tiverton Town	2-2	378	2-3†	438
V S Rugby	v	Stamford Town	2-0	550		
Walton & Hersham	v	Littlehampton Town	1-1	247	1-2	391
Warrington Town	v	Hyde United	1-0	290		
Welton Rovers	v	Worcester City	1-8	245		
Wembley	v	Windsor & Eton	1-2	126		
West Midlands Police	v	Burton Albion	0-1	270		
Whitby Town	v	Garforth Town	0-1	244		
Whitehawk	v	Bromley	0-2	135		
Whyteleafe	v	Worthing	1-2	112		
Willenhall Town	v	RC Warwick	2-1	150		
Wimborne Town	v	Weymouth	1-2	302		
Winsford United	v	Nantwich Town	3-0	386		
Wisbech Town	v	Kettering Town	0-3	1017		
Witham Town	v	Wealdstone	1-3	220		
Workington	v	Gateshead	0-1	193		
Yate Town	v	Barry Town	0-3	327		
Yeading	v	Ruislip Manor	3-1	222		

Second Qualifying Round – 28 September 1991

Home		Away	Res	Att.	Replay	
Accrington Stanley	v	Knowsley United	2-2	563	1-2†	343
Alvechurch	v	Malvern Town	3-0	81		
Bashley	v	Maidenhead United	1-1	205	0-1	252
Basingstoke Town	v	Horsham	1-1	261	1-2†	387
Bath City	v	Maesteg Park	5-2	422		
Berkhamsted Town	v	Leighton Town	2-0	243		
Billericay Town	v	Sudbury Town	3-1	472		
Bognor Regis Town	v	Burgess Hill Town	1-2	211		
Boston United	v	Tamworth	1-1	1375	0-1†	1215
Bridlington Town	v	Northallerton Town	4-0	257		
Bromley	v	Worthing	3-1	413		
Bromsgrove Rovers	v	Rushden Town	1-0	472		
Burton Albion	v	Willenhall Town	4-1	401		
Chasetown	v	Banbury United	1-1	147	2-1†	326
Chelmsford City	v	Enfield	1-1	605	1-2	665
Cheltenham Town	v	Taunton Town	8-0	473		
Colwyn Bay	v	Rhyl	2-0	758		
Crawley Town	v	Sheppey United	2-0	241		
Curzon Ashton	v	Buxton	1-0	203		
Denaby United	v	Fleetwood Town	1-0	180		
Dorchester Town	v	Witney Town	3-2	458		
Dorking	v	Gravesend & Northfleet	3-4	185		
Droylsden	v	Bootle	1-1	239	3-1	212
Dunston FB	v	Penrith	2-2	131	6-6†	283
					1-2†	517
Durham City	v	Morecambe	1-4	213		
Eastwood Hanley	v	Armthorpe Welfare	3-2	117		
Emley	v	Horwich RMI	4-2	378		
Faversham Town	v	Dover Athletic	0-0	1157	1-2	1232
Ford United	v	Dartford	0-1	323		
Frickley Athletic	v	Alfreton Town	4-1	360		
Gateshead	v	Alnwick Town	6-0	232		
Grays Athletic	v	Redbridge Forest	3-1	344		
Gresley Rovers	v	VS Rugby	3-3	774	0-3	707
Gretna	v	Bedlington Terriers	3-1	101		
Guiseley	v	Shildon	5-1	662		
Hendon	v	Baldock Town	1-2	209		
Hertford Town	v	Dulwich Hamlet	2-1	134		
Heybridge Swifts	v	Mirrlees Blackstone	1-1	142	1-0	350
Hinckley Town	v	Shepshed Albion	3-3	281	2-3	392
Kettering Town	v	Braintree Town	3-1	1609		
King's Lynn	v	Purfleet	4-2	749		
Kingstonian	v	Lewes	3-2	367		
Lincoln United	v	Oakham United	2-0	200		
Liskeard Athletic	v	Falmouth Town	5-1	286		

Home		Away	Res	Att.	Replay	
Littlehampton Town	v	Hampton	1-3	225		
Lowestoft Town	v	Harwich & Parkeston	1-0	277		
Macclesfield Town	v	Borrowash Victoria	1-2	871		
Marlow	v	Havant Town	2-1	190		
Matlock Town	v	Solihull Borough	2-1	342		
Mossley	v	Winsford United	1-1	342	0-6	359
Murton	v	Garforth Town	3-1	93		
Netherfield	v	Newcastle Blue Star	2-1	188		
North Shields	v	Conset	3-1	142		
Nuneaton Borough	v	Corby Town	1-0	667	0-1†	392
St Albans City	v	Brimsdown Rovers	1-1	338	0-2	186
Salisbury	v	Poole Town	2-0	220		
Selsey	v	Romsey Town	1-6	120		
Sittingbourne	v	Tonbridge	1-2	641		
Southport	v	Stalybridge Celtic	1-2	417		
Sutton Coldfield Town	v	Redditch United	1-3	173		
Tiptree United	v	Harlow Town	0-6	79		
Tiverton Town	v	Saltash United	0-0	278	2-1	379
Tooting & Mitcham U	v	Peacehaven & Tel	2-0	255		
Trowbridge Town	v	Mangotsfield Utd	3-0	455		
Warrington Town	v	Marine	1-1	317	0-1	217
Waterlooville	v	Thame United	3-3	147	2-3†	320
Wealdstone	v	Chesham United	2-4	745		
Weymouth	v	Barry Town	1-1	584	3-2†	455
Windsor & Eton	v	Fisher Athletic	3-2	226		
Wokingham Town	v	Erith & Belvedere	1-2	277		
Worcester City	v	Gloucester City	2-1	904		
Yeading	v	Slough Town	0-0	475	0-1	722

Third Qualifying Round – 12 October 1991

Home		Away	Res	Att.	Replay	
Alvechurch	v	Corby Town	2-0	217		
Baldock Town	v	Dartford	2-2	628	2-1†	701
Bath City	v	Worcester City	1-2	813		
Berkhamsted Town	v	Slough Town	1-4	612		
Billericay Town	v	Enfield	1-3	979		
Borrowash Victoria	v	Emley	0-3	391		
Brimsdown Rovers	v	Chesham United	2-2	412	1-2	585
Bromley	v	Dover Athletic	0-3	1010		
Bromsgrove Rovers	v	Redditch United	2-0	1050		
Burgess Hill Town	v	Gravesend & Northfleet	0-1	341		
Burton Albion	v	Shepshed Albion	3-2	704		
Chasetown	v	VS Rugby	0-0	492	0-3	605
Colwyn Bay	v	Marine	4-3	651		
Dorchester Town	v	Trowbridge Town	1-0	805		
Eastwood Hanley	v	Stalybridge Celtic	1-2	382		

22

Home		Away	Res	Att.	Replay	
Erith & Belevedere	v	Crawley Town	1-2	400		
Frickley Athletic	v	Lincoln United	0-0	477	2-3	802
Gateshead	v	Netherfield	0-0	282	3-0	
Gretna	v	Murton	3-0	143		
Guiseley	v	Denaby United	1-1	691	2-1	735
Hampton	v	Tonbridge	2-2	529	0-3†	1274
(Result after abandoned tie, 2-1, 81 minutes, floodlight failure)						
Hertford Town	v	Windsor & Eton	1-2	280		
Horsham	v	Maidenhead United	1-1	535	1-0	383
Kettering Town	v	Heybridge Swifts	3-0	1587		
King's Lynn	v	Harlow Town	2-3	1305		
Kingstonian	v	Tooting & Mitcham U	0-0	690	3-2	517
Knowsley United	v	Curzon Ashton	2-0	329		
Liskeard Athletic	v	Tiverton Town	1-3	341		
Lowestoft Town	v	Grays Athletic	1-2	679		
Marlow	v	Romsey Town	2-0	315		
Matlock Town	v	Tamworth	0-2	1149		
North Shields	v	Bridlington Town	0-2	237		
Penrith	v	Morecambe	0-3	559		
Thame United	v	Salisbury	0-4	420		
Weymouth	v	Cheltenham Town	4-0	1176		
Winsford United	v	Droylsden	3-2	681		

Fourth Qualifying Round – 26 October 1991

Home		Away	Res	Att.	Replay	
Aylesbury United	v	Chesham United	1-1	1288	3-1	1436
Baldock Town	v	Halesowen Town	1-1	927	0-1	1219
Barrow	v	Bridlington Town	0-1	1268		
Chorley	v	Emley	2-2	664	1-1	1151
(Replay abandoned after 90 mins, fog)					0-1	1380
Colchester Utd	v	Burton Albion	5-0	2147		
Colwyn Bay	v	Morecambe	0-2	781		
Enfield	v	VS Rugby	2-1	698		
Gravesend & Northfleet	v	Harlow Town	1-1	405	0-1	706
Grays Athletic	v	Atherstone United	0-2	517		
Gretna	v	Stalybridge Celtic	3-2	449		
Guiseley	v	Bishop Auckland	2-1	964		
Hayes	v	Dorchester Town	1-0	277		
Horsham	v	Crawley Town	0-0	2208	0-3	3427
Kettering Town	v	Stafford Rangers	0-0	1785	2-0	1070
Leek Town	v	Lincoln United	0-2	730		
Merthyr Tydfil	v	Windsor & Eton	1-1	521	0-1	736
Runcorn	v	Gateshead	1-0	734		
Salisbury	v	Farnborough Town	1-7	808		
Slough Town	v	Kingstonian	2-1	990		
Tamworth	v	Bromsgrove Rovers	0-1	1546		

Home		Away	Res	Att.	Replay	
Telford United	v	Knowsley United	1-0	743		
Tiverton Town	v	Dover Athletic	1-0	756		
Tonbridge	v	Yeovil Town	1-2	1483		
Welling United	v	Alvechurch	5-1	704		
Weymouth	v	Sutton United	1-1	1576	0-3	1039
Whitley Bay	v	Witton Albion	1-4	443		
Winsford United	v	Altrincham	3-2	1133		
Worcester City	v	Marlow	1-2	928		

First Round Proper – 16 November 1991

Home		Away	Res	Att.	Replay	
Aldershot	v	Enfield	0-1	2384		
Atherstone United	v	Hereford United	0-0	2588	0-3	3479
Barnet	v	Tiverton Town	5-0	3964		
Bournemouth	v	Bromsgrove Rovers	3-1	4301		
Bridlington Town	v	York City	1-2	1650		
Chester City	v	Guiseley	1-0	1851		
Colchester United	v	Exeter City	0-0	4965	0-0†	4066
(Exeter City won 4-2 on penalties)						
Crawley Town	v	Northampton Town	4-2	3370		
Emley	v	Bolton Wanderers	0-3	9035		
(at Huddersfield Town)						
Fulham	v	Hayes	0-2	6403		
Gretna	v	Rochdale	0-0	2037	1-3	4300
Halesowen Town	v	Farnborough Town	2-2	1866	0-4	1673
Huddersfield Town	v	Lincoln United	6-0	6763		
Kettering Town	v	Wycombe Wanderers	1-1	3317	2-0	5299
Kidderminster Harriers	v	Aylesbury United	0-1	1773		
Leyton Orient	v	Welling United	2-1	4858		
Maidstone United	v	Sutton United	1-0	2008		
Morecambe	v	Hull City	0-1	2853		
Peterborough United	v	Harlow Town	7-0	4341		
Runcorn	v	Tranmere Rovers	0-3	6563		
(at Tranmere Rovers)						
Slough Town	v	Reading	3-3	3990	1-2	6363
Stoke City	v	Telford United	0-0	9974	1-2	4052
West Brom Albion	v	Marlow	6-0	11,082		
Windsor & Eton	v	Woking	2-4	2534		
(Result after abandoned tie, 1-1, 69 mins, fog)						
Witton Albion	v	Halifax Town	1-1	2002	2-1†	2182
Wrexham	v	Winsford United	5-2	2964		
Yeovil Town	v	Walsall	1-1	4635	1-0†	3869

Second Round Proper – 7 December 1991

Home		Away	Res	Att.	Replay	
Aylesbury United	v	Hereford United	2-3	2913		
Enfield	v	Barnet	1-4	5121		
Hayes	v	Crawley Town	0-2	4203		
Maidstone United	v	Kettering Town	1-2	2765		
Preston North End	v	Witton Albion	5-1	6766		
Torquay United	v	Farnborough Town	1-1	2725	3-4	2285
Woking	v	Yeovil Town	3-0	4250		
Wrexham	v	Telford United	1-0	3897		

Third Round Proper – 7 January 1992

Home		Away	Res	Att.	Replay	
Blackburn Rovers	v	Kettering Town	4-1	13,821		
Brighton & Hove Albion	v	Crawley Town	5-0	18,031		
Farnborough Town (at West Ham)	v	West Ham United	1-1	23,499	0-1	23,869
Woking	v	Hereford United	0-0	4753	1-2†	8679

† after extra time

25

VAUXHALL FA TROPHY 1991-92

Colchester Double Up

The Colchester double was completed with victory at Wembley over a Witton Albion side that never really got into full swing. Backed by 20,000 or so supporters the U's were always in control of a match that never quite sparked into life. Mike Masters' strike after five minutes did much to ensure that the Colchester bandwagon stayed on the road – the confidence that was already there was simply reinforced as the U's smooth passing game never looked like letting the Northwich side back. The goal came from a long throw which player/manger McDonough flicked on and Masters did the same into the far corner of the net over Mason's outstretched hands.

Delightful wing play by Kinsella down the right was completed by Nicky Smith coming in from the left after Kinsella's low cross had evaded everyone including McGavin and Mason. The goal effectively killed the game as a spectacle, though the Cheshire side offered their supporters a glimmer of hope early in the second half when Lutkevitch – one of the smallest players on the pitch – headed home Thomas' cross from six yards. Witton had flattered to deceive in the tail end of the first half, Rose was desperately unlucky, but Barrett was equal to his shot.

McGavin might have made the game safe for Colchester when he raced away on 70 minutes to present Masters with a perfect chance which the American international put against the post.

United were reduced to ten men for the last ten minutes when Jason Cook was rightly sent off for violent play. The decision seemed to act more in the Essex side's favour as they rallied round superbly to snuff out any ideas Witton might have had of a revival. Indeed, with only seconds remaining on the clock, McGavin raced away to crown a fine personal performance with a goal scored from just inside the area to make it 3-1.

What they said:

Steve McGavin: "To turn out in a Wembley cup final with so many supporters behind us was the icing on the cake. They have supported us all season and followed us everywhere. That's reward for them." And of his last-minute strike: "The goalie made it fairly easy for me really. As I ran through he went to one side of the goal and I could see the other side and just slipped it past him."

Ever-present keeper Scott Barrett: "The Witton goal was a little bit upsetting. The guy's whipped in a good cross and their fella's got in front of the marker and just glanced it and it's gone in the far side. It made it a little bit difficult but we showed great strength and character and scored the third with ten men which is a great achievement."

First Qualifying Round – 21 September 1991

Home		Away	Res	Att.	Replay	
Accrington Stanley	v	Whitley Bay	3-2	402		
Alnwick Town	v	Southport	0-5	108		
Alvechurch	v	Gainsborough Trinity	0-1	116		
Andover	v	Bashley	1-2	207		
Barking	v	Rushden Town	4-2	125		
Bideford	v	Newport AFC	0-1	350		
Boreham Wood	v	Aveley	4-1	90		
Brandon United	v	Spennymoor United	1-1	178	0-1	292
Bridgend Town	v	Poole Town	3-1	60		
Bromley	v	Basingstoke Town	3-0	389		
Bromsgrove Rovers	v	Bedworth United	1-1	479	2-1	335
Chalfont St Peter	v	Stourbridge	3-2	80		
Chelmsford City	v	St Albans City	0-1	542		
Chesham United	v	Tamworth	1-0	650		
Congleton Town	v	Atherstone United	0-3	158		
Consett	v	Shildon	0-3	111		
Corby Town	v	Leyton-Wingate	1-3	254		
Cwmbran Town	v	Salisbury	0-1	206	(at Salisbury)	
Dorking	v	Bognor Regis Town	2-1	198		
Dudley Town	v	Redditch United	5-3	154		
Eastwood Town	v	Caernarfon Town	5-1	152		
Erith & Belvedere	v	Walton & Hersham	3-3	155	1-2	172
Ferryhill Athletic	v	Whitley Bay	0-2	124		
Goole Town	v	Warrington Town	2-1	211		
Gosport Borough	v	Croydon	4-1	130		
Grantham Town	v	Buxton	0-2	879		
Hayes	v	Baldock Town	3-1	169		
Hitchin Town	v	Grays Athletic	2-1	325		
Maidenhead United	v	Canterbury City	4-0	198		
Margate	v	Abingdon Town	1-1	318	1-0	437
Molesey	v	Marlow	2-3	82		
Moor Green	v	Radcliffe Borough	5-2	258		
Mossley	v	Alfreton Town	2-3	259		
Nuneaton Borough	v	Marine	0-0	675	2-2	675
					0-1	730
Peterlee Newtown	v	Murton	0-2	65		
Rhyl	v	Halesowen Town	1-1	385	2-1	928
Stevenage Borough	v	Wembley	2-3	333		
Taunton Town	v	Maesteg Park	6-2	245		
Ton Pentre	v	Barry Town	2-3	391		
Trowbridge Town	v	Dorchester Town	1-1	608	2-3	735
Uxbridge	v	Tooting & Mitcham United	1-2	96		
Vauxhall Motors	v	Staines Town	(walkover for Staines Town)			
Waterlooville	v	Crawley Town	3-2	197		
Weston-super-Mare	v	Saltash United	2-2	270	3-5†	227
Whickham	v	North Shields	1-2	220		

Home		Away	Res	Att.	Replay	
Whitby Town	v	*Newcastle Blue Star*	2-1	200		
Willenhall Town	v	*Colwyn Bay*	3-1	117		
Winsford United	v	*Newtown*	3-0	246		
Workington	v	*Northallerton Town*	2-2	131	0-4	163
Worksop Town	v	*Matlock Town*	1-1	149	3-3	537
					0-2	614
Yeading	v	*Fareham Town*	2-1	122		

Second Qualifying Round – 19 October 1991

Home		Away	Res	Att.	Replay	
Accrington Stanley	v	Shildon	5-2	416		
Alfreton Town	v	Atherstone United	0-3	197		
Barking	v	Chalfont St Peter	0-2	104		
Barry Town	v	Bridgend Town	2-0	217		
Bashley	v	Ashford Town	3-1	207		
Bishops Stortford	v	Boreham Wood	1-1	254	1-0	136
Bromley	v	Maidenhead United	2-0	266		
Bromsgrove Rovers	v	Hednesford Town	1-0	648		
Buxton	v	Moor Green	1-3	346		
Chesham United	v	Leyton-Wingate	1-0	532		
Dorking	v	Yeading	2-1	155		
Droylsden	v	Winsford United	1-1	347	3-1	454
Dudley Town	v	Shepshed Albion	2-1	114		
Eastwood Town	v	Rhyl	1-2	111		
Goole Town	v	Marine	1-3	251		
Gosport Borough	v	Marlow	0-2	133		
Hitchin Town	v	St Albans City	2-3	430		
Leicester United	v	Gainsborough Trinity	1-0	140		
Llanelli	v	Dorchester Town	1-3	144		
Newport AFC	v	Saltash United	5-4	521		
Northallerton Town	v	Whitley Bay	0-0	112	3-2†	420
Salisbury	v	Taunton Town	4-1	212		
Southport	v	North Shields	4-1	315		
Spennymoor United	v	Easington Colliery	1-2	122		
Staines Town	v	Heybridge Swifts	0-1	174		
Sutton Coldfield Town	v	Hayes	2-0	136		
Tooting & Mitcham Utd	v	Dulwich Hamlet	3-0	255		
Waterlooville	v	Walton & Hersham	1-1	135	0-4	198
Wembley	v	Harlow Town	0-0	58	1-0	54
Whitby Town	v	Murton	5-1	140		
Whyteleafe	v	Margate	1-2	118		
Willenhall Town	v	Matlock Town	2-3	142		

Third Qualifying Round – 30 November 1991

Home		Away	Res	Att.	Replay	
Atherstone United	v	Heybridge Swifts	1-1	345	1-0	245
Bashley	v	Carshalton Athletic	2-0	453		
Billingham Synthonia	v	Droylsden	4-1	127		
Blyth Spartans	v	Accrington Stanley	4-0	574		
Bromley	v	Weymouth	1-0	481		
Burton Albion	v	Chesham United	0-0	503	0-4	539
Chorley	v	Frickley Athletic	0-2	203		
Dagenham	v	St Albans City	3-2	454		
Dorking	v	Barry Town	2-1	256		
Dudley Town	v	Worcester City	2-3	308		
Fisher Athletic	v	Bromsgrove Rovers	1-1	—	0-2	624
Fleetwood Town	v	Seaham Red Star	4-0	161		
Gravesend & Northfleet	v	Marlow	1-3	383		
Harrow Borough	v	Bishops Stortford	2-1	285		
Hendon	v	Wealdstone	0-0	427	1-4	367
Horwich RMI	v	Marine	1-3	183		
Kingstonian	v	Dorchester Town	3-0	446		
Moor Green	v	Boston United	1-3	408		
Morecambe	v	Emley	2-2	522	4-2	512
Northallerton Town	v	Matlock Town	4-2	141		
Rhyl	v	Southport	0-3	334		
Slough Town	v	Margate	0-0	663	2-1	482
South Bank	v	Bangor City	1-1	521	0-1	284
(at Middlesbrough FC)						
Stroud	v	Newport AFC	1-3	463		
Sutton Coldfield Town	v	Cambridge City	2-1	184		
Tooting & Mitcham Utd	v	Walton & Hersham	0-0	239	1-2	258
Tow Law Town	v	Bishop Auckland	0-3	304		
VS Rugby	v	Leicester United	2-1	545		
Wembley	v	Chalfont St Peter	2-0	54		
Whitby Town	v	Easington Colliery	1-0	193		
Windsor & Eton	v	Sutton United	2-2	353	2-4	481
Wokingham Town	v	Salisbury	0-0	357	0-1	274

First Round Proper – 11 January 1992

Home		Away	Res	Att.	Replay	
Altrincham	v	Stalybridge Celtic	1-2	1256		
Atherstone United	v	Dorking	1-3	401		
Aylesbury United	v	Newport AFC	3-2	870		
Bangor City	v	Gretna	0-0	413	2-1	301
Blyth Spartans	v	Gateshead	0-0	1230	0-3†	920
(Replay at Blyth Spartans FC)						
Bromley	v	Worcester City	1-0	518		
Cheltenham Town	v	Wealdstone	3-2	768		
Colchester United	v	Kingstonian	2-2	2724	3-2	1642

29

Home		Away	Res	Att.	Replay	
Dagenham	v	Bashley	0-0	549	0-2	440
Enfield	v	Slough Town	4-0	670		
Fleetwood Town	v	Morecambe	1-1	412	0-1	452
Frickley Athletic	v	Northallerton Town	2-2	310	0-1†	359
(Replay at Frickley Athletic FC)						
Gloucester City	v	Harrow Borough	1-2	492		
Leek Town	v	Runcorn	3-3	789	1-3	713
Macclesfield Town	v	Boston United	0-0	833	2-0	947
Merthyr Tydfil	v	Dartford	1-1	750	2-1	546
Northwich Victoria	v	Hyde United	1-0	644		
Redbridge Forest	v	Bromsgrove Rovers	1-1	623	1-0	995
Southport	v	Bishop Auckland	1-0	413		
Stafford Rangers	v	Marine	0-1	718		
Sutton Coldfield Town	v	Farnborough Town	0-3	646		
Sutton United	v	Bath City	1-2	757		
Telford United	v	Guisborough Town	2-0	795		
VS Rugby	v	Kettering Town	0-1	1790		
Walton & Hersham	v	Kidderminster Harriers	0-2	426		
Welling United	v	Dover Athletic	3-2	1606		
Whitby Town	v	Barrow	0-2	739		
Witton Albion	v	Billingham Synthonia	2-2	725	2-1†	245
Wivenhoe Town	v	Marlow	1-0	223		
Woking	v	Wembley	4-2	2075		
Wycombe Wanderers	v	Salisbury	2-0	2917		
Yeovil Town	v	Chesham United	3-1	1733		

Second Round Proper – 1 February 1992

Home		Away	Res	Att.	Replay	
Bashley	v	Kettering Town	2-3	1065		
Bath City	v	Dorking	2-0	601		
Bromley	v	Yeovil Town	1-3	667		
Farnborough Town	v	Southport	5-0	1021		
Gateshead	v	Barrow	1-0	1129		
Harrow Borough	v	Stalybridge Celtic	1-3	702		
Macclesfield Town	v	Bangor City	1-0	631		
Marine	v	Wivenhoe Town	3-0	405		
Merthyr Tydfil	v	Colchester United	0-0	1211	0-1	2746
Morecambe	v	Welling United	2-1	833		
Northwich Victoria	v	Cheltenham Town	4-2	701		
Redbridge Forest	v	Enfield	2-0	843		
Runcorn	v	Kidderminster Harriers	1-1	681	2-5†	1189
Telford United	v	Northallerton Town	3-0	757		
Witton Albion	v	Aylesbury United	1-0	852		
Wycombe Wanderers	v	Woking	1-0	5801		

Third Round Proper – 22 February 1992

Home		Away	Res	Att.	Replay	
Bath City	v	Wycombe Wanderers	1-1	2899	0-2	3542
Colchester United	v	Morecambe	3-1	3206		
Marine	v	Kettering Town	2-1	1111		
Northwich Victoria	v	Macclesfield Town	0-1	1537		
Redbridge Forest	v	Farnborough Town	3-2	1353		
Telford United	v	Gateshead	0-0	1027	1-0	533
(at Blyth Spartans FC)						
Witton Albion	v	Stalybridge Celtic	1-0	1755		
Yeovil Town	v	Kidderminster Harriers	3-1	2679		

Fourth Round Proper – 14 March 1992

Home		Away	Res	Att.
Colchester United	v	**Telford United**	**4-0**	**3894**
McGavin (18), Kinsella (49), Bennett (53), Smith (63)				
Marine	v	**Redbridge Forest**	**1-1**	**1106**
Ross (63)		Cavell (84)		
Wycombe Wanderers	v	**Witton Albion**	**1-2**	**4636**
West (90 pen)		Lutkevitch (50), Thomas (89)		
Yeovil Town	v	**Macclesfield Town**	**1-2**	**4269**
Wallace (19)		Green (61), Askey (85)		

Replay

Redbridge Forest	v	**Marine**	**0-1**	**1239**
		King (49)		

Semi-Finals 1st Leg – 4 April 1992

Colchester United	v	**Macclesfield Town**	**3-0**	**5443**
Stewart (22), English (25), McDonough (70)				
Witton Albion	v	**Marine**	**2-2**	**2030**
Alford (25, 31)		Grant (38), Ross (80)		

Semi-Finals 2nd Leg – 10/11 April 1992

Macclesfield Town   v   Colchester United   1-1   1650

Timmons (20)   Cook (45)

Colchester United win 4-1 on aggregate.

Marine   v   Witton Albion   1-4   2212

Gautrey (87 pen)   Thomas (5), McCluskie (81),

                   Halliday (89), Lutkevitch (90)

Witton Albion win 6-3 on aggregate.

Final – 10 May 1992 at Wembley Stadium

Colchester United   v   Witton Albion   3-1   27,806

Masters (5), Smith (20),   Lutkevitch (57)

McGavin (90)

The Teams

Colchester United – Barrett, Donald, Roberts, Kinsella, English, Martin, Cook, Masters, McDonough (Bennett), McGavin, Smith. Sub not used: Collins.

Witton Albion – Mason, Halliday, Coathup, McNeilis, Connor, Anderson, Thomas, Rose, Alford, Grinshaw (Connor), Lutkevitch (McCluskie).

Referee: KP Barratt. Linesmen: GT Pearson, KR Tilley.

Editor's Man of the Match: Steve McGavin (Colchester United).

Vauxhall Awards and Facts

Team of the Round

First Qualifying Round	RHYL v Halesowen	1-1, 2-1
Second Qualifying Round	NORTHALLERTON v Whitley Bay	0-0, 3-2
Third Qualifying Round	SALISBURY v Wokingham	0-0, 1-0
First Round	STALYBRIDGE v Altrincham	2-1
Second Round	MORECAMBE v Welling United	2-1
Third Round	MARINE v Kettering Town	2-1
Quarter-Final	MARINE v Redbridge Forest	1-1, 1-0

Final Man of the Match   Scott Barrett (Colchester United)

Highest Attendances

5801	Wycombe Wanderers v Woking	2nd Rd	1-0
5443	Colchester United v Macclesfield Town	SF1Leg	3-0
4636	Wycombe Wanderers v Witton Albion	QF	1-2
4269	Yeovil Town v Macclesfield Town	QF	1-2

FA TROPHY FINALS 1970-1991

1970   *(Att:28,000)*
MACCLESFIELD TOWN   **2**   (Lyons, Fidler B)
TELFORD UNITED   **0**
Macclesfield Town: Cooke, Sievwright, Bennett, Beaumont, Collins, Roberts, Lyons, Fidler B, Young, Corfield, Fidler D
Telford United: Irvine, Harris, Croft, Flowers, Coton, Ray, Fudge, Hart, Bentley, Murray, Jagger

1971   *(Att:29,500)*
TELFORD UNITED   **3**   (Owen, Bentley, Fudge)
HILLINGDON   **2**   (Reeve, Bishop)
Telford United: Irvine, Harris, Croft, Ray, Coton, Carr, Fudge, Owen, Bentley, Jagger, Murray
Hillingdon: Lowe, Batt, Langley, Higginson, Newcombe, Moore, Fairchild, Bishop, Reeve, Carter, Knox

1972   *(Att: 24,000)*
STAFFORD RANGERS   **3**   (Williams 2, Cullerton)
BARNET   **0**
Stafford Rangers: Aleksic, Chadwick, Clayton, Sargeant, Aston, Machin, Cullerton, Chapman, Williams, Bayley, Jones
Barnet: McClelland, Lye, Jenkins, Ward, Embrey, King, Powell, Rerry, Flat, Easton, Plume

1973   *(Att: 23,000)*
SCARBOROUGH   **2**   (Leaske, Thompson)
WIGAN ATHLETIC   **1**   (Rogers)   *aet*
Scarborough: Garrow, Appleton, Shoulder, Dunn, Siddle, Fagan, Donoghue, Franks, Leaske (Barmby), Thompson, Hewitt
Wigan Athletic: Reeves, Morris, Sutherland, Taylor, Jackson, Gillibrand, Clements, Oats (McCunnell), Rogers, King, Worswick

1974   *(Att: 19,000)*
MORECAMBE   **2**   (Richmond, Sutton)
DARTFORD   **1**   (Cunningham)
Morecambe: Coates, Pearson, Bennett, Sutton, Street, Baldwin, Done, Webber, Roberts (Galley), Kershaw, Richmond
Dartford: Morton, Read, Payne, Carr, Burns, Binks, Light, Glozier, Robinson (Hearne), Cunningham, Halleday

1975   *(Att: 21,000)*
MATLOCK TOWN   **4**   (Oxley, Dawson, Fenoughty T, Fenoughty N)
SCARBOROUGH   **0**
Matlock Town: Fell, McKay, Smith, Stuart, Dawson, Swan, Oxley, Fenoughty N, Scott, Fenoughty T, Fenoughty M
Scarborough: Williams, Hewitt, Rettit, Dunn, Marshall, Todd, Houghton, Woodall, Davidson, Barnby, Aveyard

1976   *(Att: 21,000)*

SCARBOROUGH   3   (Woodall, Abbey, Marshall (pen))
STAFFORD RANGERS   2   (Jones 2)   **aet**

Scarborough: Barnard, Jackson, Marshall, Dunn H, Ayre (Donoghue), Dunn HA, Dale, Barmby, Woodall, Abbey, Hilley

Stafford Rangers: Arnold, Ritchie, Richards, Sargeant, Seddon, Morris, Chapman, Lowe, Jones, Hutchinson, Chadwick

1977   *(Att: 20,500)*

SCARBOROUGH   2   (Dunn (pen), Abbey)
DAGENHAM   1   (Harris)

Scarborough: Chapman, Smith, Marshall (Barmby), Dunn, Ayre, Deere, Aveyard, Donoghue, Woodall, Abbey, Dunn

Dagenham: Huttley, Wellman, Currie P, Dunwell, Moore, Currie W, Harkins, Saul, Fox, Harris, Holder

1978   *(Att: 20,000)*

ALTRINCHAM   3   (King, Johnson, Rogers)
LEATHERHEAD   1   (Cook)

Altrincham: Eales, Allan, Crossley, Bailey, Owens, King, Morris, Heathcote, Johnson, Rogers, Davidson (Flaherty)

Leatherhead: Swannell, Cooper, Eaton, Davies, Reid, Malley, Cook, Salkeld, Kelly, Baker, Boyle (Bailey)

1979   *(Att: 32,000)*

STAFFORD RANGERS   2   (Wood A 2)
KETTERING TOWN   0

Stafford Rangers: Arnold, Wood F, Willis, Sargeant, Seddon, Ritchie, Secker, Chapman, Wood A, Cullerton, Chadwick (Jones)

Kettering: Lane, Ashby, Lee, Eastall, Dixey, Suddards, Flannagan, Kellock, Phipps, Clayton, Evans (Hughes)

1980   *(Att: 26,000)*

DAGENHAM   2   (Duck, Maycock)
MOSSLEY   1   (Smith)

Dagenham: Huttley, Willman, Scales, Dunwell, Moore, Durrell, Maycock, Horan, Duck, Kidd, Jones (Holder)

Mossley: Fitton, Brown, Vaughan, Gorman, Salter, Polliot, Smith, Moore, Skeete, O'Connor, Keelan (Wilson)

1981   *(Att: 22,578)*

BISHOP'S STORTFORD   1   (Sullivan)
SUTTON UNITED   0

Bishop's Stortford: Moore, Blackman, Brame, Amith (Worrell), Bradford, Abery, Sullivan, Knapman, Radford, Simmonds, Mitchell

Sutton United: Collyer, Rogers, Green, Rains J, Rains T, Stephens (Sunnucks), Waldon, Pritchard, Cornwell, Parsons, Dennis

1982   *(Att: 18,678)*

ENFIELD   1   (Taylor)
ALTRINCHAM   0

Enfield: Jacobs, Barrett, Tone, Jennings, Waite, Ironton, Ashford, Taylor, Holmes, Oliver (Flint), King

Altrincham: Connaughton, Crossley, Davison, Bailey, Cuddy, King (Whitbread), Allan, Heathcote, Johnson, Rogers, Howard

1983 *(Att: 22,071)*
TELFORD UNITED   **2**   (Mather 2)
NORTHWICH VICTORIA 1   (Bennett)
Telford United: Charlton, Lewis, Turner, Mayman (Joseph), Walker, Easton, Barnett, Williams, Mather, Hogan, Alcock
Northwich United: Ryan, Fretwell, Murphy, Jones, Forshaw, Ward, Anderson, Abel (Bennett), Reid, Chesters, Wilson

1984 *(Att: 14,200)*
NORTHWICH VICTORIA 1   (Chesters)
BANGOR CITY   **1**   (Whelan)   **aet**
Northwich Victoria: Ryan, Fretwell, Dean, Jones, Forshaw (Power), Bennett, Anderson, Abel, Reid, Chesters, Wilson
Bangor City: Letheren, Cavanagh, Gray, Whelan, Banks, Lunn, Urquart, Morris, Carter, Howat, Sutcliffe (Westwood)

REPLAY   *(Att: 5,805)*
NORTHWICH VICTORIA 2   (Chesters (pen), Anderson)
BANGOR CITY   **1**   (Lunn)
Northwich Victoria: Ryan, Fretwell, Dean, Jones, Forshaw, Bennett, Anderson, Abel, Reid, Chesters, Wilson
Bangor: Letheren, Cavanagh, Gray, Whelan, Banks, Lunn, Urquart, Morris, Carter, Howat, Sutcliffe

1985 *(Att: 20,775)*
WEALDSTONE   **2**   (Graham, Holmes)
BOSTON UNITED   **1**   (Cook)
Wealdstone: Iles, Perkins, Bowgett, Byatt, Davies, Greenaway, Holmes, Wainwright, Donnellan, Graham (Cordice N), Cordice A
Boston United: Blackwell, Cassey, Ladd, Creane, O'Brien, Thommson, Lavereick (Mallender), Simpson, Gilbert, Lee, Cook

1986 *(Att: 15,700)*
ALTRINCHAM   **1**   (Farrelly)
RUNCORN   **0**
Altrincham: Wealands, Gardner, Densmore, Johnson, Farrelly, Conning, Cuddy, Davidson, Reid, Ellis, Anderson
Runcorn: McBride, Lee, Roberts, Jones, Fraser, Smith, Crompton S (Crompton A), Imrie, Carter, Mather, Carrodus

1987 *(Att: 23,617)*
KIDDERMINSTER HAR'S 0
BURTON ALBION   **0**
Kidderminster Harriers: Arnold, Barton, Boxall, Brazier, Collins (Pearson), Woodall, MacKenzie, O'Dowd, Tuohy, Casey, Davies
Burton Albion: New, Essex, Kamara, Vaughan, Simms, Groves, Bancroft, Land, Dorset, Redfern, Gauden

REPLAY   *(Att: 15,685)*
KIDDERMINSTER HAR'S 2   (Davies 2)
BURTON ALBION   1   (Groves)
Kidderminster Harriers: Arnold, Barton, Boxall, Brazier (Hazelwood), Collins, Woodall,
MacKenzie, O'Dowd, Tuohy, Casey, Davies
Burton Albion: New, Essex, Kamara, Vaughan, Simms, Groves, Bancroft, Land, Dorset,
Redfern (Wood), Gauden

1988   *(Att: 23,617)*
ENFIELD   0
TELFORD UNITED   0
Enfield: Pape, Cottington, Howell, Keen, Sparrow (Hayzleden), Lewis (Edmonds),
Harding, Cooper, King, Furlong, Francis
Telford United: Charlton, McGinty, Storton, Nelson, Wiggins, Mayman, Sankey, Joseph,
Stringer (Griffiths), Biggins, Norris

REPLAY   *(Att: 26,912)*
ENFIELD   3   (Furlong 2, Howell)
TELFORD UNITED   2   (Biggins, Norris (pen))
Enfield: Pape, Cottington, Howell, Keen (Edmonds), Sparrow, Lewis, Harding, Cooper,
King, Furlong, Francis
Telford United: Charlton, McGinty, Storton, Wiggins, Mayman (Cunningham, Hancock),
Sankey, Joseph, Stringer, Griffiths, Biggins, Norris

1989   *(Att: 18,102)*
TELFORD UNITED   1   (Crawley)
MACCLESFIELD   0
Telford United: Charlton, Lee, Brindley, Hancock, Wiggins, Mayman, Grainger, Joseph,
Nelson, Lloyd, Stringer. Subs: Crawley, Griffiths
Macclesfield: Zelem, Roberts, Tobin, Edwards, Hardman, Askey, Lake, Hanion, Imrie,
Burr, Timmons. Subs: Derbyshire, Kendall

1990   *(Att: 19,011)*
BARROW   3   (Gordon 2, Cowperthwaite)
LEEK TOWN   0
Barrow: McDonnell, Higgins, Chilton, Skivington, Gordon, Proctor, Doherty (Burgess),
Farrell (Gilmore), Cowperthwaite, Lowe, Ferris
Leek Town: Simpson, Elsby (Smith), Pearce, McMullen, Clowes, Coleman (Russell),
Mellow, Somerville, Sutton, Millington, Norris

1991   *(Att: 34,842)*
WYCOMBE WNDRS   2   (Scott, West)
KIDDERMINSTER HAR'S 1   (Hadley)
Wycombe Wanderers: Granville, Crossley, Cash, Kerr, Creaser, Carroll, Ryan, Stapleton,
West, Scott, Guppy (Hutchinson). Sub not used: Robinson.
Kidderminster Harriers: Jones, Kurila, McGrath, Weir, Barnett, Forsyth, Joseph (Wilcox),
Howell (Whitehouse), Hadley, Lilwall, Humphreys.

36

FA VASE 1991-92

Duck's Watershed

Guiseley arrived at Wembley to defend the FA Vase as odds-on favourites. Operating at a higher level in the Pyramid of Football than their Wessex League opponents from Wimborne – the first club side from Dorset to reach a Wembley final. A good inaugural season in the First Division of the HFS League and returning to Wembley with the Vase and experience in hand seemed to tilt the balance much too far in Guiseley's favour.

After the first period of the game, there was little to change that opinion when Ian Noteman drove home from close range on 15 minutes as the Yorkshire side played some marvellous football.

But Wimborne weathered the storm and began to find space beyond Morgan and Tetley. Tommy Killick's cross was caught by the wind and left Paul Maxted for dead before rebounding off the far post. Noteman should have made it 2-0 but blazed over the bar with the goal at his mercy. Games turn on such incidents. Almost immediately Wimborne skipper Steve Richardson, head glinting in the sun, received the ball 40 yards out, advanced five yards and hit the most unstoppable of unstoppable shots.

On the half hour, Killick made space down the left flank and crossed a ball that curled in and then out of the Guiseley defence. Sturgess rose and, despite having to stretch backwards, maintained direction to flight the ball over the keeper's hands and into the net.

Guiseley's lack of pace through the centre of the back four was exploited by Killick shortly before the interval, as he raced onto a through ball before picking his spot.

The holders had to attack in the second half, and Noteman seized his opportunity from the edge of the area when the product of a weak defensive tackle fell his way. But Wimborne didn't wobble and Killick restored their two-goal advantage with a carbon copy of Noteman's opening goal of the game. Sturgess made it five for the underdogs, driving home from 15 yards after Allan's lob through the middle had unlocked the door. Substitute Colville scored at the death, but it was Wimborne's day in a final that was as entertaining as the Guiseley v Gresley classic a year before.

After the game, Wimborne manager Alex Pike took time out in the Players' Lounge to reflect on the game. "Guiseley were their own worst enemy," he said. "At 1-0 they turned the game for us. They had a chance to go 2-0 up, didn't and then seemed to sit back and a lot of open space started to appear which we exploited fully. Our forwards did marvellously," he added, nodding in the direction of Killick and Sturgess. Pike admitted that Wimborne came close to collapsing during the first 20 minutes as Guiseley swept all before them. "We were in danger of being overawed and getting beaten and beaten well. Once we had weathered that storm and the lads settled in to their stride, we got the game plan working and started to cause them a lot of problems, especially with our pace."

It was a marvellous day for the Dorset side and made all the more enjoyable by the 5000 or so Wimborne supporters, many of whom had kitted themselves out – faces, hair and all – in black and white. Spare a thought though for Guiseley keeper Paul Maxted who provides a trivia quiz point for future reference. What goalkeeper has played in successive Wembley Cup finals and conceded a total of *nine* goals?

Extra Preliminary Round – 7 September 1991

Home		Away	Res	Att.	Replay	
Aerostructures	v	Milton United	0-1	44		
AFC Lymington	v	Bishops Cleeve	5-0	66		
Almondsbury Picksons	v	Cirencester Town	4-4	52	1-0	100
Ashford Town (Middx)	v	Hartley Wintney	3-0	50		
Ashville	v	Bamber Bridge	0-3	80		
Ayone	v	Maghull	3-2	40	(at Maghull)	
Beaconsfield United	v	Milton Keynes Borough	3-1	30		
Bemerton Heath Harleq.	v	Swindon Athletic	2-3 †	45		
Biggleswade Town	v	Wingate & Finchley	0-1	59		
Blidworth MW	v	Brodsworth MW	1-0	22		
Bloxwich Town	v	Brackley Town	4-0	25		
Brantham Athletic	v	Ely City	0-2	63		
Bridgwater Town	v	Brislington	2-0	169		
Brimsdown Rovers	v	Shillington	2-0	58		
Brockenhurst	v	BAT	4-0	70		
Burton Park Wanderers	v	Pegasus Juniors	0-2	15		
Chatteris Town	v	Woodbridge Town	1-2	89		
Christchurch	v	Fleet Town	1-3	42		
Cinderford Town	v	Backwell United	1-1	103	2-2	72
					4-2	130
Clandown	v	Wotton Rovers	1-1	27	1-2 †	45
Clipstone Welfare	v	RES Parkgate	1-1	61	1-0	30
Cobham	v	Ash United	5-1	22		
Coleshill Town	v	Holwell Sports	1-1	56	2-3	204
Deal Town	v	Eastbourne Town	1-0	190		
Diss Town	v	Clarksteel Yaxley	2-0	112		
Downham Town	v	Brightlingsea United	1-0	92		
DRG (FP)	v	Clanfield	3-4	25		
Dunkirk	v	Lincoln United	1-5	60		
Eccleshall	v	Hamlet S & L	3-1	69		
Fairford Town	v	Larkhall Athletic	2-3 †	50		
Flight Refuelling	v	Harrow Hill	5-1	23		
General Chemicals	v	Christleton	3-1	52		

38

Home		Away	Res	Att.	Replay	
Godalming Town	v	Broadbridge Heath	0-1 †	36		
Hallam	v	Hall Road Rangers	2-2	42	2-1 †	45
(at Hall Road Rangers FC)						
Harrowby United	v	Heath Hayes	5-2	57		
Hatfield Main	v	Immingham Town	2-3	35		
Heaton Stannington	v	Marske United	0-1	28		
Heswall	v	Poulton Victoria	4-0	60		
Horley Town	v	Slade Green	0-3	40		
Ipswich Wanderers	v	Wroxham	1-3	52		
(at Wroxham FC)						
Kempston Rovers	v	Langford	3-0	68		
Kidsgrove Athletic	v	Leyland DAF	*(walkover for Kidsgrove A)*			
Kings Heath	v	Highfield Rangers	3-2	42	*(at Knowle FC)*	
Knypersley Victoria	v	Atherton Collieries	3-4	45	*(at Atherton)*	
Liversedge	v	Kimberley Town	2-1 †	87		
Long Buckby	v	London Colney	2-2	25	4-1	30
Long Sutton Athletic	v	LBC Ortonians	1-2	51		
Meir KA	v	Lutterworth Town	2-1	55		
Merseyside Police	v	Westhoughton Town	4-0	50		
Mickleover RBL	v	Maltby MW	2-1	103	*(at Gresley)*	
Nettleham	v	Tadcaster Albion	0-0	46	2-0	55
Newton (WC)	v	Vauxhall Motors (WC)	1-4	20		
Northfield Town	v	Tividale	4-0	68		
Norwich United	v	Somersham Town	0-2	99		
Oadby Town	v	Pelsall Villa	1-0	60		
Old Georgians	v	Keynsham Town	0-2	40		
Old Salesians	v	Farleigh Rovers	3-2	65		
Oldswinford	v	Knowle	0-0	30	0-1	34
Oxford City	v	Wantage Town	3-1	110		
Petersfield United	v	Bedfont	1-0	75		
Pickering Town	v	Seaton Delaval ST	4-0	108		
Ponteland United	v	Sunderland IFG Roker	1-3	30		
Potters Bar Town	v	Pirton	1-0 †	72		
Priory (Eastwood)	v	Rossington Main	5-1	25		
Prudhoe East End	v	Dunston FB	2-7	91		
Radford	v	Louth United	3-2	26		
Ramsey Town	v	St Ives Town	2-1		*(at St. Ives Town)*	
Redgate Clayton	v	St Dominics	4-4	70	1-7	45
Ryde Sports	v	Kintbury Rangers	3-2	65		
St Andrews	v	Daventry Town	1-2	82		
Seaton Delaval Amateurs	v	Sunderland Vaux Ryhope	2-0	31		
Selby Town	v	Glasshoughton Welfare	1-4	107		
Sherborne Town	v	Bicester Town	3-2	45		
Shirebrook Colliery	v	Pontefract Collieries	2-1 †	150		
Stansted	v	Sawbridgeworth Town	2-1 †	148		
Stapenhill	v	Norton United	6-4	100		
Stocksbridge Park Steels	v	Bradley Rangers	2-1 †	31		

Home		Away	Res	Att.	Replay	
Stotfold	v	Bowers United	2-1	51		
Stourport Swifts	v	Bolehall Swifts	2-0	52		
The 61	v	Cockfosters	1-4	10		
Truro City	v	St Austell	0-2	180		
Viking Sports	v	Amersham Town	3-2	65		
Waltham Abbey	v	Totternhoe	3-2	41		
Waterloo Dock	v	Cheadle Town	3-1	46		
West Bromwich Town	v	Anstey Nomads	2-2	33	0-3	—
Whitehaven Miners	v	Newton Aycliffe	0-4	38		
Winslow United	v	Rayners Lane	1-3	25		
Winterton Rangers	v	Bradford PA	4-1	113		
Wolverhampton Casuals	v	Westfields	1-0	10		
Wolverton	v	Brook House	0-3	62		
Yorkshire Amateur	v	Worsboro Bridge MW	3-1	45		

Preliminary Round – 5 October 1991

Home		Away	Res	Att.	Replay	
AFC Lymington	v	Ryde Sports	1-0	58		
Almondsbury Picksons	v	Welton Rovers	0-1	62		
Annfield Plain	v	Crook Town	3-1	57		
Anstey Nomads	v	Kings Heath	2-1	85		
APV Peterborough City	v	Stratford Town	1-0	33		
Arlesey Town	v	Rainham Town	4-1	150		
Armthorpe Welfare	v	Eccleshill United	4-1	46		
Arnold Town	v	Lincoln United	0-0	190	5-0	334
Ashington	v	Penrith	1-2	46		
Ashton United	v	Lancaster City	4-0	212		
Atherton Collieries	v	Maine Road	1-1	48	1-3	61
Ayone	v	Bootle	1-1	27	3-2 †	138
Berkhamsted Town	v	Soham Town Rangers	1-0	79		
Blakenall	v	Mile Oak Rovers	8-0	89		
Blidworth MW	v	Liversedge	1-3	23		
Bloxwich Town	v	Chasetown	0-0	33	0-2	79
Boston	v	Diss Town	0-1 †	68		
Bracknell Town	v	Hoddesdon Town	0-1	48		
Bridgnorth Town	v	Irthlingborough Diamonds	4-1	80		
Bridgwater Town	v	Chippenham Town	0-2	170		
Brigg Town	v	Shirebrook Colliery	6-1	67		
Brimsdown Rovers	v	Viking Sports	0-1	66		
Broadbridge Heath	v	Oakwood	0-2	45		
Brockenhurst	v	Romsey Town	1-2	90		
Bury Town	v	LBC Ortonians	1-0	171		
Calne Town	v	Odd Down	0-1	43		
Camberley Town	v	Southwick	1-2	52		
Canvey Island	v	Witham Town	0-1	73		
Chadderton	v	Flixton	4-6 †	102		

Home		Away	Res	Att.	Replay	
Chard Town	v	Swindon Athletic	2-0	71		
Chester-le-Street Town	v	Pickering Town	2-1	105		
Chichester City	v	Chatham Town	3-0	27		
Chipstead	v	Burgess Hill Town	0-4	84		
Cinderford Town	v	Frome Town	3-0	150		
Clacton Town	v	Ely City	4-3	79		
Clanfield	v	Devizes Town	1-3	52		
Clapton	v	Haringey Borough	1-3	61		
Cleator Moor Celtic	v	Langley Park	2-6	81		
Clevedon Town	v	Flight Refuelling	7-1	110		
Clipstone Welfare	v	Winterton Rangers	0-1	100		
Clitheroe	v	Skelmersdale United	2-1	135		
Corinthian	v	Deal Town	1-0	31		
Croydon Athletic	v	Banstead Athletic	2-4	28		
Curzon Ashton	v	Blackpool (wren) Rovers	0-1	63		
Darwen	v	St Dominics	1-2	144		
Daventry Town	v	West Midlands Police	0-0	110	0-0	30
					1-2 †	60
Denaby United	v	Thackley	3-4	114		
East Cowes Victoria Ath.	v	Witney Town	1-2	40		
Eccleshall	v	Wolverhampton Casuals	2-1	46		
Egham Town	v	Malden Vale	0-1	89		
Esh Winning	v	Bedlington Terriers	1-4	45		
Evenwood Town	v	Seaton Delaval Amateurs	1-2	15		
Exmouth Town	v	Liskeard Athletic	1-0	119		
Eynesbury Rovers	v	Newmarket Town	0-0	120	0-0	110
					0-2 †	140
Feltham & Houns Boro	v	Wootton Blue Cross	5-0	30		
Flackwell Heath	v	Edgware Town	1-4	52		
Fleet Town	v	Banbury United	2-2	69	3-1	182
Ford United	v	Metropolitan Police	2-3 †	65		
Formby	v	General Chemicals	1-1	19	0-0	58
					0-1	42
Glastonbury	v	Mangotsfield United	2-4	75		
Gorleston	v	Stowmarket Town	4-2 †	134		
Halesowen Harriers	v	Holwell Sports	4-2	87		
Halstead Town	v	Basildon United	1-3	120		
Hampton	v	Ruislip Manor	1-1	145	3-2	199
Harrowby United	v	Boldmere St Michaels	1-5	77		
Hebburn	v	Norton & Stockton	2-0 †	250		
Hemel Hempstead	v	Barkingside	4-1 †	65		
Herne Bay	v	Arundel	8-1	69		
Hertford Town	v	Beaconsfield United	4-1 †	103		
Highgate United	v	Desborough Town	2-0	45		
Hinckley	v	Sandwell Borough	0-1	48		
Hinckley Town	v	Walsall Wood	1-0	74		
Horden CW	v	Darlington CB	6-1	27		

Home		Away	Res	Att.	Replay	
Horsham	v	Cove	5-1	147		
Ilkeston Town	v	Belper Town	0-3	174		
Irlam Town	v	Heswall	3-2 †	49		
Kempston Rovers	v	Cockfosters	1-3 †	79		
Kidsgrove Athletic	v	Waterloo Dock	3-1	80		
Langney Sports	v	Eastbourne United	5-2	270		
Larkhall Athletic	v	Bristol Manor Farm	1-2	49		
Leatherhead	v	Burnham	0-1	95		
Letchworth Garden City	v	Potters Bar Town	1-1	44	1-2	84
Lewes	v	Selsey	0-2	62		
Lye Town	v	Bilston Town	1-1	105	2-5	122
Malvern Town	v	Oadby Town	1-0	52		
Marske United	v	West Allotment Celtic	2-1	43		
Meir KA	v	Racing Club Warwick	0-1	35		
Mickleover RBL	v	Nettleham	3-2 †	106		
Milton United	v	Abingdon United	3-0	60		
Minehead	v	Melksham Town	4-1	102		
Mirrlees Blackstone	v	Lowestoft Town	1-4	104		
Nantwich Town	v	Wythenshawe Amateurs	1-1	148	1-2	115
Netherfield	v	Sunderland IFG Roker	1-2 †	97		
Newbury Town	v	AFC Totton	3-0	76		
Newport (IoW)	v	Oxford City	2-0	286		
Northwood	v	Long Buckby	4-1	81		
Oakham United	v	Hallam	1-5 †	73		
Old Salesians	v	Hailsham Town	2-7	51		
Oldham Town	v	Newcastle Town	1-2	30		
Ossett Albion	v	Immingham Town	2-5	48		
Pagham	v	Horsham YMCA	3-1	66		
Pegasus Juniors	v	Northampton Spencer	0-1	82		
Petersfield United	v	Tonbridge	1-7	180		
Portfield	v	Corinthian Casuals	0-1 †	40		
Prescot AFC	v	Bamber Bridge	1-3 †	132		
Priory (Eastwood)	v	Stocksbridge Park Steels	1-3	47		
Radford	v	Harworth CI	1-2	25		
Ramsey Town	v	March Town United	1-2	—		
Rayners Lane	v	Kingsbury Town	0-1 †	45		
Redhill	v	Alma Swanley	4-0	72		
Rushall Olympic	v	Stourport Swifts	5-1 †	72		
St Austell	v	Ottery St Mary	2-0	82		
St Blazey	v	Crediton United	1-2 †	75		
St Helens Town	v	Burscough	2-3	80		
Salford City	v	Merseyside Police	2-0	82		
Sheffield	v	Friar Lane OB	2-1	38		
Sheppey United	v	Faversham Town	1-4	135		
Sherborne Town	v	First Tower United	2-2	87	2-1	75
Sholing Sports	v	Swanage Town & Herston	1-2	62		
Shoreham	v	Peacehaven & Telscombe	1-3	94		

Home		Away	Res	Att.	Replay	
Shortwood United	v	Radstock Town	5-2	146		
Shotton Comrades	v	Durham City	0-6	50		
Sittingbourne	v	Beckenham Town	3-1	271		
Solihull Borough	v	Knowle	6-2	102		
Southall	v	Eton Manor	3-2 †	26	*(at Eton Manor)*	
Stamford Town	v	Bourne Town	1-0	214		
Stansted	v	Barton Rovers	3-0	105		
Stapenhill	v	Oldbury United	0-2	80		
Steyning Town	v	Epsom & Ewell	0-3	50		
Stockton	v	Dunston FB	1-2			
Stotfold	v	Tring Town	2-0	61		
Thame United	v	Horndean	6-0	111		
Three Bridges	v	Darenth Heathside	2-1 †	28		
Tilbury	v	Brook House	5-2	54		
Tiptree United	v	Downham Town	3-5	26		
Tiverton Town	v	Elmore	3-0	396		
Torpoint Athletic	v	Ilfracombe Town	1-0	88		
Torrington	v	Barnstaple Town	1-1 +	140	2-1	217
Tunbridge Wells	v	Cobham	7-6 †	105		
Vauxhall GM	v	Rocester	0-0	21	2-1	131
Vauxhall Motors (WC)	v	Atherton LR	1-2	32		
Waltham Abbey	v	Leighton Town	1-0	51		
Ware	v	Collier Row	0-2	105		
Waterloo Dock	v	Kidsgrove Athletic	1-1	80	1-1	51
					1-1	51
		at Knowsley United			1-1	63
		at Knowsley United			1-3	80
Watton United	v	Felixstowe Town	1-2	45		
Wednesfield	v	Evesham United	1-3	37		
Wellingborough Town	v	Northfield United	1-3	50		
Welwyn Garden City	v	Cheshunt	1-2	40		
West Auckland Town	v	Washington	2-0	30		
Westbury United	v	Bournemouth	0-1	98		
Whitehawk	v	Ashford Town (Middx)	2-1 †	68		
Whitstable Town	v	Lancing	4-0	103		
Wick	v	Haywards Heath Town	4-0	55		
Willington	v	Newton Aycliffe	0-4	22		
Wingate & Finchley	v	Hornchurch	5-0	106		
Woodbridge Town	v	Royston Town	0-1	167		
Worthing	v	Slade Green	1-3	130		
Worthing United	v	Ringmer	2-1	34		
Wotton Rovers	v	Keynsham Town	2-3	58		
Wroxham	v	Somersham Town	3-0	114		
Yorkshire Amateurs	v	Glasshoughton Welfare	2-3	47		

+ extra time not played

First Round – 2 November 1991

Home		Away	Res	Att.	Replay	
AFC Lymington	v	Newport (IoW)	0-1	100		
Anstey Nomads	v	Oldbury United	4-0	58		
APV Peterborough City	v	Malvern Town	3-0	—		
Arlesey Town	v	Hertford Town	1-0	150		
Armthorpe Welfare	v	Sheffield	2-4 †	43		
Atherton LR	v	Clitheroe	2-1	—		
Bamber Bridge	v	St Dominics	6-1	156		
Basildon United	v	Histon	5-3	—		
Bedlington Terriers	v	Newton Aycliffe	0-1	35		
Berkhamsted Town	v	Bury Town	2-0	63		
Billingham Town	v	Annfield Plain	4-3 †	—		
Bilston Town	v	Highgate United	1-0	64		
Blackpool (wren) Rovers	v	Ashton United	1-2	—		
Boldmere St Michaels	v	Racing Club Warwick	0-3	39		
Brigg Town	v	Stocksbridge Park Steels	5-0	52		
Burnham Ramblers	v	Haringey Borough	2-2	—	2-1	—
Burscough	v	Irlam Town	5-1	71		
Chasetown	v	Northampton Spencer	2-1 †	57		
Cheshunt	v	Waltham Abbey	2-1	55		
Chester-le-Street Town	v	Langley Park	3-3	54	3-1	97
Chippenham Town	v	Bristol Manor Farm	2-0	35		
Cockfosters	v	Kingsbury Town	1-1	65	4-1	63
Collier Row	v	Wingate & Finchley	1-0	76		
Corinthian	v	Langney Sports	1-3	18		
Corinthian Casuals	v	Malden Vale	2-3 †	45		
Crediton United	v	Torrington	1-2 †	105		
Devizes Town	v	Chard Town	0-3	38		
Didcot Town	v	Romsey Town	2-1 †	—		
Diss Town	v	Witham Town	3-1	149		
Downham Town	v	Felixstowe Town	3-3	—	0-2	65
Durham City	v	Eppleton CW	2-2	—	2-2	—
Eccleshall	v	Halesowen Harriers	4-2	51		
Epsom & Ewell	v	Chertsey Town	0-2	—		
Exmouth Town	v	Newquay	0-6	84		
Falmouth Town	v	Tiverton Town	1-3 †	245		
Faversham Town	v	Southwick	6-0	—		
Fleet Town	v	Swanage Town & Herston	4-6 †	49		
Flixton	v	Kidsgrove Athletic	1-0	35		
Garforth Town	v	Heanor Town	4-1	46		
General Chemicals	v	Maine Road	0-1	32		
Glasshoughton Welfare	v	Belper Town	0-3	—		
Glossop	v	Newcastle Town	0-1	110		
Gorleston	v	Stansted	2-1	133		
Hallam	v	Ossett Town	0-1 †	93		
Harrogate Town	v	Winterton Rangers	4-1	163		

44

Home		Away	Res	Att.	Replay	
Havant Town	v	Redhill	3-2	88		
Hebburn	v	Marske United	3-2	—		
Hemel Hempstead	v	Edgware Town	0-2	52		
Herne Bay	v	Hailsham Town	3-1	91		
Holbeach United	v	Thetford Town	2-1	70		
Horsham	v	Oakwood	1-0	—		
Keynsham Town	v	Odd Down	1-0	—		
King's Lynn	v	Lowestoft Town	2-1 †	344		
Lincoln United	v	Harworth CI	2-3	180		
Liversedge	v	Rainworth MW	3-1	44		
Mangotsfield United	v	Wimborne Town	1-2	127		
Merstham	v	Whitstable Town	0-6	—		
Metropolitan Police	v	Stotfold	1-1	35	2-0 †	98
Mickleover RBL	v	Borrowash Victoria	3-4	80		
Newbury Town	v	Eastleigh	3-0	65		
Newmarket Town	v	Stamford Town	5-0	110		
Northfield Town	v	Blakenall	1-3	49		
Northwood	v	Braintree Town	7-6 †	—		
Pagham	v	Burnham	1-0	—		
Peacehaven & Telscombe	v	Whitehawk	5-0	126		
Penrith	v	Sunderland IFG Roker	2-1	41		
Potters Bar Town	v	Hampton	0-0	64	1-4	187
Purfleet	v	Southall	6-0	45		
Raunds Town	v	Bridgnorth Town	1-1	69	2-0	90
Rossendale United	v	Ayone	5-2 †	175		
Rothwell Town	v	Evesham United	1-3	44		
Royston Town	v	March Town United	2-1	54		
Rushall Olympic	v	Hinckley Town	2-1			
Salford City	v	Vauxhall GM	2-0	55		
Sandwell Borough	v	West Midlands Police	1-2 †			
Seaton Delaval Amateurs	v	Dunston FB	1-2 †	65		
Sherborne Town	v	Thatcham Town	0-2	—		
Shortwood United	v	Clevedon Town	3-1	—		
Slade Green	v	Chichester City	4-0	—		
Solihull Borough	v	Paget Rangers	4-1	123		
Thackley	v	Immingham Town	3-1	100		
Thame United	v	Milton United	3-0	90		
Three Bridges	v	Burgess Hill Town	3-3	—	1-0	109
Tilbury	v	Hoddesdon Town	1-0	31		
Tonbridge	v	Banstead Athletic	2-1	348		
Torpoint Athletic	v	St Austell	2-0	58		
Tunbridge Wells	v	Greenwich Borough	1-2 †	—		
Viking Sports	v	Feltham & Hounslow Boro	3-1	45		
Wellington	v	Cinderford Town	1-3	50		
Welton Rovers	v	Minehead	1-0	52		
West Auckland Town	v	Horden CW	1-0	84		
Wick	v	Sittingbourne	0-2	75		

Home		Away	Res	Att.	Replay	
Witney Town	v	Bournemouth	4-3	74		
Worthing United	v	Selsey	2-1	40		
Wroxham	v	Clacton Town	3-0	64		
Wythenshawe Amateurs	v	Eastwood Hanley	0-2	—		

Second Round – 23 November 1991

Home		Away	Res	Att.	Replay	
Anstey Nomads	v	Spalding United	3-2	109		
Arlesey Town	v	Newmarket Town	0-2	120		
Ashton United	v	Maine Road	2-1	319		
Belper Town	v	Harworth CI	2-1	160		
Berkhamsted Town	v	Harwich & Parkeston	2-1	120		
Billericay Town	v	King's Lynn	4-2	404		
Bilston Town	v	APV Peterborough City	3-1	105		
Bridlington Town	v	Billingham Town	5-0	214		
Burnham Ramblers	v	East Thurrock United	5-3	119		
Burscough	v	Rossendale United	2-0	—		
Chasetown	v	Witney Town	3-2 †	105		
Chertsey Town	v	Peacehaven & Telscombe	3-2	161		
Chester-le-Street Town	v	Durham City	2-0	253		
Chippenham Town	v	Paulton Rovers	1-3	82		
Cinderford Town	v	Newquay	3-1	250		
Collier Row	v	Harefield United	4-0	—		
Dawlish Town	v	Welton Rovers	1-2	—		
Didcot Town	v	Worthing United	1-2 †	102		
Diss Town	v	Viking Sports	4-0	249		
Dunston FB	v	Thackley	3-2 †	100		
Eastwood Hanley	v	Harrogate Town	4-1	61		
Eccleshall	v	Wisbech Town	0-2	268		
Edgware Town	v	Basildon United	4-3	211		
Evesham United	v	Buckingham Town	3-1	233		
Faversham Town	v	Whitstable Town	1-0	271		
Felixstowe Town	v	Cheshunt	2-0	125		
Flixton	v	Borrowash Victoria	8-3	92		
Gorleston	v	Hampton	0-2	157		
Great Harwood Town	v	Farsley Celtic	1-1	231	0-4	260
Great Yarmouth Town	v	Cockfosters	2-1	90		
Gresley Rovers	v	Blakenall	1-0	589		
Guiseley	v	Garforth Town	2-0	601		
Harrogate RA	v	Penrith	0-1	102		
Havant Town	v	Newport (IoW)	1-2	304		
Haverhill Rovers	v	Sudbury Town	1-1	539	1-2	577
Hinckley Athletic	v	Hucknall Town	3-2	287		
Horsham	v	Littlehampton Town	2-2	—	1-0	420
Hungerford Town	v	Torpoint Athletic	2-1	171		

Home		Away	Res	Att.	Replay	
Hythe Town	v	Herne Bay	1-1	334	2-1 †	216
Knowsley United	v	Cammell Laird	1-0	—		
Langney Sports	v	Hastings Town	3-3	498	1-2	637
Liversedge	v	Bamber Bridge	3-8	113		
Malden Vale	v	Thatcham Town	2-2	—	3-2	158
Metropolitan Police	v	Royston Town	1-0	45		
Newcastle Town	v	Sheffield	3-2	80		
Newton Aycliffe	v	Hebburn	2-2	—	4-2 †	
North Ferriby United	v	West Auckland Town	1-0	—		
Northwood	v	Purfleet	3-2	—		
Ossett Town	v	Atherton LR	3-3	95	1-3	200
Pagham	v	Slade Green	3-0	—		
Potton United	v	Walthamstow Pennant	0-4	108		
Racing Club Warwick	v	Solihull Borough	1-3	141		
Raunds Town	v	Holbeach United	3-0	97		
Saffron Walden Town	v	Wroxham	3-1	150		
Salford City	v	Brigg Town	0-1	80		
Shortwood United	v	Bridport	3-1	—		
Sittingbourne	v	Tilbury	4-2 †	311		
Three Bridges	v	Greenwich Borough	2-0	77		
Tiverton Town	v	Swanage Town & Herston	2-0	241		
Tonbridge	v	Thame United	1-6	469		
Torrington	v	Keynsham Town	1-0	122		
West Midlands Police	v	Rushall Olympic	3-1 †	52		
Wimborne Town	v	Chard Town	5-2	210		
Yate Town	v	Newbury Town	3-0	215		

Third Round – 14 and 21 December 1991

Home		Away	Res	Att.	Replay	
Anstey Nomads	v	Felixstowe Town	2-1	329		
Atherton LR	v	Brigg Town	3-3	150	2-3	94
Bamber Bridge	v	Flixton	2-1	283		
Belper Town	v	Dunston FB	1-1	212	0-2	193
(First match abandoned after 90 mins, waterlogged)						
Berkhamsted Town	v	Gresley Rovers	1-2 †	337		
Billericay Town	v	Bilston Town	2-0	411		
Bridlington Town	v	Eastwood Hanley	2-3 †	153		
Burnham Ramblers	v	Chasetown	2-1	132		
Chertsey Town	v	Cinderford Town	1-1	147	0-0	285
					2-1	450
Chester-le-Street Town	v	Ashton United	2-1	175		
Collier Row	v	West Midlands Police	2-3	120		
Edgware Town	v	Hinckley Athletic	2-1	226		
Farsley Celtic	v	Guiseley	2-5	607		
Hampton	v	Newport (IoW)	0-1	226		
Hastings Town	v	Torrington	3-0	476		

Home		Away	Res	Att.	Replay	
Hungerford Town	v	Faversham Town	4-1	110		
Metropolitan Police	v	Three Bridges	2-0	51		
Newcastle Town	v	Penrith	3-2 †	121		
Newmarket Town	v	Solihull Borough	2-1	190		
Newton Aycliffe	v	Burscough	2-4 †	120		
North Ferriby United	v	Knowsley United	1-2	112		
Pagham	v	Hythe Town	1-2	171		
Paulton Rovers	v	Thame United	4-2	185		
Raunds Town	v	Diss Town	0-2	121		
Saffron Walden Town	v	Sudbury Town	1-2 †	325		
Shortwood United	v	Yate Town	2-3	150		
Tiverton Town	v	Sittingbourne	2-3	320		
Walthamstow Pennant	v	Evesham United	2-3 †	42		
Welton Rovers	v	Malden Vale	2-1	90		
Wimborne Town	v	Horsham	1-0 †	243		
Wisbech Town	v	Great Yarmouth Town	2-2	545	4-2	330
Worthing United	v	Northwood	1-2	155		

Fourth Round – 18 January 1992

Home		Away	Res	Att.	Replay	
Anstey Nomads	v	Diss Town	0-1	450		
Billericay Town	v	Yate Town	3-4 †	438		
Brigg Town	v	Bamber Bridge	4-4	410	0-1 †	1045
Burscough	v	Eastwood Hanley	0-1	314		
Chester-le-Street Town	v	Knowsley United	1-5 †	305		
Dunston FB	v	Guiseley	1-3	423		
Edgware Town	v	Welton Rovers	3-1	388		
Hythe Town	v	Evesham United	3-3 †	279	0-2	636
(Previous match abandoned at half-time, 0-0)						
Newcastle Town	v	Gresley Rovers	3-2 †	577		
Newport (IoW)	v	Burnham Ramblers	3-1 †	581		
Northwood	v	Chertsey Town	1-4	213		
Paulton Rovers	v	Hungerford Town	1-3 †	205		
Sittingbourne	v	Metropolitan Police	1-2	400		
Sudbury Town	v	Newmarket Town	3-2	758		
West Midlands Police	v	Wisbech Town	4-3	320		
Wimborne Town	v	Hastings Town	3-3	626	2-1 †	677

Fifth Round – 8 February 1992

Home		Away	Res	Att.	Replay
Bamber Bridge	v	Newport (IoW)	2-1	950	
Chertsey Town	v	Yate Town	3-1	421	
Evesham United	v	Eastwood Hanley	2-1	1202	
Guiseley	v	Edgware Town	4-0	975	

48

Hungerford Town	v	West Midlands Police	0-3	320		
Knowsley United	v	Sudbury Town	2-4	652		
Metropolitan Police	v	Diss Town	0-2	235		
Newcastle Town	v	Wimborne Town	1-1	425	0-1	912

Sixth Round – 29 February 1992

Home		*Away*	*Res*	*Att.*	*Replay*	
Chertsey Town	v	Bamber Bridge	0-1	1121		
Diss Town	v	Wimborne Town	0-0	1528	0-1	1172
Guiseley	v	Evesham United	4-0	1668		
West Midlands Police	v	Sudbury Town	1-2	1072		

Semi-Finals 1st Leg – 21 March 1992

Home		*Away*	*Res*	*Att.*
Bamber Bridge	v	Wimborne Town	0-0	2020
Guiseley	v	Sudbury Town	2-2	2142
Roberts (26), Colville (90)		Phillips (40), Ketley (50)		

Semi-Finals 2nd Leg – 28 March 1992

Wimborne Town	v	Bamber Bridge	2-0	2819
Ames (37, 80)				

Wimborne Town win 2-0 on aggregate

Sudbury Town	v	Guiseley	1-3	2987
Barker (67)		Noteman (61, 67), Tennison (81)		

Guiseley win 5-3 on aggregate

Final – 5 May 1992 at Wembley Stadium

Guiseley	v	Wimborne Town	3-5	10,772
Noteman (15, 52), Colville (89)		Richardson (27), Sturgess (30, 78), Killick (42, 57)		

The Teams

Guiseley: Maxted, Atkinson, Hogarth, Tetley (Captain) (Wilson), Morgan, Brockie, Roberts, Tennison, Noteman (Colville), Annan, Roberts.
Wimborne Town: Leonard, Langdon (Wilkins), Beacham, Allan, Taplin, Ames, Richardson (Captain), Bridle, Killick, Sturgess (Lovell), Lynn.
Referee: MJ Bodenham. Linesmen: RE Budden, UD Rennie.
Editor's Man of the Match: Steve Richardson (Wimborne) - Didn't stop working and scored a magnificent solo effort to get his side back into the game.

FA VASE FINALS 1975-1991

1975   *(Att: 9,500)*
HODDESDON TOWN   2   (Sedgwick 2)
EPSOM & EWELL   1   (Wales)
Hoddesdon Town: Galvin, Green, Hickey, Maybury, Stevenson, Wilson, Bishop, Picking,
Sedgwick, Nathan, Schofield
Epsom & Ewell: Page, Bennett, Webb, Wales, Worby, Jones, O'Connell, Walker, Tuite,
Eales, Lee

1976   *(Att: 11,858)*
BILLERICAY TOWN   1   (Aslett)
STAMFORD   0   **aet**
Billericay Town: Griffiths, Payne, Foreman, Pullin, Bone, Coughlan, Geddes, Aslett,
Clayden, Scott, Smith
Stamford: Johnson, Kwiatkowski, Marchant, Crawford, Downs, Hird, Barnes, Walpole,
Smith, Russell, Broadhurst

1977   *(Att: 14,000)*
BILLERICAY TOWN   1   (Clayden)
SHEFFIELD   1   (Coughlan og)   **aet**
Billericay Town: Griffiths, Payne, Bone, Coughlan, Pullin, Scott, Wakefield, Aslett,
Clayden, Woodhouse, McQueen. Sub: Whettell
Sheffield: Wing, Gilbody, Lodge, Hardisty, Watts, Skelton, Kay, Travis, Pugh, Thornhill,
Haynes. Sub: Strutt

Replay at Nottingham Forest (Att: 3,482)
BILLERICAY TOWN   2   (Aslett, Woodhouse)
SHEFFIELD   1   (Thornhill)
Billericay Town: Griffiths, Payne, Pullin, Whettell, Bone, McQueen, Woodhouse, Aslett,
Clayden, Scott, Wakefield
Sheffield: Wing, Gilbody, Lodge, Strutt, Watts, Skelton, Kay, Travis, Pugh, Thornhill,
Haynes

1978   *(Att: 16,391)*
BLUE STAR   2   (Dunn, Crumplin)
BARTON ROVERS   1   (Smith)
Blue Star: Halbert, Feenan, Thompson, Davidson, Dixon S., Beynon, Storey, Dixon P.,
Crumplin, Callaghan, Dunn. Sub: Diamond
Barton Rovers: Blackwell, Stephens, Crossley, Evans, Harris, Dollimore, Dunn,
Harnaman, Fossey, Turner, Smith. Sub: Cox

1979   *(Att: 17,500)*
BILLERICAY TOWN   4   (Young 3, Clayden)
ALMONDSBURY GREENWAY 1   (Price)
Billericay Town: Norris, Blackaller, Bingham, Whettell, Bone, Reeves, Pullin, Scott,
Clayden, Young, Groom. Sub: Carrigan
Almondsbury Greenway: Hamilton, Bowers, Scarrett, Sullivan, Tudor, Wookey, Bowers,
Shehean, Kerr, Butt, Price. Sub: Kilbaine

1980   *(Att: 11,500)*
STAMFORD   **2**   (Alexander, McGowan)
GUISBOROUGH TOWN   **0**
Stamford: Johnson, Kwiatkowski, Ladd, McGowan, Bliszczak I, Mackin, Broadhurst, Hall, Czarnecki, Potter, Alexander. Sub: Bliszczak S
Guisborough Town: Cutter, Scott, Thornton, Angus, Maltby, Percy, Skelton, Coleman, McElvaney, Sills, Dilworth. Sub: Harrison

1981   *(Att: 12,000)*
WHICKHAM   **3**   (Scott, Williamson, Peck og)
WILLENHALL TOWN   **2**   (Smith, Stringer)   **aet**
Whickham: Thompson, Scott, Knox, Williamson, Cook, Ward, Carroll, Diamond, Cawthra, Robertson, Turnbull. Sub: Allon
Willenhall Town: Newton, White, Dams, Woodall, Heath, Fox, Peck, Price, Matthews, Smith, Stringer. Sub: Trevor

1982   *(Att: 12,500)*
FOREST GREEN ROVERS   **3**   (Leitch 2, Norman)
RAINWORTH MINERS WELFARE   **0**
Forest Green Rovers: Moss, Norman, Day, Turner, Higgins, Jenkins, Burns, Guest, Millard, Leitch, Doughty. Sub: Dangerfield
Rainworth Miners Welfare: Watson, Hallam, Hodgson, Slater, Sterland, Oliver, Knowles, Raine, Radzki, Reah, Comerford. Sub: Robinson

1983   *(Att: 13,700)*
VS RUGBY   **1**   (Crawley)
HALESOWEN TOWN   **0**
VS Rugby: Burton, McGinty, Harrison, Preston, Knox, Evans, Ingram, Setchell, Owen, Beecham, Crawley. Sub: Haskins
Halesowen Town: Caldicott, Penn, Edmonds, Lacey, Randall, Shilvock, Hazelwood, Moss, Woodhouse, Joinson E, Joinson L. Sub: Smith

1984   *(Att: 8,125)*
STANSTED   **3**   (Holt, Gillard, Reading)
STAMFORD   **2**   (Waddicore, Allen)
Stansted: Coe, Williams, Hilton, Simpson, Cooper, Reading, Callanan, Holt, Reeves, Doyle, Gillard. Sub: Williams
Stamford: Parslow, Smitheringale, Blades, McIlwain, Lyon, Mackin, Genovese, Waddicore, Allen, Robson, Beech. Sub: Chapman

1985   *(Att: 16,715)*
HALESOWEN TOWN   **3**   (Moss, Joinson L 2)
FLEETWOOD TOWN   **1**   (Moran)
Halesowen Town: Caldicott, Penn, Sherwood, Warner, Randle, Heath, Hazelwood, Moss (Smith), Woodhouse, Joinson P, Joinson L
Fleetwood Town: Dobson, Moran, Hadgraft, Strachan, Robinson, Milligan, Hall, Trainor, Taylor (Whitehouse), Cain, Kenneley

1986   *(Att: 18,340)*
HALESOWEN TOWN   **3**   (Moss 2, Joinson L)
SOUTHALL   **0**
Halesowen Town: Pemberton, Moore, Lacey, Randle (Rhodes), Sherwood, Heath, Penn, Woodhouse, Joinson P, Joinson L, Moss

Southall: MacKenzie, James, McGovern, Croad, Holland, Powell (Richmond), Pierre, Richardson, Sweales, Ferdinand, Rowe

1987   *(Att: 4,254)*
ST HELENS   **3**   (Lay 2, Rigby)
WARRINGTON   **2**   (Reid, Cook)
St Helens: Johnston, Benson, Lowe, Bendon, Wilson, McComb, Collins (Gledhill), O'Neill, Cummins, Lay, Rigby. Sub: Deakin
Warrington: O'Brien, Copeland, Hunter, Gratton, Whalley, Reid, Brownville (Woodyer), Cook, Kinsey, Looker (Hill), Hughes

1988   *(Att: 15,000)*
COLNE DYNAMOES   **1**   (Anderson)
EMLEY   **0**
Colne Dynamoes: Mason, McFadyen, Westwell, Bentley, Dunn, Roscoe, Rodaway,Whitehead (Burke), Diamond, Anderson, Wood (Coates)
Emley: Dennis, Fielding, Mellor, Codd, Hirst (Burrows), Gartland (Cook), Carmody, Green, Bramald, Devine, Francis

1989   *(Att: 26,487)*
TAMWORTH   **1**   (Devaney)
SUDBURY   **1**   (Hubbick)   **aet**
Tamworth: Belford, Lockett, Atkins, Cartwright, McCormack, Myers, Fin, Devaney, Moores, Gordon, Stanton Subs: Rathbone, Heaton
Sudbury: Garnham, Henry, Barker G, Boyland, Thorpe, Klug, Barker D, Barton, Oldfield, Smith, Hubbick. Subs: Money, Hunt

Replay at Peterborough (Att: 11,201)
TAMWORTH   **3**   (Stanton 2, Moores)
SUDBURY   **0**
Tamworth: Belford, Lockett, Atkins, Cartwright, Finn, Myers, George, Devaney, Moores, Gordon, Stanton. Sub: Heaton
Sudbury: Garnham, Henry, Barker G, Boyland, Thorpe, Klug, Barker D, Barton, Oldfield, Smith, Hubbick. Subs: Money, Hunt

1990   *(Att: 7,932)*
BRIDLINGTON TOWN   **0**
YEADING   **0**   **aet**
Bridlington: Taylor, Pugh, Freeman, McNeil, Warburton, Brentano, Wilkes (Hall), Noteman, Gauden, Whiteman, Brattan (Brown)
Yeading: MacKenzie, Wickens, Turner, Whiskey (McCarthy), Croad, Denton, Mathews, James (Charles), Sweales, Impey, Cordery

Replay at Elland Road (Att: 5,000)
BRIDLINGTON TOWN   **0**
YEADING   **1**   (Sweales)
Bridlington: Taylor, Pugh, Freeman, McNeil, Warburton, Brentano, Wilkes (Brown), Noteman, Gauden (Downing), Whiteman, Brattan
Yeading: MacKenzie, Wickens, Turner, Whiskey, Croad (McCarthy), Schwartz, Mathews, James, Sweales, Impey (Welsh), Cordery

1991 (Att: 11,313) **aet**
GUISELEY 4 (Tennison 2, Walling, Roberts)
GRESLEY ROVERS 4 (Rathbone, Smith 2, Stokes pen)
Guiseley: Maxted, Bottomley, Hogarth, Tetley, Morgan, McKenzie, Atkinson P (Adams), Tennison, Walling, Roberts A, Roberts B (Annan)
Gresley Rovers: Aston, Barry, Elliott (Adcock), Denby, Land, Astley, Stokes, Smith, Acklam, Rathbone, Lovell (Weston)

Replay at Bramall Lane (Att: 7,885)
GUISELEY 3 (Tennison, Walling, Atkinson I)
GRESLEY ROVERS 1 (Astley)
Guiseley: Maxted, Atkinson I, Hogarth, Tetley, Morgan, McKenzie (Bottomley), Roberts A, Tennison (Noteman), Walling, Atkinson P, Roberts B
Gresley Rovers: Aston, Barry, Elliott, Denby, Land, Astley, Stokes (Weston), Smith, Acklam, Rathbone, Lovell (Adcock)

FA SUNDAY CUP 1991-92

First Round – 13 Oct 1991

Almithak v A C Sparks 3-2

Altone Steels v Birmingham Celtic 4-0

Ansells Stockland Star v A D Bulwell ...0-2

Baildon Athletic v FC Coachman 1-3

Bishopstoke AFC v Santogee 66 ....2-3 †

Bolton Woods v Oakenshaw ....2-2 †

    Replay 0-2

Borem/Wood Royals v Chequers (Herts)1-2

BRNESC v Blue Union 1-3

Carlisle United SC v Iron Bridge.........2-4

Carnforth v Britannia VNC 2-1

Chapel United v Evergreen ....2-4 †

Continental v Concord Rangers 0-0

    Replay ....1-2 †

Dereham Hobbies Sun v Shouldham Sun0-1

Dudley & Weetslade v Blyth Waterloo 5-2

Framwelgate Moor/PM v W'dlands 84 7-1

Girton Eagles v Watford Labour Club...1-4

Hanham Sunday v Bedfont Sunday 2-1

Hare v Clubmoor Nalgo 2-2

    Replay 1-2

Inter Royalle v Rolls Royce (Sunday) ...2-0

Inter Volante v Cork & Bottle 3-1

(Awarded to Cork & Bottle as Inter Volante
played an ineligible player)

Jolly Farmers v Dock 2-2

    Replay 2-1

Kenwick Dynamo v Brookvale Athletic 1-2

Littlewoods v B & A Scaffolding 2-3

Lobster v Whetley Lane 4-0

Lynemouth v Croxteth & Gilmoss RBL 0-4

Mayfield United v Stanton Dale 1-4

Netherley RBL v East Bowling Unity ...1-1

    Replay 3-3

    Replay 2-3

Old Paludians v Broad Plain House......0-5

Oxford Road Social v St Clements Hosp0-3

Phoenix v Lebeq Tavern 1-2

Priory Sports v Fryerns Community ...2-1

Queens Arms v Nenthead 0-4

Radford Park Rngrs v Bricklayers Spts 4-5 †

Rob Roy v Chesterfield Park

(Rob Roy withdrawn from Competition)

St Josephs (Luton) v BRSC Aidan ......2-1 †

Sandwell v Olympic Star 2-0

Sarton United v Somerset Ambury V E 1-0

Sawston Keys v Gamlingay OB's 3-0

Seymour v Hartlepool Lion Hotel ......3-5 †

Theale v Northfield Rangers 1-0

Western Approaches v Railway Hotel ...2-1

Second Round – 10 Nov 1991

AD Bulwell v Brookvale Athletic ....1-2†

Almithak v Lobster....................5-4†

Altone Steels v St Josephs (Luton).......0-1

Avenue Victoria Lodge v A3 0-1

B & A Scaffolding v Green Man 88.....3-0

Blue Union v East Levenshulme 2-2

    Replay....................3-2

Bricklayers Sports v Brereton Town...3-2

Broad Plain House v Inter Royalle.......2-0

Collier Row Supporter v Santogee 66..2-1

Cork & Bottle v Lodge Cottrell..........0-1

Eagle-Knowsley v Clubmoor Nalgo ...4-1

Ford Basildon v Shouldham Sunday....2-1

Framwellgate Moor & Pity Me v
Dudley &Weetslade....................2-0

Hartlepool Lion Hotel v Carnforth.......1-0

Humbledon Plains Farm v
Croxteth/Gilmoss RBL..................2-0

Iron Bridge v Chesterfield Park..........3-0

Jolly Farmers v FC Coachman

54

*(Jolly Farmers removed for playing two
contract players in previous round)*

Lee Chapel North v Concord Rangers .2-1

Nenthead v Northwood 0-1

Nicosia v East Bowling Unity 1-1

Replay 2-1

Ouzavich v Leyton Argyle 3-2

Poringland Wandrrs v Marston Sports .2-4

Ranelagh Sports v Evergreen 2-0

Reading Borough v Hanham Sunday ...1-2

Sartan Utd v St Josephs (S. Oxhey) 1-0

Sawston Keys v Bournville Warriors ..3-2

Slade Celtic v Priory Sports 2-2

Replay 1-2

(abandoned in extra time)

St Clements Hosp v Chequers (Herts)..0-1

Theale v Lebeq Tavern.......................3-0

Toshiba Sharples v Stanton Dale...........1-1

Replay 4-5

Watford Labour Club v Sandwell 1-4

Western Approaches v Oakenshaw 2-3

Third Round – 8 Dec 1991

Blue Union v Eagle-Knowsley..............0-1

Broad Plain House v Hanham Sunday .0-3

Chequers (Herts) v Sawston Keys........2-1†

Collier Row Suprtrs v Brookvale Ath. ..1-2†

FC Coachman v Frmwlgte Mr/Pity Me4-3

Ford Basildon v Sartan United 1-0

Hartlepool Lion Hotel v Almithak 3-2

Iron Bridge v Humbledon Plains Frm ..2-0

Marston Sports v B & A Scaffolding ....1-0†

Nicosia v Bricklayers Sports 0-1

Northwood v Oakenshaw 2-2

Replay 2-3

Ouzavich v Lodge Cottrell 0-2

Sandwell v Ranelagh Sports 1-4

St Josephs (Luton) v Priory Sports.......5-1

Stantondale v A3 1-2

Theale v Lee Chapel North 3-2

Fourth Round – 19 Jan 1992

A3 v Eagle-Knowsley ....2-1†

Chequers (Herts) v Theale.....................2-3

Iron Bridge v Bricklayers Sports...........0-2

Lodge Cottrell v Ford Basildon 3-0

Marston Sports v Hartlepool Lion Htl..5-3

Oakenshaw v FC Coachman 2-1

Ranelagh Sports v Hanham Sunday 2-0

St Josephs (Luton) v Brookvale Ath ....1-0†

Fifth Round – 16 Feb 1992

A3 v Oakenshaw 1-1

Replay 1-1

Replay 0-2

Lodge Cottrell v Ranelagh Sports 3-0

Marston Sports v Bricklayers Sports....2-1

Theale v St Josephs (Luton) 2-0

Semi-Finals – 22 March 1992

Lodge Cottrell v Marston Sports 0-1

Theale v Oakenshaw 2-2

Replay 2-0

Final – 3 May 1992
at Reading FC

Marston Sports   **2**
(Wells 42 pen, Walker 72)

Theale   **3**
(Parr 31 pen, Eales 81, Hambridge 85)

Att. 2,427

ENGLAND SEMI-PRO INTERNATIONALS

31 May 1979, Stafford
ENGLAND 5 (Adamson 3 (2 pens), Mutrie, Whitbread)
SCOTLAND 1
Arnold (Stafford), Thompson (Yeovil), Davison (Altrincham), Adamson (Boston), Peake (Nuneaton), Jennings (Enfield), O'Keefe (Mossley), Phillips (Nuneaton), Mutrie (Blyth), Houghton (Blyth), Whitbread (Runcorn). Sub: Simmonite (Boston) for Thompson, Watson (Wealdstone) for Houghton.

3 June 1979, Stafford
ENGLAND 1 (O'Keefe)
HOLLAND 0
Arnold (Stafford), Thompson (Yeovil), Davison (Altrincham),Adamson (Boston), Peake (Nuneaton), Jennings (Enfield), O'Keefe (Mossley), Phillips (Nuneaton), Mutrie (Blyth), Watson (Wealdstone), Whitbread (Runcorn). Sub: Simmonite (Boston) for Thompson.

4 June 1980, Veenendaal, Holland
ENGLAND 2 (Hill, Smith)
ITALY 0
Clarke (Blyth), Simmonite (Boston), Davison (Altrincham), Jennings (Enfield), Adamson (Boston), Mutrie (Blyth), Watson (Wealdstone), Whitbread (Runcorn), Smith I (Mossley), Hill (Maidstone), Mayman (Norwich). Sub: Merrick (Weymouth) for Hill.

6 June 1980, Veenendaal, Holland
SCOTLAND 4
ENGLAND 2 (Mutrie, Hill)
Parker (Yeovil), Simmonite (Boston), Davison (Altrincham), Jennings (Enfield), Merrick (Weymouth), Adamson (Boston), Mutrie (Blyth), Watson (Wealdstone), Smith (Mossley), Hill (Maidstone), Mayman (Northwich). Sub: Clarke (Blyth) for Parker, Whitbread (Runcorn) for Merrick, Phillips (Kettering) for Mayman.

7 June 1980, Veenendaal, Holland
ENGLAND 2 (Whitbread, Watson)
HOLLAND 1
Clarke (Blyth), Stockley (Nuneaton), Hill (Maidstone), Jennings (Enfield), Simmonite (Boston), Phillips (Kettering), Adamson (Boston), Watson (Wealdstone), Denham (Northwich), Mutrie (Blyth), Whitbread (Runcorn). Sub: Smith (Mossley) for Denham.

9 June 1981, Lucca, Italy
ENGLAND 2 (Davison (pen), Williams)
HOLLAND 0
Clarke (Blyth), Thompson (Maidstone), Davison (Altrincham), Barrett (Enfield), Jennings (Enfield), Sellers (Scarborough), Finnegan (Weymouth), Watson (Scarborough), Howard (Altrincham), Williams (Northwich), Rogers (Altrincham). Sub: Ovard (Maidstone) for Rogers,

11 June 1981, Empoli, Italy
ENGLAND   **0**
SCOTLAND   **0**
Clarke (Blyth), Thompson (Maidstone), Davison (Altrincham), Barrett (Enfield), Jennings (Enfield), Sellers (Scarborough), Watson (Scarborough), Finnegan (Weymouth), Watson (Scarborough), Howard (Altrincham), Williams (Northwich), Rogers (Altrincham). Sub: Johnson (Altrincham) for Finnegan, Ovard (Maidstone) for Rogers.

13 June 1981, Montecatini, Italy
ITALY   **1**
ENGLAND   **1**   (Davison (pen))
Clarke (Blyth), Thompson (Maidstone), Davison (Altrincham), Barrett (Enfield), Jennings (Enfield), Sellers (Scarborough), Johnson (Altrincham), Howard (Altrincham), Whitbread (Altrincham), Rogers (Altrincham). Sub: Ovard (Maidstone) for Whitbread.

27 April 1982, Victoria Stadium, Gibraltar
GIBRALTAR   **2**
ENGLAND   **3**   (Ashford, Camillere o.g., Stephens)
Phillips (Barnet), Barrett (Enfield), Jennings (Enfield), Waite (Enfield), Davison (Altrincham), Sellers (Scarborough), Stephens (Sutton United), Johnson (Altrincham), Ashford (Enfield), Rogers (Altrincham), Smith (Alvechurch). Sub: Howard (Altrincham) for Ashford.

1 June 1982, Aberdeen
ENGLAND   **0**
ITALY   **0**
Clarke (Blyth), Thompson (Maidstone), Davison (Altrincham), Jennings (Enfield), Barrett (Enfield), Johnson (Altrincham), Stephens (Sutton United), Watson (Scarborough), Howard (Altrincham), Williams (Scarborough), Smith (Alvechurch). Sub: Rogers (Altrincham) for Williams.

3 June 1982, Aberdeen
ENGLAND   **1**   (Ashford)
HOLLAND   **0**
Clarke (Blyth), Thompson (Maidstone), Davison (Altrincham), Jennings (Enfield), Barrett (Enfield), Johnson (Altrincham), Stephens (Sutton United), Watson (Scarborough), Howard (Altrincham), Smith (Alvechurch), Ashford (Enfield). Sub: Sellers (Scarborough) for Smith.

5 June 1982, Aberdeen
SCOTLAND   **1**
ENGLAND   **1**   (Johnson)
Clarke (Blyth), Thompson (Maidstone), Davison (Altrincham), Jennings (Enfield), Barrett (Enfield), Johnson (Altrincham), Sellers (Scarborough), Watson (Scarborough), Howard (Altrincham), Rogers (Altrincham), Ashford (Enfield). Sub: Stephens (Sutton) for Thompson.

31 May 1983, Scarborough
ENGLAND   **2**   (Sellers, Cordice)
ITALY   **0**
Richardson (Maidstone), Thompson (Maidstone), Davison (Altrincham), Robinson (Blyth), Barrett (Enfield), Sellers (Scarborough), Watson (Maidstone), Johnson (Altrincham), Cordice (Wealdstone), Williams (Telford), Ashford (Enfield).

2 June 1983, Scarborough

ENGLAND 6 (Williams, Johnson, Davison (pen), Cordice, Watson, Ashford)
HOLLAND 0

Clarke (Blyth), Thompson (Maidstone), Davison (Altrincham), Robinson (Blyth), Barrett (Enfield), Sellers (Scarborough), Watson (Maidstone), Johnson (Altrincham), Cordice (Wealdstone), Williams (Telford), Ashford (Enfield). Sub: Ironton (Enfield) for Johnson, Derbyshire (Mossley) for Watson.

4 June 1983, Scarborough

ENGLAND 2 (Davison (pen), Williams)
SCOTLAND 1

Clarke (Blyth), Thompson (Maidstone), Davison (Altrincham), Robinson (Blyth), Barrett (Enfield), Sellers (Scarborough), Watson (Maidstone), Johnson (Altrincham), Cordice (Wealdstone), Williams (Telford), Ashford (Enfield). Sub: Derbyshire (Mossley) for Johnson, Ward (Northwich) for Sellers.

27 March 1984, Newtown

WALES 2
ENGLAND 1 (Smith)

Richardson (Maidstone), Thompson (Maidstone), Robinson (Blyth), Newson (Maidstone), Davison (Altrincham), Smith (Runcorn), Morley (Nuneaton), Ironton (Enfield/Maidstone), Cordice (Wealdstone), Culpin (Nuneaton), Ashford (Enfield). Sub: Barrett (Enfield) for Thompson, Watson (Maidstone) for Ironton.

5 June 1984, Palma, Italy

ENGLAND 3 (Johnson, Davison (pen), Barrett)
HOLLAND 3

Clarke (Blyth), Thompson (Maidstone), Newson (Maidstone), Barrett (Enfield), Davison (Altrincham), Watson (Maidstone), Morley (Nuneaton), Taylor (Maidstone), Johnson (Altrincham), Williams (Telford), Ashford (Enfield).

7 June 1984, Modena, Italy

ENGLAND 2 (Williams, Ashford)
SCOTLAND 0

Clarke (Blyth), Thompson (Maidstone), Newson (Maidstone), Barrett (Enfield), Davison (Altrincham), Watson (Maidstone), Morley (Nuneaton), Taylor (Maidstone), Johnson (Altrincham), Williams (Telford), Ashford (Enfield). Sub: Cordice (Wealdstone) for Williams, Joseph (Telford) for Johnson.

9 June 1984, Reggio Emilia, Italy

ITALY 1
ENGLAND 0

Clarke (Blyth), Thompson (Maidstone), Robinson (Blyth), Newson (Maidstone), Davison (Altrincham), Watson (Maidstone), Morley (Nuneaton), Taylor (Maidstone), Johnson (Altrincham), Williams (Telford), Ashford (Enfield). Sub: Cordice (Wealdstone) for Thompson, Pearce (Harrow) for Taylor.

26 March 1985, Telford

ENGLAND 1 (Robinson)
WALES 0

Charlton (Telford), Robinson (Blyth), Glover (Maidstone), Newson (Maidstone), Turner (Telford), Newton (Burton), Joseph (Telford), Morley (Nuneaton), Ashford (Enfield), Mell

(Burton), Hooley (Frickley). Sub: Pape (Harrow) for Charlton, Culpin (Nuneaton) for Hooley, Smithers (Nuneaton) for Mell.

11 June 1985, Houten, Holland

ENGLAND   **2**   (Culpin, Barrett)
ITALY   **2**

Charlton (Telford), Constantine (Altrincham), Glover (Maidstone), Barrett (Enfield), Davison (Altrincham), Johnson (Altrincham), Joseph (Telford), Smithers (Nuneaton), Cordice (Wealdstone), Culpin (Nuneaton), Williams (Telford). Sub: Ashford (Enfield) for Williams.

13 June 1985, Utrecht, Holland

ENGLAND   **3**   (Culpin 3)
HOLLAND   **0**

Pape (Harrow), Constantine (Altrincham), Glover (Maidstone), Barrett (Enfield), Davison (Altrincham), Johnson (Altrincham), Joseph (Telford), Newton (Burton), Cordice (Wealdstone), Culpin (Nuneaton), Williams (Telford). Sub: Howell (Enfield) for Newton.

15 June 1985, Harderwijk, Holland

ENGLAND   **1**   (Williams)
SCOTLAND   **3**

Pape (Harrow), Constantine (Altrincham), Glover (Maidstone), Barrett (Enfield), Davison (Altrincham), Johnson (Altrincham), Joseph (Telford), Newton (Burton), Cordice (Wealdstone), Culpin (Nuneaton), Williams (Telford). Sub: Morley (Nuneaton) for Williams, Howell (Enfield) for Barrett.

18 March 1986, Merthyr Tydfil

WALES   **3**
ENGLAND   **1**   (Davies)

Richardson (Maidstone), Constantine (Witton), Davison (Altrincham), Howell (Enfield), Wilcox (Frickley), Stephens (Sutton), Walker (Blyth), Smithers (Nuneaton), Wilson (Frickley), Davies (Kidderminster), Casey (Kidderminster). Sub: Johnson (Altrincham) for Walker, Doherty (Weymouth) for Casey, Joseph (Telford) for Stephens, Pape (Enfield) for Richardson.

24 May 1986, Kidderminster

ENGLAND   **2**   (Johnson, Casey)
EIRE   **1**

Pape (Enfield), Shirtliff (Frickley), Davison (Altrincham), Howell (Enfield), Wilcox (Frickley), Stephens (Sutton), Walker (Blyth), Johnson (Altrincham), Ashford (Enfield), Richards (Enfield), Casey (Kidderminster). Sub: Simpson (Stafford) for Stephens, Buchanan (Blyth) for Walker.

26 May 1986, Nuneaton Borough

ENGLAND   **2**   (Wilcox, Agana)
EIRE   **1**

Richardson (Maidstone), Shirtliff (Frickley), Davison (Altrincham), Howell (Enfield), Wilcox (Frickley), Johnson (Altrincham), Clayton (Burton), Simpson (Stafford), Ashford (Enfield), Buchanan (Blyth), Agana (Weymouth). Sub: Stephens (Sutton) for Johnson, Walker (Blyth) for Howell, Casey (Kidderminster) for Buchanan.

17 March 1987, Gloucester City

ENGLAND 2 (Casey, Ashford)
WALES 2

Pape (Enfield), Shirtliff (Frickley), Thompson (Scarborough), Brazier (Kidderminster), Howell (Enfield), Jones (Weymouth), Margerrison (Barnet), Joseph (Telford), Casey (Kidderminster), Carter (Runcorn), Davies (Kidderminster). Sub: Ashford (Wycombe) for Margerrison.

18 May 1987, Dunfermline

ENGLAND 1 (Howell)
ITALY 2

Pape (Enfield), Shirtliff (Frickley), Howell (Enfield), Cuddy (Altrincham), Thompson (Scarborough), Ashford (Wycombe), Farrelly (Altrincham), Simpson (Stafford), Casey (Kidderminster), Carter (Runcorn), Davies (Kidderminster). Sub: Abbott (Welling) for Casey, Joseph (Telford) for Shirtliff.

20 May 1987, Kirkcaldy

ENGLAND 4 (Carter 4)
HOLLAND 0

Pape (Enfield), Shirtliff (Frickley), Howell (Enfield), Cuddy (Altrincham), Thompson (Scarborough), Ashford (Wycombe), Farrelly (Altrincham), Simpson (Stafford), Joseph (Telford), Carter (Runcorn), Davies (Kidderminster). Sub: Golley (Sutton) for Ashford, Humphries (Barnet) for Pape.

23 May 1987, Dunfermline

SCOTLAND 1
ENGLAND 2 (Howell, Carter)

Pape (Enfield), Cuddy (Altrincham), Howell (Enfield), Golley (Sutton), Thompson (Scarborough), Ashford (Wycombe), Simpson (Stafford), Farrelly (Altrincham), Joseph (Telford), Carter (Runcorn), Davies (Kidderminster). Sub: Abbott (Welling) for Ashford, Walker (Blyth) for Davies.

15 March 1988, Rhyl

WALES 0
ENGLAND 2 (Carter 2)

Pape (Enfield), Shirtliff (Frickley), Teale (Weymouth), Howell (Enfield), Densmore (Runcorn), Joseph (Telford), Golley (Sutton), Codnor (Barnet), Davies (Kidderminster), Carter (Runcorn), Butler (Maidstone). Sub: Brooks (Cheltenham) for Golley, Norris (Telford) for Carter, McKenna (Boston) for Pape.

29 January 1989, La Spezia, Italy

ITALY 1
ENGLAND 1 (Carter)

Pape (Enfield), Shirtliff (Frickley), Gridlett (Hendon), Howell (Enfield), Densmore (Runcorn), Lake (Macclesfield), Bancroft (Kidderminster), Joseph (Telford), Golley (Maidstone), Carter (Runcorn), Butler (Maidstone). Sub: Davies (Kidderminster) for Butler, Lee (Telford) for Shirtliff, Shearer (Cheltenham) for Lake, Beaney (Maidstone) for Pape.

21 March 1989, Kidderminster

ENGLAND 2 (Rogers, Carter)
WALES 0

60

Pape (Enfield), Shirtliff (Boston), Gridlett (Hendon), Howell (Enfield), Watts (Leytonstone), Joseph (Telford), Golley (Maidstone), Rogers (Sutton), Bancroft (Kidderminster), Carter (Runcorn), Butler (Maidstone). Sub: Cooke (Kettering) for Bancroft.

25 February 1990, Salerno, Italy
ITALY 2
ENGLAND 0
McKenna (Boston), Shirtliff (Boston), Watts (Redbridge), Howell (Enfield), Skivington (Barrow), Rogers (Sutton), Joseph (Kidderminster), Hessenthaler (Dartford), Furlong (Enfield), Carter (Runcorn), Simpson (Altrincham). Sub: Pape (Enfield) for McKenna, Bancroft (Kidderminster) for Watts, Conner (Dartford) for Hessenthaler, Cooke (Kettering) for Rogers, Hone (Welling) for Shirtliff.

6 March 1990, Merthyr Tydfil
WALES 0
ENGLAND 0
Pape (Enfield), Shirtliff (Boston), Bancroft (Kidderminster), Howell (Enfield), Skivington (Barrow), Gridlet (Barnet), Askey (Macclesfield), Hanlon (Macclesfield), Furlong (Enfield), Ashford (Redbridge), Simpson (Altrincham).

25 May 1990, Dublin
EIRE 1
ENGLAND 2 (Carter 2 (1pen))
McKenna (Boston), Shirtliff (Boston), Bancroft (Kidderminster), Watts (Redbridge), Howell (Enfield), Gridlet (Barnet), Brooks (Cheltenham), Clarke (Barnet), Carter (Runcorn), Ashford (Redbridge), Simpson (Altrincham). Sub: Rodgers (Sutton) for Simpson, Furlong (Enfield) for Ashford, Joseph (Kidderminster) for Clarke.

27 May 1990, Cork
EIRE 0
ENGLAND 3 (Ashford, Furlong, Carter)
Pape (Enfield), Shirtliff (Boston), Rogers (Sutton), Watts (Redbridge), Howell (Enfield), Gridlet (Barnet), Joseph (Kidderminster), Furlong (Enfield), Carter (Runcorn), Ashford (Redbridge), Simpson (Altrincham). Sub: McKenna (Boston) for Pape, Bancroft (Kidderminster) for Simpson, Brooks (Cheltenham) for Watts, Skivington (Barrow) for Ashford.

5 March 1991, Kettering
ENGLAND 0
ITALY 0
Pape (Enfield), Lee (Witton), Watts (Redbridge), Skivington (Barrow), Nicol (Kettering), Conner (Redbridge), Lowe (Barnet), Rogers (Sutton), Carter (Barnet), Furlong (Enfield), Showler (Altrincham). Sub: Willis (Barnet) for Furlong, Ashford (Redbridge) for Showler.

17 May 1991, Stafford
ENGLAND 1 (Carter)
WALES 2
McKenna (Boston), Lee (Witton), Bancroft (Kettering), Skivington (Barrow), Nicol (Kettering), Conner (Redbridge), Lowe (Barnet), Rogers (Sutton), Todd (Berwick), Furlong (Enfield), West (Wycombe). Sub: Carter (Barnet) for West, Showler (Altrincham) for Nicol, Humphries (Kidderminster) for Todd.

WALES   **0**
ENGLAND   **1**   (Mayes)
McKenna (Boston), Shirtliff (Boston), Watts (Redbridge), Nicol (Kettering), Connor (Redbridge), Humphreys (Kidderminster), Richardson (Redbridge), Golley (Welling), Mayes (Redbridge), Robbins (Welling), Cavell (Redbridge). Sub: Price (Stafford) for McKenna, Abbott (Welling) for Humphreys, Read (Farnborough) for Robbins.

Record Summary by Country

	P	W	D	L	F	A
Eire	4	4	0	0	9	3
Gibraltar	1	1	0	0	3	2
Holland	8	7	1	0	22	4
Italy	10	2	5	3	9	9
Scotland	8	4	2	2	15	11
Wales	9	4	2	3	11	9
Total	40	22	10	8	69	38

Scorers
Carter 13 (1 pen), Ashford 6, Davison 5 (5 pens), Williams 5, Culpin 4, Johnson 4, Adamson 3 (2 pens), Barrett 2, Casey 2, Cordice 2, Hill 2, Howell 2, Mutrie 2, Smith I. 2, Watson 2, Whitebread 2, Agana 1, Davies 1, Furlong 1, Mayes 1, O'Keefe 1, Robinson 1, Rogers 1, Sellers 1, Stephens 1, Wilcox 1, own goals 1.

GM VAUXHALL CONFERENCE

A Gnat's Whisker

In the end nine goals was all that separated Colchester and Wycombe in what proved to be the most exciting ever Vauxhall Conference championship race. Both clubs achieved a record 94 points. On the last day of the season Wycombe required a win over Witton and had to hope for United to go down at home to bottom club Barrow. It was always a very long shot but, on the other hand, the Essex club had been involved in a 4-4 see-saw game at Macclesfield a week earlier as the nerves began to show.

Both managers were quick to praise their respective sides. Roy McDonough spoke with pride on how his side had passed their way back into

Final Table 1991-92

		Home					Away					
	P	W	D	L	F	A	W	D	L	F	A	Pts
Colchester Utd....	42	19	1	1	57	11	9	9	3	41	29	94
Wycombe W........	42	18	1	2	49	13	12	3	6	35	22	94
Kettering Town ..	42	12	6	3	44	23	8	7	6	28	27	73
Merthyr Tydfil...	42	14	4	3	40	24	4	10	7	19	32	68
Farnborough T....	42	8	7	6	36	27	10	5	6	32	26	66
Telford Utd........	42	10	4	7	32	31	9	3	9	30	35	64
Redbridge F........	42	12	4	5	42	27	6	5	10	27	29	63
Boston Utd..........	42	10	4	7	40	35	8	5	8	31	31	63
Bath City	42	8	6	7	27	22	8	6	7	27	29	60
Witton Albion.....	42	11	6	4	41	26	5	4	12	22	34	58
Northwich Vic....	42	10	4	7	40	25	6	2	13	33	33	54
Welling United....	42	8	6	7	40	38	6	6	9	29	41	54
Macclesfield T....	42	7	7	7	25	21	6	9	6	25	29	52
Gateshead	42	8	5	8	22	22	4	7	10	27	35	48
Yeovil Town.......	42	8	6	7	22	21	3	8	10	18	28	47
Runcorn	42	5	11	5	26	26	6	2	13	24	37	46
Stafford Rgrs......	42	7	8	6	25	24	3	8	10	16	35	46
Altrincham..........	42	5	8	8	33	39	6	4	11	28	43	45
Kidderminster.....	42	8	6	7	35	32	4	3	14	21	45	45
Slough Town.......	42	7	3	11	26	39	6	3	12	30	43	45
Cheltenham T.....	42	8	5	8	28	35	2	8	11	28	47	43
Barrow...............	42	5	8	8	29	23	3	6	12	23	49	38

Football League status while Wanderers' Martin O'Neill said that his team had done marvellously considering they operated on a part-time basis – and that was the telling factor in the end. Colchester are the sixth club to win automatic promotion to the Football League.

The award for revival of the season goes to Redbridge Forest, for so long rooted at the foot of the Conference. Manager John Still proved conclusively that, at this level of football, money can buy success. Having bagged £100,000 from Watford for Andy Hessenthaler, Still bought perfectly and Forest shot up the table to finish in a highly respectable fifth, and also reached the Vauxhall Trophy quarter-finals.

Kettering took third spot but finished the season with upheaval. Former Arsenal and Ipswich star Brian Talbot completed a buyout at Rockingham Road and manager Peter Morris left for Boston United.

Given five years to gain Football League status by the FA of Wales, Merthyr Tydfil served notice of intent by completing an excellent season to finish fourth – a climb up the table that went almost unnoticed. It will be interesting to watch their progress in the next few years given what is at stake. Just what price will they be willing to pay when it has become a case of sink or swim?

The decline of Altrincham – one of the Conference's most consistent sides in recent times – has been sad to see. The Robins suffered the worst-ever run in their history when, from 8 February, they lost 13 consecutive Conference and Cup games and suffered the indignity of a 3-7 home defeat by Slough Town.

Cheltenham Town slipped into the Beazer Homes League having used no less than seven goalkeepers during their campaign. As Barrow were relegated, injury forced Colin Cowperthwaite to retire at the age of 32. Cowperthwaite – a folk hero at Holker Street – played over 700 games for the Bluebirds in his 15 years, scoring 281 goals in the process. Barrow's relegation is the third time they have lost Conference status. Another landmark was also achieved by Gateshead keeper Simon Smith who completed his 350th consecutive game as the season neared its close.

The price of success and failure. Double champions Colchester ended the season recording a near £500,000 loss while Stafford Rangers, who just avoided relegation, made a £99,000 profit!

Conference attendances took a drop of 100,000 on the previous season with 560,742 pushing their way through the turnstiles – an average of 1,214 per game.

The Alliance Premier League History

The Alliance Premier League was founded in 1979 with 20 clubs drawn from the Southern (13) and Northern Premier (7) Leagues. In 1981 two Isthmian clubs joined to bring the membership up to 22 clubs. The League was known as the Gola League from 1984-85 for two seasons and thereafter under its present title.

Three points for a win was introduced for 1981-82 but modified to apply to away games only for three seasons from 1983-84. Promotion to and relegation from the League has always been a feature of its structure and from 1985-86 representatives of the Southern, Northern Premier and Isthmian Leagues have normally joined at the expense of the three bottom sides.

The promotion of the League's champions to the Football League and the relegation of the 92nd Football League club to the League has been operational since 1986-87, although no club was relegated to the Conference for 1991-92 or 1992-93. With the advent of the FA Premier League, promotion from the Conference to the Football League will be to the Third Division from the 1992-93 season.

5-Year One, Two, Three Records

	First	Pts	Second	Pts	Third	Pts
1986-87	Scarborough	91	Barnet	85	Maidstone Utd	73
1987-88	Lincoln City	82	Barnet	80	Kettering	75
1988-89	Maidstone United	84	Kettering Town	76	Boston United	74
1989-90	Darlington	87	Barnet	85	Runcorn	70
1990-91	Barnet	87	Colchester Utd	85	Altrincham	82

Leading GMVC Goalscorers 1991-92

Conf	Player (Club)		FAC	BLT	VFT
29	Paul Cavell (Redbridge Forest)	plus	1	1	2
	(including 7 League goals for Boston United)				
	Terry Robins (Welling United)	plus	–	–	1
27	Gary Jones (Boston United)	plus	2	1	1
26	Roy McDonough (Colchester United)	plus	1	–	2
21	Simon Read (Farnborough Town)	plus	9	2	3
	Karl Thomas (Witton Albion)	plus	3	1	4
20	Dave Webley (Merthyr Tydfil)	plus	–	–	–
19	Gary Abbott (Welling United)	plus	5	–	1
	Jon Graham (Kettering Town)	plus	3	–	–
	Steve McGavin (Colchester United)	plus	2	2	3
	Ken McKenna (Altrincham)	plus	–	1	–
	Malcolm O'Connor (Northwich Victoria)	plus	–	2	1
	Paul Randall (Bath City)	plus	3	2	1
18	Keith Scott (Wycombe Wanderers)	plus	–	1	1
16	Gary Bennett (Colchester United)	plus	–	–	2
	Richard Hill (Kettering Town)	plus	1	–	2
	Mickey Spencer (Yeovil Town)	plus	1	3	4
	Ceri Williams (Merthyr Tydfil)	plus	1	1	1

FAC=FA Cup. BLT=Bob Lord Trophy. VFT=Vauxhall Football Trophy.

ANNUAL AWARDS

Player of the Year:	Steve McGavin (Colchester United)
Manager of the Year:	Roy McDonough (Colchester United)
Goalscorers of the Year:	Terry Robbins (Welling United)
	Paul Cavell (Redbridge Forest)

The Mail on Sunday Team of the Year

Position	Player	Club
Goalkeeper	John McKenna	Boston United
Right Back	Paul Shirtliff	Boston United
Centre Backs	Andy Kerr	Wycombe Wanderers
	Glyn Creaser	Wycombe Wanderers
Left Back	Paul Watts	Redbridge Forest
Midfield	Steve Thompson	Wycombe Wanderers
	Eammon Collins	Colchester United
	Paul Richardson	Redbridge Forest
Forwards	Steve McGavin	Colchester United
	Paul Cavell	Redbridge Forest
	Terry Robbins	Welling United

The Mail on Sunday Manager of the Month Awards

Month	Manager	Club
September	Martin O'Neill	Wycombe Wanderers
October	Ted Pearce	Farnborough Town
November	Gerry Daly	Telford United
December	Peter Morris	Kettering Town
January	Ted Pearce	Farnborough Town
February	John Still	Redbridge Forest
March	Peter O'Brien	Witton Albion
April	Martin O'Neill	Wycombe Wanderers

The Mail on Sunday Goalscorer of the Month Awards

Month	Player	Club
September	Malcolm O'Connor	Northwich Victoria
October	Paul McKinnon	Slough Town
November	Terry Robbins	Welling United
December	Gary Bennett	Colchester United
January	Darryl McCarthy	Runcorn
February	Paul Cavell	Redbridge Forest
March	David Leaworthy	Farnborough Town
April	Keith Scott	Wycombe Wanderers

The Mail on Sunday Goals Jackpot Awards

Month	Club	Goals/Game
September	Colchester United	2.55
October	Slough Town	3.25
November	Welling United	2.60
December	Colchester United	2.50
January	Northwich Victoria	2.25
February	Redbridge Forest	3.67
March	Redbridge Forest	2.00
April	Colchester United	3.17

Leading Goalscorers by Club

Club	Player	Total	Con	FA	BLT	VFT
Altrincham	Ken McKenna	20	19	–	1	–
Barrow	John Brady	11	11	–	–	–
Bath City	Paul Randall	25	19	3	2	1
Boston United	Gary Jones	31	27	2	1	1
Cheltenham Town	Kevin Willetts	12	9	2	1	–
Colchester United	Roy McDonough	29	26	1	–	2
Farnborough Town	Simon Read	35	21	9	2	3
Gateshead	Alan Lamb	14	14	–	–	–
Kettering Town	Jon Graham	22	19	3	–	–
Kidderminster Har.	Peter Howell	14	9	–	2	3
Macclesfield Town	Andrew Green	9	8	–	–	1
	Colin Lambert	9	8	–	–	1
Merthyr Tydfil	Dave Webley	20	20	–	–	–
Northwich Victoria	Malcolm O'Connor	22	19	–	2	1
Redbridge Forest	Paul Cavell	22	22	–	–	–
Runcorn	Steve Saunders	14	12	–	–	2
Slough Town	Paul McKinnon	19	15	4	–	–
Stafford Rangers	Wayne Simpson	6	6	–	–	–
Telford United	Tim Langford	16	12	1	–	3
Welling United	Terry Robbins	30	29	–	–	1
Witton Albion	Karl Thomas	29	21	3	1	4
Wycombe Wanderers	Keith Scott	20	18	–	1	1
Yeovil Town	Mickey Spencer	24	16	1	3	4

FAC=FA Cup. BLT=Bob Lord Trophy. VFT=Vauxhall Football Trophy.

Championship Shield – 10 September 1992

Wycombe Wanderers   Barnet   1-0
West (57 pen)

A penalty 12 minutes into the second half by Mark West secured the James V. Thompson Championship Shield for Wycombe. Wanderers were well worth their win and become the first FA Trophy winners to take the Shield in four years.

GMVC RESULTS 1991-92

	Altrincham	Barrow	Bath City	Boston United	Cheltenham	Colchester Utd	Farnborough T	Gateshead	Kettering Towi	Kidderminster I	Macclesfield
Altrincham	•	1-1	4-0	2-4	2-1	1-2	1-1	1-1	1-1	1-1	3-1
Barrow	0-2	•	2-0	2-2	0-0	1-1	0-1	1-1	0-0	5-1	2-0
Bath City	3-2	2-1	•	2-0	5-1	0-0	1-2	1-1	1-1	0-1	1-1
Boston United	2-1	4-1	2-0	•	3-3	0-4	0-1	4-0	0-3	1-1	1-5
Cheltenham Town	0-2	0-0	1-0	1-1	•	1-1	4-3	3-2	3-1	1-2	2-3
Colchester United	3-3	5-0	1-2	1-0	4-0	•	2-3	2-0	3-1	3-0	2-0
Farnborough Town	3-0	5-0	5-0	5-0	1-1	0-2	•	3-1	1-3	2-1	4-2
Gateshead	5-0	1-1	1-2	2-1	2-1	0-2	0-2	•	0-0	0-3	2-0
Kettering Town	5-0	3-2	0-1	1-3	3-0	2-2	1-2	1-1	•	2-1	2-0
Kidderminster Har	1-0	1-2	2-2	1-3	3-1	2-2	1-1	5-3	2-3	•	1-1
Macclesfield Town	1-1	0-1	0-1	0-1	3-3	4-4	1-2	1-0	0-2	0-0	•
Merthyr Tydfil	3-1	2-1	0-0	2-0	3-1	2-0	1-0	1-4	4-1	2-1	3-2
Northwich Victoria	1-2	6-1	1-1	1-1	3-1	1-1	1-1	1-1	4-3	3-1	2-1
Redbridge Forest	0-1	2-2	1-3	1-4	1-2	2-1	2-0	2-1	4-0	5-0	0-0
Runcorn	2-2	2-2	3-1	2-2	2-1	1-3	1-1	1-1	0-0	4-1	0-0
Slough Town	2-3	1-0	0-2	3-1	1-3	2-4	0-5	2-0	2-0	3-1	0-3
Stafford Rangers	1-2	0-0	2-2	0-1	2-2	3-3	0-1	1-3	1-2	2-0	1-1
Telford United	4-2	4-2	0-2	1-2	2-1	0-3	1-2	1-1	1-1	3-1	0-1
Welling United	2-2	5-3	0-5	1-3	1-1	4-1	1-0	2-2	2-3	3-2	2-1
Witton Albion	2-0	0-1	2-2	1-0	4-2	2-2	4-1	0-3	1-0	2-1	1-1
Wycombe Wanderers	4-2	3-2	1-0	2-1	2-2	1-2	2-1	2-1	1-0	2-0	2-0
Yeovil Town	2-1	2-0	1-1	1-1	1-1	0-1	2-2	1-0	0-1	1-1	0-1

	Merthyr Tydfil	Northwich Vic	Redbridge F	Runcorn	Slough Town	Stafford Rgrs	Telford United	Welling United	Witton Albion	Wycombe Wds	Yeovil Town
Altrincham	1-1	0-1	0-3	2-2	3-7	3-0	2-3	1-2	2-2	0-4	2-1
Barrow	2-2	0-2	0-1	2-3	3-4	0-0	3-0	6-1	0-1	0-1	0-0
Bath City	0-0	2-0	0-0	3-1	2-1	1-2	1-2	2-3	0-2	1-1	3-1
Boston United	2-0	0-2	2-1	2-1	3-1	2-2	1-2	5-1	3-2	2-2	1-3
Cheltenham Town	1-2	1-0	0-7	4-1	1-0	0-0	2-1	3-2	0-1	2-1	1-1
Colchester United	2-0	1-0	1-0	2-1	4-0	2-0	2-0	3-1	3-1	3-0	4-0
Farnborough Town	0-0	2-4	0-2	0-2	2-1	1-1	2-0	1-1	1-1	1-3	0-0
Gateshead	0-1	2-0	0-1	1-1	2-1	0-0	0-2	1-1	1-1	2-3	1-0
Kettering Town	3-1	1-0	3-2	3-0	2-3	2-1	3-0	1-1	0-1	1-1	2-0
Kidderminster Har	2-2	1-0	5-1	2-1	3-3	2-1	1-2	1-3	1-0	1-0	1-1
Macclesfield Town	3-0	•	0-0	3-0	0-1	1-0	2-1	1-1	1-0	3-1	1-2
Merthyr Tydfil	•	2-1	2-2	2-0	1-2	1-2	2-2	2-1	3-0	1-2	2-2
Northwich Victoria	4-1	•	0-2	3-0	3-0	4-3	1-1	1-2	3-1	0-1	1-0
Redbridge Forest	1-1	4-3	•	1-2	4-0	0-0	1-0	2-0	3-1	0-5	0-0
Runcorn	1-1	3-1	1-0	•	1-0	0-0	0-3	2-2	2-1	1-2	1-4
Slough Town	0-0	•	4-0	1-0	•	•	0-3	0-3	1-0	0-2	0-0
Stafford Rangers	0-0	2-1	3-0	1-0	1-1	•	3-2	0-0	2-1	0-2	1-0
Telford United	1-2	1-4	3-3	2-1	2-2	4-1	•	2-1	2-1	1-3	1-0
Welling United	1-2	6-1	2-2	1-2	0-2	1-1	3-1	•	1-1	1-2	3-1
Witton Albion	3-2	1-1	2-0	1-3	2-1	6-0	1-1	2-2	•	•	3-1
Wycombe Wanderers	4-0	2-0	1-0	1-0	3-0	3-0	6-1	4-0	4-0	•	1-0
Yeovil Town	1-1	2-1	0-1	1-4	1-0	0-1	0-2	3-0	2-1	1-0	•

69

ATTENDANCES 1991-92

	Altrincham	Barrow	Bath City	Boston United	Cheltenham T	Colchester Utc	Farnborough	Gateshead	Kettering Tow	Kidderminster	Macclesfield T
Altrincham	•	930	771	908	862	905	694	842	1293	842	767
Barrow	1301	•	1440	1018	1240	1480	1384	1521	1384	1109	1158
Bath City	590	485	•	401	657	1101	759	632	699	544	523
Boston United	891	775	1008	•	1164	2635	1134	639	2919	1319	951
Cheltenham Town	980	742	800	894	•	1157	846	701	1006	872	783
Colchester United	2849	7193	2416	3229	2643	•	2954	897	6303	3033	2333
Farnborough Town	1113	982	680	724	773	3069	•	675	1086	822	615
Gateshead	386	747	355	271	343	530	415	•	420	5050	375
Kettering Town	1347	1750	2379	3207	1336	4100	993	1497	•	1532	1367
Kidderminster Har	1128	1256	928	1009	2158	1828	1175	1051	1243	•	1326
Macclesfield Town	1301	502	578	869	834	886	752	369	940	851	•
Merthyr Tydfil	317	576	917	589	835	1032	517	575	570	422	588
Northwich Victoria	747	615	707	654	484	1042	543	540	665	1015	802
Redbridge Forest	514	332	475	472	360	2327	743	428	726	479	472
Runcorn	907	629	531	575	438	883	595	489	637	544	661
Slough Town	860	611	608	732	659	2226	784	730	698	832	588
Stafford Rangers	680	1139	895	681	667	961	1052	707	1089	1102	994
Telford United	1235	1034	1092	841	684	1109	1017	717	890	1430	1199
Welling United	777	763	806	726	759	1837	1164	748	636	815	5050
Witton Albion	825	690	742	749	759	1045	838	593	887	792	1308
Wycombe Wanderers	3245	3699	4263	2580	3060	5184	2275	2603	4069	3913	3821
Yeovil Town	1919	2573	3340	1823	1963	2385	1959	2222	1929	2111	2110

	Merthyr Tydfil	Northwich Vic	Redbridge F	Runcorn	Slough Town	Stafford Rgrs	Telford United	Welling Unite	Witton Albion	Wycombe Wd	Yeovil Town
Altrincham	896	693	479	1049	884	1201	507	537	1059	1166	937
Barrow	1268	1217	1049	1087	1035	1547	1113	1129	1026	1438	1281
Bath City	629	510	614	575	600	862	524	626	5509	1386	1504
Boston United	1312	1218	1058	864	721	839	901	755	1187	1706	1240
Cheltenham Town	1080	518	909	450	821	808	738	1197	1059	1320	912
Colchester United	4148	3218	4773	2617	3197	2139	2964	2933	2842	5083	2979
Farnborough Town	682	796	721	932	762	811	786	975	560	2236	685
Gateshead	328	346	286	530	292	202	264	307	273	912	344
Kettering Town	1616	1513	1304	1519	1830	1318	1664	1962	1508	2918	1257
Kidderminster Har	1014	929	1045	1078	1541	1136	1992	1168	1074	2037	1305
Macclesfield Town	568	905	460	1065	879	522	838	338	1015	693	701
Merthyr Tydfil	•	587	702	592	586	886	426	632	632	1088	618
Northwich Victoria	689	•	823	603	444	745	886	729	2809	1043	654
Redbridge Forest	502	623	•	812	673	452	509	763	437	2891	503
Runcorn	404	733	446	•	533	688	686	577	838	951	474
Slough Town	521	628	910	799	•	658	877	907	610	3703	584
Stafford Rangers	945	733	709	762	690	•	943	637	817	1381	758
Telford United	1303	1738	835	913	691	1179	•	698	935	1520	766
Welling United	759	548	615	712	866	822	848	•	914	1337	704
Witton Albion	885	1902	851	278	814	912	875	712	•	1242	783
Wycombe Wanderers	3339	2750	2285	2688	5162	3202	4283	3910	6035	•	2901
Yeovil Town	1587	1992	1832	1821	1763	2339	2116	2127	1659	2901	•

Attendance Summaries by Club

Club	Psn	Total Home	90-91	Ave	90-91	Total Away	Ave
Wycombe Wdrs	2	75,726	(57,673)	3,606	(2,746)	38,952	1,855
Colchester United	1	71,783	(62,833)	3,418	(2,992)	37,722	1,796
Yeovil Town	15	44,471	(55,421)	2,118	(2,639)	22,349	1,064
Kettering Town	3	37,917	(53,831)	1,806	(2,563)	30,089	1,433
Kidderminster Har	19	27,421	(25,132)	1,306	(1,197)	24,924	1,187
Barrow	22	26,225	(29,928)	1,249	(1,425)	28,023	1,334
Boston United	8	25,236	(28,820)	1,202	(1,372)	22,952	1,093
Telford United	6	21,826	(26,425)	1,039	(1,258)	25,918	1,234
Farnborough Town		20,485		975		22,593	1,076
Slough Town	20	19,425	(24,537)	925	(1,168)	24,790	1,180
Witton Albion	10	19,182		913		27,839	1,326
Cheltenham Town	21	18,593	(21,689)	885	(1,033)	22,678	1,080
Stafford Rangers	17	18,342	(24,679)	873	(1,175)	22,968	1,094
Altrincham	18	18,222	(29,076)	868	(1,385)	23,912	1,139
Welling United	12	17,661	(20,695)	841	(985)	23,413	1,115
Northwich Victoria	11	17,166	(15,706)	817	(748)	23,997	1,143
Macclesfield Town	13	15,866	(20,757)	756	(988)	23,246	1,107
Redbridge Forest	7	15,116		720		22,706	1,081
Bath City	9	14,771	(18,868)	703	(898)	25,731	1,225
Merthyr Tydfil	4	13,658	(15,706)	650	(824)	24,475	1,165
Runcorn	16	13,219	(15,316)	629	(729)	22,289	1,061
Gateshead	14	8,431	(12,324)	401	(587)	19,176	913
Total		560,742		1,214			

All Time Top GMVC Attendance

Att	Match	Date
9,432	Lincoln City v Wycombe Wanderers	02/05/88
7,542	Lincoln City v Boston United	04/04/88
7,193	Colchester United v Barrow	02/05/92
6,986	Colchester United v Altrincham	20/04/91
6,303	Colchester United v Kettering Town	28/04/92

GMVC – Football League Ups and Downs

Season	Promoted	Relegated
1986-87	Scarborough	Lincoln City
1987-88	Lincoln City	Newport County
1988-89	Maidstone United	Darlington
1989-90	Darlington	Colchester United
1990-91	Barnet	No club relegated
1991-92	Colchester United	No club relegated

GMVC Sequences 1991-92

Highest Scorers

4	Paul Cavell	Cheltenham v REDBRIDGE FOREST	29.02.92
	Dennis Greene	Altrincham v WYCOMBE WDRS	11.04.92
	David Leworthy	FARNBOROUGH v Macclesfield	10.04.92
	Roy McDonough	Slough Town v COLCHESTER UTD	26.08.91
	Terry Robbins	WELLING UTD v Northwich Victoria	26.02.92

Highest Aggregate Scores

3-7	Altrincham v Slough Town	19.10.91
5-3	Welling United v Barrow	30.11.91
5-3	Kidderminster Harriers v Gateshead	24.08.91
4-4	Macclesfield Town v Colchester United	25.04.92

Largest Home Wins

6-0	Witton Albion v Stafford Rangers	08.02.92
6-1	Wycombe Wanderers v Telford United	12.10.91
6-1	Barrow v Welling United	28.09.91
6-1	Northwich Victoria v Barrow	24.09.91
6-1	Welling United v Northwich Victoria	26.02.92

Largest Away Wins

0-7	Cheltenham Town v Redbridge Forest	29.02.92
0-5	Redbridge Forest v Wycombe Wanderers	30.04.92
0-5	Slough Town v Farnborough Town	20.04.92
0-5	Welling United v Bath City	21.03.92

Matches Without a Defeat

15 Colchester United; 12 Colchester United; 10 Bath City, Kettering Town, Merthyr Tydfil.

Matches Without a Win

14 Slough Town; 11 Cheltenham Town, Kidderminster Harriers, Redbridge Forest, Witton Albion.

Consecutive Victories

7 Redbridge Forest, Wycombe Wanderers (twice); 6 Colchester United; 5 Colchester United, Kettering Town, Telford United.

Consecutive Defeats

9 Altrincham; 6 Slough Town; 5 Cheltenham Town, Redbridge Forest, Witton Albion.

BOB LORD TROPHY

1st Round 1st Leg

Bath City Randall 25, 88 (2 pens)	**Slough Town** Hill 82	2-1	404
Farnborough Town Coombes 9 (pen), Reid 16, 74	**Yeovil Town** Spenser 41, 89	3-2	461
Northwich Victoria O'Conner 12, 34	**Stafford Rangers**	2-0	501
Redbridge Forest Conner 50, Sowerby 87	**Boston United**	2-0	202
Cheltenham Town Caisey 6, 55, Willetts 50 (pen), Kurilla 82 (og)	**Kidderminster H.** Davies 46, Humphreys 57	4-2	675
Gateshead Bell 20, Corner 24 (pen), Butler 53	**Witton Albion**	3-0	260

1st Round 2nd Leg

Stafford Rangers Pearson 61	**Northwich Victoria** Vaughan 73 *Northwich Vic. won 3-1 on agg.*	1-1	540
Witton Albion Thomas 3, Hill 44, Lutkevitch 62, McCluskie 104, 113	**Gateshead** *Witton Albion won 5-3 on agg.*	5-0	501
Yeovil Town Carroll 3, 67, Boulton 85	**Farnborough Town** *Yeovil Town won 5-3 on agg.*	3-0	1473
Boston United Casey 4, Cavell 36, Shirtliff 49, Jones 66	**Redbridge Forest** *Boston United won 4-2 on agg.*	4-0	746
Slough Town Knight 45, Joseph 76	**Bath City** *Slough won 3-2 on agg.*	2-0	584
Kidderminster Harriers Howell 10, Davies 28, Whitehouse 60	**Cheltenham Town** Fox 80 *5-5 on agg. Kidderminster won on away goals.*	3-1	733

2nd Round

Altrincham Brady 64, 90	**Barrow** Doherty 62	2-1	589
Colchester United McGavin 16, Collins 45, Kinsella 77, 87	**Kettering Town**	4-0	1296
Northwich Victoria Graham 5, 20, Butler 89	**Boston United** Nesbitt 58, 77	3-2	474
Telford United Brindley 17	**Macclesfield Town** Timmons 14, Dawson 94	1-2	597

| Merthyr Tydfil | Wycombe Wdrs | 1-3 | 526 |
| Williams 70 | Crossley 15, Hutchinson 23, Gooden 73 | | |

| Runcorn | Witton Albion | 2-2 aet | 850 |
| Redmond 20, Hawtin 120 | McCluskie 65, 107 | | |

| Slough Town | Kidderminster H. | 0-1 | 408 |
| | Howell 77 | | |

| Yeovil Town | Welling United | 2-0 | 1430 |
| Batty 24 (pen), Spenser 45 | | | |

Replay

| Witton Albion | Runcorn | 0-2 | 503 |
| | Withers 56, McCarthy 65 | | |

3rd Round

Colchester United	Wycombe Wdrs	2-6	919
Restarick 35, McGavin 87	West 28, 89, Scott 51, Hutchinson 62, 66		
	Creaser 76		

| Macclesfield Town | Altrincham | 1-1 | 447 |
| Green 6 | Hughes 90 | | |

| Runcorn | Northwich Victoria | 2-1 | 558 |
| Withers 59, McCarthy 65 | Graham 61 | | |

| Kidderminster Harriers | Yeovil Town | 1-2 | 681 |
| Howell 38 | Shail 88, Carroll 110 | | |

Replay

| Altrincham | Macclesfield Town | 3-1 | 524 |
| Daws 13, Anderson 24, McKenna 31 | Askey 85 | | |

Semi-Finals 1st leg

| Runcorn | Altrincham | 2-1 | 534 |
| Hill 72, McCarthy 75 | Shaw 44 | | |

| Yeovil Town | Wycombe Wdrs | 0-0 | 1816 |

Semi-Finals 2nd leg

Altrincham	Runcorn	1-3	605
Lee 44	Disley 2, 16, Richards 24		
	Runcorn won 5-2 on agg.		

| Wycombe Wdrs | Yeovil Town | 2-0 | 1883 |
| Creaser 69, Greene 89 | *Wycombe won 2-0 on agg.* | | |

Final 1st leg

| Runcorn | Wycombe Wdrs | 1-0 | 853 |
| Saunders 21 | | | |

Final 2nd leg

| Wycombe Wanderers | Runcorn | 2-0 | 2519 |
| Guppy 16, Carroll 74 | *Wycombe won 2-1 on agg.* | | |

DIVISION 3

COLCHESTER UNITED – GMVC
Champions 1991-92

Formed as a professional club in 1937 as successors to an older, amateur club, Colchester Town. From the Southern League they were elected to the Football League Third Division (South) in 1950. Relegated to Division Four five times, promoted to Division Three four times. Lost their League place in 1990, but regained it in 1992. Won GMVC and Trophy double 1991-92.

Ground: Layer Road Ground, Colchester, Essex, CO2 7JJ

Phone: 0206-574042   **Info Line:** 0839-664410

Manager: Roy McDonough **Secretary:** Mrs D.Elwood **Chairman:** J. Bowdidge

Colours: Navy Blue & White Stripes, Navy Blue, White **Change:** All Red

Nickname: The U's

5-Year Record

		P	W	D	F	A	Pts	Psn	Cup	FAT
87-88	FL4	46	19	10	47	51	67	9	3	–
88-89	FL4	46	12	14	60	78	50	22	4	–
89-90	FL4	46	11	10	46	75	43	24	2	–
90-91	CONF	42	25	10	68	35	85	2	2	QF
91-92	CONF	42	28	10	98	40	94	1	1	W

Major Honours: GMVC 91/2 RU 90/1. FAT 91/2.

Record Transfer Fee Received: £150,000 for Paul McGee (Wimbledon) 90

League Appearances and Goalscorers 91-92

(Details listed in the following order: Appearances, substitute appearances, goals)
P. Abrahams 0,3,0; S. Barrett 42,0,1; G. Bennett 31,7,16; E. Collins 29,4,2; J. Cook 27,2,2; W. Donald 38,2,0; S. Elliott 33,4,3; T. English 37,1,5; Goodwin 0,3,0; M. Grainger 9,2,0; Gray 1,1,0; M. Kinsella 37,5,3; R. McDonough 40,0,26; S. McGavin 39,0,19; D. Martin 8,1,0; M. Masters 7,7,7,; I. Phillips 1,2,0; S. Restarick 1,5,0; P. Roberts 34,0,1; N. Smith 42,0,8; I. Stewart 6,3,2; and M. Walsh 0,1,0. (22 players) Three own goals.

Biggest Home Win: 5-0 v Barrow/Bath City

Biggest Home Defeat: 2-3 v Farnborough Town

Biggest Away Win: 4-0 v Boston United

Biggest Away Defeat: 1-4 v Welling United

Ground Capacity: 14,000 (2,000)

Record: 19,073 v Reading FAC1 1948. Non-Lge: 7,193 v Barrow GMVC 1992

Rail: Colchester North (4 miles from ground).

Directions: Follow signs to Colchester on A12/A604 and then follow signs to Layer (B1026) into Layer Road.

GMVC CLUBS

ALTRINCHAM

Founded in 1903 and members of the Manchester League until joining the Lancashire Combination Second Division in 1911. Promoted to Division One in 1912 but left to become founder members of the Cheshire County League in 1919. Founder members of the Northern Premier League in 1968 and completed a hat-trick of foundations in 1979 when they were inaugural members of the Alliance Premier League.

Ground: Moss Lane, Altrincham, Cheshire, WA15 8AP

Phone: 061-928-1045 **Info Line:** 0898-664845

Manager: Gerry Quinn **Secretary:** Mrs J.Baldwin **Chairman:** Bill King

Colours: Red/White Stripes, Black, White **Change:** Sky Blue **Nickname:** Robins

5-Year Record

		P	W	D	F	A	Pts	Psn	Cup	FAT
87-88	CONF	42	14	10	59	59	52	14	1	QF
88-89	CONF	40	13	10	51	61	49	14	2	QF
89-90	CONF	42	12	13	59	48	49	16	4q	1
90-91	CONF	42	23	13	87	46	82	3	1	SF
91-92	CONF	42	11	12	61	82	45	18	4q	1

Major Honours: APL 79/80, 90/1; APLC 80/1; APLS 81/2; APLS RU 79/80; FAT 77/8, 85/6; BLT 80/1; BLT RU 79/80; NPLC 69/70; NPLS 79/80.

Record Transfer Fee Received: no details for Paul Edwards (Crewe Alex.)

Record Transfer Fee Paid: no details for Gary Simpson (Boston United)

League Appearances and Goalscorers 91-92

(Details listed in the following order: Appearances, substitute appearances, goals)

G. Anderson 31,0,10; S. Berryman 11,0,0; J. Brady 18,3,4; P. Burns 8,4,2; M. Carter 2,1,0; T. Chilton 4,0,0; M. Davies 4,0,0; N. Daws 39,2,4; P. Densmore 34,2,0; T. Edwards 36,1,2; S. Gresty 0,1,0; M. Hayde 9,3,0; M. Hughes 8,13,2; B. Kilshaw 3,4,0; A. Lee 30,1,0; M. Lewis 23,2,2; A. McDonald 10,4,2; K. McKenna 35,0,19; T. Miller 1,0,0; A. Reid 34,0,1; S. Roberts 6,0,0; P. Rowlands 22,1,1; S. Rudge 20,5,1; N. Shaw 29,4,10; J. Wealands 20,0,0; H. Wiggins 24,4,0; and S. Worrall 1,1,0. (27 players) One own goal.

Biggest Home Win: 4-0 v Bath City

Biggest Home Defeat: 3-7 v Slough Town

Biggest Away Win: 3-2 v Slough Town

Biggest Away Defeat: 0-5 v Kettering Town/Kidderminster Harriers

Ground Capacity: 10,000 (1,000)

Record: 10,275 v Altrinchan Boys, English Schools Shield, 1925

Rail: Altrincham (½ miles from ground). **Directions:** From South: leave M6 at Junction 19 (Manchester Airport sign) and A556 into Altrincham. From North: leave M6 at Junction 20 on to M56. Leave M56 at Junction 7 for Altrincham and A56 into Altrincham. From town centre the ground is approximately half a mile along Moss Lane from the railway station.

BATH CITY

Formed in 1889. Joined the Western League in 1908 and became Southern League members in 1921. Relegated to Division One in 1965, 1967 and 1972, they were promoted back to the Premier Division in 1966, 1969 and 1974. In 1979 they were founder members of the Alliance Premier League. Relegated to the Beazer Homes League in 1988, they were promoted back to the Conference in 1990.

Ground: Twerton Park, Twerton, Bath, Avon, BA2 1DB
Phone: 0225-423087/313247　　　　**Info Line:** 0898-884474
Manager: Tony Ricketts　**Secretary:** P.Britton　**Chairman:** R.Stock
Colours: Black and White Stripes, Black, Black/White　**Change:** All Yellow
Nickname: City

5-Year Record

		P	W	D	F	A	Pts	Psn	Cup	FAT
87-88	CONF	42	9	10	48	76	37	20	3	2
88-89	BHLP	42	15	13	66	51	58	9	2	1
89-90	BHLP	42	30	8	81	28	98	2	1	3
90-91	CONF	42	10	12	55	61	42	20	4q	3
91-92	CONF	42	16	12	54	51	60	9	3q	3

Major Honours: SL 58/9, 77/8, 89/90; SL RU 61/2, 89/90; SLD1 RU 68/9; SLC 78/9; SL v NPL 77/8.
Record Transfer Fee Received: £57,000 for Jason Dodds (Southampton) 89
Record Transfer Fee Paid: £10,000 for Tony Ricketts (Yeovil Town)
League Appearances and Goalscorers 91-92
(Details listed in the following order: Appearances, substitute appearances, goals)
P. Bailey 1,0,0; C. Banks 39,0,2; M. Boyle 33,7,10; K. Brown 28,2,2; A. Churchward 31,0,0; R. Cousins 31,0,3; R. Crowley 33,3,2; G. Dicks 22,0,0; J. Gill 13,8,1; I. Hedges 40,0,3; P. Hirons 0,2,0; S. Kean 9,1,1; S. Lundon 12,5,0; A. Mings 20,4,2; S. Painter 0,1,0; D. Payne 1,1,0; J. Preston 11,0,0; D. Radford 5,1,0; P. Randall 32,2,19; A. Ricketts 25,3,0; D. Singleton 23,12,1; A. Theobald 1,1,0; I. Weston 25,0,1; and G. Withey 35,4,6. (24 players)
Biggest Home Win: 5-1 v Cheltenham Town
Biggest Home Defeat: 0-3 v Welling United
Biggest Away Win: 5-0 v Welling United
Biggest Away Defeat: 0-5 v Colchester United
Ground Capacity: 10,300 (730)　　　　**Record:** 18,020 v Brighton FAC3 1960
Rail: Bath Spa (2 miles from ground).
Directions: Just off the A36/A4 main Bristol to Bath road – Lower Bristol Road.

BOSTON UNITED

Formed in 1934 when they joined the Midland League. Moved to the Southern League in 1958 but transferred to the Central Alliance League in 1960 and then to the reformed Midland in 1961. Resigned in 1964, and in 1966 re-emerged as United Counties Leaguers, moving on to the West Midlands (Regional) League after one season. Northern Premier League founders in 1968 and Alliance Premier League founder members in 1979.

Ground: York Street Ground, York Street, Boston, Lincolnshire
Phone: 0205-365524/5   **Info Line:** 0898-121539
Manager: Peter Morris **Secretary:** J.Blackwell **Chairman:** P.Malkinson
Colours: Off Gold , Black, Off Gold **Change:** White with Red/Blue Trim
Nickname: Pilgrims

5-Year Record		P	W	D	F	A	Pts	Psn	Cup	FAT
87-88	CONF	42	14	7	60	75	49	16	4q	2
88-89	CONF	40	22	8	61	51	74	3	3q	3
89-90	CONF	42	13	8	48	67	47	18	3q	1
90-91	CONF	42	12	11	55	69	47	18	1	1
91-92	CONF	42	18	9	71	66	63	8	2q	1

Major Honours: NPL 72/3, 73/4, 76/7, 77/8; NPL RU 71/2; NPLC 73/4, 75/6; NPLC RU 77/8; NPLS 73/4, 76/7, 77/8; FAT RU 79/80; SLNPL 76/7; SLNPL RU 73/4, 77/8.

Record Transfer Fee Received: £20,000 Gregg Fee (Sheffield Wednesday)
Record Transfer Fee Paid: £20,000 for Paul Richardson (Barnet) 7/91

League Appearances and Goalscorers 91-92
(Details listed in the following order: Appearances, substitute appearances, goals)
S. Adams 35,3,2; G. Beech 0,1,0; P. Casey 34,2,1; P. Cavell 11,0,7; S. Collins 38,1,0; G. Evans 0,1,0; M. Fletcher 0,1,1; M. Hardy 35,1,4; L. Howarth 10,0,0; G. Jones 41,1,27; L. Lamont 1,0,0; J. McGinlay 12,7,4; J. McKenna 41,0,0; A. Moore 20,6,1; S. Myles 3,1,0; M. Nesbitt 12,4,3; M. North 1,0,1; M. Nuttell 23,0,9; S. Raffell 21,2,0; D. Reddin 0,1,0; G. Retallick 7,7,0; P. Richardson 8,0,0; Smith 0,1,0; P. Shirtliff 38,0,0; S. Stoutt 34,3,7; C. Swailes 28,2,1; and R. Toone 9,9,2. (27 players) One own goal.

Biggest Home Win: 5-1 v Welling United
Biggest Home Defeat: 1-5 v Macclesfield Town
Biggest Away Win: 4-1 v Redbridge Forest
Biggest Away Defeat: 0-5 v Farnborough Town
Ground Capacity: 14,000 (2,000)
Record: 10,086 v Corby Town, Floodlight opening 1955
Rail: Boston (10 minutes from ground), also Peterborough or Grantham.
Directions: From North: A17 from Sleaford to Boston. Over railway crossing bear right to lights over bridge. Through lights to York Street. From South: A16 from Spalding to Boston. Turn right at first set of traffic lights over bridge. Through lights to York Street.

BROMSGROVE ROVERS

Formed in 1885. Members of the Birmingham Combination from 1908, they joined the Birmingham & District – later West Midland (Regional) – League in 1953. Moved to the Southern League in 1972 and in 1986 were promoted to the Premier Division.

Ground: Victoria Ground, Birmingham Road, Bromsgrove, Worcs
Phone: 0527-78260   **Nickname:** Rovers
Manager: Robert Hope   **Secretary:** B.A. Hewings   **Chairman:** C. Lloyd
Colours: Red, Black, Red   **Change:** Green, White, Green

5-Year Record		P	W	D	F	A	Pts	Psn	Cup	FAT
87-88	BHLP	42	22	11	65	39	77	4	1q	3
88-89	BHLP	42	14	16	68	56	58	10	1	1
89-90	BHLP	42	17	10	56	48	61	10	1	1
90-91	BHLP	42	20	11	68	49	71	5	4q	3q
91-92	BHLP	42	27	9	78	34	90	1	1	1

Major Honours: SLP 91/2: SLP RU 86/7: SLMD 85/6.
Record Transfer Fee Received: £10,000 Steve Smith (Walsall)
League Appearances and Goalscorers 91-92
(Details listed in the following order: Appearances, substitute appearances, goals)
S. Brighton 40,0,1; S. Burgher 7,0,0; S. Cooksey 37,0,0; S. Cooper 8,4,0; M. Crisp 39,1,12; S. Cunningham 8,4,1; T. Daly 31,2,7; B. Durkin 5,13,2; I. Gandy 2,0,0; C. Hanks 36,3,22; J. Hussey 0,1,0; K. James 2,5,0; P. Masefield 2,6,1; R. Moran 3,0,0; M. O'Connor 33,1,6; S. O'Meara 37,1,9; M. Pugh 0,3,0; K. Richardson 39,0,0; D. Rolfe 1,6,1; J. Ross 0,1,0; J. Skelding 42, 0,0; R. Sweeney 0,2,0; S. Stott 33,1,9; S. Volrath 0,2,0; P. Wardle 12,8,0; P. Webb 36,1,4; and M. Whitehouse 4,11,0. (27 players).

Biggest Home Win: 7-0 v Fisher Athletic
Biggest Home Defeat: 0-2 v Cambridge City/Gloucester City
Biggest Away Win: 3-0 v Crawley Town
Biggest Away Defeat: 1-3 v Burton Albion
Ground Capacity: 4,800 (375)
Record: 7,563 v Worcester City, Birmingham Senior Cup 1987/8
Rail: Bromsgrove.
Directions: The Victoria Ground is situated on the north side of Bromsgrove on the Birmingham Road (A38) opposite petrol station.

DAGENHAM and REDBRIDGE

Formed in the 1992 close season on the amalgamation of Dagenham (founded 1949) and Redbridge Forest. The Forest club was formed by the amalgamation of Leytonstone Ilford and Walthamstow Avenue (1900) in 1988. Leytonstone (1886) and Ilford (1881) joined together in 1979 and the Redbridge Forest name was first used in 1989.

Ground: Victoria Road, Dagenham, Essex, RM10 7XL

Phone: 081-592-1549   **Nickname:** The Stones

Manager: John Still   **Secretary:** Ken Mizen   **Chairman:** David Andrews

Colours: Red with Blue Trim, Royal Blue, Red

Change: Yellow and Green

5-Year Record

Leytonstone Ilford

		P	W	D	F	A	Pts	Psn	Cup	FAT
87-88	VLP	42	20	11	59	43	71	4	4q	3q
88-89	VLP	42	26	11	76	37	89	1	2q	3q

Redbridge Forest

		P	W	D	F	A	Pts	Psn	Cup	FAT
89-90	VLP	42	16	11	65	62	59	11	1q	3
90-91	VLP	42	29	6	74	43	93	1	3q	3
91-92	CONF	42	18	9	69	56	63	7	2q	QF

Dagenham

		P	W	D	F	A	Pts	Psn	Cup	FAT
87-88	CONF	42	5	6	37	104	21	22	1	1
88-89	VLP	42	11	12	53	68	45	18	1	1
89-90	VLP	42	17	15	54	43	66	6	4q	1
90-91	VLP	42	13	11	62	68	50	14	4q	3q
91-92	DLP	42	15	16	70	59	61	9	1q	1

Major Honours: Leytonstone, Ilford, Walthamstow Avenue, Leytonstone Ilford and Redbridge Forest all Isthmian League champions.

Record Transfer Fee Received: £100,000 for Andy Hessenthaler (Watford) 9/91

Record Transfer Fee Paid: £10,000 for Gary Blackford (Barnet) 1/91

League Appearances and Goalscorers 91-92 (Redbridge Forest)

(Details listed in the following order: Appearances, substitute appearances, goals)

N. Ashford 9,3,0; K. Barrett 10,1,0; I. Bennett 18,0,0; G. Blackford 21,1,2; J. Broom 19,5,2; P. Cavell 28,0,22; M. Cawston 2,0,0; R. Cherry 6,3,1; M. Cole 1,3,0; S. Connor 42,0,3; K. Davidson 7,3,0; I. Docker 6,3,0; M. Ebdon 22,0,7; K. Foster 9,0,0; L. Fulling 1,0,0; R. Garvey 11,3,2; N. Grice 4,0,1; H. Hayrettin 5,0,1; A. Hessenthaler 3,0,1; A. Hopping 1,0,0; P. Hucker 6,0,0; P. Jackman 8,0,0; D. Jacques 33,1,0; B. Mayes 30,4,6; A. Owers 7,2,0; T. Pamphlett 39,0,4; P. Richardson 27,0,3; D. Riley 7,0,2; L. Scott 3,0,0; K. Shoemake 3,0,0; C. Sowerby 8,1,1; T. Sullivan 0,1,0; P. Taylor 1,1,0; M. Walsh 24,5,9; and P. Watts 40,0,2. (35 players)

Biggest Home Win: 5-0 Redbridge Forest v Kidderminster

Biggest Home Defeat: 0-5 Redbridge Forest v Wycombe Wanderers

Biggest Away Win: 7-0 Redbridge Forest v Cheltenham
Biggest Away Defeat: 1-5 Redbridge Forest v Kidderminster
Ground Capacity: 7,500 (450)   **Record:** Dagenham: 7,100 v Reading
FAC2R 1968. Redbridge Forest: 2,891 v Wycombe CONF 4/92
Rail: Dagenham East (Underground 500 yards from ground).
Directions: Victoria Road runs off the A1112 between the A12 and A13.

FARNBOROUGH TOWN

Founded in 1967, first playing in the Surrey Senior League Division One in 1968. Promoted to the Premier Division in 1971 and moved to the London Spartan League in 1972. On moving to a new ground at Cherrywood Road changed leagues, becoming Athenians in 1976-77 and Isthmians the next season. Promoted to the Premier Division in 1985. Promoted to the Conference in 1989 but relegated after only one season, being allocated to the Southern League. Returned to the Conference a season later.

Ground: John Roberts Ground, Cherrywood Road, Farnborough, Hants, GU14 8UD
Phone: 0252-541469/541171   **Nickname:** Boro
Manager: Ted Pearce **Secretary:** Terry Parr **Chairman:** Charlie Mortimore
Colours: All Yellow with Blue Trim   **Change:** White with Red Trim, White, Red

5-Year Record		P	W	D	F	A	Pts	Psn	Cup	FAT
87-88	VLP	42	17	11	63	60	62	8	1	1
88-89	VLP	42	24	9	85	61	81	2	4q	2q
89-90	CONF	42	10	12	60	73	42	21	1	3
90-91	BHLP	42	26	7	79	43	85	1	1	2
91-92	CONF	42	18	12	68	543	66	5	3	3

Major Honours: BHL 90/1; VOL R 89/90; IST D1 84/5. D2 78/9; ATH D2 76/7; LSP 72/3, 73/4, 74/5.
League Appearances and Goalscorers 91-92
(Details listed in the following order: Appearances, substitute appearances, goals)
K. Baker 35,2,0; S. Baker 16,0,0; P. Batey 9,0,0; B. Broome 32,2,5; A. Bye 37,0,3; A. Cockram 3,1,1; D. Coleman 10,0,0; A. Coles 2,2,0; A. Comfort 6,1,1; D. Coney 20,0,6; P. Coombs 8,3,4; G. Cooper 4,0,1; T. Dalton 9,0,0; M. Doherty 17,3,5; M. Fleming 16,7,0; G. Hobson 3,0,0; D. Holmes 37,3,4; J. Horton 28,10,3; P. Hucker 11,0,0; D. Leworthy 19,0,12; Lovell 3,5,0; J. Power 21,0,0; S. Read 34,2,21; A. Rogers 17,4,1; W. Stamp 17,0,0; G. Stevens 1,2,0; P. Thompson 1,0,0; M. Turkington 7,1,0; and J. Wigmore 36,2,1. (29 players)
Biggest Home Win: 5-0 v Barrow/Boston United
Biggest Home Defeat: 2-4 v Northwich Victoria
Biggest Away Win: 5-0 v Slough Town
Biggest Away Defeat: 1-4 v Witton Albion

Ground Capacity: 4,000 (300)   Record: 3,069 v Colchester, CONF 11/91
Rail: Farnborough (Main), Farnborough North.
Directions: From M3 (Junction 4) along A325, turn into Prospect Avenue
(signed FT FC), second right into Cherrywood Road.

GATESHEAD

Present club formed in 1977 and took the Northern Premier League place of
the former Gateshead club. Promoted to the Conference in 1983, they were
relegated to the Northern Premier in 1985 only to return to the Conference in
1986. Relegated in 1987, they re-entered the Conference again in 1990.
Ground: The International Stadium, Neilson Road, Gateshead, NE10 0EF
Phone: 091-478-3883   Info Line:
Manager: Tommy Cassidy Secretary: Clare Tierney Chairman: J. Gibson
Colours: White, Black, Black   Change: Blue, White, Blue
Nickname: Tynesiders

5-Year Record		P	W	D	F	A	Pts	Psn	Cup	FAT
87-88	NPLP	42	11	7	52	71	40	18	1q	2T
88-89	HFSP	42	7	13	36	70	34	21	2q	3q
89-90	HFSP	42	22	10	78	58	76	2	3q	2q
90-91	CONF	42	14	6	52	92	48	17	1q	2
91-92	CONF	42	12	12	49	57	48	14	4q	3

Major Honours: NPL 82/3, 85/6; NPL RU 89/90; NPLC RU 89/90; NPLS
86/7.
Record Transfer Fee Received: £3,000 for Jimmy McGinley (Sunderland)
Record Transfer Fee Paid: £6,500 for Richard Toone (Boston Utd) 2/91
League Appearances and Goalscorers 91-92
(Details listed in the following order: Appearances, substitute appearances, goals)
B. Askew 4,0,0; D. Bell 40,1,1; G. Brabin 0,2,0; C. Butler 21,12,4; S.
Chambers 10,0,2; D. Corner 35,0,4; S. Cuthbert 10,2,4; K. Davies 2,1,0; A.
Dixon 5,0,1; K. Dixon 9,8,3; P. Emson 2,2,1; M. Farrey 31,3,0; G. Forrest
30,2,1; A. Gourlay 2,0,1; N. Granycome 22,2,1; N. Grayson 14,0,3; S.
Guthrie 4,0,1; B. Halliday 28,0,1; B. Healey 13,0,2; S. Higgins 13,0,0; M.
Hopkinson 0,1,0; I. Johnson 7,1,0; A. Lamb 26,0,14; G. Leishman 5,0,0;
P. Linacre 11,6,4; T. Lowery 8,0,0; I. McInerney 2,0,0; S. O'Brien 11,2,0;
N. Peverell 2,2,0; N. Saddington 17,0,0; D. Scope 2,0,0; S. Smith 42,0,0;
C. Veart 28,7,1; K. Wharton 1,0,0; and D. Wheatley 3,5,0. (35 players)
Biggest Home Win: 4-0 v Altrincham
Biggest Home Defeat: 0-3 v Kidderminster Harriers
Biggest Away Win: 4-1 v Merthyr Tydfil
Biggest Away Defeat: 3-5 v Kidderminster Harriers
Ground Capacity: 12,000 (12,000)
Record: 5,012 v Newcastle United, Testimonial 8/84

Rail: Newcastle Central (2 miles from ground).
Directions: Follow A1(M) to the end of motorway, then take first exit to join A6115. Continue on this road for 3 miles passing one roundabout. Stadium is located on the right.

KETTERING TOWN

Founded in 1876, Kettering joined the Midland League in 1892. From 1900 the club had intermittent Southern League experience, for some of the period playing in the Northants County League (later the United Counties League), the Central Alliance, the Birmingham & District League and local junior football. They joined the Southern League for the fourth time in 1950. Three times relegated from the top section but promoted back each time, they were Alliance Premier League founder members in 1979.

Ground: Rockingham Road, Kettering, Northants, NN16 9AW
Phone: 0536-83028   **Info Line:** 0898-888639
Manager: Dave Cusack   **Secretary:** G.T.Ellitson   **Chairman:** Brain Talbot
Colours: All Red   **Change:** All Blue
Nickname: Poppies
5-Year Record

		P	W	D	F	A	Pts	Psn	Cup	FAT
87-88	CONF	42	22	9	68	48	75	3	1q	2
88-89	CONF	40	23	7	56	39	76	2	4	2
89-90	CONF	42	18	12	66	53	66	5	1	1
90-91	CONF	42	23	11	67	45	80	4	4q	3
91-92	CONF	42	20	13	72	50	73	3	3	3

Major Honours: SLP 78/9; SLC 74/5; GMACC 87; APL RU 78/9; APLC RU 88/9; APLS RU 81; FAT RU 78/9.
Record Transfer Fee Received: £60,000 for Cohen Griffith (Cardiff City)
Record Transfer Fee Paid: £17,500 for Gary Jones (Grantham) 1/90
League Appearances and Goalscorers 91-92
(Details listed in the following order: Appearances, substitute appearances, goals)
P. Bancroft 26,5,3; D. Barker 4,0,0; P. Bastock 24,0,0; D. Bloodworth 10,2,0; P. Brown 38,1,10; S. Butterworth 8,0,1; T. Christie 19,2,5; P. Cotton 4,2,0; P. Cox 1,0,0; P. Culpin 4,0,0; H. Curtis 17,0,0; P. Emson 2,1,1; P. Gavin 15,0,3; J. Graham 30,8,19; R. Hill 41,0,16; L. Howarth 6,0,0; R. Huxford 42,0,1; P. Jones 16,3,0; D. Keast 26,7,1; P. Nicol 42,0,2; M. North 4,4,6; G. Price 17,2,0; K. Shoemake 18,0,0; T. Slack 37,1,1; R. Walker 5,0,1; Waller 2,5,0; and M. Walsh 5,0,0. (27 players). Two own goals.
Biggest Home Win: 5-0 v Altrincham
Biggest Home Defeat: 1-3 v Boston United
Biggest Away Win: 3-0 v Cheltenham
Biggest Away Defeat: 0-4 v Redbridge Forest
Ground Capacity: 6,500 (1,250)

Record: 6,950 v Northampton Town, FAC1 1990
Rail: Kettering (1 mile from ground).
Directions: Located on A6003 Kettering to Oakham road about one mile from town centre.

KIDDERMINSTER HARRIERS

The Athletics Club came into being in 1877, turning to soccer in 1886 and amalgamating with Kidderminster Olympic in 1890. Birmingham League founder members and long-term participants, returning in 1960 after periods in the Birmingham Combination and Southern Leagues. Moved from the West Midland League to the Southern in 1972 and in 1983 they were promoted to the Gola League.

Ground: Aggborough, Hoo Road, Kidderminster, DY10 1NB
Phone: 0562-823931   **Info Line:** 0898-121547
Manager: Graham Allner   **Secretary:** R.Mercer   **Chairman:** D.Reynolds
Colours: Red and White Halves, White, White
Change: Yellow and Blue, Blue, Blue   **Nickname:** The Harriers

5-Year Record		P	W	D	F	A	Pts	Psn	Cup	FAT
87-88	CONF	42	18	15	75	66	69	7	2	2
88-89	CONF	40	21	6	68	57	69	5	4q	3
89-90	CONF	42	15	9	64	67	54	13	1	QF
90-91	CONF	42	14	10	56	67	52	13	1	F
91-92	CONF	42	12	9	56	77	45	19	1	3

Major Honours: FAT 86/7, RU 90/91; WFAC RU 85/6, 88/9; SLC 79/80; SLP RU 82/3.
Record Transfer Fee Received: £60,000 for Paul Jones (Woves) 6/91
Record Transfer Fee Paid: £17,000 for Antone Joseph, 12/89
League Appearances and Goalscorers 91-92
(Details listed in the following order: Appearances, substitute appearances, goals)
D. Barnett 20,0,2; D. Benton 38,1,2; P. Bradley 0,1,0; M. Carroll 2,4,0; M. Coogan 0,1,0; P. Davies 30,3,4; M. Davis 3,1,0; R. Forsyth 14,1,3; C. Gillett 10,3,0; P. Grainger 8,0,3; R. Green 40,0,0; B. Hackett 4,0,0; D. Hadley 18,2,1; J. Hanson 3,3,0; P. Howell 27,4,9; D. Humphreys 35,2,7; A. Joseph 35,4,1; A. Kurila 5,1,1; S. Lilwall 24,4,3; J. McGrath 35,0,0; G. MacKenzie 11,0,0; D. Mulholland 5,0,0; D. Stedman 2,0,0; J. Taylor 1,1,0; M. Weir 37,0,4; M. Whitehouse 19,1,10; B. Wilcox 30,2,5; and M. Wolsey 6,4,0. (28 players) One own goal.
Biggest Home Win: 5-0 v Altrincham
Biggest Home Defeat: 1-3 v Boston United/Welling United
Biggest Away Win: 3-0 v Gateshead
Biggest Away Defeat: 0-5 v Redbridge Forest
Ground Capacity: 10,000 (400)   **Record:** 9,155 v Hereford Utd, FAC1 48/9
Rail: Kidderminster (½ mile from ground).

Directions: From North and Midlands: A456 turn-off from M5, 10 miles to Kidderminster (mostly dual carriageway), turn left at first set of lights (into Chester Road), turn right at next set of lights, turn into Hoo Road (before ring road). From South: Kidderminster turn-off from M5, 12 miles to Kidderminster (mostly dual carriageway), turn right at first island approaching Kidderminster, first turning left into Hoo Road.

MACCLESFIELD TOWN

Founded in 1874 as Macclesfield, they have occuppied their Moss Rose Ground since 1891. Founder members of the Cheshire County League (1919) and participants until being founder members of the Northern Premier League in 1968. Promoted to the Conference in 1987.

Ground: Moss Rose Gd, London Road, Macclesfield, Cheshire, SK11 7SP
Phone: 0625-511545/24324   **Info Line:** 0898-121546
Manager: Peter Wragg   **Secretary:** B.Lingard   **Chairman:** A.Brocklehurst
Colours: Blue, White, Blue   **Change:** White, Black, Red
Nickname: The Silkmen

5-Year Record		P	W	D	F	A	Pts	Psn	Cup	FAT
87-88	CONF	42	18	9	64	62	63	11	3	QF
88-89	CONF	40	17	10	63	57	61	7	4q	F
89-90	CONF	42	17	15	56	41	66	4	1	2
90-91	CONF	42	17	12	63	52	63	7	4Q	1
91-92	CONF	42	13	13	50	50	52	13	2q	SF

Major Honours: FAT 69/70; FAT RU 88/9; NPL 68/9, 69/70, 85/6; NPLC 85/6; NPLPC 86.
Record Transfer Fee Received: £40,000 Mike Lake (Sheffield Utd) 1988
Record Transfer Fee Paid: £6,000 for George Shepherd (Hyde United)
League Appearances and Goalscorers 91-92
(Details listed in the following order: Appearances, substitute appearances, goals)
J. Askey 33,0,5; S. Bimson 12,1,2; D. Boughey 1,2,0; P. Clayton 10,11,1; J. Dawson 5,10,1; M. Dempsey 33,1,1; M. Doherty 15,0,6; E. Edwards 38,0,3; R. Ellis 14,9,2; M. Farrelly 26,1,1; S. Farrelly 39,0,0; A. Green 25,0,8; S. Hanlon 38,0,2; D. Heesom 11,0,0; T. Hopley 2,3,2; J. Imrie 1,0,0; P. Johnson 34,0,1; P. Kendall 13,1,0; C. Lambert 38,1,8; M. Rutter 1,0,0; G. Shepherd 31,0,0; J. Timmons 31,5,4; G. Tobin 8,1,0; and A. Zelem 3,1,0. (24 players) Three own goals.
Biggest Home Win: 3-0 v Merthyr Tydfil/Runcorn United
Biggest Home Defeat: 0-2 v Kettering Town
Biggest Away Win: 5-1 v Boston United
Biggest Away Defeat: 2-4 v Colchester United
Ground Capacity: 6,000 (600)   **Record:** 8,900 v Stockport, FAC1 12/67
Rail: Macclesfield (1 mile from ground).
Directions: At south end of town on main road to Leek (A523).

MERTHYR TYDFIL

Formed in 1945 and joined the Southern League in the competition's second post-war season. They were re-organised into the First Division in 1959; promoted to the Premier Division in 1961; relegated to the First in 1964; promoted again in 1971; and relegated again in 1972. After the regionalised period they found themselves in the lower section again in 1982. Promoted to the Premier Division in 1988, and promoted to the Conference in 1989.

Ground: Penydarren Park, Merthyr Tydfil, Mid Glam, CF47 8RF

Phone: 0685-384102   **Info Line:** 0898-884533

Manager: Wynford Hopkins **Secretary:** Brian Davies **Chairman:** J.Reddy

Colours: White, Black, Black   **Change:** Red, White, Red

Nickname: The Martyrs

5-Year Record		P	W	D	F	A	Pts	Psn	Cup	FAT
87-88	BHLM	42	30	4	102	40	94	1	1	1
88-89	BHLP	42	26	7	104	58	85	1	1	3
89-90	CONF	42	16	14	67	63	62	9	2	1
90-91	CONF	42	16	9	62	61	57	9	2	2
91-92	CONF	42	18	14	59	56	68	4	4q	2

Major Honours: WFAC 48/9, 50/1, 86/7; SL(BHL) 47/8, 49/50, 50/1, 51/2, 53/4, 88/8, 89/90; SL RU 52/3, 70/71; SL(BHL)D1 87/8; SLD1 RU 78/; SLC 47/8, 50/1.

Record Transfer Fee Received: £12,000 for Ray Pratt (Exeter City)

Record Transfer Fee Paid: no details

League Appearances and Goalscorers 91-92

(Details listed in the following order: Appearances, substitute appearances, goals)
G. Abraham 8,0,0; A. Beattie 35,4,0; T. Boyle 41,0,2; E. Chiverton 3,7,1; M. Coates 7,2,1; D. D'Auria 31,4,5; S. Davey 6,2,1; P. Evans 7,0,0; C. Hemming 10,0,0; T. Hutchinson 29,1,2; T. James 36,0,0; R. Lewis 23,0,0; J. Morgan 1,1,0; K. Rogers 27,5,5; J. Sherwood 7,2,0; I. Thompson 6,1,1; M. Tucker 32,5,4; G. Wager 31,0,0; D. Webley 36,2,20; C. Williams 37,1,16; M. Williams 36,0,0; D. Withers 2,2,1; and G. Wood 11,0,0. (23 players).

Biggest Home Win: 4-1 v Kettering Town

Biggest Home Defeat: 1-4 v Gateshead

Biggest Away Win: 2-1 v Cheltenham Town/Telford United/Welling United

Biggest Away Defeat: 0-4 v Wycombe Wanderers

Ground Capacity: 10,000 (1,500)   **Record:** 21,000 v Reading, FAC 1949

Rail: Merthyr Tydfil (½ mile from ground).

Directions: From South (A470): Express Way to Merthyr, through town centre, follow signs to Tregenna Hotel, Park Terrace. From North: Heads of the Valley road to town centre, bear right at traffic lights, follow signs for Tregenna Hotel, Park Terrace.

NORTHWICH VICTORIA

Founded in 1874, the club were Football League Division Two founder members in 1892. After two seasons they left the League and played in the Combination and Manchester League. Cheshire County League founder members in 1919, Northern Premier League founders in 1968 and Alliance Premier League founder members in 1979.

Ground: The Drill Field, Drill Field Road, Northwich, Cheshire, CW9 5HN
Phone: 0606-41450   **Info Line:** 0898-664813
Manager: Sammy McIlroy   **Secretary:** D.R.Nuttall   **Chairman:** D.H.Stone
Colours: Green and White, White, White **Change:** Claret, Sky Blue, Claret
Nickname: Vics

5-Year Record		P	W	D	F	A	Pts	Psn	Cup	FAT
87-88	CONF	42	10	17	46	57	47	17	2	1
88-89	CONF	40	14	11	64	65	53	10	2	2
89-90	CONF	42	15	5	51	67	50	15	1	2
90-91	CONF	42	13	13	65	75	52	12	4q	QF
91-92	CONF	42	16	6	63	48	54	11	1q	3

Major Honours: FAT 83/4; FAT RU 82/3; WFAC RU 1881/2, 1888/9; BLT 79/80; APLS 80; NPL RU: 76/7; NPLC 72/3; NPLC RU 78/9.
Record Transfer Fee Received: £35,000 for Shaun Teale (Weymouth) 9/87
Record Transfer Fee Paid: £10,000 for Malcolm O'Connor (Hyde) 8/88
League Appearances and Goalscorers 91-92
(Details listed in the following order: Appearances, substitute appearances, goals)
G. Ainsworth 14,0,4; T. Ball 8,0,0; S. Berryman 12,0,0; C. Blain 24,3,4; C. Blundell 36,0,1; A. Bullock 22,0,0; A. Butler 33,2,4; P. Donnelly 6,1,0; G. Easter 14,1,3; Edwardson 4,2,1; A. Feeley 13,0,1; A. Graham 13,6,3; S. Gresty 0,3,0; L. Hackett 1,0,0; M. Hancock 33,0,0; T. Hancock 2,0,0; A. Hemmings 34,5,11; S. Holland 7,4,2; M. Jones 41,0,0; D. Lenton 2,1,0; S. Locke 42,0,1; M. McCarrick 5,0,0; S. McIlroy 7,0,0; M. O'Connor 40,0,19; D. O'Gorman 7,1,2; J. Stringer 20,1,6; M. Vaughan 21,4,0; and M. Wrench 1,1,0. (28 players). One own goal.
Biggest Home Win: 6-1 v Barrow
Biggest Home Defeat: 1-3 v Bath City
Biggest Away Win: 4-1 v Telford United
Biggest Away Defeat: 1-6 v Welling United
Ground Capacity: 16,000 (600)   **Record:** 12,000 v Watford, FAC4 1977
Rail: Northwich (1 mile from ground).
Directions: M6 Junction 19. Take Chester road to roundabout and head for Bus Station (6 miles from M6). Ground adjacent to Bus Station.

RUNCORN

Formed in 1918, Runcorn were founder members of the Cheshire League and its first champions in 1919. Left to become founder members of the Northern Premier League in 1968. Joined the Alliance Premier League in its third season, 1981-82, and were champions in their first season.

Ground: Canal Street, Runcorn, Cheshire, WA7 1RZ
Phone: 0928-560076   **Info Line:** 0898-664814
Manager: John Carroll   **Secretary:** D.Bignall   **Chairman:** David Robinson
Colours: Yellow, Green, Yellow   **Change:** Red and White, Red, Red
Nickname: Linnets

5-Year Record		P	W	D	F	A	Pts	Psn	Cup	FAT
87-88	CONF	42	21	11	68	47	74	4	2	3
88-89	CONF	40	19	8	77	53	65	6	2	1
89-90	CONF	42	19	13	59	62	70	3	4q	3
90-91	CONF	42	16	10	69	67	58	8	1	2
91-92	CONF	42	13	13	50	63	46	16	1	2

Major Honours: APL 81/2; APLS 82/3, 84/5; BLT 82/3, 84/5; RU 91/2; FAT RU 85/6; NPL 75/6, 80/1; NPLS 80/1, 81/2.
Record Transfer Fee Received: £40,000 for Mark Carter (Barnet) 2/91
League Appearances and Goalscorers 91-92
(Details listed in the following order: Appearances, substitute appearances, goals)
T. Abrahams 0,3,0; J. Bates 27,0,0; G. Brabin 31,0,3; I. Brady 7,1,1; S. Byrne 20,0,0; J. Carroll 20,0,1; S. Carter 1,0,0; A. Diggle 1,1,0; M. Disley 2,0,1; K. Hagan 1,1,0; M. Hanchard 5,0,1; I. Harold 30,0,0; C. Hawtin 8,5,0; M. Henshaw 7,4,0; G. Hill 38,0,2; P. Hughes 1,0,0; J. Imrie 3,1,0; King 0,1,0; S. Lundon 11,5,2; D. McCarthy 24,0,8; P. Mullen 36,0,0; J. Pallidino 16,0,0; I. Redman 19,6,2; Richards 14,4,0; T. Rigby 0,2,0; J. Routledge 2,0,0; S. Saunders 35,0,12; P. Shaughnessy 37,2,11; P. Varden 0,6,0; J. Wall 9,0,1; J. Waring 0,2,0; B. Wellings 9,6,1; A. Williams 24,0,0; and P. Withers 24,14,4. (34 players).

Biggest Home Win: 4-1 v Kidderminster Harriers
Biggest Home Defeat: 1-3 v Colchester United
Biggest Away Win: 4-1 v Yeovil Town
Biggest Away Defeat: 1-4 v Cheltenham Town
Ground Capacity: 8,400 (250)   **Record:** 10,011 v Preston NE, FAC3 1939
Rail: Runcorn (2 miles from ground).
Directions: From South: M56 (Junction 11) follow signs for Warrington for 1 mile, left at roundabout (signposted Widnes, Liverpool). Stay on this road for approx 4 miles, exit at Runcorn Old Town. From North: M62 (Junction 7) follow signs for Widnes/Runcorn. Go over Widnes/Runcorn bridge. Exit for Runcorn Old Town.

SLOUGH TOWN

Slough FC emerged from the amalgamation of several clubs in 1890 and played in the Southern Alliance and Great Western Suburban League. In 1920 they joined the Spartan League. During the Second World War they amalgamated with Slough Centre to become Slough United and in 1945 they became founder members of the Corinthian League. In 1947 Slough Centre reformed and the remaining part of the club became Slough Town. Absorbed into the Athenian League in 1963, they joined the Isthmian set-up in 1973. Promoted into the top section at the first attempt, they stayed there until promoted to the Conference in 1990.

Ground: Wexham Park Stadium, Wexham Road, Slough, SL2 5QR
Phone: 0753-523358   **Info Line:** 0898-446885
Manager: Alan Davies   **Secretary:** R.B.S.Hayward   **Chairman:** Tony Abbott
Colours: Amber and Navy broad hoops, Navy Blue, Navy Blue
Change: Royal Blue, White   **Nickname:** The Rebels

5-Year Record		P	W	D	F	A	Pts	Psn	Cup	FAT
87-88	VLP	42	21	9	67	41	72	3	4q	2
88-89	VLP	42	24	6	72	42	78	3	4q	1
89-90	VLP	42	27	11	85	38	92	1	1	1
90-91	CONF	42	13	6	51	80	45	19	2q	1
91-92	CONF	42	13	6	56	82	45	20	1	1

Major Honours: IPL 81/2, 89/90; ILD2 RU 73/4; ACDC 75/6, 80/1; ILCS RU 81/2.
Record Transfer Fee Received: £20,000 for Eric Young (Brighton)
Record Transfer Fee Paid: £18,000 for Colin Fielder (Farnborough) 8/91
League Appearances and Goalscorers 91-92
(Details listed in the following order: Appearances, substitute appearances, goals)
D. Anderson 37,0,8; T. Booker 4,0,0; J. Brown 0,1,0; T. Bunting 27,0,0; P. Burns 3,0,0; T. Dell 4,1,0; G. Donnellan 27,0,0; C. Fielder 38,0,0; S. Hemsley 11,1,0; S. Hickey 2,6,0; M. Hill 31,1,0; F. Joseph 4,2,2; T. Knight 21,0,0; T. Lynch 1,0,0; P. McKinnon 35,0,15; M. Mallinson 29,0,1; C.Moussaddik 3,0,0; E. O'Connor 14,6,3; A. Pluckrose 36,0,6; M. Putnam 6,2,0; B. Rake 1,0,0; S. Scott 11,2,2; J. Sitton 4,0,0; P. Stacey 33,0,1; N. Stanley 18,7,2; S. Thompson 23,0,10; M. Turkington 10,0,1; R. Watkiss 9,0,0; and S. Whitby 20,3,0. (29 players). One own goal.
Biggest Home Win: 4-0 v Redbridge Forest
Biggest Home Defeat: 0-5 v Farnborough Town
Biggest Away Win: 7-3 v Altrincham
Biggest Away Defeat: 0-4 v Colchester United/Redbridge Forest
Ground Capacity: 7,000 (395)   **Record:** 5,000 v Millwall, FAC1 1982
Rail: Slough (2 miles from ground).   **Directions:** From North: M40 Junction 1. Follow A412 for 3 miles, turn right, signposted Wexham Park Hospital. Club ½ mile south of Hospital. From East: M4 Junction 5. Follow A4 for 2 miles, turn right A412, turn left, signposted Hospital. From West: M4 Junction 6. At A4 turn right, follow signs for Wexham Park Hospital.

STAFFORD RANGERS

Probably formed around 1876. Members of the North Staffordshire League, then played in the Birmingham League 1900-12, Birmingham Combination 1912-21, and Birmingham League again until the Second World War. Revived by supporters in 1946, they returned to the Birmingham Combination but switched to the Cheshire County League in 1952. Northern Premier League founder members in 1968, they were Alliance Premier League founder members in 1979. Apart from 1983-85 they have been at Conference level ever since.

Ground: Marston Road, Stafford, ST16 3BX

Phone: 0785-42750   **Info Line:** 0898-664839   **Nickname:** Boro

Manager: Dennis Booth   **Secretary:** Mrs A.Meddings   **Chairman:** J. Horton

Colours: Black & White, White, White   **Change:** All Yellow with Red Trim

5-Year Record

		P	W	D	F	A	Pts	Psn	Cup	FAT
87-88	CONF	42	20	9	79	58	69	6	2q	3
88-89	CONF	42	11	9	49	54	40	19	1	1
89-90	CONF	42	12	12	50	62	48	17	1	SF
90-91	CONF	42	12	14	51	50	50	15	1	1†
91-92	CONF	42	10	16	41	59	46	17	4q	1

† Tie awarded to opponents

Major Honours: NPL 71/2, 84/5; FAT 71/2, 78/9; FAT RU 75/6; BLT 85/6; NPLS 84/5.

Record Transfer Fee Received: £100,000 Stan Colleymore (C. Palace) 1990

Record Transfer Fee Paid: £11,000 for Steve Butterworth (VS Rugby) 12/90

League Appearances and Goalscorers 91-92

(Details listed in the following order: Appearances, substitute appearances, goals)
S. Anastasi 4,1,0; C. Baker 0,2,0; G. Berry 7,0,0; J. Berks 2,1,0; P. Berks 11,5,1; M. Booth 7,1,1; Boyle 3,0,0; M. Bradshaw 34,3,1; D. Bremner 7,0,0; Brown 5,1,0; Brough 5,0,0; S. Butterworth 1,0,0; N. Callaghan 7,0,0; J. Dawson 8,1,1; P. Devlin 26,0,3; Edwards 7,0,3; S. Essex 37,0,1; D. Foreman 10,0,4; D. Harle 5,0,0; Harman 4,0,0; C. Heggs 4,0,1; C. Hemming 22,0,0; A. Hodkinson 3,0,1; V. Hollier 1,0,0; D. Hope 8,10,1; P. Jones 9,0,0; Lindsey 8,3,0; I. Miller 12,1,1; K. Mower 2,0,0; D. Newman 3,3,0; B. Palgrave 15,2,2; J. Pearson 27,4,0; R. Price 42,0,0; Roberts 1,0,0; S. Rooney 1,0,0; W. Simpson 39,0,6; Straw 1,3,0; M. Tuohy 12,0,2; Wareing 0,2,0; Wells 6,1,1; M. Whitehouse 1,1,0; P. Wilson 5,0,0; J. Withe 2,0,1; J. Wolverson 6,0,2; and F. Wood 36,1,3. (45 players) 3 own goals.

Biggest Home Win: 3-2 v Telford United/Witton Albion

Biggest Home Defeat: 1-3 v Gateshead

Biggest Away Win: 1-0 v Yeovil Town

Biggest Away Defeat: 0-6 v Witton Albion

Ground Capacity: 9,500 (426)   **Record:** 8,536 v Rotherham, FAC3 1/75

Rail: Stafford (2 miles from ground).   **Directions:** M6 Junction 14, follow signs for Stafford and Stone, straight over the island, third exit right, signposted Common Road. Ground is straight ahead.

STALYBRIDGE CELTIC

Founded in 1911. In 1921 they moved via the Lancashire Combination and the Central League to be founder members of the Football League Division Three (North). Dropped out after a couple of seasons and joined the Cheshire County League. Became founder members of the North West Counties League in 1982 and, in 1987, founder members of the Northern Premier League First Division. Promoted to the Premier Division in 1988 and to the Conference in 1992.

Ground: Bower Fold, Mottram Road, Stalybridge, Cheshire
Phone: 061-338-2828   **Nickname:** Celtic
Manager: Phil Wilson   **Secretary:** Martin Torr   **Chairman:** Ray Connor
Colours: All Royal Blue   **Change:** All Red

5-Year Record		P	W	D	F	A	Pts	Psn	Cup	FAT
87-88	NPL1	36	22	6	72	42	72	2	1q	3q
88-89	HFSP	42	9	13	46	81	40	19	1q	2q
89-90	HFSP	42	12	9	48	61	45	17	1q	1q*
90-91	HFSP	40	22	11	44	26	77	2	1q	2q
91-92	HFSP	42	26	14	84	33	92	1	4q	3

* Tie awarded to opponents

Major Honours: NPL 91/2; NPL RU 90/1; NPL D1 RU 87/8.
Record Transfer Fee Received: £4,000 Eamon O'Keefe (Plymouth Agy)
Record Transfer Fee Paid: £1,200 Paul Higginbottom (Glossop)
HFS League Appearances and Goalscorers 91-92
(Details listed in the following order: Appearances, substitute appearances, goals)
J. Aspinall 42,0,7; G. Bauress 31,0,5; P. Bennett 41,0,4; R. Blackman 32,1,1; C. Booth 0,1,0; K. Booth 33,1,0; J. Brown 39,0,8; M. Burrell 13,5,1; C. Camden 42,0,31; D. Coyne 1,0,0; P. Dixon 40,1,1; N. Edmonds 4,3,0; M. Edwards 8,2,5; M. Filson 1,0,0; P. Higginbottom 14,0,3; R. Hughes 41,0,0; S. Leicester 28,6,5; K. O'Connell 4,1,1; S. O'Shea 5,2,0; E. Priest 14,7,6; C. Sharratt 15,4,1; J. Smith 14,0,3; A. Woan 0,5,0. (23 players).
Biggest Home Win: 7-0 v Goole Town
Biggest Home Defeat: 1-2 v Hyde United
Biggest Away Win: 4-1 v Bishop Auckland
Biggest Away Defeat: 1-3 v Gainsborough Trinity
Capacity: 7,500 (500)   **Record:** 9,753 v WBA, FAC1R 1922
Rail: Stalybridge (1 mile from ground).
Directions: M1 or Sheffield: Woodhead Pass to Mottram and Stalybridge. M62: Oldham, Ashton-under-Lyne, Stalybridge. From Manchester, Mancunian Way, Ashton Old Road, Ashton-under-Lyne, Stalybridge.

TELFORD UNITED

Wellington Town were founded in the 1870s and after a period of minor football became Birmingham & District League members in 1898. Moved in 1938 to the Cheshire County League and in 1958 to the Southern League. Apart from the regionalised first season, they spent their Southern League career in the top section, changing their name to Telford United in 1969. Constant members of the Conference since it was founded as the Alliance Premier League in 1979.

Ground: Bucks Head Ground, Watling Street, Wellington, Telford, Shropshire, TF1 2NJ

Phone: 0952-223838   **Info Line:** 0898-121545

Manager: Gerry Daly   **Secretary:** M.J.Ferriday   **Chairman:** Tony Esp

Colours: White, Blue, White   **Change:** Yellow, Red, Red

Nickname: The Lilywhites

5-Year Record		P	W	D	F	A	Pts	Psn	Cup	FAT
87-88	CONF	42	20	10	65	50	70	5	1	F
88-89	CONF	40	13	9	37	43	48	16	1	W
89-90	CONF	42	15	13	56	63	58	12	1	3
90-91	CONF	42	20	7	62	52	67	6	1	1
91-92	CONF	42	19	7	62	66	64	6	2	QF

Major Honours: WFAC 01/2, 05/6, 39/40; FAT 70/1, 82/3; FAT RU 69/70, 87/8, 88/9; SLC 70/1.

Record Transfer Fee Received: £50,000 for Stephen Norris (Scarborough)

Record Transfer Fee Paid: £10,000 for Paul Mayman (Northwich Victoria)

League Appearances and Goalscorers 91-92

(Details listed in the following order: Appearances, substitute appearances, goals)

D. Acton 38,0,0; R. Alleyne 6,2,1; G. Amos 1,1,0; I. Benbow 34,1,12; C. Brindley 39,1,6; I. Brown 6,4,1; D. Burke 2,0,0; C. Carr 1,0,0; K. Charlton 1,0,0; S. Clarke 20,4,3; A. Cooke 3,8,1; P. Culan 1,0,2; C. Downes 1,0,0; D. Duffy 1,1,0; P. Dyson 35,0,5; S. Fergusson 23,1,3; G. Fitzpatrick 1,1,0; R. Forsyth 9,0,0; A. Garratt 5,3,0; S. Gilman 7,1,0; P. Grainger 27,0,0; B. Hackett 7,3,0; P. Hughes 1,0,0; J. Humphreys 30,4,0; T. Langford 35,1,12; M. Myers 38,0,10; S. Nelson 31,0,0; S. Parrish 15,1,1; M. Perks 1,0,0; J. Robertson 1,0,0; B. Ross 3,0,1; D. Ryan 1,0,0; P. Whitehouse 4,0,0; T. Whittington 25,0,4; J. Withe 5,4,0; and S. Worrall 4,6,0. (36 players).

Biggest Home Win: 4-1 v Stafford Rangers

Biggest Home Defeat: 1-4 v Northwich Victoria

Biggest Away Win: 3-0 v Slough Town

Biggest Away Defeat: 1-6 v Wycombe Wanderers

Ground Capacity: 8,500 (1,222)   **Record:** 13,000 v Shrewsbury, B'ham Lge 36

Rail: Wellington - Telford West (1 mile from ground).

Directions: M54 Junction 6 to B5061 (Watling Street).

WELLING UNITED

Founded in 1963. Progressed rapidly once they gained senior status, joining the Spartan League in 1976; the Athenian League in 1978; and the Southern League in 1981. They were promoted to the Conference in 1986.

Ground: Park View Road, Welling, Kent

Phone: 081-301-1196   **Info Line:** 0898-800654

Manager: Nicky Brigden   **Secretary:** B.Hobbins   **Chairman:** P.Websdale

Colours: Red, Red, White   **Change:** All Sky Blue

Nickname: The Wings

5-Year Record		P	W	D	F	A	Pts	Psn	Cup	FAT
87-88	CONF	42	11	9	50	72	42	19	2	1
88-89	CONF	40	14	11	45	46	53	11	3	QF
89-90	CONF	42	18	10	62	50	64	6	2	2
90-91	CONF	42	3	15	55	57	54	11	1	3
91-92	CONF	42	14	12	69	79	54	12	1	2

Major Honours: SLP 85/6; SLMC 85/6.

Record Transfer Fee Received: £15,000 for Gary Abbott (Barnet) 1989

Record Transfer Fee Paid: £30,000 for Gary Abbott (Enfield) 1989/90

League Appearances and Goalscorers 91-92

(Details listed in the following order: Appearances, substitute appearances, goals)

G. Abbott 38,1,19; P. Barron 25,0,0; L. Berry 30,0,0; T. Booker 1,3,0; W. Brown 23,6,3; R. Burgess 7,2,0; N. Clemmence 29,5,1; J. Francis 23,0,1; J. Glover 21,1,1; M. Golley 27,3,2; L. Harrison 7,0,0; M. Hone 30,4,0; G. Howell 7,0,1; D. Monteith 0,1,0; J. Parsons 1,0,0; N. Ransom 39,1,3; T. Reynolds 31,2,1; T. Robbins 42,0,29; S. Robinson 32,1,0; G. Stapely 2,0,0; N. Sullivan 7,0,0; and S. White 40,0,4. (22 players). Two own goals.

Biggest Home Win: 6-1 v Northwich Victoria

Biggest Home Defeat: 0-5 v Bath City

Biggest Away Win: 3-0 v Slough Town

Biggest Away Defeat: 1-6 v Barrow

Ground Capacity: 5,500 (500)   **Record:** 3,850 v Blackburn, FAC3 1/89

Rail: Welling SR (¾ mile from ground).

Directions: M25, then A2 towards London taking Welling turn-off. Ground ¾ mile ahead.

WITTON ALBION

Formed in 1890, they joined the Lancashire Combination in 1912. In 1919 they were founder members of the Cheshire County League and they stayed there until joining the Northern Premier League in 1979. They moved to their current ground in 1990 and were promoted to the Conference for the first time in 1991.

Ground: Wincham Pk, Chapel St, Windham, Northwich, Cheshire, CW9 6DA
Phone: 0606 43008   **Nickname:** Albion
Manager: Peter O'Brien   **Secretary:** David Leather   **Chairman:** D. Shirley
Colours: Red and White Stripes, Black, Red   **Change:** All Blue

5-Year Record		P	W	D	F	A	Pts	Psn	Cup	FAT
87-88	NPLP	42	16	12	61	47	60	11	1q	3
88-89	HFSP	42	22	13	67	39	79	3	3q	1
89-90	HFSP	42	22	7	67	39	73	3	4q	2
90-91	HFSP	42	28	9	81	31	93	1	1	SF
91-92	CONF	42	16	10	63	60	58	10	2	F

Major Honours: HFSP 90/1; PRC 90/1; FAT RU 91/2.
Record Transfer Fee Received: £11,500 Paul Henderson (Chester City). £35,000 Mike Whitlow and Neil Parsley (Leeds United)

(HFS Loans) League Appearances and Goalscorers 91-92
(Details listed in the following order: Appearances, substitute appearances, goals)
C. Alford 15,5,4; S. Anderson 30,1,5; J. Burndred 3,0,0; L. Coatup 26,4,0; Jim Connor 26,2,1; Joe Connor 31,10,6; P. Cuddy 12,1,0; C. Dyson 1,3,0; M. Edwards 2,6,0; S. Ellis 4,1,1; D. Fuller 3,0,0; A. Grimshaw 34,0,3; M. Halliday 17,0,0; D. Heesom 12,1,0; J. Hill 9,0,1; R. Hooton 8,1,0; M. Hughes 11,1,1; T. Hughes 1,0,0; M. Jackson 1,0,0; T. Jarvis 0,1,0; P. Lodge 4,0,0; M. Lutkevitch 20,11,3; J. McCluskie 20,10,9; A. McDonald 3,0,0; S. McNeilis 39,0,2; K. Mason 35,0,0; D. Morgan 7,0,0; A. Newell 1,0,0; J. Palidino 3,0,0; C. Rose 13,0,1; G. Stewart 29,5,5; K. Thomas 34,1,21; P. Wilson 5,3,0; and A. Zelem 3,0,0. (34 players)

Biggest Home Win: 6-0 v Stafford Rangers
Biggest Home Defeat: 0-3 v Gateshead
Biggest Away Win: 2-0 v Bath City
Biggest Away Defeat: 0-4 v Wycombe Wanderers
Capacity: 5,000 (650)   **Record:** 10,000 v Northwich, Ches. Cty Lge 1947/8
Rail: Northwich (1½ miles from ground).
Directions: M6 Junction 19. A556 towards Northwich for 3 miles. Turn right at beginning of dual carriageway on to A559. Turn right at cross-roads (A559 Warrington and Wincham). After another ¾ mile turn left opposite Black Greyhound Inn into Wincham Lane, ground ¾ mile on left immediately after crossing Canal Bridge.

WOKING

Founded in 1889. Played in the West Surrey League from 1895. They joined the Isthmian League in 1911 and had been there ever since. They were relegated in 1983 and again in 1985, but were promoted to Division One in 1987 and to the Premier Division in 1990.

Ground: Kingfield Sports Ground, Kingfield, Woking, Surrey, GU22 9AA
Phone: 0483-772740 **Nickname:** Cards
Manager: Geoff Chapple **Secretary:** Philip Ledger **Chairman:** Ted Hills
Colours: Red with White Trim, White with Red Trim, White with Red Trim
Change: All Yellow with Blue trim

5-Year Record		P	W	D	F	A	Pts	Psn	Cup	FAT
87-88	VL1	42	25	7	91	52	82	3	3q	3q
88-89	VL1	40	24	10	72	30	82	3	1	3
89-90	VL1	42	30	8	102	39	98	2	2	3
90-91	VLP	42	24	10	84	39	82	4	4	1
91-92	DLP	42	30	7	96	25	97	1	3	2

Major Honours: ILP 91/2; ILD1 RU 89/90; ILD1 81/2.
Record Transfer Fee Received: £25,000 Mark Harris (Crystal Palace)
Record Transfer Fee Paid: £5,000 Fred Hyatt (Burnham)
Diadora League Appearances and Goalscorers 91-92
(Details listed in the following order: Appearances, substitute appearances, goals)
T. Baron 42,0,6; P. Barrowcliffe 0,2,0; L. Batty 42,0,3; M. Biggins 34,3,7; D. Brown 31,2,4; A. Cockram 3,0,0; N. Collier 9,3,2; A. Cowler 38,0,0; S. Devine 2,0,1; G. Friel 38,2,28; J. Hunt 2,0,0; T. Lynch 1,2,0; G. McPherson 0,2,0; S. Milton 28,7,16; S. Mitchell 35,0,0; P. Mulvaney 1,5,0; S. Paris 0,1,0; D. Parker 2,0,0; A. Parr 34,3,8; A. Perry 1,9,1; B. Pratt 33,1,5; A. Russell 13,0,1; M. Smith 0,4,0; F. Vines 9,2,3; R. Walkes 3,2,1; C. White 0,1,0; L. Wye 33,2,3; and S. Wye 28,0,4. (28 players). Four own goals.
Biggest Home Win: 5-0 v Basingstoke and v Enfield
Biggest Home Defeat: 1-2 v Bromley
Biggest Away Win: 7-1 v Wivenhoe Town
Biggest Away Defeat: 0-2 v Sutton United
Capacity: 6,000 (650) **Record:** 6,000 v Swansea, FAC2R 1978
Rail: Woking (1½ miles from ground).
Directions: M25 Junction 10. Follow towards Woking, and then towards Kingfield.

WYCOMBE WANDERERS

Formed in 1884, they were Southern League members from 1986 to 1908. Great Western Suburban Leaguers before the First World War, they were in the Spartan League for the first two post-war seasons. They joined the Isthmian League in 1921 and were promoted to the Conference in 1985. Relegated after just one season, they returned to the Conference in 1987.

Ground: Adams Park, Hillbottom Rd., Sands, High Wycombe, Bucks, HP12 4HJ
Phone: 0494-472100   **Info Line:** 0898-446855
Manager: Martin O'Neill **Secretary:** John Goldsworthy **Chairman:** I.Beeks
Colours: Light Blue/Dark Blue Quarters, Dark Blue, Light Blue
Change: All Yellow   **Nickname:** The Blues

5-Year Record		P	W	D	F	A	Pts	Psn	Cup	FAT
87-88	CONF	42	11	13	50	76	46	18	1q	1
88-89	CONF	40	20	11	68	52	71	4	4q	QF
89-90	CONF	42	17	10	64	56	61	10	4q	1
90-91	CONF	42	21	11	75	46	74	5	2	W
91-92	CONF	42	30	4	84	35	94	2	1	QF

Major Honours: IL 55/6, 56/7, 70/1, 71/2; IL RU 57/8, 59/60, 69/70; ILD1 73/4, 74/5; ILD1 RU 75/6, 76/7; FAAm 30/1; FAAm RU 56/7; VOLP 82/3, 86/7; ACDC 84/5; ACDC RU 82/3, 83/4; ILCVS 83/4, 85/6, 87/8; FAT 90/1; GMVC RU 91/2; BLT 91/2.

Record Transfer Fee Paid: £32,000 for Nicky Evans (Barnet) 1989

League Appearances and Goalscorers 91-92
(Details listed in the following order: Appearances, substitute appearances, goals)
D. Carroll 38,1,4; K. Casey 9,5,5; G. Cooper 4,3,0; J. Cousins 41,0,1; G. Covington 3,0,0; G. Creaser 42,0,4; M. Crossley 22,1,0; J. Deakin 8,4,0; T. Gooden 0,6,0; D. Greene 11,5,10; S. Guppy 38,1,7; S. Hutchinson 11,12,4; P. Hyde 42,0,0; P. Johnson 8,0,0; A. Kerr 34,0,4; M. Nuttell 9,1,6; K. Ryan 10,3,1; K. Scott 32,1,18; G. Smith 24,3,2; S. Stapleton 38,0,5; S. Thompson 11,0,1; S. Walford 6,0,0; and M. West 21,3,9. (23 players). Two own goals.

Biggest Home Win: 6-1 v Telford United
Biggest Home Defeat: 1-2 v Colchester United
Biggest Away Win: 5-0 v Redbridge Forest
Biggest Away Defeat: 0-3 v Colchester United
Ground Capacity: 6,000 (1,300)
Record: 6,035 v Witton Albion (GMVC) 02/05/92
Rail: High Wycombe (3 miles from ground).
Directions: M40 Junction 4. Follow A4010 towards Aylesbury. Continue across four mini-roundabouts until double mini-roundabout. Turn left into Lane End Road. Hill Bottom Road ¾ mile on right. Ground at end of Industrial Estate.

YEOVIL TOWN

Formed in 1895 as Yeovil Casuals, they became simply Yeovil in 1908 and, on joining the Western League in 1919, became Yeovil and Petters United. Joined the Southern League in 1922. Changed their name to Yeovil Town just after the Second World War. They were founder members of the Alliance Premier League in 1979. Relegated to the Isthmian arm of the Pyramid in 1985, they were promoted back in 1988.

Ground: Huish Park, Boundary Road, Yeovil, Somerset, BA22 8YF
Phone: 0935-23662   **Info Line:** 0898-333092
Manager: Steve Rutter   **Secretary:** R.L.Brinsford   **Chairman:** Bryan Moore
Colours: White, Green, White   **Change:** All Sky Blue
Nickname: The Glovers

5-Year Record		P	W	D	F	A	Pts	Psn	Cup	FAT
87-88	VLP	42	24	9	66	34	81	1	3	2
88-89	CONF	40	15	11	68	67	56	9	2	2
89-90	CONF	42	17	12	62	54	63	7	1	3
90-91	CONF	42	13	11	58	58	50	14	1	1
91-92	CONF	42	11	14	40	49	47	15	2	QF

Major Honours: SL 54/5, 64/5, 70/1; SL RU 23/4, 31/2, 34/5, 69/70, 72/3; SLC 48/9, 54/5, 60/1, 65/6; VOL 87/8; VOL RU 85/6, 86/7; ACDC 67/8; BLT 89/90; ILCS 86/7.
Record Transfer Fee Received: £12,000 for Paul Doherty (Runcorn)
Record Transfer Fee Paid: £15,000 for Joe Jackson (Worcester) 9/90
League Appearances and Goalscorers 91-92
(Details listed in the following order: Apperances, substitute apperances, goals)
P. Batty 30,7,0; M. Boulton 2,6,2; R. Carroll 29,5,6; D. Coles 23,0,0; R. Cooper 26,6,0; P. Conning 37,2,1; A. Dixon 0,3,0; P. Ferns 26,1,0; D. Fry 13,0,0; S. Harrower 37,0,0; Henderson 2,2,0; M. Hervin 6,0,0; B. McDermott 29,5,4; M. McEvoy 8,5,0; H. Pritchard 8,5,2; D. Robinson 8,0,3; J. Rowbotham 5,0,0; P. Rowland 4,0,0; S. Rutter 36,1,1; M. Shail 39,0,1; S. Sivell 2,0,0; M. Spencer 39,1,16; A. Wallace 32,0,3; and P. Wilson 20,1,1. (24 players).

Biggest Home Win: 3-0 v Welling United
Biggest Home Defeat: 1-4 v Runcorn
Biggest Away Win: 4-1 v Slough Town
Biggest Away Defeat: 0-4 v Colchester United
Ground Capacity: 9,000 (5,000)
Record: 5,093 v Newcastle United, ground opening 8/90
Rail: Yeovil Pen Mill – Bristol/Westbury to Weymouth Line (2½ miles from ground). Yeovil Junction – Waterloo/Salisbury to Exeter Line (4 miles from ground).   **Directions:** Leave A303 at Cargate roundabout and take B3088 signposted Yeovil. Take first exit at next roundabout and first exit again at next roundabout into Boundary Road.

RELEGATED CLUBS

BARROW

League Appearances and Goalscorers 91-92

(Details listed in the following order: Appearances, substitute appearances, goals)
P. Atkinson 19,11,3; M. Ballantyne 9,0,2; J. Brady 15,0,11; M. Brown 9,7,3;
D. Burgess 4,8,0; P. Campbell 0,5,0; T. Chilton 21,0,0; C. Cowperthwaite 15,1,3;
N. Doherty 41,0,7; P. Doolan 22,1,0; B. Gilmour 2,5,1; N. Kelly 21,0,0; S. Knox
13,5,0; P. McDonnell 42,0,0; S. McHugh 7,0,0; K. McNall 18,0,5; T. McPhillips
5,0,0; G. Messenger 32,0,3; D. Nolan 7,3,0; P. Power 17,1,1; K. Procter 21,2,2;
P. Rowlands 15,0,3; M. Rutter 5,7,0; G. Skivington 32,0,0; P. Slater 36,1,2;
S. Todhunter 16,0,0; and D. Wheatley 18,0,4. (27 players). Two own goals.

CHELTENHAM TOWN

League Appearances and Goalscorers 91-92

(Details listed in the following order: Appearances, substitute appearances, goals)
M. Barrett 11,0,0; P. Bloomfield 13,12,0; P. Brogan 22,1,0; S. Brooks 35,0,5; M.
Buckland 29,2,7; D. Butler 10,0,0; K. Casey 23,0,4; R. Clark 9,0,1; M. Coates
6,0,1; M. Davies 6,0,0; P. Evans 3,1,1; M. Fox 4,0,0; D. Fry 3,0,0; M. Gansel
0,2,0; M. Gayle 3,0,0; C. Henry 5,2,0; A. Horlick 0,2,0; R. Hoult 3,0,0; L.
Howells 26,0,2; N. Jordan 8,0,1; T. Lange 6,0,0; G. Livingstone 3,0,0; P.
Masefield 7,0,0; W. Matthews 5,0,0; P. Mortimore 0,2,0; A. Nicholls 11,0,0; M.
Olson 2,0,0; S. Owen 24,0,2; D. Perrett 11,6,3; S. Phillips 1,0,0; B. Powell 0,1,0;
J. Purdie 26,0,7; S. Reck 9,3,0; J. Smith 15,0,6; N. Smith 17,0,1; L. Stobart
16,1,1; D. Taggart 6,3,0; P. Tester 5,1,0; P. Turnbull 0,3,1; J. Upshall 0,1,0; A.
Vircavs 34,0,3; C. Warren 1,3,0; K. Willetts 40,0,9; and J. Wring 4,4,0. (44
players). One own goal.

Ever Present Players

Colchester United	S. Barrett, N. Smith
Boston United	G.Jones
Redbridge Forest	S. Connor
Gateshead	S. Smith
Northwich Victoria	S. Locke
Stafford Rangers	R. Price
Wycombe Wanderers	G. Creaser, P. Hyde
Promoted Clubs	
Stalybridge Celtic	J. Aspinal, C. Camden
Woking	T. Baron, L. Batty

DIADORA LEAGUE

Woking's Walkover

It was scant reward for Enfield that they beat Champions Woking 2-0 on the final Saturday of the season. It was Woking's fifth consecutive game without a win but the shouting had long been over. Despite the Cardinals' final run-in, they still finished their Premier Division campaign a massive 18 points clear of rivals Enfield who clinched the runners-up spot for the second successive season. The two-horse race at the top had been a tight affair but Woking opened up more than daylight when they dismantled the E's 5-0 at Kingfield.

Woking's downfall last year had been their magnificent FA Cup run. Victory at WBA and a narrow defeat at Everton took their toll. But the Surrey club learned from that and, despite the distraction of another marvellous Cup run, they maintained their advantage in the League. The Cardinals secured their first-ever title a full month before the end of the season, beating Kingstonian 3-1 in front of 3073 spectators.

Spare a thought for Enfield, who were also runners-up in the Isthmian League Cup, losing 3-1 to Grays Athletic. Sutton United finished in third place, above Chesham United on goal difference.

Considering that St Albans have failed to win 35 of their last 48 home matches during the past two seasons, they did well to finish mid-table despite an abysmal start to the season.

Bishop's Stortford had their worst season for many a year – they have won a trophy of some sort for the past seven seasons – and slip into Division One. Bognor Regis Town avoid the drop courtesy of Dagenham's inevitable merger with the club eater – Redbridge Forest (et al).

In Division One, Stevenage Borough won promotion as Champions for a second successive season under the guidance of Paul Fairclough. Striker Martin Gittings' haul of 29 League goals played a large part in the Hertfordshire club's meteoric rise which included a period of 15 consecutive wins up until the penultimate game of the season. Their place in the Premier Division will ensure some very interesting and highly charged local derbies during 1992-93. Borough's home record in the past two years makes very interesting reading:

P41 W39 D2 L0 F136 A26 Pts 119

Had Boreham Wood won their final match of the season at Wembley, they would have been among those derbies. As it was, Wood went down 1-0 and Dulwich Hamlet clinched third spot with a 1-0 win at Hitchin. Yeading comfortably took the runners-up spot seven points ahead of Hamlet but 14 behind Borough.

Maidenhead United's winning goal at Abingdon Town on New Year's Day was their 1000th in the Isthmian League.

Purfleet completed a championship and cup double, taking the Division Two crown ahead of Lewes by six points. They also picked up the Loctite Trophy, coming from 2-0 down to beat Egham Town 3-2. Purfleet's promotion therefore maintains their unusual record of never having played in the same division of the Isthmian League in successive seasons since being elected for 1988-89. In fact, since the club's formation as recently as 1985, they have only ever played in the same division two years running when in 1986-87 and 1987-88 they were members of the Essex Senior League.

Billericay clinched the third promotion spot from Leatherhead to return to Division One, having been relegated at the end of the 1987-88 season.

Southwick – one of two clubs resigning from the League – finished one from bottom ahead of Newbury Town who failed to win for 29 successive games and lost their last 12, conceding a massive 117 goals in their 42 games.

In Division Three, the season reached the last day with Chertsey Town needing a win over Horsham Town to pip Edgware Town for the championship. They failed, going down by the odd goal in seven. Edgware took advantage of their slip to beat Feltham and Hounslow 2-0 and move two points clear at the top. Edgware were the top scorers across all four divisions, finding the back of the onion bag on no less than 106 occasions. Tilbury took the third promotion spot.

The fears of Andy Curry, Eastbourne United's chairman at the start of the season, were fully realised. With debts of over £40,000, the club finished bottom of Division Three and have had to resign from the League.

Diadora Ups, Downs, Ins and Outs

Club	Division	Position	Movement
Woking	Premier	1st	Promoted to GMVC
Dagenham	Premier		Resigned – Merged with Redbridge Forest
Bishop's Stortford	Premier	22nd	Relegated to Division One
Stevenage Borough	One	1st	Promoted to Premier
Yeading	One	2nd	Promoted to Premier
Dulwich Hamlet	One	3rd	Promoted to Premier
Purfleet	Two	1st	Promoted to Division One
Lewes	Two	2nd	Promoted to Division One
Billericay Town	Two	3rd	Promoted to Division One
Southwick	Two		Resigned
Edgware Town	Three	1st	Promoted to Division Two
Chertsey Town	Three	2nd	Promoted to Division Two
Tilbury	Three	3rd	Promoted to Division Two
Hampton	Three	4th	Promoted to Division Two
Eastbourne United	Three		Resigned
Aldershot Town	–		Elected to Division Three
East Thurrock United	ESL	3rd	Elected to Division Three
Farnham Town	DAirL	1st	Elected to Division Three
Leighton Town	SML	1st	Elected to Division Three
Northwood	SpL	1st	Elected to Division Three

ADT Healthquest Charity Shield

Woking...................................3	Redbridge Forest ....1 aet
Barron 53, 95, Biggins 100	Davidson 42 Att: 1397

The Isthmian League History

The Isthmian League was founded in 1905 with just six clubs. There was a gradual increase in size and by 1963, when four prominent Athenian Leaguers joined, it had grown to 20 clubs. Membership reached 22 clubs for the first time in 1972.

In 1973 a 16-club Division Two was added, which grew to 22 clubs in 1975. These divisions were renamed as the Premier and First Divisions in 1977 when a new Division Two of 17 clubs was added. In 1983-84 all three divisions comprised 22 clubs.

For the 1984-85 season Division Two was split into a North and South Division, but for 1991-92 a single Division Two returned, with the clubs finishing in the bottom half of the regionalised tables in 1990-91 forming a new Division Three. While feeder leagues serve the lowest division, the League champions are normally promoted to the Conference, with a club normally being relegated from the Conference joining the Premier Division.

Diadora took over sponsorship in 1991. Former sponsors have been Rothmans, Berger, Servowarm and Vauxhall.

5-Year One, Two, Three Records

Premier Division

	1st	Pts	2nd	Pts	3rd	Pts
1986-87	Wycombe W	101	Yeovil Town	92	Slough Town	77
1987-88	Yeovil Town	81	Bromley	76	Slough Town	72
1988-89	Ley'stone Ilf	89	Farnborough T	81	Slough Town	78
1989-90	Slough Town	92	Wokingham T	89	Aylesbury Utd	84
1990-91	Redbridge For	93	Enfield	89	Aylesbury Utd	83

Division One

	1st	Pts	2nd	Pts	3rd	Pts
1986-87	Ley'stone Ilf	95	Leyton-Win.	82	Bracknell Town	81
1987-88	Marlow	101	Grays Ath	100	Woking	82
1988-89	Staines Town	87	Basingstoke T	83	Woking	82
1989-90	Wivenhoe T	100	Woking	98	Southwick	84
1990-91	Chesham Utd	89	Bromley	80	Yeading	77

Division Two (North)

	1st	Pts	2nd	Pts	3rd	Pts
1986-87	Chesham Utd	90	Wolverton	83	Haringey Bor	79
1987-88	Wivenhoe Town	88	Collier Row	79	Tilbury	69
1988-89	Harlow Town	90	Purfleet	78	Tring Town	76
1989-90	Heybridge Sw	87	Aveley	85	Hertford Town	83
1990-91	Stevenage Bor	107	Vauxhall Motors	82	Billericay Town	74

Division Two (South)

	1st	Pts	2nd	Pts	3rd	Pts
1986-87	Woking	88	Marlow	88	Dorking	84
1987-88	Chalfont St P	87	Met Police	86	Dorking	86
1988-89	Dorking	100	Whyteleafe	84	Finchley	72
1989-90	Yeading	91	Molesey	83	Abingdon Town	75
1990-91	Abingdon Town	94	Maidenhead Utd	92	Egham Town	87

LEAGUE CUP

An own goal by Mark Keen gave Grays the lead in the Isthmian League Cup final. Further goals from John Campbell and Winston Whittingham took Athletic's lead to 3-0 before Mark Kane replied for Enfield. It was Grays' first success in the Cup.

5-Year Finals List

Year	Teams	Score	Venue
1986-87	Bognor Regis v Hendon	3-2	Windsor & Eton
1987-88	Yeovil Town v Hayes	3-1	Basingstoke
1988-89	B. Stortford v Farnborough Town	1-0	Hayes
1989-90	Aveley v St Albans City	3-0	Dagenham
1990-91	Woking v Carshalton Athletic	2-1	Kingstonian

The 'Isthmian League Cup' was first competed for during the 1974-75 season when Tilbury beat Croydon 3-1 over two legs. It was known as the 'AC Delco Cup' from 1985-86 until 1990-91.

Preliminary Round

Abingdon v Hemel Hempstead 2-0
Barton v Clapton 3-2
Billericay v Petersfield 4-1
Bracknell v Harefield 0-1
Chertsey v Tring 1-0
Collier Row v Ruislip Manor 1-4
Eastbourne v Southwick ....† 2-2
    Replay......................................6-0
Edgware v Ware ....† 0-1
Hertford v Purfleet 2-1
Horsham v Feltham & Hounslow 4-1
Hungerford v Berkhamstead 2-4
Leatherhead v Banstead Ath 1-2
Lewes v Hornchurch ....† 0-0
    Replay......................................3-2
Maidenhead v Kingsbury ....† 2-3
Malden Vale ....w/o
Rainham v Epson & Ewell...............4-2
Saffron Walden v Newbury ....† 2-2
    Replay......................................0-2
Southall v Met Police 3-1
Thame v Camberley 1-2
Tilbury v Hampton 1-0
Witham v Flackwell ....† 1-2

Worthing v Egham Town ....† 1-1
    Replay......................................2-4

1st Round

Abingdon v Harefield.......................2-0
Aveley v Hayes 1-3
Bishop's Stortford v Hertford ....† 1-0
Banstead Athletic v Grays Athletic ...1-2
Barking v Southwick 4-3
Barton v Woking 1-3
Basingstoke v Dagenham 1-0
Carshalton v Croydon......................3-2
Chalfont St Peter v Hendon ....† 4-6
Chertsey v Aylesbury 2-0
Chesham v Tooting & Mitcham ......† 2-2
    Replay......................................3-2
Dorking v Malden Vale 2-1
Egham Town v Boreham Wood 2-0
Heybridge v Kingstonian 1-0
Hitchin Town v Billericay Town......† 1-2
Lewes v Camberley 3-0
Leyton-Wingate v Bromley 1-2
Marlow v Wokingham 2-1
Molesey v Kingsbury 1-0
Rainham v Bognor Regis 1-0
Royston v Berkhamsted 0-2

103

Ruislip Manor v St Albans City 0-3
Saffron Walden v Enfield 0-2
Southall v Tilbury 1-3
Staines v Flackwell.....................2-0
Sutton v Stevenage 2-1
Uxbridge v Harlow 0-3
Ware v Horsham ....† 2-2
  Replay.....................................2-1
Whyteleafe v Wivenhoe 2-1
Windsor & Eton v Wembley 4-1
Yeading v Dulwich Hamlet............† 2-1

2nd Round

Abingdon v Lewes 2-0
Barking v Heybridge 2-1
Berkhamsted v Carshalton 1-6
Chersey v Enfield 1-4
Dorking v Molesey ....† 3-3
  Replay.....................................2-0
Egham Town v Billericay 0-1
(Billericay removed for breach of rules)
Harlow v Grays Athletic..................4-0
Harrow v Basingstoke 3-1
Hayes v Yeading 1-0
Hertford v Sutton 0-5
Marlow v Windsor & Eton ....† 3-4
St Albans City v Bromley 4-1
Staines v Chesham 0-1
Tilbury v Hendon 3-0
Ware v Whyteleafe 2-1
Woking v Rainham.......................4-1

3rd Round

Abingdon v Sutton 1-2
Chesham v Woking 1-2

Dorking v Grays Athletic 3-4
Enfield v Hayes 2-3
Harrow v Carshalton 0-1
St Albans City v Tilbury 5-0
Ware v Barking 2-0
Windsor & Eton v Egham ....† 0-0
  Replay (abd 90 mins).................0-0
  Replay.....................................3-1

4th Round

Carshalton v Ware ....† 2-2
  Replay.....................................0-1
Egham Town v Grays Athletic 1-4
Sutton v St Albans City ....† 2-3
Woking v Enfield 0-2

Semi-Finals 1st Leg

St Albans City v Grays Athletic.........2-2
Ware v Enfield 1-2

Semi-Finals 2nd Leg

Enfield v Ware 0-0
   Enfield won 2-1 on agg
Grays Athletic v St Albans City.........1-0
   Grays won 3-2 on agg

Final

at Dagenham FC
Grays Athletic 3
   Keen (og 44), Whittingham 52,
   Campbell 57
Enfield 1
   Kane 66
Att: 1264

League Cup Attendance Summaries 1991-92

Round	Matches	Total	Average
Preliminary	26	3,193	123
First	34	6,905	203
Second	17	3,693	217
Third	10	2,459	246
Fourth	5	2,547	509
Semi-Finals	4	1,836	459
Final	1	1,264	
Total	**97**	**21,897**	**226**

LOCTITE CUP

Goals in each half from Scott and Browne gave Sutton United their first Loctite Cup success at the expense of runaway League Champions Woking.

The 'Isthmian League Full Members Cup' is known as the 'Loctite Cup' and entry is compulsory for all Full Members of the Isthmian Football League, ie members of the Premier and First Divisions.

1st Round

Aveley v St Albans City	1-6
Aylesbury United v Barking	1-3
Basingstoke v Croydon	1-0
Harrow Boro v Heybridge Swifts	2-2

Harrow won 7-6 on pens

Hendon v Chalfont St. Peter	2-1
Hitchin Town v Abingdon Town	0-3
Tooting & Mitcham v Stevenage B ...	†1-2
Windsor & Eton v Harlow Town	2-3
Wokingham Tn v Bishop's Stortford	2-0
Yeading v Kingstonian	†3-2

2nd Round

Barking v Dagenham	1-5
Boreham Wood v Yeading	1-2
Bromley v Bognor Regis	0-1
Dorking v Harrow Borough	3-4
Enfield v Molesey	†2-3
Harlow Town v Hayes	2-4
Hendon v Abingdon Town	1-2
Leyton-Wingate v Chesham	0-4
Maidenhead United v Basingstoke	2-2

Basingstoke won 3-2 on pens

Marlow v Carshalton	1-2
St Albans City v Wokingham Town	1-3
Staines Town v Dulwich Hamlet	0-3
Sutton United v Whyteleafe	4-0
Uxbridge v Grays Athletic	†4-2
Wivenhoe v Stevenage Borough	0-4
Woking v Walton & Hersham	2-1

3rd Round

Carshalton v Abingdon Town	2-1
Chesham v Woking	2-5
Dagenham v Yeading	0-2

Dulwich Hamlet v Bognor Regis	0-0

Dulwich won 5-4 on pens

Harrow Borough v Wokingham Town	2-0
Hayes v Uxbridge	1-3
Molesey v Stevenage Borough	4-4

Molesey won 3-0 on pens

Sutton United v Basingstoke	3-2

4th Round

Dulwich Hamlet v Sutton United	0-0

Sutton won 5-4 on pens

Harrow Borough v Carshalton	†0-2
Molesey v Uxbridge	†1-0
Woking v Yeading	1-0

Semi-Finals

Harrow Borough v Woking	0-2
Sutton United v Molesey	4-1

Final

at Hayes FC, 5 May

Sutton United	2

Scott A 18, Browne 58

Woking	0

LOCTITE TROPHY

Egham saw a 2-0 lead disappear as Purfleet stormed back to lift the Loctite Trophy at Gander Green Lane. Mark Butler and Brett Smith put the Surrey side ahead with goals after six and 34 minutes. However, Alan Brett started the Purfleet revival on 35 minutes and Nigel Jeyes levelled the scores two minutes after the interval. Geoff Wood scored what proved to be the winner six minutes later. Purfleet's Jason Spiteri missed a spot kick in the closing minutes.

The Isthmian League Associate Members Cup, which is called the Loctite Trophy, is compulsory for all 44 Associate Members of the Isthmian Football League, ie members of Divisions Two and Three.

1st Round

Banstead v Eastbourne 7-1
Barton Rovers v Horsham ....† 3-2
Collier Row v Lewes 4-3
Cove v Berkhamsted 4-0
Epsom & Ewell v Hertford...............3-1
Hampton v Hornchurch 2-1
Hemel Hempstead v Harefield 0-2
Leatherhead v Ware 1-3
Ruislip Manor v Witham Town 1-0
Tilbury v Purfleet...........................0-2
Tring Town v Camberley Town.........1-2

2nd Round

Banstead v Southall 0-1
Barton Rovers v Southwick 10-2
Bracknell v Newbury 1-1
Newbury won 5-3 on pens
Chertsey v Kingsbury......................1-3
Clapton v Ruislip Manor ....† 1-3
Collier Row v Saffron Walden 2-4
Cove v Hampton.............................2-1
Epsom & Ewell v Royston 4-1
Flackwell v Egham..........................0-1
Harefield v Camberley 2-1
Hungerford v Malden Vale..............0-1
Met Police v Feltham & Hounslow ...1-2
Petersfield v Rainham 2-1
Purfleet v Edgware 2-0
Thame v Billericay 1-0
Ware v Worthing 2-3

3rd Round

Egham Town v Harefield 3-0
Epsom & Ewell v Cove 0-1
Feltham & H. v Ruislip Manor 1-0
Kingsbury v Barton Rovers 0-2
Newbury v Purfleet 0-5
Petersfield v Thame 1-2
Saffron Walden v Southall 1-4
Worthing v Malden Vale 0-6

4th Round

Malden Vale v Barton Rovers 6-0
Egham Town v Thame 1-2
Cove v Saffron Walden 0-2
Purfleet v Ruislip Manor 3-0

Semi-Finals

Malden Vale v Egham Town 2-2
Saffron Walden v Purfleet 0-2
Replay
Egham Town v Malden Vale 4-3

Final

at Sutton United FC, 14 May
Egham Town 2
    Butler 6, Smith B 34
Purfleet 3
    Brett 36, Jeyes 47, Wood G. 53
Att: 241

PREMIER DIVISION

Final Table 1991-92

	P	W	D	L	F	A	Pts
Woking	42	30	7	5	96	25	97
Enfield	42	24	7	11	59	45	79
Sutton United	42	19	13	10	88	51	70
Chesham United	42	20	10	12	67	48	70
Wokingham Town	42	19	10	13	73	58	67
Marlow	42	20	7	15	56	50	67
Aylesbury United	42	16	17	9	69	46	65
Carshalton Athletic	42	18	8	16	64	67	62
Dagenham	42	15	16	11	70	59	61
Kingstonian	42	17	8	17	71	65	59
Windsor & Eton	42	15	11	16	56	56	56
Bromley	42	14	12	16	51	57	54
St Albans City	42	14	11	17	66	70	53
Basingstoke Town	42	14	11	17	56	65	53
Grays Athletic	42	14	11	17	53	68	53
Wivenhoe Town	42	16	4	22	56	81	52
Hendon	42	13	9	20	59	73	48
Harrow Borough	42	11	13	18	58	78	46
Hayes	42	10	14	18	52	63	44
Staines Town	42	11	10	21	43	73	43
Bognor Regis Town	42	9	11	22	51	89	38
Bishop's Stortford	42	7	12	23	41	68	33

Leading Premier League Goalscorers

Friel, G. (Woking) 28; Bolton, J. (Carshalton Ath.) 22; Thompson, D.
(Wokingham Town) 19; Westley, G. (Enfield) 19; Beste, R. (Carshalton
Ath.) 18; Whittingham, W. (Grays Ath.) 18.

Promotions and Relegations

Club	Position	Movement
Woking	Champions	Promoted to GMVC
Bishop's Stortford	22nd	Relegated to Division One

Clubs Joining Premier Division

Club	Position	From
Stevenage Borough	Champions	Division One
Yeading	Runners-up	Division One
Dulwich Hamlet	3rd	Division One

PREMIER DIVISION RESULTS 1991-92

	Aylesbury Utd	Basingstoke	B. Stortford	Bognor Regis	Bromley	Carshalton A	Chesham Utd	Dagenham	Enfield	Grays Ath	Harrow B.
Aylesbury United	•	2-1	0-0	1-1	1-2	0-0	1-2	1-1	1-1	3-1	7-1
Basingstoke	0-0	•	1-1	1-1	2-3	0-2	2-2	2-2	1-2	1-2	0-1
Bishop's Stortford	1-0	0-1	•	1-2	0-0	1-0	0-0	0-4	0-1	3-0	2-0
Bognor Regis Town	2-2	1-2	1-1	•	5-1	1-0	0-6	1-0	0-1	2-2	2-2
Bromley	0-0	2-0	1-0	1-4	•	3-1	0-1	0-1	0-1	2-3	0-2
Carshalton Athletic	1-0	2-1	2-2	4-0	1-0	•	3-0	0-3	1-1	2-2	1-0
Chesham United	0-2	2-1	2-1	1-3	1-1	4-0	•	0-1	0-2	2-2	1-0
Dagenham	2-4	2-2	3-0	4-1	0-1	1-1	3-0	•	2-1	2-0	5-2
Enfield	2-2	0-2	1-0	3-1	5-1	2-1	3-2	3-5	•	2-2	3-0
Grays Athletic	3-3	1-0	3-1	1-2	2-1	1-2	1-3	2-2	0-4	•	0-0
Harrow Borough	0-4	5-1	3-2	4-1	1-3	1-2	1-1	2-2	1-2	0-2	•
Hayes	0-0	0-1	1-0	4-1	4-1	3-2	0-0	4-0	2-0	4-0	1-1
Hendon	1-2	0-2	0-1	3-1	0-2	1-1	2-3	0-1	1-0	1-2	2-2
Kingstonian	0-1	0-1	2-3	0-1	0-4	4-1	3-1	2-2	3-0	4-1	3-1
Marlow	0-0	2-4	1-0	2-1	4-2	2-0	3-0	2-0	0-1	1-0	1-0
St Albans City	3-3	1-1	3-2	2-3	0-1	1-2	1-2	1-2	1-2	1-2	6-0
Staines Town	0-0	4-1	2-2	0-1	1-1	1-0	1-5	2-2	0-1	0-1	0-0
Sutton United	1-2	1-2	2-2	5-0	2-1	2-4	1-2	5-3	2-3	5-0	1-1
Windsor & Eton	2-3	1-3	1-0	1-0	3-2	3-0	1-0	0-1	1-1	1-2	4-0
Wivenhoe Town	0-3	4-1	1-0	4-0	1-2	0-0	1-0	4-0	5-0	1-1	1-4
Woking	2-1	5-0	3-0	3-1	1-4	3-0	2-1	3-1	2-0	3-1	2-0
Wokingham Town	4-0	1-1	0-0	3-1		0-0	1-0	1-1	1-1	3-1	1-1

	Hayes	Hendon	Kingstonian	Marlow	St Albans City	Staines Town	Sutton United	Windsor & E.	Wivenhoe Tn	Woking	Wokingham Tn
Aylesbury United	0-0	4-1	0-1	1-0	2-0	0-1	4-4	4-0	1-1	0-4	4-0
Basingstoke	4-2	0-1	1-0	2-0	1-1	2-0	0-2	0-2	5-1	0-3	3-3
Bishop's Stortford	1-1	1-3	1-3	2-0	1-1	1-2	0-2	1-1	1-2	1-2	1-5
Bognor Regis Town	3-4	1-4	2-2	0-1	2-4	2-2	0-0	0-1	3-0	1-2	0-0
Bromley	0-0	1-1	0-2	0-0	2-0	1-1	2-2	0-0	2-1	0-2	3-2
Carshalton Athletic	3-1	5-4	4-4	2-1	1-2	1-3	2-1	0-0	0-2	0-2	3-2
Chesham United	2-2	0-0	3-2	3-0	3-1	4-0	1-0	2-2	2-2	0-0	4-0
Dagenham	3-3	0-1	1-2	4-1	0-0	1-0	0-0	2-2	1-0	0-0	0-1
Enfield	2-0	1-0	4-0	0-2	3-1	0-0	3-1	0-0	1-0	1-0	0-1
Grays Athletic	0-0	0-0	1-2	1-2	2-0	1-1	0-2	2-2	4-1	0-2	1-1
Harrow Borough	2-4	1-1	1-1	2-1	2-2	6-1	1-1	3-1	1-0	1-3	1-2
Hayes	•	3-0	0-0	1-3	0-1	5-0	0-6	0-2	0-2	2-2	2-1
Hendon	1-0	•	4-1	1-2	3-5	0-2	0-0	1-1	2-0	1-2	1-2
Kingstonian	2-1	5-0	•	4-1	0-0	4-0	1-0	1-1	3-0	0-3	1-1
Marlow	1-1	4-0	2-1	•	1-2	•	1-2	1-2	1-2	0-3	0-3
St Albans City	0-0	1-1	2-2	2-0	•	4-0	1-0	1-2	1-2	0-2	1-3
Staines Town	3-2	1-3	1-2	1-0	1-2	•	1-3	0-3	3-0	2-0	0-2
Sutton United	1-2	4-2	2-2	3-2	2-3	1-2	•	4-1	4-2	2-0	5-0
Windsor & Eton	2-0	1-4	3-0	0-0	2-3	3-1	2-2	•	4-1	0-3	1-0
Wivenhoe Town	2-0	2-1	2-0	1-3	1-2	3-0	0-1	0-3	•	1-7	2-0
Woking	4-1	1-1	3-1	4-1	4-1	2-2	1-0	2-0	2-0	•	0-1
Wokingham Town	5-2	2-1	0-1	2-3	4-1	1-3	3-3	0-1	6-0	0-3	•

	Aylesbury Utd	Basingstoke	B. Stortford	Bognor Regis	Bromley	Carshalton A	Chesham Utd	Dagenham	Enfield	Grays Ath	Harrow B.
Aylesbury United	•	473	464	546	536	411	1318	702	902	459	490
Basingstoke	416	•	359	685	498	514	614	381	482	321	381
Bishop's Stortford ...	303	301	•	231	298	235	318	367	474	328	320
Bognor Regis Town ...	243	345	214	•	352	215	240	185	290	175	240
Bromley	431	482	505	340	•	429	439	433	518	568	324
Carshalton Athletic ...	300	389	274	266	441	•	383	263	396	366	335
Chesham United	960	550	569	478	400	409	•	613	662	445	421
Dagenham	441	451	462	449	609	421	370	•	527	381	435
Enfield	735	462	520	512	816	720	451	501	•	570	484
Grays Athletic	292	357	234	275	452	304	465	494	393	•	309
Harrow Borough	243	2178	267	295	302	203	389	232	501	289	•
Hayes	275	218	242	207	254	190	329	171	352	235	337
Hendon	363	199	240	175	306	236	327	244	363	205	372
Kingstonian	550	375	489	505	625	515	429	503	889	625	555
Marlow	501	245	240	181	275	212	430	260	430	227	240
St Albans City	436	421	485	546	388	418	578	328	1502	331	398
Staines Town	336	324	295	283	415	274	446	252	571	191	406
Sutton United	530	629	418	706	790	1146	767	634	890	517	558
Windsor & Eton	282	304	188	259	254	322	307	232	246	243	303
Wivenhoe Town	296	283	184	207	309	196	196	193	328	247	203
Woking	2218	1701	2369	1608	1521	1402	2305	1374	3125	1689	1451
Wokingham Town	426	452	230	324	325	282	475	345	280	272	450

	Hayes	Hendon	Kingstonian	Marlow	St Albans City	Staines Town	Sutton United	Windsor & E.	Wivenhoe Tn	Woking	Wokingham Th
Aylesbury United	802	687	742	819	602	567	509	603	758	2165	573
Basingstoke	367	502	533	251	341	394	594	460	451	1578	631
Bishop's Stortford	334	394	367	244	295	285	388	276	304	723	311
Bognor Regis Town	208	226	240	230	270	260	408	260	212	580	215
Bromley	463	413	557	384	489	532	783	335	422	1545	451
Carshalton Athletic	300	369	686	365	308	211	1398	285	367	893	368
Chesham United	374	674	591	764	460	395	304	505	491	1299	525
Dagenham	287	426	625	379	319	328	435	393	307	883	372
Enfield	372	522	399	312	717	649	708	570	599	1182	406
Grays Athletic	333	264	425	230	397	206	341	303	339	1012	295
Harrow Borough	406	411	401	284	292	288	324	297	252	1139	241
Hayes	•	242	241	238	309	291	392	266	199	1148	233
Hendon	266	•	329	241	271	265	388	233	183	751	243
Kingstonian	357	550	•	776	635	488	1491	676	549	2071	757
Marlow	301	340	404	•	510	272	444	302	255	1020	385
St Albans City	536	510	341	303	•	296	366	308	638	828	481
Staines Town	321	299	525	403	291	•	492	352	254	1410	324
Sutton United	479	667	865	695	734	617	•	551	611	1658	823
Windsor & Eton	317	273	405	225	256	225	342	•	201	1184	258
Wivenhoe Town	265	234	193	196	253	242	343	154	•	393	194
Woking	1484	1629	3073	1289	1912	1209	2327	1962	1973	•	1867
Wokingham Town	306	282	432	407	348	289	347	464	217	1081	•

Attendance Summaries by Club

Club	Psn	Total	Home 90-91	Ave	90-91	Away Total	Ave
Woking	1	39,488	(30,885)	1,880	(1,471)	24,543	1,169
Sutton United	3	15,285	(18,366)	728	(875)	13,124	625
Aylesbury United	7	15,128	(19,876)	720	(946)	10,577	504
Kingstonian	10	14,410	(17,923)	686	(853)	12,374	589
Enfield	2	12,207	(15,378)	581	(732)	14,121	672
Chesham United	4	11,889	(–)	566	(–)	11,576	551
Bromley	12	10,843	(–)	516	(–)	10,166	484
Basingstoke Town	14	10,753	(7,997)	512	(381)	11,139	530
St Albans City	13	10,438	(9,224)	497	(439)	10,009	477
Dagenham	9	9,300	(8,956)	443	(426)	8,707	415
Harrow Borough	18	9,234	(6,285)	440	(299)	9,012	429
Carshalton Athletic	8	8,963	(7,417)	427	(353)	9,054	431
Staines Town	20	8,464	(7,197)	403	(343)	8,309	396
Wokingham Town	5	8,034	(6,732)	383	(321)	9,953	474
Grays Athletic	15	7,720	(9,637)	368	(459)	8,684	414
Marlow	6	7,474	(6,754)	356	(322)	9,035	430
Bishop's Stortford	22	7,096	(6,718)	338	(320)	9,248	440
Windsor & Eton	11	6,626	(6,011)	316	(286)	9,555	455
Hayes	19	6,369	(6,482)	303	(309)	8,878	423
Hendon	17	6,200	(6,754)	295	(322)	9,914	472
Bognor Regis Tn	21	5,608	(4,919)	267	(234)	9,078	432
Wivenhoe Town	16	5,109	(7,996)	243	(381)	9,582	456

Total Attendance:	1991-92	236,638		1990-91	(208,470)	
Average Attendance:	1991-92	512		1990-91	(451)	

Best Attendances at 10 Grounds 1991-92

3,125	Woking	v	Enfield	30/11/91
2,165	Aylesbury United	v	Woking	28/12/91
2,071	Kingstonian	v	Woking	20/08/91
1,658	Sutton United	v	Woking	18/04/92
1,578	Basingstoke Town	v	Woking	15/02/92
1,545	Bromley	v	Woking	25/01/92
1,502	St Albans City	v	Enfield	01/01/92
1,410	Staines Town	v	Woking	21/12/91
1,398	Carshalton Athletic	v	Sutton United	01/01/92
1,299	Chesham United	v	Woking	28/08/91

Premier League Top Scorers By Club

Club	Player	Tot	Lg	IC	LC
Aylesbury United	Cliff Hercules	17	17	–	–
	Darren Collins	17	17	–	–
Basingstoke Town	Richard Smart	15	15	–	–
	(including 12 for Kingstonian)				
Bishop's Stortford	Peter Petrou	9	9	–	–
Bognor Regis Town	Kevin Maddock	9	9	–	–
Bromley	Paul McMenemy	11	10	1	–
Carshalton Athletic	Jim Bolton	29	22	6	1
Chesham United	Micky Banton	14	12	1	1
Dagenham	Leo West	18	18	–	–
Enfield	Graham Westley	25	19	5	1
Grays Athletic	Winston Whittingham	21	18	2	1
Harrow Borough	Steve Conroy	16	14	–	2
Hayes	John Lawford	18	18	1	–
	(including 5 Lg and 1 IC for Bishop's Stortford)				
Hendon	Mark Xavier	18	12	4	2
Kingstonian	Richard Cherry	19	16	1	2
	(including 1 Lg and 1IC for Grays Athletic)				
Marlow	David Lay	11	10	–	1
St Albans City	Steve Clarke	24	14	8	2
Staines Town	Gary Crawshaw	10	10	–	–
Sutton United	Dominic Feltham	22	17	3	2
Windsor & Eton	Richard Evans	19	17	2	–
Wivenhoe Town	Steve Restarick	11	11	–	–
Woking	George Friel	32	28	2	2
Wokingham Town	David Thompson	21	19	–	2

*Tot=Total number of goals; Lg=League; IC=Isthmian League Cup;
LC=Loctite Cup.*

William Hill Manager of Month Awards

Month	Manager	Club
September	Geoff Chapple	Woking
October	George Wakeling	Bromley
November	Geoff Chapple	Woking
December	John Mitchell	St Albans City
January	Eddie McCluskey	Enfield
February	Roy Merryweather	Wokingham Town
March	Geoff Chapple	Woking
April	Gerald Aplin	Chesham United

PREMIER DIVISION CLUBS

AYLESBURY UNITED

Founded by an amalgamation of the Printing Works and Night Schools Clubs. Once a Spartan League side, they were Delphian League founder members in 1951, moving on to the Athenian on the absorption of that League in 1963. The club joined the Southern League in 1976 and moved to a new out-of-town ground in 1986. Promoted to the Conference in 1988 but relegated to the Vauxhall League after one season.

Ground: The Stadium, Buckingham Road, Aylesbury, Bucks, HP19 3QL
Phone: 0296-436350   **Nickname:** The Ducks   **Founded:** 1897
Manager: Trevor Gould **Secretary:** Tony Graham   **Chairman:** N. Stonell
Colours: Green and White Hoops, White, Green   **Change:** All Red

5-Year Record		P	W	D	F	A	Pts	Psn	Cup	FAT
87-88	BHLP	42	27	8	79	55	89	1*	1	1
88-89	CONF	40	9	9	43	71	36	20	2	2
89-90	VLP	42	25	9	86	30	84	3	2	2
90-91	VLP	42	24	11	90	47	83	3	1	2
91-92	DLP	42	16	17	69	46	65	7	2	2

* On goal difference
Ground Capacity: 7,800 (400)   **Record:** 6,000 v England, friendly 6/88
Rail: Aylesbury (1 mile from ground).
Directions: Opposite Horse & Jockey PH on A413 Buckingham Rd.

BASINGSTOKE TOWN

The club were Hampshire League members from 1900 until 1971 when they joined the Southern League. In 1947 they moved to an out-of-town site – the Camrose Ground. They were in the Southern League's top section from 1985 until 1987 when they moved to the Isthmian League set-up. Spent one season in the Premier Division before relegation but were promoted back from Division One at the first attempt.

Ground: The Camrose Grd, Western Way, Basingstoke, Hants, RG24 6HW
Phone: 0256-461465   **Nickname:** Stoke   **Founded:** 1896
Manager: Fred Callaghan **Secretary:** David Knight   **Chairman:** G. Hill
Colours: Blue with Gold Trim, Blue, Blue   **Change:** Gold, Black, Black

5-Year Record		P	W	D	F	A	Pts	Psn	Cup	FAT
87-88	VLP	42	6	17	37	71	35	22	4q	2q
88-89	VL1	40	25	8	85	36	83	2	2q	1

89-90	VLP	42	18	9	65	55	63	8	2	1q
90-91	VLP	42	12	7	57	95	43	18	4q	1q
91-92	DLP	42	14	11	56	65	53	14	2q	1q

Ground Capacity: 6,000 (840)   **Record:** 4,091 v Northampton Tn, FAC1
Rail: Basingstoke (1½ miles from ground).
Directions: M3 Junction 6, then follow A30. Ground off Winchester Rd.

BOGNOR REGIS TOWN

Founded in October 1883 and played in the West Sussex and Brighton &
Hove Leagues before joining the Sussex County in 1927. They joined the
Southern League in 1972, but in 1981 moved to the Isthmian League, being
elected to Division One and gaining promotion at the first attempt.

Ground: Nyewood Lane, Bognor Regis, West Sussex, PO21 2TY
Phone: 0243-828683   **Nickname:** The Rocks   **Founded:** 1883
Manager: no details **Secretary:** Martin Jones **Chairman:** Stanley Rowlands
Colours: White with Green Trim, Green, White **Change:** All Yellow/Red Trim

5-Year Record		P	W	D	F	A	Pts	Psn	Cup	FAT
87-88	VLP	42	14	9	41	57	51	16	1	1q
88-89	VLP	42	17	11	38	49	62	9	2	1q
89-90	VLP	42	9	14	37	67	41	19	4q	3q
90-91	VLP	42	12	8	44	71	44	17	2q	1
91-92	DLP	42	9	11	51	89	38	21	2q	1q

Ground Capacity: 6,000 (243)   **Record:** 3,642 v Swansea, FAC1R 1984
Rail: Bognor Regis (1 mile from ground).
Directions: Follow seafront westward from the pier. Continue past Aldwich
Shopping Centre and turn right into Nyewood Lane. Entrance on left.

BROMLEY

Initially played in the South London League. Founder members of the
Southern League Second Division in 1894 but after two seasons switched to
the London League. Movement saw Kent and more London League action
before being Spartan League founder members in 1907. Isthmian Leaguers
from 1908 to 1911, they then returned to the Kent League. After the First
World War they joined the Athenian League. In 1938 their Hayes Lane
ground was opened and in 1952 they returned to the Isthmian League.
Relegated from the top division in 1975, 1984 and again in 1990, they
returned to the Premier Division in 1991.

Ground: Hayes Lane, Bromley, Kent, BR2 9EF
Phone: 081-460-5291   **Nickname:** Lillywhites   **Founded:** 1892
Manager: George Wakeling **Secretary:** J.Cooper **Chairman:** G.Beverly

Colours: White, Black, White   Change: Red, Black

5-Year Record		P	W	D	F	A	Pts	Psn	Cup	FAT
87-88	VLP	42	23	7	68	40	76	2	3q	2q
88-89	VLP	42	13	15	61	48	54	14	3q	1
89-90	VLP	42	7	11	32	69	32	21	4q	3q
90-91	VL1	42	15	14	62	37	80	2	2q	2
91-92	DLP	42	14	12	51	57	54	12	3q	2

Ground Capacity: 8,500 (2,000)   **Record:** 12,000 v Nigeria, Friendly, 9/49
Rail: Bromley South (1 mile from ground).
Directions: M25, Junction 4. A21 to Bromley.

CARSHALTON ATHLETIC

Formed in 1905 by the amalgamation of Mill Lane Mission (1903) and Carshalton St Andrews (1897). Originally in the Southern Suburban League, they were founder members of the Surrey Senior League in 1922 and of the Corinthian League in 1946. They switched to the Athenian League in 1956 and in 1973 were founder members of the Isthmian League Division Two. Promoted to the top section in 1977, they have stayed there ever since.

Ground: War Memorial SG, Colston Avenue, Carshalton, Surrey, SM5 2EX
Phone: 081-642-8425   **Nickname:** Robins   **Founded:** 1903
Manager: Billy Smith   **Secretary:** Ron McLean   **Chairman:** Trevor Cripps
Colours: White with Maroon Trim, Maroon with White Trim, White
Change: Maroon, White, White

5-Year Record		P	W	D	F	A	Pts	Psn	Cup	FAT
87-88	VLP	42	16	13	49	41	61	9	1	2q
88-89	VLP	42	19	15	59	36	72	4	2q	2
89-90	VLP	42	19	5	63	59	59*	10	2q	3q
90-91	VLP	42	17	7	80	67	64	9	2q	1
91-92	DLP	42	18	8	64	67	62	8	1q	3q

* Three points deducted

Ground Capacity: 8,000 (200)   **Record:** 8,200 v Tooting & Mitcham 1951
Rail: Carshalton (300 yards from ground).
Directions: From station turn left into North Street and then first right into Camden Road. At end cross over West Street into Colston Avenue.

CHESHAM UNITED

Formed by the amalgamation of Chesham Town (1879) and Chesham Generals (1887), the club were members of the Spartan League until 1947 when they joined the Corinthian League. They became Athenian Leaguers in 1963 and were Isthmian League Division Two founder members in 1973.

They were relegated in 1986 but promoted back to Division One in 1987. Promoted to the top division for the first time in 1991.

Ground: The Meadow, Amy Lane, Amersham Rd, Chesham, Bucks, HP5 1NE
Phone: 0494-783964   **Nickname:** United   **Founded:** 1919
Manager: Gerald Aplin **Secretary:** A.Greenham **Chairman:** Bill McGowan
Colours: Claret and Blue Stripes, Claret, Blue **Change:** no details

5-Year Record		P	W	D	F	A	Pts	Psn	Cup	FAT
87-88	VL1	42	12	10	69	77	46	18	Pr	1q
88-89	VL1	42	12	9	54	67	45	14	1q	2q
89-90	VL1	42	15	12	46	49	57	10	Pr	1q
90-91	VL1	42	27	8	7	102	37	1	2q	1
91-92	DLP	42	20	10	67	48	70	4	4q	1

Ground Capacity: 5,000 (150)   **Record:** 5,000 v Camb. Utd, FAC3 12/79
Rail: Chesham (¼ mile from ground).
Directions: Located on the A416 – follow Amersham signs from Chesham.

DULWICH HAMLET

Founded in 1893, they competed in local leagues, joining the Isthmian League from the Southern Suburban League in 1907. Isthmian Leaguers since that time, they were relegated in 1977, promoted to the top section in 1978, relegated for a second time in 1990, but promoted again last season.

Ground: Dog Kennel Hill, Dulwich
Phone: **Nickname:** The Hamlet **Founded:** 1893
Manager: Jim Cannon **Secretary:** Terry Stephens **Chairman:** Steve Dye
Colours: Blue and Pink Stripes, Blue, Blue   **Change:** All Yellow

5-Year Record		P	W	D	F	A	Pts	Psn	Cup	FAT
87-88	VLP	42	10	11	46	64	41	18	1q	3q
88-89	VLP	42	12	12	58	57	48	17	4q	1q
89-90	VLP	42	6	8	32	80	26	22	4q	1q
90-91	VL1	42	16	11	67	54	59	12	1q	1q
91-92	DL1	40	22	9	71	40	75	3	2q	2q

Ground Capacity: **Record:** (First season at ground)
Rail: East Dulwich.
Directions: Located 200 yards from East Dulwich Station.

ENFIELD

Founded as Enfield Spartans, adopting their current name on joining the North Middlesex League in 1900. London League members from 1905, they were Athenian League founder members in 1912. In 1936 they moved to their current home and in 1963 joined the Isthmian League. Joined the Alliance Premier League for the 1981-82 season, being relegated in 1990.

Ground: The Stadium, Southbury Road, Enfield, Middx, EN1 1YQ
Phone: 081-363-2858   **Nickname:** The E's   **Founded:** 1893
Manager: Eddie McCluskey   **Secretary:** Alan Diment   **Chairman:** T. Unwin
Colours: White, Blue, Blue   **Change:** All Yellow

5-Year Record		P	W	D	F	A	Pts	Psn	Cup	FAT
87-88	CONF	42	15	10	68	78	55	12	4q	W
88-89	CONF	40	14	8	62	67	50	13	2	2
89-90	CONF	42	10	6	52	89	36	22	4q	2
90-91	VLP	42	26	11	83	30	89	2	3q	2
91-92	DLP	42	24	7	59	45	79	2	2	2

Ground Capacity: 8,500 (820)   **Record:** 10,000 v Tottenham, f.o., 1963
Rail: Southbury Road (½ mile from ground).   **Directions:** Located at junction of A10 and A110 (Enfield). Five minutes from M25/A10 junction.

GRAYS ATHLETIC

Founded in 1890 and took occupation of their Bridge Road ground in 1894. Athenian League founder members in 1912, they reappeared after the First World War in the London League. After the Second World War they were Corinthian League founder members and first champions. Moved to the Athenian again in 1958 and in 1983 joined the Isthmian League set-up. They were the first champions of Division Two (South) in 1985 and promoted to the Premier Division in 1988.

Ground: The Recreation Ground, Bridge Road, Grays, Essex, RM17 6BZ
Phone: 0375-377753   **Nickname:** The Blues   **Founded:** 1890
Managers: Jeff & Fred Saxton   **Secretary:** Jeff Saxton   **Chairman:** F. Harris
Colours: Royal Blue, White, Royal Blue   **Change:** Silver, Grey, Black

5-Year Record		P	W	D	F	A	Pts	Psn	Cup	FAT
87-88	VL1	42	30	10	74	25	100	2	1q	3q
88-89	VLP	42	19	13	62	47	70	5	1	2q
89-90	VLP	42	19	13	59	44	70	5	1q	1q
90-91	VLP	42	20	8	66	53	68	6	3q	2q
91-92	DLP	42	14	11	53	68	53	15	4q	1q

Ground Capacity: 5,500 (350)   **Record:** 9,500 v Chelmsford FAC 1959
Rail: Grays (1 mile from ground).
Directions: A13 towards Southend, turn right at traffic lights towards Grays. Bridge Road after ½ mile on left.

HARROW BOROUGH

Formed as Roxonian. Moved to their Earlsmead Ground and joined the Spartan League in 1934. In 1938 they adopted the name Harrow Town. In 1958 they joined the Delphian League and were absorbed into the Athenian League in 1963. In 1967 their name was changed to Harrow Borough and in 1975 they were elected to the Isthmian League. Promoted to the top section in 1979, they have stayed there ever since.

Ground: Earlsmead, Carlyon Avenue, South Harrow, Middx, HA2 8SS
Phone: 081-422-5221   **Nickname:** The Boro   **Founded:** 1933
Manager: George Borg **Secretary:** Peter Rogers **Chairman:** Martin Murphy
Colours: All Red   **Change:** All Light Blue

5-Year Record		P	W	D	F	A	Pts	Psn	Cup	FAT
87-88	VLP	42	15	11	53	58	56	12	2q	2
88-89	VLP	42	9	13	53	75	40	19	1q	3q
89-90	VLP	42	11	10	51	79	43	18	1q	2
90-91	VLP	42	10	8	57	84	38	20	1q	3q
91-92	DLP	42	11	13	58	78	46	18	1q	2

Ground Capacity: 4,750 (200)   **Record:** 3,000 v Wealdstone, FAC 46
Rail: Northolt Park (½ mile from the ground).
Directions: Take A40 and exit in direction of South Harrow. Left at lights; right at roundabout; fifth right.

HAYES

Originally founded as a boys' team – Botwell Mission. Played in the Great Western Suburban League 1919-24, moving to their Church Road ground in 1921. Spartan League members from 1924, changing their name to Hayes in 1929 and being elected to the Athenian League in 1930. Moved to the Isthmian League in 1971 and have stayed in the top section since that time.

Ground: Townfield House, Church Road, Hayes, Middx, UB3 2LE
Phone: 081-573-4598   **Nickname:** The Missioners **Founded:** 1909
Manager: Clive Griffiths   **Secretary:** John Price   **Chairman:** Derek Goodall
Colours: Red and White Stripes, Black, Black   **Change:** Blue and White

5-Year Record		P	W	D	F	A	Pts	Psn	Cup	FAT
87-88	VLP	42	20	9	62	48	69	6	1	1q
88-89	VLP	42	18	12	61	47	66	8	1	3q
89-90	VLP	42	14	11	61	59	53	14	1	1q
90-91	VLP	42	20	5	60	57	65	8	2	1
91-92	DLP	42	10	14	52	63	44	19	2	2q

Ground Capacity: 9,500 (450)   **Record:** 15,370 v Bromley, FAAmC 2/51
Rail: Hayes and Harlington (1 mile from ground).   **Directions:** M4, exit A312.

HENDON

Founded in 1908 as Hampstead Town. Reached the Athenian League in 1919 via the Finchley, Middlesex and London Leagues. In 1933 they changed their name to Golders Green Town and in 1946 changed again to their present title. Moved to the Isthmian League in 1963 and have stayed in the top section since that time.

Ground: Claremont Road, Cricklewood, London, NW2 1AE
Phone: 081-458-3093   **Nickname:** Dons   **Founded:** 1908
Manager: Gwyn Walters   **Secretary:** Michael Cox   **Chairman:** Victor Green
Colours: Green, White, Green   **Change:** All Yellow

5-Year Record		P	W	D	F	A	Pts	Psn	Cup	FAT
87-88	VLP	42	16	12	62	58	60	10	2q	2
88-89	VLP	42	13	17	51	68	56	12	1	1
89-90	VLP	42	15	10	54	63	55	12	4q	1
90-91	VLP	42	12	10	48	62	46	15	2q	3q
91-92	DLP	42	13	9	59	73	48	17	2q	3q

Ground Capacity: 8,000 (500)   **Record:** 9,000 v Northampton, FAC 52
Rail: Brent Cross (Underground ½ mile from ground).
Directions: M1/A406 roundabout. Take minor exit towards Refuge Centre. At second mini roundabout turn right into Claremont Rd. Continue for about 1 mile – ground on left.

KINGSTONIAN

Formed on the amalgamation of Old Kingstonians and Kingston Town, themselves the two parts of a "split" Kingston and Surbiton YMCA formed in 1885. Joined the Athenian League in 1919, then the Isthmian in 1929. Relegated from the Premier Division in 1979, they were promoted back in 1985 and have been there ever since.

Ground: Kingsmeadow Stadium, 422A Kingston Road, Kingston-Upon-Thames, Surrey, KT1 2HL
Phone: 081-547-3336   **Nickname:** The K's   **Founded:** 1885
Manager: Chris Kelly   **Secretary:** William McNully   **Chairman:** no details
Colours: Red and White Hoops, Black, Black   **Change:** All White

5-Year Record		P	W	D	F	A	Pts	Psn	Cup	FAT
87-88	VLP	42	14	12	47	53	54	14	1q	2q
88-89	VLP	42	19	11	54	37	68	6	3q	1
89-90	VLP	42	24	9	87	51	81	4	1q	QF
90-91	VLP	42	21	12	86	57	75	5	4q	3q
91-92	DLP	42	17	8	71	65	59	10	4q	1

Ground Capacity: 6,500 (1,200)   **Record:** 1,930 v Barrow, FAT4 3/90

Rail: Kingston (1 mile from ground).
Directions: On A307 Kingston to Richmond road. Kingsmeadow is signposted.

MARLOW

Known in their early days as Great Marlow. Joined the Spartan League in 1908 but for 1911-12 moved to the Great Western Suburban League. In 1924 they moved to the Reading & District League, returning to the Spartan in 1928. In 1965 they became Athenians, joining the top division in 1973. Joined the Isthmian League Division Two (North) in 1984, transferred to the South Section in 1985, then promoted twice in consecutive seasons.
Ground: Alfred Davis Memorial Gd, Oak Tree Rd, Marlow, Bucks, SL7 3ED
Phone: 0628-483970   **Nickname:** The Blues   **Founded:** 1870
Manager: David Russell **Secretary:** Paul Burdell **Chairman:** M. Eagleton
Colours: Royal Blue with White Trim, Royal Blue, Royal Blue
Change: All Gold and Black

5-Year Record		P	W	D	F	A	Pts	Psn	Cup	FAT
87-88	VL1	42	32	5	100	44	101	1	2q	1
88-89	VLP	42	9	11	48	83	38	20	2q	3q
89-90	VLP	42	11	13	42	59	46	17	4q	2q
90-91	VLP	42	18	13	72	49	67	7	4q	3q
91-92	DLP	42	20	7	56	50	67	6	1	1

Ground Capacity: 8,000 (500)   **Record:** no details
Rail: Marlow (1 mile from ground).
Directions: M4 or M40 take A404 to Marlow. Follow A4135 towards town centre. At Esso Garage turn right into Maple Rise. Ground in opposite road.

ST ALBANS CITY

Formed in 1908 and immediately joined the Spartan League. They became Athenians in 1920 and moved to the Isthmian League three seasons later. They were relegated in 1974 and again in 1983, but were promoted to Division One in 1984 and to the Premier Division in 1986.
Ground: Clarence Park, Hatfield Road, St Albans, Herts, AL1 4NF
Phone: 0727-64296   **Nickname:** Saints   **Founded:** 1908
Manager: John Mitchell **Secretary:** Steve Trulock **Chairman:** B. Tominey
Colours: Yellow with Blue Trim, Blue, Yellow **Change:** Blue, Yellow, Blue

5-Year Record		P	W	D	F	A	Pts	Psn	Cup	FAT
87-88	VLP	42	15	6	60	69	51	15	1q	1q
88-89	VLP	42	12	9	51	59	45	17	2q	1q
89-90	VLP	42	13	10	49	59	49	15	1q	1q

| 90-91 | VLP | 42 | 11 | 12 | 60 | 74 | 45 | 16 | 1q | 1q |
| 91-92 | DLP | 42 | 14 | 11 | 66 | 70 | 53 | 13 | 2q | 3q |

Ground Capacity: 7,000 (1,000)   **Record:** 9,757 v Ferryhill Ath., FAAmC 1926
Rail: St Albans City (300 yards from ground).
Directions: M25 Junction 22. Across two roundabouts towards city. At first lights turn right. Left at next lights. Right at second lights into Clarence Road. Ground located inside Clarence Park.

STAINES TOWN

Formed as Staines Albany. Merged around 1905 with St Peter's Institute. Emerged after the First World War as Staines Lagonda. Joined the Spartan League in 1924 and became Staines Town in 1925. Moved to Wheatsheaf Park in 1951. Members of the Parthenon League until becoming Hellenic League founder members in 1953. Moved to the Spartan League in 1958 and to the Athenian in 1971. Founder members of the Isthmian League Division Two in 1973. Promoted in 1975 and 1989, relegated in 1984.

Ground: Wheatsheaf Park, Wheatsheaf Lane, Staines, Middx, TW18 2PD
Phone: 0784-455988   **Nickname:** Swans   **Founded:** 1892
Manager: Wayne Wanklyn **Secretary:** Len Gregory **Chairman:** Alan Boon
Colours: Old Gold with Royal Blue Trim, Blue, Blue   **Change:** Blue and White Stripes, White, White

5-Year Record		P	W	D	F	A	Pts	Psn	Cup	FAT
87-88	VL1	42	19	11	71	48	68	5	Pr	1q
88-89	VL1	40	26	9	79	29	87	1	3q	2q
89-90	VLP	42	14	6	53	69	48	16	4q	1
90-91	VLP	42	10	10	46	79	39 *	19	1q	1q
91-92	DLP	42	11	10	43	73	43	20	1q	2q

One point deducted
Ground Capacity: 2,000 (700)
Record: 2,500 v Banco di Roma, Anglo-Italian Cup, 10/75
Rail: Staines (¾ mile from ground).
Directions: Off Laleham Road (B376) from town centre.

STEVENAGE BOROUGH

Founded in 1976, they joined the United Counties League in 1980 and were promoted to the top section after their first season. Moved to the Vauxhall Opel League in 1984 and promoted to the First Division in 1986. Relegated in 1988, they have been promoted twice since then.

Ground: Stevenage Stadium, Broadhall Way, Stevenage, Herts, SG2 8RH
Phone: 0438-367059   **Nickname:** The Boro   **Founded:** 1976
Manager: Paul Fairclough **Secretary:** Ron Berners **Chairman:** Ken Vale

Colours: Red and White Stripes, White, White **Change:** All Yellow with Red Trim

5-Year Record		P	W	D	F	A	Pts	Psn	Cup	FAT
87-88	VL1	42	11	9	36	64	42	21	1q	3q
88-89	VL2N	42	20	13	84	55	73	4	2q*	(VPr)
89-90	VL2N	42	22	6	60	45	72	4	1q	(V3)
90-91	VL2N	42	34	5	122	28	107	1	1q	(V1)
91-92	DL1	40	30	6	95	37	96	1	1q	1q

Tie awarded to opponents

Ground Capacity: 5,000 (480)   **Record:** 3,000, Charity, 5/80

Rail: Stevenage (1 mile from ground).

Directions: A1(M) Junction 7. On B197 from 2nd roundabout.

SUTTON UNITED

Sutton gained senior status and a South Suburban League place in 1910. Joined the Athenian League in 1921, moving to an expanded Isthmian League in 1963. Always in the top division, they declined promotion to the Conference in 1985 but accepted it the following season. Relegated in 1991.

Ground: Boro Sports Ground, Gander Green Lane, Sutton, Surrey, SM1 2EY

Phone: 081-644-5120   **Nickname:** U's   **Founded:** 1898

Manager: Alan Gane   **Secretary:** B. Williams   **Chairman:** D. Hermitage

Colours: All Amber   **Change:** All White

5-Year Record		P	W	D	F	A	Pts	Psn	Cup	FAT
87-88	CONF	42	16	18	77	54	66	8	3	1
88-89	CONF	40	12	15	64	54	51	12	4	2
89-90	CONF	42	19	6	68	64	63	8	1	1
90-91	CONF	42	10	9	62	82	39	21	1	1
91-92	DLP	42	19	13	88	51	70	3	1	1

Ground Capacity: 8,000 (1,000) **Record:** 14,000 v Leeds Utd, FAC3 1/70

Rail: West Sutton (adjacent to ground).

Directions: M25 Junction 8. Take A217 to Sutton. Follow A217 signs towards London. Right at second set of lights into Gander Green Lane.

WINDSOR AND ETON

Played one Southern League game in 1895. Disbanded in 1901 but re-emerged in 1902 when Windsor & Eton Temperance (formed 1900) adopted the current name. Pre-First World War members of the Great Western Suburban, Athenian and Spartan Leagues, they were Corinthian League founders in 1945. Moved to the Metropolitan and District League before becoming Delphian Leaguers and then Athenians again. In 1981 they joined the Isthmian League Division Two and were promoted in 1983 and, to the Premier Division, in 1984.

Ground: Stag Meadow, St. Leonards Road, Windsor, Berks, SL4 3DR
Phone: 0753-860656   **Nickname:** The Royalists   **Founded:** 1891
Manager: Alf Coulton   **Secretary:** C. Cherry   **Chairman:** M. Broadley
Colours: Red with Green Piping, Red, White   **Change:** White, Black, White

5-Year Record		P	W	D	F	A	Pts	Psn	Cup	FAT
87-88	VLP	42	16	17	59	43	65	7	1q	1
88-89	VLP	42	14	13	52	50	55	13	3q	3
89-90	VLP	42	13	15	51	47	54	13	3q	2
90-91	VLP	42	15	10	48	63	55	12	3q	1
91-92	DLP	42	15	11	56	56	56	11	1	3q

Ground Capacity: 5,000 (350)   **Record:** 8,500
Rail: Windsor & Eton Central (1½ miles from ground).
Directions: M4 Junction 6. Follow A332 towards Windsor. Left at lights.
Opposite Stag & Hounds public house.

WIVENHOE TOWN

Formed as Wivenhoe Rangers. Played locally, moving from the Colchester &
East Essex League to the Essex & Suffolk Border League in 1971 and to the
Essex Senior League in 1979. Joined the Isthmian League set-up in 1986.
Promoted to Division One in 1988 and to the Premier Division in 1990.
Ground: Broad Lane Ground, Elmstead Road, Wivenhoe, Essex, CO7 7HA
Phone: 0206-225380   **Nickname:** The Dragons   **Founded:** 1925
Manager: Steve Foley   **Secretary:** Richard Adler   **Chairman:** D. Whymark
Colours: Blue, White, White   **Change:** no details

5-Year Record		P	W	D	F	A	Pts	Psn	Cup	FAT
87-88	VL2N	42	26	10	105	42	88	1	1q	(V1)
88-89	VL1	40	22	6	62	44	72	5	1q	3q
89-90	VL1	42	31	7	94	36	100	1	4q	2
90-91	VLP	42	16	11	69	66	59	10	2q	3
91-92	DLP	42	16	4	56	81	52	16	1q	2

Ground Capacity: 3,000 (200)   **Record:** 1,912 v Runcorn, FAT2 1990
Rail: Wivenhoe (1 mile from ground).
Directions: Leave Colchester in direction of Clacton. Take Wivenhoe exit
and ground is visible.

WOKINGHAM TOWN

Played in local soccer, moving to their Finchampstead Road ground in 1906.
Joined the Metropolitan & District League in 1954, the Delphian in 1957 and
the Corinthian in 1959. They were absorbed into the Athenian League in
1963, switching to the Isthmian in 1973. They were promoted to the top
section in 1982 and have stayed there ever since.

Ground: Finchampstead Road, Wokingham, Berks, RG11 2NR
Phone: 0734-780253   **Nickname:** The Town   **Founded:** 1875
Manager: Roy Merryweather   **Secretary:** J. Aulsberry   **Chairman:** G. Gale
Colours: Amber, Black, Black   **Change:** Red, White, Red

5-Year Record		P	W	D	F	A	Pts	Psn	Cup	FAT
87-88	VLP	42	21	7	62	52	70	5	4q	SF
88-89	VLP	42	15	11	60	54	56	11	3q	1
89-90	VLP	42	26	11	67	34	89	2	4q	2
90-91	VLP	42	15	13	58	54	58	11	3q	1
91-92	DLP	42	19	10	73	58	67	5	2q	3q

Ground Capacity: 4,000 (200)
Record: 3,475 v Norton Woodseats, FAAmCup 57/8
Rail: Wokingham (½ mile from ground).
Directions: From town centre turn left into Denmark Street. Follow to Finchampstead Road.

YEADING

Formed in 1965. From local leagues and the Middlesex League they joined the Spartan League in 1984 and were promoted to the Premier Division in 1985. Joined Division 2 (South) of the Vauxhall League in 1987 and have been promoted twice since.

Ground: The Warren, Beaconsfield Road, Hayes, Middx
Phone: 081-848-7362   **Nickname:** The Dinc   **Founded:** 1965
Manager: Gordon Bartlett   **Secretary:** Peter Bickers   **Chairman:** P. Spurden
Colours: Red and Black Stripes, Black, Black   **Change:** All Yellow

5-Year Record		P	W	D	F	A	Pts	Psn	Cup	FAT
87-88	VL2S	42	19	10	83	56	67	10	1q	(V2)
88-89	VL2S	40	13	9	47	63	46*	15	Pr	(V2)
89-90	VL2S	40	29	4	86	37	91	1	2q	(VW)
90-91	VL1	42	23	8	75	45	77	3	1q	3q
91-92	DL1	40	24	10	83	34	82	2	2q	2q

Two points deducted

Ground Capacity: 5,000 (100)   **Record:** 1,546 v Hythe, FAVsf 1990
Rail: Hayes (2 miles from ground).
Directions: A4020 Uxbridge Road. Turn right towards Southall, right into Springfield Road and left into Beaconsfield Road.

DIVISION ONE

Final Table 1991-92

	P	W	D	L	F	A	Pts
Stevenage Borough	40	30	6	4	95	37	96
Yeading	40	24	10	6	83	34	82
Dulwich Hamlet	40	22	9	9	71	40	75
Boreham Wood	40	22	7	11	65	40	73
Wembley	40	21	6	13	54	43	69
Abingdon Town	40	19	8	13	60	47	65
Tooting & Mitcham United	40	16	13	11	57	45	61
Hitchin Town	40	17	10	13	55	45	61
Walton & Hersham	40	15	13	12	62	50	58
Molesey	40	16	9	15	55	61	57
Dorking	40	16	7	17	68	65	55
Barking	40	14	11	15	51	54	53
Chalfont St Peter	40	15	6	19	62	70	51
Leyton-Wingate	40	13	11	16	53	56	50
Uxbridge	40	13	8	19	47	62	47
Maidenhead United	40	13	7	20	52	61	46
Harlow Town	40	11	9	20	50	70	42
Croydon	40	11	6	23	44	68	39
Heybridge Swifts	40	8	9	23	33	71	33
Whyteleafe	40	7	10	23	42	78	31
Aveley	40	8	3	29	33	95	27

Leading Division One Goalscorers

Gittings, M. (Stevenage B.) 29; Grainger, P. (Dorking) 22; Portway, S. (Barking) 21; Collins, J. (Tooting) 19; Kuhne, S. (Uxbridge) 19.

Promotions and Relegations

Club	Position	Movement
Stevenage Borough	Champions	Promoted to Premier Division
Yeading	Runners-up	Promoted to Premier Division
Dulwich Hamlet	3rd	Promoted to Premier Division

Clubs Joining Division One

Club	Position	From
Bishop's Stortford	22nd	Relegated from Premier Division
Purfleet	Champions	Promoted from Divsion Two
Lewes	Runners-up	Promoted from Divsion Two
Billericay Town	3rd	Promoted from Divsion Two

Division One Top Scorers By Club

Club	Player	Tot	Lg	IC	LC
Abingdon Town	Paul Bradbury	20	13	3	1
Aveley	Stewart Harvey	8	8	–	–
Barking	Steve Portway	22	21	–	1
Boreham Wood	Jimmy Hughes	15	14	1	–
	(inc 1 Lg and 1 IC for Stevenage Borough)				
Chalfont St Peter	Ansill Bushay	13	13	–	–
	Steve Darlington	13	13	–	–
Croydon	Matt Norris	13	12	1	–
Dorking	Phil Grainger	26	22	2	2
Dulwich Hamlet	Matt Norris	19	18	1	–
	(inc 12 Lg and 1 IC for Croydon)				
Harlow Town	Paul Battram	17	14	1	2
Heybridge Swifts	Wayne Adcock	7	4	1	2
Hitchin Town	Paul Quarmain	11	11	–	–
Leyton-Wingate	Micky Fredricks	10	10	–	–
Maidenhead United	Benny Laryea	18	17	–	1
Molesey	Michael Rose	13	11	1	1
Stevenage Borough	Martin Gittings	36	29	1	6
Tooting & Mitcham U	John Collins	21	19	2	–
Uxbridge	Steve Kuhne	21	19	–	2
Walton & Hersham	Steve Griffiths	11	11	–	–
	(inc 1 Lg for Sutton United)				
Wembley	Kenny Page	10	9	1	–
Whyteleafe	Ian Cox	9	7	2	–
Yeading	Hector Welsh	17	17	–	–

Tot=Total number of goals; Lg=League; IC=Isthmian League Cup; LC=Loctite Cup.

William Hill Manager of Month Awards

Month	Manager	Club
September	Keith Hull	Heybridge Swifts
October	Jim Cannon	Dulwich Hamlet
November	Trevor Ford	Tooting & Mitcham
December	Derek Parsons	Walton & Hersham
January	Gordon Bartlett	Yeading
February	Paul Fairclough	Stevenage Borough
March	Trevor Butler	Abingdon Town
April	Jim Cannon	Dulwich Hamlet

DIVISION ONE RESULTS 1991-92

	Abingdon Tn	Aveley	Barking	Boreham Wood	Chalfont St P	Croydon	Dorking	D. Hamlet	Harlow Town	Heybridge Sw	Hitchin Town
Abingdon Town	•	3-0	2-2	1-2	1-0	1-0	2-0	2-1	2-1	7-1	2-2
Aveley	0-1	•	2-1	1-2	1-0	0-4	2-0	2-5	0-4	0-0	1-0
Barking	1-0	5-1	•	2-0	4-2	3-3	2-1	2-0	0-1	0-0	0-2
Boreham Wood	2-0	4-0	1-1	•	3-0	3-0	3-3	1-1	2-0	4-1	3-0
Chalfont St Peter	1-3	1-2	1-2	1-1	•	1-1	3-2	1-2	0-0	1-0	1-1
Croydon	0-0	1-0	1-3	0-1	2-3	•	3-4	0-4	0-3	1-2	2-0
Dorking	3-0	3-1	2-2	0-1	2-3	1-0	•	3-1	1-0	3-0	4-0
Dulwich Hamlet	1-1	2-3	3-0	1-0	1-3	6-1	3-4	•	1-0	0-1	3-1
Harlow Town	0-1	2-1	0-2	2-3	2-4	2-1	0-2	2-0	•	0-1	2-1
Heybridge Swifts	1-1	5-2	1-1	2-1	1-3	1-1	0-2	0-2	1-0	•	1-0
Hitchin Town	1-0	4-2	1-0	0-3	0-2	1-0	1-2	0-1	0-0	2-0	•
Leyton-Wingate	1-2	3-2	0-3	0-2	3-1	2-4	1-3	1-1	3-3	1-1	1-3
Maidenhead United	0-2	2-1	4-0	0-1	2-1	4-2	0-3	0-4	1-1	3-1	2-4
Molesey	4-1	5-0	2-0	2-0	5-1	3-2	2-1	1-1	7-1	3-1	2-0
Stevenage Borough	2-1	3-0	1-1	0-1	1-3	1-0	2-2	2-2	2-3	2-0	0-0
Tooting & Mitcham U.	1-2	1-0	0-0	2-3	2-0	1-2	1-1	1-2	1-3	1-1	1-1
Uxbridge	1-1	4-2	3-2	2-1	1-2	1-0	1-0	0-1	2-2	0-0	2-1
Walton & Hersham	2-1	3-1	2-1	1-0	2-2	2-3	2-0	3-2	1-0	0-1	3-2
Wembley	1-3	1-1	1-3	2-2	2-0	1-0	0-1	1-4	1-3	1-3	0-2
Whyteleafe	1-3	1-1	1-3	2-2	2-0	2-3	0-1	1-4	1-3	1-3	0-2
Yeading	2-1	3-0	1-0	0-1	5-0	4-2	3-2	0-1	3-0	4-0	0-2

Team	Leyton-Win	Maidenhead U	Molesey	Stevenage B	Tooting & M	Uxbridge	Walton & H	Wembley	Whyteleafe	Yeading
Abingdon Town	0-0	1-2	3-2	4-0	1-1	1-2	1-0	1-0	0-3	1-3
Aveley	1-5	1-0	1-1	0-4	0-2	0-4	0-1	0-2	0-1	0-2
Barking	2-2	2-0	1-1	1-3	0-3	0-1	0-1	1-1	2-1	1-1
Boreham Wood	3-1	1-0	2-1	0-3	4-0	3-0	2-3	1-2	2-2	2-4
Chalfont St Peter	1-2	0-1	2-0	0-0	2-0	2-1	1-1	0-1	2-3	0-3
Croydon	2-0	1-0	0-1	0-1	1-1	1-2	0-3	0-1	0-2	1-1
Dorking	3-3	0-2	0-2	3-1	1-3	0-3	3-0	1-0	0-1	1-1
Dulwich Hamlet	1-0	2-1	0-1	0-2	0-1	2-1	0-1	1-0	1-1	0-0
Harlow Town	2-1	2-2	0-1	0-3	2-2	1-5	2-3	2-5	0-0	0-0
Heybridge Swifts	1-3	0-3	0-2	1-1	2-3	2-0	0-0	1-3	3-1	0-2
Hitchin Town	3-1	2-0	1-1	2-2	0-1	2-0	0-0	4-0	0-0	1-0
Leyton-Wingate	•	1-2	0-0	0-3	2-1	4-0	1-3	2-1	3-0	0-2
Maidenhead United	3-2	•	1-2	1-1	0-3	2-1	1-2	0-0	1-2	2-4
Molesey	0-0	1-3	•	3-2	2-1	4-1	0-3	1-2	2-1	2-2
Stevenage Borough	4-1	2-0	3-2	•	2-1	2-0	3-2	2-0	4-0	0-1
Tooting & Mitcham U.	1-0	2-1	0-0	3-1	•	2-0	0-1	0-1	3-1	0-3
Uxbridge	0-2	2-2	2-3	1-3	1-1	•	2-1	0-0	2-0	0-3
Walton & Hersham	1-1	2-2	0-1	2-3	1-1	4-0	•	0-1	4-1	2-2
Wembley	2-1	1-2	0-2	0-1	1-3	0-1	3-0	•	1-1	0-0
Whyteleafe	1-1	0-2	1-1	0-1	1-0	1-1	0-3	1-3	•	1-1
Yeading	0-0	2-2	6-2	4-0	1-1	1-2	2-1	2-1	5-2	•

DIVISION ONE CLUBS

ABINGDON TOWN

Ground: Culham Road, Abingdon, Oxon, OX14 3BT
Phone: 0235-21684   **Nickname:** Over The Bridge   **Founded:** 1889
Manager: Trevor Butler   **Secretary:** Dave Sharp   **Chairman:** Brian Tonkin
Colours: Yellow with Green Trim, Green with Yellow Trim, Yellow
Change: All Blue
Ground Capacity: 2,000 (80)   **Record:** 1,400 v Oxford City, FAC 9/60
Rail: Culham (2 miles from ground).
Directions: On A415 ½ mile from town centre.

AVELEY

Ground: Mill Field, Mill Road, Aveley, Essex, RM15 4TR
Phone: 0708-865940   **Nickname:** The Millers   **Founded:** 1927
Manager: Tommy Lee   **Secretary:** Ken Sutliff   **Chairman:** Tony Wallace
Colours: Royal Blue, White, White   **Change:** Red, White, White
Ground Capacity: 7,500 (400)   **Record:** 2,623 v Wycombe W, FAC 1978
Rail: Rainham/Purfleet (½ mile from ground).
Directions: Near Sandy Lane on A13.

BARKING

Ground: Mayesbrook Park, Lodge Avenue, Dagenham, Essex, IG3 9EG
Phone: 081-595-6511   **Nickname:** The Blues   **Founded:** 1880
Manager: David Patient   **Secretary:** Mike Roberts   **Chairman:** John Knight
Colours: Blue, White, Blue   **Change:** All White with Blue Trim
Ground Capacity: 4,200 (200)   **Record:** 1,900 v Aldershot FAC2 1988
Rail: Upney (Underground 1½ miles from ground).
Directions: Mayesbrook Park is about 1 mile along the A1153 from the A13 Thatched Cottage roundabout.

BILLERICAY TOWN

Ground: New Lodge, Blunts Wall Road, Billericay, Essex, CM12 9SA
Phone: 0277-652188   **Nickname:** Town   **Founded:** 1880
Manager: John Kendall   **Secretary:** Len Dewson   **Chairman:** Brian Cornes
Colours: Royal Blue with White Trim, White, Royal Blue with White Trim
Change: Yellow, Black, Black   **Rail:** Billericay (¾ mile from ground).
Directions: M25 Junction 28. Via Shenfield (A129), right at first lights. M25 Junction 29. Via Basildon (A129), left at second set of lights.

BISHOP'S STORTFORD

Ground: George Wilson Stadium, Rhodes Av, B. Stortford, Herts, CM23 3JN
Phone: 0279-654140/656538   **Nickname:** Bishops   **Founded:** 1874
Manager: John Radford   **Secretary:** Jim Gill   **Chairman:** Jim Gill
Colours: Blue and White Stripes, Blue, Blue   **Change:** All Red
Ground Capacity: 6,000 (228)
Record: 6,000: v Middlesbrough FAC3 1/83 v Peterborough FAC2 12/72
Rail: Bishop's Stortford (½ mile from ground).
Directions: M11 Junction 8. A120 towards Bishop's Stortford. Take South Street to South Road and Rhodes Avenue. About ½ mile on left.

BOREHAM WOOD

Ground: Broughinge Road, Borehamwood, Herts, WD6 5AL
Phone: 081-953-5097   **Nickname:** The Wood   **Founded:** 1948
Manager: Trevor Harvey   **Secretary:** Tony Perkins   **Chairman:** Phil Wallace
Colours: White, Black, Red   **Change:** Red, Red, Black
Ground Capacity: 5,000 (220)   **Record:** 2,500 v St. Albans, FAAmC 1970/1
Rail: Elstree & Borehamwood (1 mile from ground).
Directions: M25, A1 towards London. Exit at first turn-off towards Borehamwood. Located off roundabout near BBC studios.

CHALFONT ST PETER

Ground: The Playing Fields, Amersham Rd, Chalfont St Peter, Bucks, SL9 7BQ
Phone: 0753-885797   **Nickname:** The Saints   **Founded:** 1926
Manager: Tony O'Driscoll   **Secretary:** Mal Keenan   **Chairman:** David Ward
Colours: White, Green, Green   **Change:** All Yellow
Ground Capacity: 2,500 (200)   **Record:** 2,500 v Watford, benefit 4/85
Rail: Gerrards Cross (2 miles from ground).
Directions: Off A413 between Ambulance Station and Community Centre.

CROYDON

Ground: Croydon Sports Arena, Albert Road, S. Norwood, London, SE25 4QL
Phone: 081-654-3462   **Nickname:** Blues   **Founded:** 1953
Manager: Dave Boyton   **Secretary:** Geoff Beeson   **Chairman:** N. Moran
Colours: All Blue   **Change:** All Red
Ground Capacity: 8,000 (450)   **Record:** 1,450 v Wycombe W, FAC4q 1975
Rail: Norwood Junction (200 yards).
Directions: Albert Rd is situated just off the junction of the A215 and A213.

DORKING

Ground: Meadowbank, Mill Lane, Dorking, Surrey, RH4 1DX
Phone: 0306-884112   **Nickname:** The Chicks   **Founded:** 1977
Manager: Martin Collins **Secretary:** Brian Stone **Chairman:** Tom Howes
Colours: Green and White Hoops, White, White **Change:** Blue, White, Red
Ground Capacity: 600 (150)   **Record:** 4,500 v Folkestone, 1954/5
Rail: Dorking (½ mile from ground).
Directions: From town centre turn right at Woolworth's into Mill Lane.

HARLOW TOWN

Ground: Harlow SC, Hammarskjold Road, Harlow, Essex, CM20 2JF
Phone: 0279-444183   **Nickname:** The Owls   **Founded:** 1879
Manager: Dave Edwards **Secretary:** G. Auger **Chairman:** Alan Howick
Colours: All Red with White Trim   **Change:** White, White, Blue
Ground Capacity: 10,000 (450)   **Record:** 9,723 v Leicester C., FAC4 1/80
Rail: Harlow Town (½ mile from ground).
Directions: not known

HEYBRIDGE SWIFTS

Ground: Scraley Road, Heybridge, Maldon, Essex
Phone: 0621-852978   **Nickname:** Swifts   **Founded:** 1880
Manager: Gary Hill **Secretary:** Dennis Fenn **Chairman:** Michael Gibson
Colours: Black and White Stripes, Black, Red **Change:** Orange, White, White
Ground Capacity: 5,000 (200)   **Record:** 2,500, Charity 1990
Rail: Witham (6 miles from ground).
Directions: Head towards Maldon from Colchester Road, through Heybridge
village. Then right in direction of Tolleshunt D'Arcy (Scraley Road). Ground
on right-hand side.

HITCHIN TOWN

Ground: Top Field, Fishponds Road, Hitchin, Herts, SG5 1NU
Phone: 0462-434483   **Nickname:** The Canaries   **Founded:** 1865
Manager: Steve Norris **Secretary:** Alan Sexton **Chairman:** T. Barratt
Colours: Yellow, Green, Yellow   **Change:** All Red
Ground Capacity: 4,000 (400)
Record: 7,878 v Wycombe W, FAAmC3 2/56
Rail: Hitchin (1 mile from ground).
Directions: On A505 1 mile from town centre.

LEWES

Ground: The Dripping Pan, Mountfield Road, Lewes, Sussex, BN7 1XN
Phone: 0273-472100   **Nickname:** The Rooks   **Founded:** 1885
Manager: Brian Donnelly **Secretary:** D. J. Quinn **Chairman:** D. J. Quinn
Colours: Red and Black Hoops, Black, Red   **Change:** Yellow, Blue
Ground Capacity: 5,000 (400) **Record:** 2,500 v Newhaven SxCtyLg 1947
Rail: Lewes.
Directions: From station turn left. Left into Mountfield Road. Ground about 100 yards on left hand side.

LEYTON

Ground: 282 Lea Bridge Road, Leyton, London, E10 7LD
Phone: 081-539-5405   **Nickname:** not known   **Founded:** 1975
Manager: Kevin Moran **Secretary:** Alan Hunter **Chairman:** George Gross
Colours: Blue, White, Blue   **Change:** White, Blue, White
Ground Capacity: 3,000 (200)   **Record:** 500 v Wickham, FAV6 1984
Rail: Leyton or Blackhorse Road Underground (1½ miles from ground).
Directions: Located on the Lea Bridge Road behind the Hare and Hounds PH.

MAIDENHEAD UNITED

Ground: 1 York Road, Maidenhead, Berks, SL6 1SQ
Phone: 0628-24739   **Nickname:** Tanners   **Founded:** 1869
Manager: John Clements **Secretary:** Stan Payne **Chairman:** Jim Parsons
Colours: White, Black, White   **Change:** All Red
Ground Capacity: 1,500 (100)   **Record:** 9,401 v Southall, FAAm C 1936
Rail: Maidenhead (400 yards from ground).
Directions: In town centre. Two minutes walk from cark parks.

MOLESEY

Ground: 412 Walton Road, West Molesey, Surrey, KT8 0JG
Phone: 081-979-4823   **Nickname:** Moles   **Founded:** 1950
Manager: Tony Dunne **Secretary:** John Chambers **Chairman:** Gary Mayne
Colours: White, Black, Black   **Change:** Yellow, Blue, Yellow
Ground Capacity: 4,800 (400) **Record:** 1,255 v Sutton, Surrey Snr Cup sf 1966
Rail: Hampton Court (1 mile from ground).
Directions: A3, take A309 at Hook. Turn right at Marquis of Grandby PH to Hampton Court Station. Left through Molesey. Ground on left after 1 mile.

PURFLEET

Ground: Essex Hotel & L.C., Ship Lane, Grays, Essex, RM15 4HB
Phone: 0708-868901   **Nickname:** None   **Founded:** 1985
Manager: Gary Calder   **Secretary:** N. Posner   **Chairman:** H. South
Colours: Green, Green, Yellow   **Change:** All Yellow
Ground Capacity: 2,500 (300)   **Record:** 980 v West Ham 1989
Rail: Purfleet (2 miles from ground).
Directions: M25 or A13 to Dartford Tunnel roundabout. Take Ship Lane –
signposted ground located on right.

TOOTING AND MITCHAM UNITED

Ground: Sandy Lane, Mitcham, Surrey, CR4 2HD
Phone: 081-648-3248   **Nickname:** Terrors   **Founded:** 1932
Manager: Bob Langford   **Secretary:** Chris Jackson   **Chairman:** Jack Payne
Colours: White, Black, Red   **Change:** All Light Blue
Ground Capacity: 7,500 (1,900)   **Record:** 15,000 v Wimbledon 1951
Rail: Tooting (¼ mile from ground).
Directions: Off Streatham Road near the Swan Hotel.

UXBRIDGE

Ground: Honeycroft, Horton Road, West Drayton, Middx, UB7 8HX
Phone: 0895-443557   **Nickname:** Reds   **Founded:** 1871
Manager: Mick Harvey **Secretary:** Alan Brown **Chairman:** Alan Holloway
Colours: Red, White, Red   **Change:** All Sky Blue
Ground Capacity: 5,000 (200)   **Record:** 1,000 v Arsenal, f.o. 1981
Rail: West Drayton (1 mile from ground).
Directions: From West Drayton Station: Turn right, first right into Horton
Road. Ground 1 mile on left.

WALTON AND HERSHAM

Ground: Sports Ground, Stompond Lane, Walton-on-Thames, Surrey
Phone: 0932-245263   **Nickname:** Swans   **Founded:** 1896
Manager: Chris Wainwright **Secretary:** Gerry Place **Chairman:** Nick Swindley
Colours: Red and White, White, Red **Change:** All Blue
Ground Capacity: 6,500 (500)   **Record:** 6,500 v Brighton, FAC 1973/4
Rail: Walton-on-Thames (½ mile from ground).
Directions: ¼ mile south of Walton-on-Thames town centre on A244 to
Esher.

WEMBLEY

Ground: Vale Farm, Watford Road, Sudbury, Wembley, Middx, HA0 4UR
Phone: 081-904-8169   **Nickname:** The Lions **Founded:** 1946
Manager: Tony Waugh **Secretary:** Mrs J. Gumm **Chairman:** Brian Gumm
Colours: Red, White, Red   **Change:** All Sky Blue
Ground Capacity: 3,000 (250)   **Record:** 2,000 v Hendon, Mid Snr Cup, 59/60
Rail: Sudbury (400 yards from ground).
Directions: Watford Road is part of the A404 and runs on from Harrow Road when driving north from High Road, Wembley.

WHYTELEAFE

Ground: 15 Church Road, Whyteleafe, Surrey, CR3 0AR
Phone: 081-660-5491   **Nickname:** Leafe   **Founded:** 1946
Manager: Steve Kember **Secretary:** Syd Maddex **Chairman:** A. Lidbury
Colours: Green and White, Green, White   **Change:** Yellow, Black, Black
Ground Capacity: 5,000 (200)   **Record:** not known
Rail: Whyteleafe (600 yards from ground).
Directions: A22 to Whyteleafe.

Division One Home Attendances By Club

Club	Total	Ave	90/91	%+/-
Abingdon Town	4,962	248	281	-13.3
Aveley	1,970	99	145	-46.4
Barking	2,143	107	195	-82.2
Boreham Wood	2,845	142	144	-1.4
Chalfont St Peter	2,509	125	188	-50.4
Croydon	2117	106	122	-15.0
Dorking	3,430	172	216	-25.5
Dulwich Hamlet	2,970	149	195	-30.8
Harlow Town	1,910	96	114	-18.7
Heybridge Swifts	3,147	157	170	-8.2
Hitchin Town	6,599	330	337	-14.2
Leyton-Wingate	2,310	116	198	-70.6
Maidenhead United	4,335	217	246	-13.3
Molesey	1,958	98	101	-3.0
Stevenage Borough	12,859	643	485	+32.5
Tooting & Mitcham United	2,973	149	169	-13.4
Uxbridge	2,344	117	126	-7.6
Walton & Hersham	2,975	149	197	-32.2
Wembley	2,383	119	99	+20.2
Whyteleafe	2,153	108	138	-27.7
Yeading	2,883	144	129	+11.6

DIVISION TWO

Final Table 1991-92

	P	W	D	L	F	A	Pts
Purfleet	42	27	8	7	97	48	89
Lewes	42	23	14	5	74	36	83
Billericay Town	42	24	8	10	75	44	80
Leatherhead	42	23	6	13	68	40	75
Ruislip Manor	42	20	9	13	74	51	69
Egham Town	42	19	12	11	81	62	69
Metropolitan Police	42	20	9	13	76	58	69
Saffron Walden Town	42	19	11	12	86	67	68
Hemel Hempstead	42	18	10	14	63	50	64
Hungerford Town	42	18	7	17	53	58	61
Barton Rovers	42	17	8	17	61	64	59
Worthing	42	17	8	17	67	72	59
Witham Town	42	16	11	15	56	61	59
Banstead Athletic	42	16	10	16	69	58	58
Malden Vale	42	15	12	15	63	48	57
Rainham Town	42	14	13	15	53	48	55
Ware	42	14	9	19	58	62	51
Berkhamsted Town	42	13	11	18	56	57	50
Harefield United	42	11	7	24	47	66	40
Southall	42	8	7	27	39	93	31
Southwick	42	6	2	34	29	115	20
Newbury Town	42	4	8	30	30	117	20

Leading Scorers Division Two

Butler, M. (Egham Town) 31; Jones, S. (Billericay Town) 29; Camp, R. (Barton Rovers) 25; Wood, J. (Purfleet) 22.

Promotions and Relegations

Club	Position	Movement
Purfleet	Champions	Promoted to Division One
Lewes	Runners-up	Promoted to Division One
Billericay Town	3rd	Promoted to Division One
Southwick		Resigned

Division Two Top Scorers By Club

Club	Player	Tot	Lg	IC	LT
Banstead Athletic	Gary Grabban	25	23	1	1
Barton Rovers	Richard Camp	28	25	–	3
Berkhamsted Town	Ian Ranger	12	12	–	–
Billericay Town	Steve Jones	32	29	3	–
Egham Town	Mark Butler	36	31	2	3
Harefield United	Pedro Herbert	9	9	–	–
Hemel Hempstead	Phillip Reid	15	15	–	–
Hungerford Town	Tim Brooks	9	9	–	–
Leatherhead	Clifton Soares (inc 6 Lg for Newbury Town)	11	11	–	–
Lewes	Kevin Crooks	15	14	1	–
Malden Vale	Mick Browne	16	13	–	3
Metropolitan Police	John Nicholson	14	13	1	–
Newbury Town	James Rowland	6	6	–	–
	Clifton Soares	6	6	–	–
Purfleet	Jeff Wood	26	22	–	4
Rainham Town	Steve Kirby	14	12	2	–
Ruislip Manor	Pedro Herbert (inc 9 for Harefield United)	21	21	–	–
Saffron Walden Town	Tony Welch	19	18	–	1
	Mark Simpson	19	15	1	3
Southall	Lee Budd	10	7	2	1
Southwick	Paul Smith	6	4	2	–
Ware	Sean Brett	25	15	8	2
Witham Town	Jason Thompson (inc 6 Lg and 2 LT for Purfleet)	12	10	–	2
Worthing	Paul Boxall	23	20	1	2

Tot=Total number of goals; Lg=League; IC=Isthmian League Cup; LT=Loctite Trophy.

William Hill Manager of Month Awards

Month	Manager	Club
September	Stuart Todd	Ware
October	Bobby Knock	Banstead Athletic
November	Micky Burns	Leatherhead
December	David Evans	Hemel Hempstead
January	Gary Calder	Purfleet
February	Wilf Tranter	Hungerford Town
March	John Kendall	Billericay Town
April	John Kendall	Billericay Town

DIVISION TWO RESULTS 1991-92

Home \ Away	Banstead Ath	Barton Rovers	Berkhamsted	Billericay Town	Egham Town	Harefield Utd	Hemel Hemp	Hungerford T	Leatherhead	Lewes	Malden Vale
Banstead Athletic	•	1-1	2-2	1-0	0-0	2-1	1-1	0-1	2-1	2-3	3-1
Barton Rovers	0-2	•	2-1	0-0	0-1	2-0	0-3	2-3	0-3	0-1	2-1
Berkhamsted Town	3-1	4-1	•	2-3	1-2	1-3	1-2	2-3	1-0	0-0	0-3
Billericay Town	2-0	4-0	2-0	•	2-2	1-1	0-0	4-1	0-3	3-1	3-0
Egham Town	3-1	0-2	1-1	2-2	•	2-0	3-1	1-3	0-1	3-1	2-1
Harefield United	1-2	0-1	1-1	1-1	0-3	•	4-0	1-0	2-3	2-1	0-0
Hemel Hempstead	4-1	1-1	1-0	0-0	1-2	2-0	•	1-3	0-0	1-1	3-1
Hungerford Town	0-0	0-0	2-1	1-0	1-3	2-1	2-2	•	0-0	1-1	2-0
Leatherhead	0-1	1-0	0-2	2-1	0-3	1-0	4-0	1-0	•	1-1	1-0
Lewes	2-2	1-2	3-2	3-0	4-1	4-0	2-0	2-0	0-1	•	1-1
Malden Vale	1-0	1-0	1-0	1-2	3-3	4-1	1-0	3-2	1-2	2-3	•
Metropolitan Police	3-2	3-5	3-0	1-1	2-1	0-1	1-2	0-2	2-1	0-3	2-2
Newbury Town	1-3	5-0	1-1	0-1	4-3	5-1	1-1	0-1	2-2	0-3	0-4
Purfleet	2-0	2-1	3-1	0-1	2-0	1-0	0-1	3-0	1-1	2-3	1-0
Rainham Town	2-1	1-3	0-0	0-1	1-1	1-0	2-2	4-0	2-1	1-1	1-1
Ruislip Manor	1-0	1-2	0-1	0-1	1-2	1-3	0-1	2-4	3-0	0-1	2-1
Saffron Walden	1-1	2-1	2-0	0-1	2-5	0-2	1-3	1-0	2-4	2-4	4-2
Southall	1-6	0-3	1-1	0-2	1-0	1-3	1-0	2-0	0-4	0-1	0-0
Southwick	1-3	4-1	0-1	1-1	1-0	1-0	1-0	2-0	0-6	0-2	0-3
Ware	1-2	2-4	1-1	4-0	1-1	0-2	0-2	5-1	3-1	0-0	1-1
Witham Town	1-4	5-1	0-0	1-1	1-0	1-3	1-0	2-0	1-1	2-2	0-0
Worthing	1-4	5-1	1-1	5-4	1-1	1-0	1-1	5-1	1-2	2-2	0-0

	Met Police	Newbury Town	Purfleet	Rainham Town	Ruislip Manor	Saffron Walden	Southall	Southwick	Ware	Witham Town	Worthing
Banstead Athletic	0-1	7-1	3-3	0-0	3-4	1-2	4-1	2-0	1-1	0-1	0-2
Barton Rovers	2-1	1-1	1-2	1-1	1-1	2-3	5-1	3-0	3-0	1-1	3-0
Berkhamsted Town	3-0	1-0	1-1	0-1	2-5	1-4	2-0	5-1	4-0	2-0	3-0
Billericay Town	3-2	7-0	0-2	1-1	4-3	2-1	1-0	4-0	1-0	4-1	3-1
Egham Town	4-2	1-1	3-4	2-3	3-2	1-1	5-0	5-4	1-1	5-1	1-3
Harefield Utd	2-1	2-0	2-4	1-0	0-0	0-1	1-1	5-2	1-2	1-0	0-1
Hemel Hempstead	1-1	6-1	1-1	2-0	2-0	0-1	4-0	0-2	6-3	0-1	2-2
Hungerford Town	1-0	1-1	1-2	1-0	2-1	1-1	1-2	2-1	0-2	0-1	4-1
Leatherhead	0-1	4-0	3-1	0-0	0-3	0-0	4-0	2-1	1-2	2-0	3-0
Lewes	2-2	5-0	1-3	0-0	0-2	4-0	3-0	0-0	2-1	1-0	9-1
Malden Vale	1-1	3-0	0-2	1-1	1-1	4-1	1-1	4-1	3-1	1-2	2-1
Metropolitan Police	•	0-0	0-6	2-0	1-0	2-2	6-1	4-1	3-0	5-1	1-0
Newbury Town	0-1	•	1-0	1-3	1-2	1-7	1-0	4-1	1-3	2-4	1-2
Purfleet	1-3	4-1	•	1-2	1-2	3-2	2-0	1-0	2-1	1-2	3-2
Rainham Town	1-1	3-0	1-2	•	2-0	2-3	3-0	1-0	4-1	2-0	2-0
Ruislip Manor	3-1	3-1	1-4	2-0	•	3-3	1-0	1-0	4-1	2-0	2-1
Saffron Walden	3-2	1-2	3-2	2-3	3-3	•	2-3	0-2	0-4	3-3	3-1
Southall	0-4	4-0	0-4	0-0	1-0	2-3	•	0-2	1-0	2-3	4-1
Southwick	1-2	1-2	0-2	0-2	0-4	0-2	0-0	•	9-1	0-2	0-4
Ware	2-0	2-0	1-4	0-4	1-1	1-6	4-0	0-4	•	1-2	2-0
Witham Town	2-3	3-0	2-0	4-2	1-1	1-2	4-0	3-3	2-0	•	1-1
Worthing	3-0	4-1	3-2	2-0	2-1	3-2	4-1	1-0	0-1	0-0	•

DIVISION TWO CLUBS

BANSTEAD ATHLETIC
Ground: Merland Rise, Tadworth, Surrey, KT20 5JG
Phone: 0737-350982   **Nickname:** The A's   **Founded:** 1944
Colours: Amber with Black Trim, Black, Black   **Change:** Red and White
Rail: Tattenham Corner.
Directions: M25, A217 to Tadworth. Follow signs towards swimming pool, the ground is located nearby.

BARTON ROVERS
Ground: Sharpenhoe Road, Barton-le-Cley, Bedford, MK45 4SD
Phone: 0582-882607   **Nickname:** Rovers   **Founded:** 1898
Colours: White, Royal Blue, Royal Blue   **Change:** Yellow, Royal Blue, Royal Blue
Rail: Harlington (4½ miles from ground).
Directions: M1 Junction 12. Right at top of slip road. Continue through Harlington and Sharpenhoe until you reach Barton. Ground can be seen on right.

BERKHAMSTED TOWN
Ground: Broadwater, Lower Kings Road, Berkhamsted, Herts, HP4 2AA
Phone: 0442-826815   **Nickname:** Lilywhites   **Founded:** 1895
Colours: White, Black, Black   **Change:** All Sky Blue
Rail: Berkhamsted (ground next to station).
Directions: A41 to Berkhamsted. Ground next to station.

EGHAM TOWN
Ground: Tempest Road, Egham, Surrey, TW20 8BB
Phone: 0784-435226   **Nickname:** Town   **Founded:** 1963
Colours: Blue with Yellow sleeves, Blue, Blue with Amber tops
Change: All White with Blue and Gold trim
Rail: Egham (1½ miles from ground).
Directions: M25 Staines exit. Left at Police Station, left at next junction, first left after Prince Alfred public house.

HAMPTON
Ground: Beveree Stadium, Beaver Close, off Station Road, Hampton, Middx, TW12 2BX
Phone: 081-979-2456   **Nickname:** Beavers   **Founded:** 1920
Colours: Blue and Red Stripes, Red, Blue   **Change:** Yellow and Red

Rail: Hampton (500 yards from ground).
Directions: M3 Junction 1. A308 to High Street.

HAREFIELD UNITED
Ground: Preston Park, Breakspear Road North, Harefield, Middx, UB9 6DG
Phone: 0895-823474   Nickname: The Hare   Founded: 1868
Colours: Red and White Stripes, Black, Black and Red
Change: All Sky and Navy Blue
Rail: Denham (2 miles from ground).
Directions: M25 Junction 17. Follow signs for Swakeleys roundabout on
A40 and turn off on B467 following signs to Harefield.

HEMEL HEMPSTEAD
Ground: Vauxhall Road, Adeyfield, Hemel Hempstead, Herts, HP2 4HW
Phone: 0442-42081   Nickname: Hemel   Founded: 1885
Colours: All Red   Change: All Blue
Rail: Hemel Hempstead (1½ miles from ground).
Directions: M1 Junction 8. Across two roundabouts and right into Leverstock
Green Road. Vauxhall Road first on left.

HUNGERFORD TOWN
Ground: Bulpit Lane, Hungerford, Berks, RG17 0AY
Phone: 0488-682939   Nickname: Crusaders   Founded:1886
Colours: White, Navy Blue, White   Change: All Red
Rail: Hungerford (¾ miles from ground).
Directions: M4 Junction 14. A4, turn right. Turn left at Bear Hotel. Left into
Priory Road after town centre (A338), second left into Bulpit Lane.

LEATHERHEAD
Ground: Fetcham Grove, Guildford Road, Leatherhead, Surrey, KT22 9AS
Phone: 0372-372634   Nickname: Tanners   Founded: 1946
Colours: Green, White, Green   Change: White, Black, Black
Rail: Leatherhead (½ mile from ground).
Directions: M25 Junction 9. Follow signs to Leisure Centre.

MALDEN VALE
Ground: Grand Drive, Raynes Park, London, SW20 9NB
Phone: 081-542-2193   Nickname: The Vale   Founded: 1967
Colours: Royal Blue with White Trim, Navy Blue, Red Change: All Red
Rail: Raynes Park (500 yards from ground).
Directions: Grand Drive (B279) is off of Bushey Road by Bushey Mead Park
driving towards Raynes Park along from Kingston Road.

METROPOLITAN POLICE

Ground: Metropolitan Police (Imber Court) Sports Club, Ember Lane, East Molesey, Surrey, KT8 0BT
Phone: 081-398-1267   **Nickname:** The Blues   **Founded:** 1919
Colours: All Blue   **Change:** All Red
Rail: Thames Ditton (½ mile from ground).
Directions: A3, A308 to Scilly Isles roundabout. Turn right into Hampton Court Way. Left at roundabout into Imber Court Road.

NEWBURY TOWN

Ground: Town Ground, Faraday Road, Newbury, Berks, RG13 2AD
Phone: 0635-40048   **Nickname:** The Town   **Founded:** 1887
Colours: Amber, Black, Black   **Change:** Red and White
Rail: Newbury (½ mile from ground).
Directions: A34 Robin Hood roundabout. Take A4 towards Reading. Right at lights into Faraday Road.

RAINHAM TOWN

Ground: Essex Hotel & L.C., Ship Lane, Grays, Essex, RM15 4HB
Phone: 0708-868901   **Nickname:** The Reds   **Founded:** 1945
Colours: Red and White, Red, Red   **Change:** All Blue
Rail: Purfleet (2 miles from ground).
Directions: M25 or A13 to Dartford Tunnel roundabout. Take Ship Lane – signposted ground located on right.

RUISLIP MANOR

Ground: Grosvenor Vale, off West End Road, Ruislip, Middx, HA4 6JQ
Phone: 0895-637487   **Nickname:** The Manor   **Founded:** 1938
Colours: White, Black, Black   **Change:** All Yellow
Rail: Ruislip Manor Underground (Metropolitan line – ½ mile from ground)
Directions: From station turn left and then first right (Shenley Ave). Third left (Cranley Drive).

SAFFRON WALDEN TOWN

Ground: Catons Lane, Saffron Walden, Essex, CB10 2DU
Phone: 0799-22789   **Nickname:** The Bloods   **Founded:** 1872
Colours: Red and Black Stripes, Black with Red Trim, Black with Red Trim
Change: All Yellow with Red Trim
Rail: Audley End (ground 3 miles from station).
Directions: M11 Junction 9. Take third exit at roundabout (B184). Follow signs to town. Left at Museum Street and left into Catons Lane. (Beware the one-way system! *Ed.*)

SOUTHALL

Ground: Western Road, Southall, Middx, UB2 5HX
Phone: 081-574-1084   **Nickname:** The Fowlers   **Founded:** 1871
Colours: All Red and White   **Change:** Grey and White
Rail: Southall (½ mile from ground).
Directions: From A4020 Uxbridge Road turn into South Road (A3005).
Follow on through into The Green and then King Street. Western Road is first
major right-hand turn.

WARE

Ground: Buryfield, Park Road, Ware, Herts, SG12 0AJ
Phone: 0920-463247   **Nickname:** Blues   **Founded:** 1892
Colours: Blue and White Stripes, Blue, Red   **Change:** All Amber and Black
Rail: Ware (1 mile from ground).
Directions: A10, A602 & B1001. Ground behind Banks Radio factory.

WITHAM TOWN

Ground: Spa Road, Witham, Essex, CM8 1UN
Phone: 0376-500146   **Nickname:** The Town   **Founded:** 1947
Colours: Red and Black Stripes, Black, Black   **Change:** All Blue
Rail: Witham (¾ mile from ground).
Directions: A12 to Witham. Left at lights. Right at end – ground just beyond
railway bridge.

WORTHING

Ground: Woodside Road, Worthing, West Sussex, BN14 7HQ
Phone: 0903-39575   **Nickname:** The Rebels   **Founded:** 1886
Colours: All Red   **Change:** All White
Rail: Worthing.
Directions: To the north of the sea-front and town centre.

DIVISION THREE

Final Table 1991-92

	P	W	D	L	F	A	Pts
Edgware Town	40	30	3	7	106	44	93
Chertsey Town	40	29	4	7	115	44	91
Tilbury	40	26	9	5	84	40	87
Hampton	40	26	5	9	93	35	83
Horsham	40	23	8	9	92	51	77
Cove	40	21	9	10	74	49	72
Flackwell Heath	40	19	12	9	78	50	69
Thame United	40	19	7	14	73	46	64
Epsom & Ewell	40	17	11	12	55	50	62
Collier Row	40	17	9	14	67	59	60
Royston Town	40	17	7	16	59	58	58
Kingsbury Town	40	12	10	18	54	61	46
Hertford Town	40	12	10	18	55	73	46
Petersfield United	40	12	9	19	45	67	45
Camberley Town	40	11	8	21	52	69	41
Feltham & Hounslow	40	11	7	22	53	78	40
Bracknell Town	40	10	7	23	48	90	37
Hornchurch	40	8	7	25	40	87	31
Tring Town	40	9	4	27	35	94	31
Clapton	40	9	3	28	47	93	30
Eastbourne United	40	5	5	30	34	121	20

Leading Scorers Division Three

Thompson, N. (Cove) 28; Ewing, G. (Hampton) 27; Whitehead, D.
(Hertford Town) 27; Wood, T. (Flackwell Heath) 27.

Promotion and Relgation

Club	Position	Movement
Edgware Town	Champions	Promoted to Division Two
Chertsey Town	Runners-up	Promoted to Division Two
Tilbury	3rd	Promoted to Division Two
Hampton	4th	Promoted to Division Two
Eastbourne United		Resigned

Marc Morris of Wingate & Finchley (left) and Brendon Quill of the now defunct Wolverton battle it out in a Campri South Midlands League game at Summers Lane. Photo: Bruce Smith

Battle of Bedford. Gabs Arpaia (centre) and Aaron Coker (falling back) at full stretch as Town play United. Photo: Keith Mayhew.

Robert Smith on patrol for VS Rugby against Kettering Town in the FA Trophy first round. Photo: Tony Eyre.

Farnborough's Simon Reed bursts through the West Ham United defence during their fabulous FA Cup third round tie at Upton Park. Photo: M. Floate.

Beazer Homes League action – Waterlooville v Bashley. Rickey Burnside (white) and John Cidozie (stripes). Photo: Peter Haynes.

Welling United's Gary Abbott gasps as he sees his glancing header fly narrowly wide of the Cheltenham Town upright. Photo: Mike Floate.

Steve Bateman (left) of Chesham United beats Marlow's Rodney Jack to the ball during their Diadora League encounter. Photo: Bruce Smith.

Gary Brabin of Runcorn (right) has more than a chip on his shoulder as Kidderminster's David Barnett fights for supremacy. Photo: Dave Howarth.

Party time. Wimborne celebrate with the FA Vase in the Players' Lounge at Wembley. Photo: Bruce Smith.

Andover defender Thomson (3) thwarts a Bashley attack during their FA Trophy tussle at Portway Stadium. Photo: Dennis Nicholson.

FA Cup action as Billericay Town's Steve Jones leads the charge at a corner. The Enfield defence look bemused! Photo: Bruce Smith.

Ford United's Dave Jenkins crosses despite the close attention of Canvey Island's Lewis Harvey in the Essex Senior League. Photo: Mike Floate.

Chris "Buffalo" Camden of Stalybridge Celtic (dark shirt) charges to beat Mossley's Chris Malloy to the ball. Photo: Dave Howarth.

Division Three Top Scorers By Club

Club	Player	Tot	Lg	IC	LT
Bracknell Town	Justin Day	14	13	–	1
Camberley Town	Keith Hoad	11	11	–	–
Chertsey Town	Peter Skeritt	24	24	–	–
Clapton	Peter Mason	14	13	1	–
Collier Row	Tony Samuels	20	17	–	3
Cove	Nigel Thompson	31	28	–	3
Eastbourne United	John Craig	5	5	–	–
Edgware Town	Steve Newing	26	26	–	–
Epsom & Ewell	Andy Webster	24	18	–	6
Feltham & Hounslow	Tony Nicholson	10	9	–	1
Flackwell Heath	Tony Wood	28	27	1	–
Hampton	Gary Ewing	27	27	–	–
Hertford Town	David Whitehead	27	27	–	–
Hornchurch	Brian Weekes	13	13	–	–
Horsham	Mark Dunk	17	16	1	–
Kingsbury Town	Mark Ivers	15	14	–	1
Petersfield United	Phillip Vaughan	9	7	–	2
Royston Town	Kevin Lowe	8	8	–	–
Thame United	David Watson	14	14	–	–
Tilbury	Mark Phillips	26	24	2	–
Tring Town	Mark Dewick	9	9	–	–

Tot=Total number of goals; Lg=League; IC=Isthmian League Cup; LT=Loctite Trophy.

William Hill Manager of Month Awards

Month	Manager	Club
September	Peter Evans	Horsham
October	Brian Ridler	Edgware Town
November	Jim Kelman	Chertsey Town
December	Chick Botley	Cove
January	Mark Fewings	Hampton
February	Jim Kelman	Chertsey Town
March	Nicky Phillips	Tilbury
April	Mark Fewing	Hampton

DIVISION THREE RESULTS 1991-92

	Bracknell T	Camberley T	Chertsey Town	Clapton	Collier Row	Cove	Eastbourne Utd	Edgware Town	Epsom & Ew	Feltham & H	Flackwell H
Bracknell Town	•	4-2	0-4	1-0	1-1	2-0	4-3	1-5	1-1	1-2	1-3
Camberley Town	2-3	•	0-2	1-0	0-3	0-1	4-1	2-3	3-1	3-2	2-3
Chertsey Town	2-0	4-0	•	10-1	1-2	2-1	5-1	4-2	0-1	4-1	4-0
Clapton	1-0	0-1	0-3	•	3-1	0-3	5-1	0-5	0-1	0-1	2-4
Collier Row	5-0	3-0	2-3	2-0	•	3-3	3-0	2-2	1-3	1-0	2-1
Cove	4-0	1-4	4-2	2-0	4-1	•	2-0	1-2	1-3	1-1	4-3
Eastbourne United	2-1	2-1	0-3	0-1	3-0	1-2	•	1-1	0-1	2-0	1-5
Edgware Town	2-1	1-1	3-1	4-0	2-2	3-1	9-1	•	2-0	2-0	3-4
Epsom & Ewell	1-1	2-1	2-3	3-1	1-1	1-1	2-0	0-1	•	3-1	2-2
Feltham & Hounslow	1-1	2-2	1-3	3-2	2-3	2-2	1-1	0-1	2-2	•	4-3
Flackwell Heath	3-0	0-1	0-0	4-0	1-0	5-0	1-2	0-2	3-0	3-1	•
Hampton	4-0	0-0	0-0	3-2	0-3	5-0	5-0	0-1	3-0	2-4	0-0
Hertford Town	2-1	6-2	0-3	5-3	4-1	0-0	0-2	1-4	2-2	3-4	1-1
Hornchurch	1-1	3-0	1-3	0-1	2-1	0-3	3-0	1-4	1-3	4-2	1-1
Horsham	7-0	0-0	1-2	4-1	5-1	1-2	3-0	4-0	5-1	2-0	1-1
Kingsbury Town	0-0	0-2	1-1	0-1	1-0	4-1	0-0	0-3	1-1	2-0	0-3
Petersfield United	0-1	1-0	2-0	2-0	0-1	1-0	2-2	1-2	0-1	2-0	0-3
Royston Town	1-0	2-1	1-3	4-1	3-0	1-2	2-0	0-4	2-1	0-1	1-1
Thame United	6-1	2-1	0-3	4-2	0-1	2-3	4-0	1-2	1-0	1-1	0-1
Tilbury	2-0	6-1	2-2	4-1	1-0	1-0	3-3	2-1	3-2	2-0	0-1
Tring Town	3-1	0-4	0-7	3-3	2-1	0-0	3-1	1-4	1-3	1-0	0-1

	Hampton	Hertford Town	Hornchurch	Horsham	Kingsbury Town	Petersfield Utd	Royston Town	Thame United	Tilbury	Tring Town
Bracknell Town	0-5	0-1	5-1	1-4	2-1	1-1	1-1	1-2	2-2	3-0
Camberley Town	0-1	0-0	2-2	3-1	0-2	1-2	1-2	0-2	0-0	3-0
Chertsey Town	4-3	2-0	4-2	3-4	0-1	1-1	3-0	1-0	4-2	5-0
Clapton	1-3	4-0	0-1	2-2	0-0	1-2	2-0	0-1	0-4	6-0
Collier Row	2-1	6-2	2-0	0-2	4-1	1-1	0-3	3-3	2-1	1-0
Cove	2-1	3-1	2-0	3-0	2-3	0-0	2-0	1-1	0-6	5-0
Eastbourne United	0-6	1-3	2-1	0-1	0-8	2-3	1-3	0-3	0-6	0-3
Edgware Town	2-1	5-0	3-2	2-4	2-0	4-0	2-0	2-3	1-2	5-0
Epsom & Ewell	1-1	3-1	2-0	0-1	2-0	3-1	1-0	1-0	0-0	2-0
Feltham & Hounslow ..	0-3	1-2	0-1	2-0	1-0	0-1	0-4	1-6	1-2	4-0
Flackwell Heath	2-1	0-0	6-0	3-1	4-1	3-0	2-2	3-1	3-2	1-2
Hampton	•	4-2	6-0	0-0	2-0	3-0	2-0	2-0	3-0	1-1
Hertford Town	0-3	•	4-1	2-2	1-1	0-0	0-0	0-3	2-0	0-1
Hornchurch	1-3	2-0	•	1-1	1-0	3-1	1-0	1-1	2-4	2-0
Horsham	1-2	2-1	5-1	•	4-2	3-1	4-2	3-0	1-2	1-0
Kingsbury Town	0-0	1-1	1-2	1-0	•	2-2	0-3	2-2	1-2	1-0
Petersfield United	2-1	2-0	3-2	1-1	1-5	•	0-3	0-3	2-3	6-1
Royston Town	0-2	3-3	1-0	2-4	4-2	3-2	•	0-4	2-2	3-0
Thame United	1-1	2-0	3-0	0-1	5-1	2-0	1-2	•	1-3	2-0
Tilbury	0-2	3-0	2-0	1-1	3-0	1-0	1-0	2-0	•	3-0
Tring Town	0-2	0-2	4-1	2-3	1-2	4-1	0-1	0-0	1-2	•

147

DIVISION THREE CLUBS

ALDERSHOT TOWN
Ground: Recreation Ground, High Street, Aldershot, Hants, GU11 1TW
Phone: 0252-20211   **Nickname:** The Shots   **Founded:** 1992
Colours: Red with Blue trim, Blue   **Change:** not known
Rail: Aldershot
Directions: not known

BRACKNELL TOWN
Ground: Larges Lane, Bracknell, Berks, RG12 3AN
Phone: 0344-423255   **Nickname:** The Robins   **Founded:** 1894
Colours: All Red   **Change:** All Sky Blue
Rail: Bracknell (400 yards from ground).
Directions: Turn left at Tyre Co. at the Met Office Roundabout (A329). Ground next to Cricket Club.

CAMBERLEY TOWN
Ground: Krooner Park, Krooner Road, off Frimley Road, Camberley, Surrey, GU15 2QP
Phone: 0276-65392   **Nickname:** Town   **Founded:** 1969
Colours: All Red   **Change:** All Sky Blue
Rail: Camberley or Frimley (both 1 mile from ground).
Directions: M3 Junction 4. Keep left take and A321 to shops. Krooner Road on left past mini-roundabout.

CHERTSEY TOWN
Ground: Alwyns Lane, Chertsey, Surrey, KT19 9DW
Phone: 0932-561744   **Nickname:** The Curlews   **Founded:** 1890
Colours: Blue and White Stripes, White, Blue   **Change:** All Yellow
Rail: Chertsey (½ mile from ground).
Directions: Off Windsor Street at the north end of the town's shopping centre.

CLAPTON
Ground: Old Spotted Dog Ground, Upton Lane, Forest Gate, London, E7 9NP
Phone: 081-552-4729   **Nickname:** The Tons   **Founded:** 1878
Colours: Red and White Stripes, Black, Black   **Change:** All Dark Green
Rail: Forest Gate (BR) or Plaistow (District Line).

Directions: Upton Lane runs adjacent to West Ham Park and off of the Portway-Plashett Road junction (B165).

COLLIER ROW

Ground: Sungate, Collier Row Road, Romford, Essex, RM5 2BH
Phone: 0708-722766   **Nickname:**   **Founded:** 1929
Colours: Red, Black, Black   **Change:** All Silver Grey
Rail: Romford (4 miles from ground).
Directions: A12 from London. Left at Moby Dick public house (signposted Collier Row) lights. Turn right at next roundabout. Ground set back 200 yards on right-hand side.

COVE

Ground: Oak Farm Field, off Romayne Close, Cove, Farnborough, Hants
Phone: 0252-543615   **Nickname:**   **Founded:** 1897
Colours: Amber, Black with Amber Stripe, Amber   **Change:** not known
Rail: Farnborough Main (2 miles from ground).
Directions: From M3 (Junction 4) along A325, turn into Prospect Avenue (signposted Farnborough Town FC) to bottom, left at roundabout following signs to Cove FC.

EAST THURROCK UNITED

Ground: Rookery Hill, Corringham, Essex
Phone: 0375-644166   **Nickname:** Rocks   **Founded:** 1969
Colours: Amber and Black   **Change:** All Blue
Rail: Basildon or Stanford le Hope (Both 1 mile from ground).
Directions: A1014 (from A13 London-Southend road) at Stanford le Hope. Proceed for just over 2 miles. Ground located on left.

EDGWARE TOWN

Ground: White Lion Ground, High Street, Edgware, Middx, HA8 5AQ
Phone: 081-952-6799   **Nickname:** Town   **Founded:** 1939
Colours: All Green   **Change:** not known
Rail: Edgware (Underground).
Directions: From station turn left and left again at lights. Ground on right.

EPSOM AND EWELL

Ground: West Street, Ewell, Surrey, KT19 1XU
Phone: 081-393-7077   **Nickname:** E's   **Founded:** 1917
Colours: All Royal Blue   **Change:** not known
Rail: Ewell West (400 yards from ground).
Directions: A24 Epsom Road. West Street is located in Epsom Village.

FARNHAM TOWN

Ground: Memorial Ground, Babbs Mead, West Street, Farnham, Surrey
Phone: 0252-715305   **Nickname:**   **Founded:** 1921
Colours: Claret and Blue   **Change:** Yellow and Black
Rail: Farnham (1 mile from ground).
Directions: A31 Farnham by-pass. Take A325 (West Street) at roundabout and then first right.

FELTHAM & HOUNSLOW BOROUGH

Ground: Feltham Sports Arena, Shakespeare Ave, Feltham, Middx, TW13 4RQ
Phone: 081-890-6119/6905   **Nickname:**   **Founded:** 1991
Colours: Blue and White Hoops, Blue, White   **Change:** All Red
Rail: Feltham (400 yards from ground).
Directions: M3/M4 – A316 Hanworth Road. Turn left into Burns Avenue and then second left into Shakespeare Avenue.

FLACKWELL HEATH

Ground: Wilks Park, Heath End Road, Flackwell Heath, High Wycombe, Bucks, HP10 9EA
Phone: 06285-23892   **Nickname:**   **Founded:** 1907
Colours: Red, White, Red   **Change:** Yellow and Black
Rail: High Wycombe (4½ miles from ground).
Directions: M40 Junction 3. Follow signs to Flackwell Heath. Ground situated at rear of Magpie public house at Heath End.

HERTFORD TOWN

Ground: Hertingfordbury Park, West Street, Hertford, Herts, SG13 8EZ
Phone: 0992-583716   **Nickname:** The Blues **Founded:** 1927
Colours: All Blue   **Change:** All Yellow
Rail: Hertford North (Moorgate) or Hertford East (Liverpool St) (ground about 1 mile from both).
Directions: A1M Junction 4. Follow signs to Hertford. Look out for Trimoco Garage on right of dual carriageway. Go around next roundabout and come back. West Street on left (club signposted).

HORNCHURCH

Ground: The Stadium, Bridge Avenue, Upminster, Essex, RM14 2LX
Phone: 04022-20080   **Nickname:** Urchins   **Founded:** 1923
Colours: All White with Red Trim   **Change:** All Yellow
Rail: Upminster Bridge (BR) (½ mile from ground).
Directions: 1 mile east of town centre on A124. Bridge Avenue on right after railway bridge.

HORSHAM

Ground: Queen Street, Horsham, West Sussex, RH13 5AD
Phone: 0403-52310   **Nickname:** The Hornets   **Founded:** 1885
Colours: Lincoln Green and Amber, Green, Amber   **Change:** All White
Rail: Horsham (1 mile from ground).
Directions: not known

LEIGHTON TOWN

Ground: Bell Close, Lake Street, Leighton Buzzard, Beds
Phone: 00525-373311   **Nickname:** Town   **Founded:** 1885
Colours: Red and White Stripes, White, Red   **Change:** All Blue
Rail: Leighton Buzzard.
Directions: Leighton by-pass. Second right – continue to mini-roundabout.
Entrance to ground on roundabout by Camden Motors.

KINGSBURY TOWN

Ground: Silver Jubilee Park, Townsend Lane, Kingsbury, London, NW9 0DE
Phone: 081-205-1645   **Nickname:** Town   **Founded:** 1927
Colours: All Blue   **Change:** All White
Rail: Kingsbury (Underground – 1 mile from ground).
Directions: Take Kingsbury Road from Edgware Road. At top of hill turn left
into Townsend Lane.

NORTHWOOD

Ground: Chestnut Avenue, Northwood, Middx
Phone: 0927-427148   **Nickname:**   **Founded:** 1900
Colours: All Red   **Change:** All Blue
Rail: Northwood Hills (½ mile from ground).
Directions: A404 Pinner-Rickmansworth Road. Chestnut Avenue is located
on left before a large bridge, ½ mile past Northwood Hills roundabout.

PETERSFIELD UNITED

Ground: Love Lane, Petersfield, Hants, GU31 4BW
Phone: 0730-62177   **Nickname:** The Reds   **Founded:** 1889
Colours: Red and Black, White, Red **Change:** White, Red, Red
Rail: Petersfield (¾ mile from ground).
Directions: Located off A3, Tor Way, circulatory system in town.

ROYSTON TOWN

Ground: Garden Walk, Royston, Herts, SG8 7HP
Phone: 0763-241204   **Nickname:** The Crows   **Founded:** 1875
Colours: Red and White Stripes, Red, Red   **Change:** Red, Black
Rail: not known
Directions: A1 to A505, Royston and on to by-pass. At second roundabout turn right and then second left.

THAME UNITED

Ground: Windmill Road, Thame, Oxon, OX9 3NR
Phone: 0844-213017   **Nickname:**   **Founded:** 1883
Colours: All Red and Black   **Change:** All Blue
Rail: Haddenham & Thame Parkway (BR) (1½ miles from ground).
Directions: Turn into Nelson Street from Market Square.

TILBURY

Ground: Chadfields, St. Chad's Road, Tilbury, Essex, RM18 8NL
Phone: 03752-3093   **Nickname:** Dockers   **Founded:** 1900
Colours: Black and White Stripes, Black, White   **Change:** All Red
Rail: Tilbury Town (1½ miles from ground).
Directions: M25 Junction 30/31. Take Tilbury Docks turn. Follow turn off to Chadwell St Mary. Ground on right.

TRING TOWN

Ground: Pendley Sports Centre, Cow Lane, Tring, Herts, HP23 5NS
Phone: 044282-3075   **Nickname:**   **Founded:** 1904
Colours: Red and White, White, Red **Change:** All Blue
Rail: Tring (1½ miles from ground).
Directions: A41 – Cow Lane located just after start of A41M.

BEAZER HOMES LEAGUE

Rovers Reign

The Beazer Homes League is developing a habit of producing exciting championship races. Bromsgrove Rovers took a crown that hardly seemed likely as November drew to a close. At that point they had collected 16 points from their opening 12 matches, recording just four victories in the process. But, in an amazing turnabout, the Worcestershire side recorded 23 wins in their remaining 30 games to win the title by six points. But, despite such a sustained surge of form, Rovers did not lead the table until the penultimate Saturday of the season.

Cambridge City and VS Rugby had shared the top spot until Christmas, Bashley then burst onto the scene for the first seven weeks of the New Year. VS maintained their challenge and were favourites to win promotion to the Conference until Dover became the fourth club to top the Premier Division as the season entered the final straight. The 1990 champions' surge proved to be too late and Rovers' 3-0 win over Bashley secured them the title. Bromsgrove's 2-2 at Dover in the final weeks of the season attracted an attendance of 4,035, the highest in the League since 1982 when 5,432 watched Bedworth and Nuneaton.

At the foot of the table, the writing was on the wall for Gravesend after early season 9-0 and 8-2 defeats, while Fisher suffered relegation for the second successive season. Poole Town dropped back into the Southern Division after just two seasons in the top flight and Wealdstone found themselves in the fourth relegation spot on the last day of the season. The Stones had started the season with high hopes and a new home in their joint ownership of Vicarage Road. One of the revivals of the season came from Burton Albion who were three points adrift at the foot of the table come Christmas. A change of manager produced a change in fortune and 13 wins in the second half of the season lifted them to the fringe of the prize money.

In the Midland Division, new boys Solihull Borough took the title at their very first attempt with a six-point cushion. Runners-up Hednesford Town pushed them all the way but lost their chance of the championship following a 6-1 defeat at the hands of Borough in the final phase. Town also reached the Welsh Cup final, going down through a 59th-minute goal to Cardiff City in front of 10,000 spectators at Cardiff Arms Park.

The Southern Division championship was much more clear cut, Hastings United led the table for all but three weeks of the season. Weymouth clinched the runners-up spot on the final day of the season in front of an ecstatic 2,167 crowd. Hythe, who had been a challenger to Weymouth, dropped to 13th spot and have withdrawn from the competition. For 1991-92 Stroud FC have reverted to their former name – Forest Green Rovers.

In the traditional season curtain raiser Farnborough Town (1990-91 champions) took on the Southern League Cup holders (Chelmsford City) in the Champions Match and ran out comfortable winners 6-1. Dover Athletic beat Dorchester Town to take the 1991-92 Challenge Cup, now sponsored by Barclays Commercial Services.

The spectre of the Welsh League hung over Barry Town and Newport AFC but both clubs remain in the Pyramid of Football by moving home in to Gloucester and Worcester respectively.

Gosport Borough lost their place, being relegated to the Wessex League, but Dudley and Canterbury City earned reprieves following the resignations of Hythe Town and Alvechurch. Coming into the fold for 1992-93 are Gresley Rovers, Evesham and Weston-super-Mare. The inclusion of Gresley will appease many, after the club has produced a successful and exciting side only to have missed out on ground grading in the past.

Crawley Town progressed to the third round of the FA Cup, going down at Brighton & Hove Albion but returning from the Goldstone Ground £110,000 the richer.

Sportique Managers of the Season

Premier Division	Bobby Hope	Bromsgrove Rovers
Midland Division	Ralph Punsheon	Solihull Borough
Southern Division	Peter Sillett	Hastings Town

Beazer Homes League Honours

Premier Division Champions	Bromsgrove Rovers
Midland Division Champions	Solihull Borough
Southern Division Champions	Hastings Town
Championship Match Winners	Farnborough Town
Barclays Commercial Service Cup Winners	Dover Athletic
Merit Cup Winners	Solihull Borough

1991-92 Championship Match

| Farnborough Town | 6 | Chelmsford City | 1 |

Docherty 42, 89, Comford 45 (pen),   Dennis Greene 63
Horton 55, 87, 90   Att: 459

The Southern League History

A two-division Southern League was formed for the 1893-94 season, consisting of nine and seven clubs respectively. The format has changed considerably over the years consequent upon the withdrawal of amateur clubs; the participation of reserve sides; and the creation of a Third Division of the Football League formed by the members of the Southern League's Division One in 1920.

Predominantly a competition for Football League reserve sides between the Wars. The League emerged from the Second World War as a single division of mainly first teams. The League expanded, 13 clubs joining in 1958 and, following a regionalised season, a Premier and a First Division were introduced for 1959-60.

The First Division was regionalised in 1971 (South and North) but between 1979-80 and 1982-83 the whole competition was regionalised, with Midland and South Divisions. In 1983 it returned to the Premier Division and regionalised Division One (Midland and South) format.

While feeder Leagues serve Division One, the League champions are normally promoted to the Conference, with a club relegated from the Conference joining the Premier Division. Prior to 1983 two Southern Leaguers were normally promoted. Beazer Homes have been sponsors of the League since 1987-88.

5-Year One, Two, Three Records

Premier Division

	1st	Pts	2nd	Pts	3rd	Pts
1986-87	Fisher Athletic	86	Bromsgrove R	83	Aylesbury Utd	83
1987-88	Aylesbury Utd	89	Dartford	89	Cambridge City	80
1988-89	Merthyr Tydfil	85	Dartford	82	VS Rugby	79
1989-90	Dover Athletic	102	Bath City	98	Dartford	=87
1990-91	Farnborough T	85	Gloucester City	83	Cambridge City	77

Southern Division

	1st	Pts	2nd	Pts	3rd	Pts
1986-87	Dorchester Tn	77	Ashford Town	76	Woodford Town	72
1987-88	Dover Athletic	94	Waterlooville	91	Salisbury	83
1988-89	Chelmsford C	95	Gravesend	87	Poole Town	83
1989-90	Bashley	82	Poole Town	77	Buckingham Tn	76
1990-91	Buckingham T	83	Trowbridge T	78	Salisbury	77

Midland Division

	1st	Pts	2nd	Pts	3rd	Pts
1986-87	V S Rugby	80	Leicester United	79	Merthyr Tydfil	75
1987-88	Merthyr Tydfil	94	Moor Green	86	Grantham Town	85
1988-89	Gloucester City	92	Atherstone Utd	87	Tamworth	87
1989-90	Halesowen Tn	92	Rushden Town	89	Nuneaton Boro	85
1990-91	Stourbridge	90	Corby Town	85	Hednesford Tn	82

BARCLAYS COMMERCIAL SERVICES CUP

Notes: † after extra time; a.g. denotes team won tie on away goals; * denotes that this leg was a replay – first game abandoned due to reason given.

Preliminary Round

	1st Leg	2nd Leg	Agg.	Notes
Grantham Town v Leicester United	1-2	3-1	4-3	
Newport I.O.W. v Poole Town	3-3	5-1	8-4	

1st Round

	1st Leg	2nd Leg	Agg.	Notes
Alvechurch v Redditch United	1-2	3-1 †	4-3	
Ashford Town v Fisher Athletic	3-0	0-1	3-1	
Atherstone United v Grantham Town	0-0	0-3	0-3	
Bilston Town v Halesowen Town	3-2	0-2	3-4	
Braintree Town v Cambridge City	2-2	0-5	2-7	
Bridgnorth Town v Dudley Town	4-2	0-3	4-5	
Bromsgrove Rovers v Worcester City	3-3	4-1	7-4	
Buckingham Town v Burnham	3-2	3-2	6-4	
Canterbury City v Hastings Town	2-5	2-1	4-6	
Chelmsford v Bury Town	1-0	0-1	1-1	5-3 on pens
Crawley Town v Hythe Town	3-2	2-1	5-3	
Dartford v Gravesend & Northfleet	3-0	1-3	4-3	
Dover Athletic v Sittingbourne	2-0	2-0	4-0	
Gosport Borough v Fareham Town	0-1	1-1	1-2	
Havant Town v Weymouth	0-0	0-0	0-0	4-2 on pens
King's Lynn v Sudbury Town	3-4	1-3	4-7	
Margate v Erith & Belvedere	3-2	0-2	3-4	
Moor Green v Stourbridge	2-1	0-0	2-1	
Newport A.F.C. v Barry Town	0-2	2-1	2-3	
Newport I.O.W v Dorchester Town	1-2	1-5	2-7	
Nuneaton Borough v Corby Town	1-1	0-2	1-3	
RC Warwick v Hednesford Town	1-2	2-3	3-5	
Salisbury v Andover	1-0	1-0	2-0	
Solihull Borough v Bedworth United	0-0	3-1	3-1	
Stroud v Yate Town	2-3	3-1	5-4	
Sutton Coldfield v Burton Albion	0-0	0-1 †	0-1	
Tamworth v Hinckley Town	4-1	3-0	7-1	
Towbridge City v Gloucester City	1-0	0-2	1-2	
VS Rugby v Rushden Town	3-1	4-1	7-2	
Waterlooville v Bashley	4-4	2-0	6-4	
Wealdstone v Baldock Town	2-0	5-0	7-0	

Witney Town v Dunstable 0-1   1-3   1-4

2nd Round

Barry Town v Gloucester City 1-1   0-2   1-3
Buckingham Town v Chelmsford City 0-1   1-1 †   1-2
Burton Albion v Alvechurch....................2-1   4-2   6-3
Corby Town v Grantham Town 1-3   3-2 †   4-5
Crawley Town v Ashford Town 1-1   0-6   1-7
Dover Athletic v Hastings Town 0-0   1-1   1-1   Dover ag
Dunstable v Wealdstone 2-1   1-4 †   3-5
Erith & Belvedere v Dartford 0-1   0-4   0-5
Havant Town v Fareham Town 2-1   2-1   4-2
Hednesford Town v Halesowen Town 3-0   4-1   7-1
Moor Green v Bromsgrove Rovers...........0-0   0-5   0-5
Solihull Borough v Dudley Town.............1-2   4-0   5-2
Stroud v Dorchester Town 1-2   0-6   1-8
Sudbury Town v Cambridge City 1-2   0-4   1-6
VS Rugby v Tamworth 2-1   5-1   7-2
Waterlooville v Salisbury 0-2   1-3   1-5

3rd Round

Bromsgrove Rovers v Hednesford Town .1-1   1-0   2-1
Chelmsford City v Ashford Town 2-0   1-1   3-1
Dover Athletic v Dartford..........................1-1   2-0   3-1
Havant Town v Dorchester Town.............0-1   2-2 †† 2-3
Salisbury v Gloucester City 1-2   2-0   3-2
Solihull Borough v Burton Albion.............0-2   1-1   1-3
VS Rugby v Grantham Town 0-1   1-2   1-3
Wealdstone v Cambridge City 1-1   1-2   2-3
††This match was replayed after 1-2 score.

4th Round

Burton Albion v Bromsgrove Rovers 0-6   0-3   0-9
Cambridge City v Grantham Town............5-0   2-1   7-1
Dover Athletic v Chelmsford City 3-2   2-0   5-2
Salisbury v Dorchester Town....................0-1   0-2   0-3

Semi-Finals

Cambridge City v Dover Athletic..............3-4   0-2   3-6
Dorchester Town v Bromsgrove Rovers...4-1   1-2   5-3

Final

Dover Athletic v Dorchester Town 1-0   3-0   4-0

PREMIER DIVISION

Final Table 1991-92

	P	W	D	L	F	A	Pts
Bromsgrove Rovers	42	27	9	6	78	34	90
Dover Athletic	42	23	15	4	66	30	84
VS Rugby	42	23	11	8	70	44	80
Bashley	42	22	8	12	70	44	74
Cambridge City	42	18	14	10	71	53	68
Dartford	42	17	15	10	62	45	66
Trowbridge Town	42	17	10	15	69	51	61
Halesowen Town	42	15	15	12	61	49	60
Moor Green	42	15	11	16	61	59	56
Burton Albion	42	15	10	17	59	61	55
Dorchester Town	42	14	13	15	66	73	55
Gloucester City	42	15	9	18	67	70	54
Atherstone United	42	15	8	19	54	66	53
Corby Town	42	13	12	17	66	81	51
Waterlooville	42	13	11	18	43	56	50
Worcester City	42	12	13	17	56	59	49
Crawley Town	42	12	12	18	62	67	48
Chelmsford City	42	12	12	18	49	56	48
Wealdstone	42	13	7	22	52	69	46
Poole Town	42	10	13	19	46	77	43
Fisher Athletic	42	9	11	22	53	89	38
Gravesend & Northfleet	42	8	9	25	39	87	33

Promotions and Relegations

Club	Position	Movement
Bromsgrove Rovers	Champions	Promoted to GMVC
Wealdstone	19th	Relegated to Southern Division
Poole Town	20th	Relegated to Southern Division
Fisher Athletic	21st	Relegated to Southern Division
Gravesend & Northfleet	22nd	Relegated to Southern Division

Clubs Joining Premier Division

Club	From
Solihull Borough	Midland Division
Hednesford Town	Midland Division
Hastings	Southern Division
Weymouth	Southern Division

Leading Premier Division Goalscorers by Club

Club	Top scorers
Atherstone United	Green 12; Wilson 6; Tolley 5.
Bashley	Whale 13; Lovell 10; Baird 9.
Bromsgrove Rovers	Hanks 19; O'Meara 9; Stott 9; Crisp 9.
Burton Albion	Jones 10; Gocan 10; Roberts 8.
Cambridge City	Ryan 13; Lockhart 11; Grogan 7.
Chelmsford City	Dennis Greene 12; David Green 8; Brown 7.
Corby Town	Murphy 13; Hofbauer 9; Genovese 8.
Crawley Town	Hulme 9; Venables 8; Wittington 4; Churchill 4.
Dartford	Quaile 11; Leslie 9; Hunt 7.
Dorchester Town	Daiz 26; Manson 12; Coates 3; Green 3; Masters 3.
Dover Athletic	Rogers 13; Blewden 8; Little 8.
Fisher Athletic	Malcolm 11; Sansom 9; Booker 5.
Gloucester City	Eaton 15; Penny 8; Talboys 7; Townsend 7.
Gravesend & Northfleet	Fordred 7; Cotter 6; Flint 4; Watkins 4.
Halesowen Town	Harrison 10; Flynn 9; Hazlewood 7; Massey 7.
Moor Green	Taylor 10; Davies 8; Fearon 8.
Poole Town	Dent 18; Funnell 6; Maloney 6.
Trowbridge Town	Adams 12; Freeguard 10; Harris 8; Iddles 8.
VS Rugby	Boyland 15; Crawley 13; Rosegreen 12.
Waterlooville	Boyce 12; Hore 8; Moran 7.
Wealdstone	Hopson 8; Donnellan 5; Hippolyte 5.
Worcester City	Kearns 16; Robinson 15; Wolverson 6.

PREMIER DIVISION RESULTS 1991-92

Home \ Away	Atherstone Utd	Bashley	Bromsgrove R	Burton Albion	Cambridge C	Chelmsford C	Corby Town	Crawley Town	Dartford	Dorchester T	Dover Athletic
Atherstone United	•	1-3	2-0	3-2	0-1	3-0	3-4	1-2	0-0	4-2	1-1
Bashley	4-0	•	0-1	1-1	1-1	0-0	3-1	2-0	3-0	0-1	2-0
Bromsgrove Rovers	2-0	3-0	•	3-1	0-2	2-1	3-0	5-1	1-0	5-1	0-0
Burton Albion	0-2	1-0	3-1	•	2-0	1-2	3-1	1-0	0-1	1-2	0-1
Cambridge City	4-1	0-1	1-0	3-1	•	3-0	1-0	1-3	2-0	0-3	2-2
Chelmsford City	1-0	1-1	1-1	3-1	6-1	•	1-0	0-0	1-2	1-3	0-1
Corby Town	3-1	3-2	1-3	1-2	2-2	1-0	•	3-4	2-2	1-4	1-1
Crawley Town	3-1	1-3	0-3	1-2	2-2	3-0	1-1	•	1-1	1-4	0-0
Dartford	4-1	1-0	1-1	0-3	2-2	0-2	1-5	3-2	•	1-1	0-0
Dorchester Town	0-1	0-1	1-2	2-1	1-3	2-3	0-0	0-4	1-1	•	2-3
Dover Athletic	1-0	3-2	2-2	1-1	3-0	3-0	1-1	2-1	0-1	2-1	•
Fisher Athletic	2-0	2-3	1-3	0-2	1-1	3-1	2-1	2-2	0-0	6-5	0-4
Gloucester City	1-1	3-1	1-2	0-2	1-1	3-1	3-2	4-1	1-1	2-1	0-1
Gravesend&Northfleet	1-1	1-2	0-1	4-1	0-0	0-1	1-1	1-1	1-0	1-1	2-0
Halesowen	1-1	1-2	1-1	0-2	3-2	2-1	1-1	4-2	1-3	2-2	1-0
Moor Green	2-3	2-0	1-1	5-3	2-2	3-2	2-0	1-1	0-0	0-1	1-1
Poole Town	0-1	1-1	0-2	3-0	1-1	2-0	2-0	2-1	3-3	0-1	1-1
Trowbridge Town	1-2	2-0	1-1	1-0	3-1	1-1	0-0	2-1	0-0	3-4	0-1
VS Rugby	3-1	0-2	1-3	0-4	1-1	0-0	1-4	0-2	0-5	3-1	0-2
Waterlooville	1-0	0-0	1-1	1-0	2-3	1-1	3-0	0-2	2-2	2-2	0-2
Wealdstone	1-0	1-2	1-3	0-4	3-1	2-0	1-2	2-1	2-0	2-1	0-2
Worcester City	1-1	1-3	1-1	1-1	2-1	2-1	1-2	2-1	2-0	5-1	1-1

	Fisher Athletic	Gloucester City	Gravesend N	Halesowen	Moor Green	Poole Town	Trowbridge T	VS Rugby	Waterlooville	Wealdstone	Worcester City
Atherstone United ...	2-2	0-3	2-1	4-0	1-1	3-0	0-3	2-0	1-4	2-0	1-3
Bashley	3-1	2-1	3-0	2-3	3-0	3-0	2-0	3-1	1-2	1-1	2-2
Bromsgrove Rovers ..	7-0	0-2	1-0	1-0	5-3	3-1	3-1	1-2	1-0	1-0	2-0
Burton Albion	0-2	4-3	2-1	0-0	2-0	5-2	1-3	0-0	0-4	1-1	1-1
Cambridge City	4-0	4-2	3-1	2-1	2-0	5-1	3-0	1-1	0-0	3-0	1-1
Chelmsford City	3-0	0-0	2-3	0-0	3-1	1-1	1-1	1-1	2-3	2-6	0-1
Corby Town	2-1	2-2	2-1	0-4	1-6	2-1	1-1	4-2	1-1	0-1	3-1
Crawley Town	0-0	5-2	0-1	2-0	1-2	3-3	1-0	1-1	2-0	1-1	2-2
Dartford	1-0	2-0	5-0	1-1	1-3	4-0	2-0	2-3	2-1	4-1	1-0
Dorchester Town	3-1	4-2	1-1	0-0	2-2	2-1	2-2	2-1	0-0	3-0	3-3
Dover Athletic	2-0	4-0	3-0	0-1	1-1	1-0	3-1	1-3	3-2	1-0	3-1
Fisher Athletic	•	3-0	2-2	0-1	4-0	1-0	0-4	1-2	2-1	2-0	0-1
Gloucester City	2-0	•	0-1	1-8	1-3	5-1	2-2	2-3	1-0	3-2	0-0
Gravesend&Northfleet	4-2	1-0	•	1-1	2-0	2-2	0-1	0-4	1-2	1-1	0-0
Halesowen	3-2	0-2	1-1	•	2-0	2-2	1-0	1-2	1-2	1-1	2-1
Moor Green	3-0	5-1	2-0	3-2	•	1-2	1-0	0-0	0-0	0-1	2-1
Poole Town	1-1	2-1	9-0	1-1	2-2	•	1-0	0-4	0-2	0-0	1-0
Trowbridge Town.....	6-0	1-1	1-1	3-2	2-1	3-1	•	0-1	1-1	3-2	1-2
VS Rugby	3-0	2-1	3-1	1-0	2-1	2-2	1-0	•	2-0	3-2	2-0
Waterlooville	1-1	1-0	0-1	1-0	0-1	3-1	1-0	0-4	•	0-1	3-1
Wealdstone	4-4	3-2	2-1	2-1	1-0	0-1	3-1	0-3	2-0	•	1-4
Worcester City	1-1	0-3	6-2	1-2	1-2	0-1	1-2	2-0	0-0	1-0	•

PREMIER ATTENDANCES 1991-92

	Atherstone Utd	Bashley	Bromsgrove R	Burton Albion	Cambridge C	Chelmsford C	Corby Town	Crawley Town	Dartford	Dorchester T	Dover Athletic
Atherstone United	•	304	527	440	329	264	495	298	275	256	362
Bashley	323	•	326	405	376	283	202	754	407	224	548
Bromsgrove Rovers	639	1565	•	484	603	717	564	660	806	1224	552
Burton Albion	575	768	692	•	621	594	708	642	545	637	571
Cambridge City	221	345	351	326	•	397	274	312	325	271	659
Chelmsford City	854	503	537	719	752	•	525	622	511	635	801
Corby Town	206	295	360	334	327	283	•	289	244	294	293
Crawley Town	617	424	466	431	505	511	421	•	687	379	611
Dartford	507	538	601	569	501	718	542	647	•	284	1407
Dorchester Town	597	953	1107	587	401	737	468	434	480	•	562
Dover Athletic	1067	1795	4035	1208	1093	1216	1249	901	1642	1252	•
Fisher Athletic	181	317	195	180	214	326	207	228	514	265	507
Gloucester City	411	458	875	337	694	650	734	328	420	353	662
Gravesend&Northfleet	465	476	432	499	402	768	533	448	836	455	932
Halesowen	672	1015	1330	1112	580	713	717	914	1002	686	951
Moor Green	276	332	486	538	254	249	241	3774	327	271	418
Poole Town	251	604	242	181	135	228	155	203	166	585	172
Trowbridge Town	434	878	540	530	550	404	546	553	719	516	594
VS Rugby	923	836	813	719	753	414	476	481	766	416	998
Waterlooville	254	236	241	114	220	210	196	245	134	153	250
Wealdstone	324	347	422	373	431	502	407	453	510	311	634
Worcester City	756	389	2438	664	757	660	714	670	514	747	886

	Fisher Athletic	Gloucester City	Gravesend N	Halesowen	Moor Green	Poole Town	Trowbridge T	VS Rugby	Waterlooville	Wealdstone	Worcester City
Atherstone United ...	156	230	326	495	376	278	314	545	301	206	301
Bashley	284	496	403	284	224	653	545	425	248	363	341
Bromsgrove Rovers ...	538	744	625	1765	867	1117	797	554	668	768	1297
Burton Albion	429	685	943	692	574	482	706	791	595	454	541
Cambridge City	332	390	342	304	248	207	310	518	264	317	270
Chelmsford City	827	567	522	575	799	592	417	746	512	796	689
Corby Town	334	246	234	232	446	543	267	472	150	480	361
Crawley Town	606	517	463	438	475	330	453	523	677	516	418
Dartford	406	412	1152	524	514	443	460	610	644	525	605
Dorchester Town	752	1049	509	465	667	640	576	655	746	800	401
Dover Athletic	1544	930	1441	854	1323	943	1114	1666	1024	1212	1188
Fisher Athletic	•	207	422	131	371	213	151	363	218	371	210
Gloucester City......	810	•	553	796	585	749	549	543	574	779	483
Gravesend&Northfleet	435	430	•	337	495	453	493	548	452	502	523
Halesowen	762	660	666	•	800	739	696	1276	739	1047	908
Moor Green	341	453	342	665	•	318	302	518	250	282	458
Poole Town	169	153	137	182	127	•	323	229	224	179	220
Trowbridge Town	310	443	448	456	515	429	•	719	556	618	498
VS Rugby	471	355	599	485	586	749	554	•	443	678	674
Waterlooville	294	252	125	143	586	265	256	217	•	286	224
Wealdstone	546	489	429	607	456	427	412	324	353	•	435
Worcester City......	647	1103	893	1366	673	567	880	1215	561	680	•

Sportique Manager of the Month Awards

Month	Manager	Club
August	Jimmy Knox	VS Rugby
September	Chris Kinnear	Dover Athletic
October	Bob Markin	Dartford
November	John Murphy	Trowbridge Town
December	Trevor Parker	Bashley
January	Danny O'Leary	Chelmsford City
February	Bobby Hope	Bromsgrove Rovers
March	Chris Kinnear	Dover Athletic

Attendance Summaries by Club

Club	Psn	Home Total	90-91	Ave	90-91	Away Total	Ave
Dover Athletic	2	28,697	(25,822)	1,367	(1,230)	13,370	637
Halesowen	8	17,985	(24,719)	856	(1,177)	11,796	562
Worcester City	16	17,780	(19,921)	847	(948)	11,045	526
Bromsgrove Rovers	1	17,554	(18,295)	836	(871)	17,016	810
Dorchester Town	11	13,586	(16,453)	647	(783)	10,214	486
Chelmsford City	18	13,501	(15,984)	643	(761)	10,844	516
Burton Albion	10	13,245	(14,137)	631	(673)	10,750	512
VS Rugby	3	13,189	(10,224)	628	(486)	13,457	641
Dartford	6	12,609	(13,032)	600	(620)	11,830	563
Gloucester City	12	12,343	(19,880)	588	(946)	10,811	515
Trowbridge Town	7	11,256		536		10,575	504
Moor Green	9	11,095	(8,043)	528	(383)	11,707	557
Gravesend & North'	22	10,914	(10,198)	520	(485)	11,574	551
Crawley Town	17	10,468	(9,338)	498	(444)	13,856	660
Wealdstone	19	9,192	(10,987)	438	(523)	11,859	565
Bashley	4	8,114	(8,392)	386	(399)	13,378	637
Atherstone United	13	7,078	(8,458)	337	(402)	10,553	503
Cambridge City	5	6,983	(8,898)	333	(428)	10,498	500
Corby Town	14	6,690		319		10,374	494
Fisher Athletic	21	5,791	(13,683)	276	(652)	10,993	523
Waterlooville	15	4,901	(6,659)	233	(317)	10,199	486
Poole Town	20	4,865	(9,038)	232	(430)	11,137	530
Totals		257,836		558			

PREMIER DIVISION CLUBS

ATHERSTONE UNITED

Formed in 1979 and joined Division One of the West Midlands (Regional) League. Promoted to the top section in 1982. Moved to the Beazer Homes League in 1987 and promoted to the Premier Division in 1989.
Ground: Sheepy Road, Atherstone, Warwickshire, CV9 3AD
Phone: 0827-717929   **Nickname:** The Adders   **Founded:** 1979
Manager: Joe Gallagher   **Secretary:** K.J. Allen   **Chairman:** Alan Bates
Colours: Red and White, Red, Red   **Change:** Yellow, Blue, Blue

5-Year Record		P	W	D	F	A	Pts	Psn	Cup	FAT
87-88	BHLM	42	22	10	93	56	76	4	1	(V5)
88-89	BHLM	42	26	9	85	38	87	2	2q	1
89-90	BHLP	42	19	10	60	52	67	6	1q	1q
90-91	BHLP	42	14	10	55	58	53	15	2	3q
91-92	BHLP	42	15	8	54	66	53	13	1	1

Ground Capacity: 7,500 (400)   **Record:** 2,816 v VS Rugby, FAC1 1987
Rail: Atherstone (1 mile from ground).   **Directions:** Ground ½ mile north of town centre on the B4116 Twycross/Ashby road.

BASHLEY

Founded in 1947. Gained senior status and a Hampshire County League place in 1983. Promoted to Division Two of the League after two seasons, they were Wessex League founder members in 1986. In 1989 they joined the BHL Southern Section and were champions and promoted at the first attempt.
Ground: Bashley Rec., Bashley Road, New Milton, Hants, BH25 5RY
Phone: 0425-620280   **Nickname:** The Bash   **Founded:** 1947
Manager: Trevor Parker   **Secretary:** S. G. Hynds   **Chairman:** T.R. Adams
Colours: Yellow and Black Stripes, Black, Black
Change: Blue and White Stripes, White, White

5-Year Record		P	W	D	F	A	Pts	Psn	Cup	FAT
87-88	WSX	36	26	6	91	26	84	1	-	(VSF)
88-89	WSX	32	26	4	87	24	82	1	3q	(VQF)
89-90	BHLS	42	25	7	80	47	82	1	1q	(V5)
90-91	BHLP	42	15	12	56	52	57	10	4q	1q
91-92	BHLP	42	22	8	70	44	74	4	2q	2

Ground Capacity: 4,000 (200)   **Record:** 3,500 v Emley, FAVsf, 3/88
Rail: New Milton.
Directions: M27 turn-off to New Forest, Lyndhurst A35 to Bournemouth, take B3058, follow road to Rising Sun, Wootton, keep on to Bashley.

BURTON ALBION

Formed in 1950 and joined the Birmingham & District League. Moved to the Southern League in 1958. Promoted to the top section in 1966, 1972 and 1974, they were relegated in 1970, 1973 and 1977. In 1979 became Northern Premier League founder members. Moved to the Beazer Homes League Premier Division in 1987.

Ground: Eton Park, Princess Way, Burton-on-Trent, DE14 2RU
Phone: 0283-44303 **Nickname:** Brewers **Founded:** 1950
Manager: Eric Avins **Secretary:** David Twigg **Chairman:** S. Brassington
Colours: All Yellow **Change:** All Red

5-Year Record		P	W	D	F	A	Pts	Psn	Cup	FAT
87-88	BHLP	42	11	14	62	74	47	16	1	1
88-89	BHLP	42	18	10	79	68	64	8	4q	2
89-90	BHLP	42	20	12	64	40	72	4	4q	1
90-91	BHLP	42	15	15	59	48	60	7	4q	2
91-92	BHLP	42	15	10	59	61	55	10	4q	3q

Ground Capacity: 8,000 (300) **Record:** 5,860 v Weymouth, SLC Final 64
Rail: Burton-on-Trent.
Directions: M1-A50, turn right at mini roundabout (Derby), left at next island. M42/A38, take second turn for Burton, right at island.

CAMBRIDGE CITY

Founded as Cambridge Town in 1908 from a split from Cambridge St Mary's FC. Were an Amateur Football Alliance Club in the Southern Amateur League, but joined the Spartan League in 1935. Became Athenian Leaguers and changed to their current name in 1950 but adopted professionalism and moved to the Southern League in 1958. Relegated from the top section twice, they were last promoted in 1986.

Ground: City Ground, Milton Road, Cambridge, CB4 1UY
Phone: 0223-357973 **Nickname:** City Devils **Founded:** 1908
Manager: Stephen Fallon **Secretary:** Martin Carter **Chairman:** D. Rolph
Colours: White, Black, White **Change:** All Sky Blue

5-Year Record		P	W	D	F	A	Pts	Psn	Cup	FAT
87-88	BHLP	42	24	8	84	43	80	3	2q	2
88-89	BHLP	42	20	10	72	51	70	5	2q	3q
89-90	BHLP	42	17	11	76	46	62	8	3q	3q
90-91	BHLP	42	21	14	63	43	77	3	3q	2q
91-92	BHLP	42	18	14	71	53	68	5	1q	3q

Ground Capacity: 5000 (400) **Record:** 12,500 v Leytonstone, FAAmC 1956
Rail: Cambridge. **Directions:** 50 yards on left from beginning of the A1134 Cambridge to Ely road.

CHELMSFORD CITY

Formed in 1938 as a professional club on the demise of the city's amateur club. Immediately joined the Southern League where they have been ever since. Relegated from the top section in 1977 and 1988 they were promoted back in 1979 and 1989.

Ground: The Stadium, New Writtle Street, Chelmsford, Essex, CM2 0RP
Phone: 0245-353052 **Nickname:** City **Founded:** 1938
Manager: Joe Sullivan **Secretary:** Mrs Y. Fawcett **Chairman:** D. Wakeling
Colours: Claret and White, Claret, Claret **Change:** Sky Blue

5-Year Record		P	W	D	F	A	Pts	Psn	Cup	FAT
87-88	BHLP	42	11	10	60	75	43	19	1	3q
88-89	BHLS	42	30	5	106	38	95	1	4q	1q
89-90	BHLP	42	11	10	52	72	43	18	4q	1q
90-91	BHLP	42	11	15	57	68	48	18	1	1q
91-92	BHLP	42	12	12	49	56	48	18	2q	1q

Ground Capacity: 2,500 (300) **Record:** 16,480 v Colchester U, SLge 9/49
Rail: Chelmsford.
Directions: From London A12, A1016 to Chelmsford. New Writtle Street is off New London Road. Follow signs to the Essex County Ground which is next to the football ground.

CHELTENHAM TOWN

Formed in 1892, joined the Birmingham Combination in 1932 and moved to the Southern League in 1935. Relegated in 1962 and 1969, they were promoted to the Premier Division in 1964, 1977 and, a season after regionalisation, 1983. They joined the Vauxhall Conference in 1985 but were relegated last season.

Ground: Whaddon Road, Cheltenham, Glos, GL52 5NA
Phone: 0242-513397 **Info Line:** 0898-333-96 **Nickname:** The Robins
Manager: Dave Lewis **Secretary:** not known **Chairman:** David Courtney
Colours: Red and White, Black, Red **Change:** White with Red Trim

5-Year Record		P	W	D	F	A	Pts	Psn	Cup	FAT
87-88	CONF	42	11	20	64	67	53	13	1	QF
88-89	CONF	40	12	12	55	58	48	15	2q	2
89-90	CONF	42	16	11	58	60	59	11	3q	3
90-91	CONF	42	12	12	54	72	48	16	1	3
91-92	CONF	42	10	13	56	82	43	21	3q	2

Ground Capacity: 7,000 (1,200) **Record:** 8,326 v Reading FAC
Rail: Cheltenham – Lansdown (2 miles from ground)
Directions: From North: M5 Junction 10; From South: M5 Junction 11 – follow signs to Cheltenham, then take A46 (Winchcombe and Broadway). Ground situated off Prestbury Road.

CORBY TOWN

United Counties Leaguers until moving to the Midland League in 1952. Joined the Southern League in 1958. Promoted to the Premier Division in 1965, they were relegated in 1968 but, after the period of regionalisation, were re-organised back into the top division in 1982. Relegated in 1990 but promoted to the Premier again after just one season.

Ground: Rockingham Triangle Stadium, Rockingham Rd, Corby, NN17 2AE
Phone: 0536-401007   **Nickname:** The Steelmen   **Founded:** 1948
Manager: Elwyn Roberts **Secretary:** J. Wiseman **Chairman:** T. McConnachie
Colours: White, Black, Black   **Change:** All Yellow

5-Year Record		P	W	D	F	A	Pts	Psn	Cup	FAT
87-88	BHLP	42	16	8	61	64	56	10	1q	1
88-89	BHLP	42	14	11	55	59	53	16	1q	3q
89-90	BHLP	42	10	6	57	77	36	20	1q	1q
90-91	BHLM	42	27	4	99	48	85	2	3q	1q
91-92	BHLP	42	13	12	66	81	51	14	3q	1q

Ground Capacity: 3,000 (1,150)   **Record:** 2,240 v Watford, Pre-season, 1986
Rail: Kettering (8 miles from ground).
Directions: Northern outskirts of town at junction of A6003 and A6116 above village of Rockingham. Ground opposite entrance to Rockingham Castle grounds.

CRAWLEY TOWN

After many seasons of local football the club joined the Sussex County League in 1951. In 1956 they moved to the Metropolitan & District League and in 1963 joined the Southern League. Promoted in 1969, they were relegated in 1970 but returned to the Premier Division in 1984.

Ground: Town Mead, Ifield Avenue, West Green, Crawley, Sussex
Phone: 0293-21800   **Nickname:** The Reds   **Founded:** 1896
Manager: Steve Wicks   **Secretary:** Stan Markham   **Chairman:** John Maggs
Colours: Red, Red, White   **Change:** Blue, Blue, White or Blue

5-Year Record		P	W	D	F	A	Pts	Psn	Cup	FAT
87-88	BHLP	42	17	14	73	63	65	6	1q	2
88-89	BHLP	42	14	16	61	56	58	12	4q	3q
89-90	BHLP	42	13	12	53	57	51	15	1q	3q
90-91	BHLP	42	12	12	45	67	48	19	2q	2q
91-92	BHLP	42	12	12	62	67	48	17	3	1q

Ground Capacity: 2,500 (250)   **Record:** 3,256 v Wimbledon, FAC4Q 11/69
Rail: Crawley.
Directions: M23 Junction 10. Turn right on to A264 for Horsham, turn left at second roundabout, over mini-roundabout, turn right at next roundabout into Ifield Avenue. Ground 150 yards on the right behind the fire station.

DARTFORD

Founder members of the Kent League in 1894, they eventually settled in the Southern League as from 1927. Relegated in 1961; promoted in 1962; relegated again in 1966; promoted again in 1970; relegated for a third time in 1975; then promoted from the regionalised Southern Division to the Alliance Premier League in 1981. They returned to the Southern League in 1982, went back into the Conference in 1984, but were relegated to the Southern in 1986.

Ground: Watling Street, Dartford, Kent, DA2 6EN

Phone: 0322-73639   **Nickname:** The Darts   **Founded:** 1888

Manager: Bobby Makin   **Secretary:** B.H. Bundock   **Chairman:** R. Walker

Colours: Black and White Hoops, White, White

Change: Red and White Hoops, White, Red

5-Year Record		P	W	D	F	A	Pts	Psn	Cup	FAT
87-88	BHLP	42	8	8	79	39	89	2	4q	1
88-89	BHLP	42	25	7	79	33	82	2	1	SF
89-90	BHLP	42	26	9	80	35	87	3	1	1
90-91	BHLP	42	15	9	61	64	54	13	4q	2
91-92	BHLP	42	17	15	62	45	66	6	3q	1

Ground Capacity: 5,250 (678)   **Record:** 11,004 v Leyton Orient, FAC1 1948

Rail: Dartford SR.

Directions: Leave M25 at Dartford Tunnel, Stone turn-off from North use M1/M10/M25 Dartford Toll Tunnel road. No parking facilities at Dartford.

DORCHESTER TOWN

After many seasons of local football, joined the Western League in 1947. In 1972 they joined the Southern League First Division. They were promoted in 1978, relegated in 1984, but returned to the top division in 1987.

Ground: The Avenue Stadium, Dorchester, Dorset, DT1 2RY

Phone: 0305-262451   **Nickname:** The Magpies   **Founded:** 1880

Manager: Paul Arnold   **Secretary:** A.E. Miller   **Chairman:** P.J. Aiken

Colours: Black and White Stripes, Black, Black   **Change:** All Sky Blue

5-Year Record		P	W	D	F	A	Pts	Psn	Cup	FAT
87-88	BHLP	42	14	14	51	57	56	11	1q	1q
88-89	BHLP	42	14	16	56	61	58	13	3q	1
89-90	BHLP	42	16	7	52	67	55	13	1	1q
90-91	BHLP	42	15	12	47	54	57	11	2q	3q
91-92	BHLP	42	14	13	66	73	55	11	4q	3q

Ground Capacity: 7,210 (710)   **Record:** 1,860 v Weymouth, League 1990/1

Rail: Dorchester South.

Directions: Half mile to south side of town centre, ground immediately on junction of town by-pass with A354.

DOVER ATHLETIC

Formed in 1983 on the demise of Dover FC, taking that club's Southern League Southern Section place. In 1988 they were South Division champions and promoted to the top section. Premier Division champions in 1990, they failed to meet the necessary requirements for promotion to the Conference.

Ground: Crabble Athletic Ground, Lewisham Road, River, Dover, Kent
Phone: 0304-822373   **Nickname:** The Lilywhites   **Founded:** 1983
Manager: Chris Kinnear   **Secretary:** J.F. Durrant   **Chairman:** J.T. Husk
Colours: White, Black, Black   **Change:** Yellow, Green, Yellow

5-Year Record		P	W	D	F	A	Pts	Psn	Cup	FAT
87-88	BHLS	40	28	10	81	28	94	1	1q	1q
88-89	BHLP	42	19	12	65	47	69	6	4q	2
89-90	BHLP	42	32	6	87	27	102	1	3q	3
90-91	BHLP	42	21	11	56	37	74	4	4q	2
91-92	BHLP	42	23	15	66	30	84	2	4q	1

Ground Capacity: 4,000 (1,500)   **Record:** not known
Rail: Dover Priory.
Directions: Main A2 from London/Canterbury road to first roundabout. Fourth exit down the hill to roundabout, left, right at first set of traffic lights.

GLOUCESTER CITY

Played in several Gloucestershire Leagues before joining the Birmingham Combination in 1932. In 1939 they joined the Southern League. They were re-organised into the lower division in 1959; promoted in 1969; relegated in 1971; re-organised into the top division on the end of regionalisation in 1982; relegated in 1985 and promoted again in 1989.

Ground: Meadow Park, Sudmeadow Road, Hempsted, Gloucester, GL2 6HS
Phone: 0452-23883   **Nickname:** The Tigers   **Founded:** 1883
Manager: Brian Godfrey   **Secretary:** Ken Turner   **Chairman:** George Irvine
Colours: All Yellow   **Change:** White, Black, Black

5-Year Record		P	W	D	F	A	Pts	Psn	Cup	FAT
87-88	BHLM	42	18	14	86	62	68	8	1q	1
88-89	BHLM	42	28	8	95	37	92	1	3q	3q
89-90	BHLP	42	17	11	80	68	62	9	2	3q
90-91	BHLP	42	23	14	86	49	82	2	4q	3
91-92	BHLP	42	15	9	67	70	54	12	2q	1

Ground Capacity: 5,000 (600)   **Record:** 3,877 v Cardiff, FAC2R 12/90
Rail: Gloucester.
Directions: Take A40 into city centre towards the historic docks area, then Severn Road, then right into Hempsted Lane and right into Sudmeadow Road. Ground is on the left 50 yards up the road.

HALESOWEN TOWN

Early members of the Birmingham & District League, but members of the Birmingham Combination for the period between the Wars. Re-joined the Birmingham & District – later the West Midlands (Regional) – League in 1946, moving on to the Southern League in 1986. Promoted to the Premier Division in 1990.

Ground: Grove Recreation Ground, Stourbridge Rd/Old Hawne La, Halesowen
Phone: 021-550-2179   **Nickname:** Yeltz   **Founded:** 1873
Manager: John Morris **Secretary:** Stuart Tildsley **Chairman:** Ron Moseley
Colours: Blue, White, Blue   **Change:** Red, White or Black, Red

5-Year Record		P	W	D	F	A	Pts	Psn	Cup	FAT
87-88	BHLM	42	18	15	79	59	69	6	1	1q
88-89	BHLM	42	25	10	85	42	85	4	1	1q
89-90	BHLM	42	28	8	100	49	92	1	1	1q
90-91	BHLP	42	17	9	73	67	60	8	1	1q
91-92	BHLP	42	15	15	61	49	60	8	1	1q

Ground Capacity: 4,500 (420)   **Record:** 5,000 v Hendon, FAC1 11/54
Rail: Old Hill Birmingham/Stourbridge.
Directions: M5 Junction 3. A456 to first roundabout (turn right), at second roundabout take second left into Old Hawne Lane ground 400 yards on left.

HASTINGS TOWN

Formed around 1895 as Hastings and St. Leonards, they joined the Sussex County League in 1921. Were in local football between 1927 and 1952 when they rejoined the County League. Success in the League came after changing their name , and in 1985 they took Hastings United's place in the Southern League and took up occupation too of their ground.

Ground: The Pilot Field, Elphinstone Road, Hastings, East Sussex, TN34 2AX
Phone: 0424-444635   **Nickname:** Town   **Founded:** 1898
Manager: Peter Sillett **Secretary:** Richard Cosens **Chairman:** David Nessling
Colours: All White   **Change:** All Yellow

5-Year Record		P	W	D	F	A	Pts	Psn	Cup	FAT
87-88	BHLS	40	14	10	60	70	52	12	Pr	(V1)
88-89	BHLS	42	21	11	75	48	74	7	2q	(V1)
89-90	BHLS	42	20	9	64	54	69	8	1q	(V4)
90-91	BHLS	40	18	11	66	46	65	7	Pr	(V5)
91-92	BHLS	42	28	7	80	37	91	11	1q	(V4)

Ground Capacity: 10,000 (500) **Record:** 1,200 v Weymouth, BHL, 1991/2
Rail: Hastings.   **Directions:** From A21 turn left into St Helen's Road. Turn left into St. Helen's Park Road (about 1 mile) which leads into Downs Road. Go to the end of this road and at T-junction turn left. Ground is immediately on the right.

HEDNESFORD TOWN

Formed in 1880. Early members of the Birmingham Combination and Birmingham District League. Rejoined the Combination in 1945, they returned to the Birmingham & District (later the West Midlands (Regional)) and, apart from two seasons in the 1970s in the Midland Counties League, stayed there until joining the Southern League in 1984.

Ground: Cross Keys Ground, Hill Street, Hednesford, Staffs

Phone: 05438-2870   **Nickname:** The Pitmen   **Founded:** 1880

Manager: John Baldwin   **Secretary:** Bob Cooper   **Chairman:** Mike Smith

Colours: White, Black, Black   **Change:** All Yellow

5-Year Record		P	W	D	F	A	Pts	Psn	Cup	FAT
87-88	BHLM	42	11	10	43	18	43	18	Pr	2q
88-89	BHLM	42	12	15	49	57	51	15	Pr	1q
89-90	BHLM	42	11	14	50	62	47	17	Pr	1q
90-91	BHLM	42	25	7	79	47	82	3	2q	1q
91-92	BHLM	42	26	13	81	37	91	2	1q	2q

Ground Capacity: 3,500 (500)   **Record:** 10,000 v Walsall, FAC5Q 1919/20

Rail: Hednesford.

Directions: M6 Junction 11. Continue to Cannock, take A460 to Hednesford, after 2 miles turn right opposite Shell garage; ground at the bottom of the hill on the right.

MOOR GREEN

Formed in 1901 by members of the Ashfield CC, they had three pre-Second World War seasons in the Central Amateur League. After the War they competed in the Birmingham Combination and when that was disbanded joined the Birmingham & District League. In 1965 they moved to the Worcestershire (later Midland) Combination and in 1983 joined the Southern League. Promoted to the Premier Division in 1988 for the first time.

Ground: Sherwood Road, Hall Green, Birmingham, B28 0EX

Phone: 021-777-2757   **Nickname:** The Moors   **Founded:** 1901

Manager: Bob Faulkner   **Secretary:** Brian Smith   **Chairman:** Brian Smith

Colours: Light Blue, Dark Blue, Light Blue   **Change:** All Green

5-Year Record		P	W	D	F	A	Pts	Psn	Cup	FAT
87-88	BHLP	42	26	8	91	49	86	2	4q	2q
88-89	BHLP	42	14	13	58	70	55	15	4q	1q
89-90	BHLP	42	18	7	62	59	61	11	1q	2q
90-91	BHLP	42	15	6	64	75	51	16	1q	1
91-92	BHLP	42	15	11	61	59	6	9	1q	3q

Ground Capacity: 2,500 (250)   **Record:** 5,000 v Romford, FAAmC11951

Rail: Hall Green and Yardley Wood.

Directions: Off Highfield Road, which is off the main A34 Birmingham to Stratford Road, at Hall Green, South Birmingham, 4 miles from M42.

SOLIHULL BOROUGH

Formed in 1951, they joined the Midland Combination from local football in 1969. Recently left their Widney Lane ground to share at Moor Green pending occupation of a new stadium. Elected to Beazer Homes League for 1990-91 season and won promotion to Premier Division in first season.

Ground: Moor Green FC, Sherwood Road, Hall Green, Birmingham, B28 0EX
Phone: 021-777-2757 **Nickname:** The Borough **Founded:** 1951
Manager: Ralph Punsheon **Secretary:** J. France **Chairman:** J. Hewitson
Colours: All Red **Change:** Yellow and Blue

5-Year Record		P	W	D	F	A	Pts	Psn	Cup	FAT
87-88	MC	36	14	6	62	65	34	11	–	(VPr)
88-89	MC	34	7	6	41	72	20	17	–	(V1)
89-90	MC	38	16	3	53	52	51	10	–	(V1)
90-91	MC	40	24	6	74	35	78	2	1q	(VPr)
91-92	BHLM	42	29	10	92	40	97	1	2q	(V3)

Ground Capacity: 2,500 (300) **Record:** not known
Rail: Hall Green and Yardley Wood.
Directions: Off Highfield Road, which is off the main A34 Birmingham to Stratford road at Hall Green, South Birmingham, 4 miles from M42.

TROWBRIDGE TOWN

Founder members of the Western League in 1892, they moved into an expanded Southern League in 1958 and were promoted to the Alliance Premier League from third place in the Midland Division in 1981. They were relegated after three seasons and fell further, into the Southern's Division One, in 1985. Promoted back into the BHL Premier Division in 1991.

Ground: Frome Road, Trowbridge, Wilts, BA14 0DB
Phone: 0225-752076 **Nickname:** The Bees **Founded:** 1880
Manager: John Murphy **Secretary:** Jeff Hooper **Chairman:** John Fitchin
Colours: Old Gold, Black, Black **Change:** All White

5-Year Record		P	W	D	F	A	Pts	Psn	Cup	FAT
87-88	BHLM	42	14	3	53	82	45	16	1q	2q
88-89	BHLS	42	19	7	59	52	64	10	1q	1q
89-90	BHLS	42	20	9	79	64	69	7	2q	(VPr)
90-91	BHLS	40	22	12	67	31	78	2	2q	(VSF)
91-92	BHLP	42	17	10	69	51	61	7	3q	1q

Ground Capacity: 5,000 (200) **Record:** 9,009 v Weymouth, FAC4Q 49
Rail: Trowbridge.
Directions: Follow inner relief-road signs to Frome. Ground is on left past Ship Inn.

VS RUGBY

Valley Sports (Rugby) formed in 1956. After local soccer they joined the United Counties League in 1969. As VS Rugby they were West Midland (Regional) League members from 1975, moving on to the Southern League in 1983. Promoted to the Premier Division in 1987.

Ground: Butlin Road, Rugby, Warwickshire, CV21 3ST
Phone: 0788-543692 **Nickname:** The Valley **Founded:** 1956
Manager: Jimmy Knox **Secretary:** Kevin Horrigan **Chairman:** R.Gallimore
Colours: Sky Blue, Navy Blue, Sky Blue **Change:** All White with Red Trim

5-Year Record		P	W	D	F	A	Pts	Psn	Cup	FAT
87-88	BHLP	42	10	16	52	57	46	17	2	2q
88-89	BHLP	42	24	7	64	43	79	3	4q	1q
89-90	BHLP	42	19	12	51	35	69	5	4q	3q
90-91	BHLP	42	16	11	56	46	59	9	2q	2
91-92	BHLP	42	23	11	70	44	80	3	4q	1

Ground Capacity: 5,000 (400) **Record:** 3,961 v Northampton, FAC1R 1984
Rail: Rugby.
Directions: Butlin Road is off the B5414 on the east side of Rugby close to Junction 1 of M6, the A5, and Junctions 18 and 20 of M1.

WATERLOOVILLE

They were Hampshire League members from 1953 to 1971, when they moved to the Southern League. Promoted to the top section in 1972, they were relegated in 1973. On the ending of the League's regionalisation they found themselves in the top section again, only to be relegated after one year in 1983. They moved back into the top section in 1988.

Ground: Jubilee Park, Aston Park, Waterlooville, PO7 7XG
Phone: 0705-263423 **Nickname:** The Ville **Founded:** 1910
Manager: Ernie Bradwell **Secretary:** M. Richards **Chairman:** F. Faulkner
Colours: White, White, Blue **Change:** All Yellow

5-Year Record		P	W	D	F	A	Pts	Psn	Cup	FAT
87-88	BHLS	40	27	10	88	33	91	2	2q	3q
88-89	BHLP	42	13	13	61	63	52	17	1	1q
89-90	BHLP	42	13	10	63	81	49	16	1q	1q
90-91	BHLP	42	11	13	51	70	46	20	1q	1q
91-92	BHLP	42	13	11	43	56	50	15	2q	2q

Ground Capacity: 4,000 (500) **Record:** 4,500 v Wycombe W, FAC1 1976
Rail: Havant (4 miles from ground). **Directions:** Take town by-pass road (B2150), turn right at Asda roundabout, along dual carriageway to next roundabout and return back towards town. Aston Park Road is the first left.

WEYMOUTH

Founded in 1890 they joined the Western League in 1907 and had a Southern League period in the 1920s before returning to the Western. They joined the Southern for a second time in 1949. Always members of the top section, they were Alliance founder members in 1979. Moved to their present ground in 1987 and relegated to the BHL in 1989. Further relegated in 1991, but promoted last season.

Ground: Wessex Stadium, Radipole Road, Weymouth, Dorset, DT4 0TJ
Phone: 0305-785558   **Nickname:** The Terras   **Founded:** 1889
Manager: Len Drake   **Secretary:** S.Charlton
Colours: Maroon, Sky Blue, Sky Blue   **Chairman:** A. Caswell
                                              Change: All White

5-Year Record		P	W	D	F	A	Pts	Psn	Cup	FAT
87-88	CONF	42	18	9	53	43	63	10	4q	1
88-89	CONF	40	7	10	37	70	31	21	4q	2
89-90	BHLP	42	11	13	50	70	46	17	3q	2
90-91	BHLP	42	4	9	50	88	24	22	3q	3q
91-92	BHLS	42	22	12	64	35	78	2	4q	3q

Ground Capacity: 10,000 (900) **Record:** 5,500 v Man. Utd 1987, grd opening
Rail: Weymouth.   **Directions:** Approach Weymouth on Dorchester road (A354), turn right at first roundabout to town centre, turn right at next roundabout (signposted) and ground is straight on.

WORCESTER CITY

Early members of the Birmingham & District League, City joined the Southern League in 1938. Relegated in 1967 and 1974, they were promoted to the top division in 1968 and 1977, becoming Alliance Premier League founder members in 1979. They lost their place in 1985 and returned to the Southern League.

Ground: St George's Lane, Barbourne, Worcester, WR1 1QT
Phone: 0905-23003   **Nickname:** City   **Founded:** 1908
Manager: Martin Bennett   **Secretary:** G. Jukes   **Chairman:** B. Connally
Colours: Blue and White, Blue, Blue   **Change:** All Red

5-Year Record		P	W	D	F	A	Pts	Psn	Cup	FAT
87-88	BHLP	42	22	6	58	48	72	5	1	3q
88-89	BHLP	42	20	13	72	49	73	4	4q	1
89-90	BHLP	42	15	10	62	63	54 †	14	3q	1
90-91	BHLP	42	18	12	55	42	66	6	3q	3q
91-92	BHLP	42	12	13	56	59	49	16	4q	1

Ground Capacity: 10,000 (1,500) **Record:** 17, 042 v Sheff. Utd, FAC4 1959
Rail: Foregate Street.   **Directions:** M1 Junction 6. Take Kidderminster road to roundabout. Turn left into Worcester, at first set of lights turn right and then third left.   *†One point deducted*

MIDLAND DIVISION

Final Table 1991-92

	P	W	D	L	F	A	Pts
Solihull Borough	42	29	10	3	92	40	97
Hednesford Town	42	26	13	3	81	37	91
Sutton Coldfield Town	42	21	11	10	71	51	74
Barry Town	42	21	6	15	88	56	69
Bedworth United	42	16	15	11	67	63	63
Nuneaton Borough	42	17	11	14	68	53	62
Tamworth	42	16	12	14	66	52	60
Rushden Town	42	16	12	14	69	63	60
Stourbridge	42	17	8	17	85	62	59
Newport A.F.C.	42	15	13	14	72	60	58
Yate Town	42	14	15	13	65	64	57
Bilston Town	42	15	10	17	56	67	55
Grantham Town	42	11	17	14	59	55	50
King's Lynn	42	13	11	18	61	68	50
Hinckley Town	42	14	8	20	61	87	50
Leicester United	42	12	13	17	56	63	49
Bridgnorth Town	42	12	12	18	61	74	48
Racing Club Warwick	42	11	14	17	45	61	47
Stroud	42	14	4	24	66	88	46
Redditch United	42	12	8	22	52	92	44
Alvechurch	42	11	10	21	54	88	43
Dudley Town	42	8	9	25	41	92	33

Leading Midland League Goalscorers

Burton, C. (Solihull Borough) 28; Burr, S. (Hednesford Town) 27; Hallam, M. (Leicester United) 26; O'Connor, J. (Hednesford Town) 25.

Promotions and Relegations

Club	Position	Movement
Solihull Borough	Champions	Promoted to Premier Division
Hednesford Town	Runners-up	Promoted to Premier Division
Alvechurch	21st	Resigned

Clubs Joining Midland Division

Club	From
Gresley Rovers	West Midlands League
Evesham United	Influence Midland Football Combination
Weston-super-Mare	Great Mills Western League

Leading League Goalscorers by Club

Club	Top scorers
Alvechurch	Treharne 10; Healey 8; Richardson 8.
Barry Town	Summers 23; Hunter 10; Williams 10.
Bedworth United	Hardwick 19; McBean 17; Taylor 6.
Bilston Town	Richards 8; Baker 7; Streete 5; Williams 5.
Bridgnorth Town	Balshaw 10; Clarke 9; Comerford 7; Meredith 7.
Dudley Town	Baker 5; Young 5; Smith 4.
Grantham Town	Hurst 15; Whitehurst 7; Cooke 5; Dorsett 5.
Hednesford Town	Burr 23; O'Connor 20; King 6.
Hinckley Town	Akeredolu 15; Simmonds 10; Donaldson 7.
King's Lynn	Gallagher 13; Rawcliffe 10; Topliss 5.
Leicester United	Hallam 25; Liquorish 9; Beckford 5.
Newport A.F.C	Green 23; Lillygreen 12; Price 7.
Nuneaton Borough	Twigger 22; Straw 15; Anastasi 5.
Racing Club Warwick	Emery 8; Derby 6; Watts 6.
Redditch United	Campbell 7; Judd 5; Warner 4.
Rushden Town	Green 19; Belfon 18; Kirkup 11.
Solihull Borough	Burton 25; Carter 10; Canning 9; Hawker 9.
Stourbridge	E. Wright 18; Barrows 13; H. Wright 13.
Stroud	Peacey 16; Bayliss 10; Townsend 9.
Sutton Coldfield Town	Smith 18; Morrison 16; Hunter 5.
Tamworth	Gordon 13; Bodkin 10; Smith 8.
Yate Town	Thaws 22; Thompson 8; Hewlett 6.

Sportique Manager of the Month Awards

Month	Manager	Club
August	John Relish	Newport AFC
September	Ralph Punsheon	Solihull Borough
October	Tony Wilcox	Barry Town
November	Ralph Punsheon	Solihull Borough
December	John Baldwin	Hednesford Town
January	John Baldwin	Hednesford Town
February	Ian Love	Barry Town
March	John Chambers	Stourbridge

MIDLAND DIVISION RESULTS 1991-92

	Alvechurch	Barry Town	Bedworth Utd	Bilston Town	Bridgnorth T	Dudley Town	Grantham Town	Hednesford T	Hinckley Town	King's Lynn	Leicester Utd
Alvechurch	•	0-5	1-3	1-0	2-2	2-1	0-0	1-3	0-0	1-1	1-3
Barry Town	2-1	•	3-1	3-1	1-4	0-1	1-3	0-2	10-0	1-1	2-1
Bedworth United	1-2	0-4	•	3-3	0-0	2-2	3-2	1-1	3-1	2-2	0-2
Bilston Town	1-3	3-0	3-0	•	1-1	1-4	2-2	0-4	1-2	3-1	2-1
Bridgnorth Town	2-2	3-2	0-3	2-3	•	3-1	2-4	0-4	2-3	2-0	1-3
Dudley Town	0-0	0-6	0-3	0-2	0-1	•	1-1	1-2	0-1	2-0	0-0
Grantham Town	2-2	0-1	1-1	2-2	1-2	6-0	•	0-0	2-2	0-0	1-1
Hednesford Town	6-0	3-0	0-1	3-0	1-0	0-0	2-1	•	2-0	2-1	3-3
Hinckley Town	1-3	1-2	1-3	1-1	2-3	3-0	2-4	1-1	•	0-4	0-0
King's Lynn	4-3	3-2	1-3	0-0	3-5	2-0	4-1	0-0	1-1	•	2-5
Leicester United	2-0	1-1	2-3	0-0	1-1	2-0	1-3	0-1	2-0	4-5	•
Newport AFC	3-0	1-0	1-1	1-1	2-1	3-1	1-1	0-2	5-1	3-1	0-1
Nuneaton Borough	5-2	0-1	3-1	2-1	1-1	5-0	1-0	1-2	2-0	1-0	2-0
Racing Club Warwick	0-0	1-1	2-2	4-1	3-2	1-2	1-0	1-3	0-1	0-1	1-0
Redditch United	1-2	0-4	1-1	1-0	1-1	0-0	1-1	1-2	2-1	0-2	0-1
Rushden Town	1-0	0-3	0-1	3-1	0-0	3-3	1-1	1-1	3-1	2-0	3-3
Solihull Borough	2-1	2-1	0-1	2-1	2-1	5-1	2-0	6-1	4-1	1-1	0-0
Stourbridge	5-1	2-2	3-1	3-1	3-3	5-1	2-0	1-3	3-1	4-0	2-1
Stroud	5-2	2-1	2-1	0-1	4-1	4-0	2-0	0-3	0-2	2-3	5-0
Sutton Coldfield Town	3-2	3-1	2-6	0-1	1-0	3-1	0-2	2-0	1-2	2-1	0-1
Tamworth	2-0	2-3	2-2	0-1	0-0	1-1	2-0	2-3	0-2	2-1	3-0
Yate Town	5-1	0-1	2-2	4-0	0-0	3-3	2-2	2-3	1-1	0-0	1-1

	Newport AFC	Nuneaton B	RC Warwick	Redditch Utd	Rushden Town	Solihull Boro	Stourbridge	Stroud	Sutton C'field	Tamworth	Yate Town
Alvechurch	2-0	1-0	1-3	0-0	3-2	2-1	2-4	1-2	2-2	2-3	2-0
Barry Town	2-2	2-1	5-0	4-0	1-1	1-3	2-1	4-1	2-1	0-2	1-2
Bedworth United	3-2	0-0	2-1	1-0	0-0	0-2	1-3	3-1	1-1	1-0	0-0
Bilston Town	2-2	0-1	4-2	0-2	3-0	0-2	0-4	4-1	0-1	2-1	2-1
Bridgnorth Town	1-1	0-1	0-4	1-2	1-4	0-3	0-1	5-2	1-2	1-4	0-0
Dudley Town	2-1	2-0	2-3	1-2	1-4	0-2	2-1	0-2	1-6	3-2	2-3
Grantham Town	3-3	1-1	1-0	2-1	4-1	0-1	0-0	0-1	0-2	2-1	1-2
Hednesford Town	2-1	2-2	2-1	3-0	2-1	1-1	1-1	3-1	1-1	0-0	1-1
Hinckley Town	1-3	2-2	1-4	4-2	1-3	4-5	3-2	3-0	1-2	1-0	4-1
King's Lynn	3-1	2-1	1-0	4-0	3-3	1-3	0-2	2-0	2-2	2-4	1-2
Leicester United	0-0	2-1	2-1	1-0	1-3	1-3	1-1	2-2	0-1	0-1	0-1
Newport AFC	•	3-2	5-0	5-0	2-1	1-1	0-4	1-0	2-2	0-3	2-2
Nuneaton Borough	2-0	•	0-1	3-2	1-1	1-1	2-2	2-0	1-1	3-3	1-2
Racing Club Warwick	0-2	0-0	•	4-1	2-2	0-4	2-0	2-0	0-0	0-0	1-2
Redditch United	0-5	0-2	4-1	•	4-4	0-4	2-1	2-1	0-2	1-3	2-0
Rushden Town	0-3	1-1	2-1	5-0	•	2-2	3-1	2-0	1-2	3-2	2-0
Solihull Borough	3-1	2-3	4-0	1-1	2-0	•	1-0	2-1	3-1	2-1	4-1
Stourbridge	2-3	3-1	1-2	5-0	2-3	1-1	•	2-1	2-3	4-1	1-1
Stroud	2-3	4-1	0-0	4-5	2-5	1-2	2-1	•	0-2	3-2	1-2
Sutton Coldfield Town	1-1	3-2	0-0	3-2	0-0	2-3	2-1	5-0	•	1-1	3-0
Tamworth	1-0	2-3	0-0	1-1	1-0	1-1	1-0	4-0	0-1	•	2-2
Yate Town	1-5	1-0	1-1	5-0	1-2	3-4	3-1	0-0	3-0	1-3	•

MIDLAND DIVISION CLUBS

BARRY TOWN

Ground: St George's Lane, Barbourne, Worcester, WR1 1QT
Phone: 0446-731171   **Nickname:** The Linnets   **Founded:** 1923
Manager: Ian Love   **Secretary:** Alan Whelan   **Chairman:** N. O'Hallovon
Colours: Green, Navy, Green   **Change:** All Red
Ground Capacity: 10,000 (1,500)   **Record:** (First season at Worcester)
Rail: Forgate Street.
Directions: M1 Junction 6. Take Kidderminster road to roundabout. Turn left into Worcester, at first set of lights turn right and then third left.

BEDWORTH UNITED

Ground: The Oval, Miners' Welfare Park, Bedworth, Warwicks, CV12 8NN
Phone: 0203-314302   **Nickname:** The Greenbacks   **Founded:** 1947
Manager: Brendon Phillips   **Secretary:** B. Jacques   **Chairman:** Alan Robinson
Colours: Green, White, Green   **Change:** Yellow, Green, Yellow
Ground Capacity: 4,000 (300)   **Record:** 5,127 v Nuneaton B, 2/82
Rail: Bedworth.   **Directions:** M6 Junction 3. B4113 to Bedworth, 1½ miles from Junction 3, adjacent to leisure centre.

BILSTON TOWN

Ground: Queen Street, Bilston, West Midlands, WV14 7EX
Phone: 0902-744653   **Nickname:** not known   **Founded:** 1895
Manager: Steve Bowater   **Secretary:** Morris Baker   **Chairman:** A. Hickman
Colours: Tangerine, Black, Tangerine   **Change:** All White
Ground Capacity: 7,000 (350)   **Record:** v Wolverhampton, 1953/4, f.o.
Rail: Wolverhampton.   **Directions:** M6 Junction 10. A454 Wolverhampton, pick up A563 Bilston, and after approx 1¼ miles turn left at Beckett Street.

BRIDGNORTH TOWN

Ground: Crown Meadow, Innage Lane, Bridgnorth, Shropshire, WV16 6PZ
Phone: 0746-762747/766064   **Nickname:** Town   **Founded:** 1946
Manager: Billy Ball   **Secretary:** Gordon Thomas   **Chairman:** J. Heseltine
Colours: Blue, White, Blue   **Change:** All Red
Ground Capacity: 1,600 (400)   **Record:** 1,600 v South Shields, FA Vase
Rail: Wolverhampton.   **Directions:** Through High Street, fork left into Innage Lane, ground 200 yards on left.

DUDLEY TOWN

Ground: The Round Oak Stadium, John Street, Brierly Hill, West Midlands
Phone: 0384-263478 **Nickname:** The Robins **Founded:** 1893
Manager: Paddy Page **Secretary:** Tony Turpin **Chairman:** N.D. Jeynes
Colours: Red, White, Black   **Change:** All Yellow
Ground Capacity: 3,000 (204)   **Record:** 1,000 v Tamworth, 1989
Rail: Stourbridge.
Directions: From Dudley take the A461 towards Stourbridge for about two miles. On entering Brierly Hill turn right on to the B4180 and into John Street. Stadium entrance is 200 yards on right.

EVESHAM UNITED

Ground: Common Road, Evesham, Worcs
Phone: 0386-2303 **Nickname:** not known **Founded:** 1945
Manager: not known **Secretary:** not known **Chairman:** not known
Colours: Red and White Stripes, Red, Red **Change:** White with Black Stripe, Black, Black
Ground Capacity: 2,000 (350)   **Record:** 1,400 v Aston Villa, Friendly
Rail: Evesham.
Directions: From Birmingham, on entering Evesham turn left into Swan Lane. Common Road off Swan Lane.

FOREST GREEN ROVERS

Ground: The Lawn, Nympsfield Road, Forest Green, Nailsworth, Glos
Phone: 045-383-4860 **Nickname:** Rovers **Founded:** 1898
Manager: Bobby Jones **Secretary:** D. Roberts **Chairman:** A. Coburn/T. Horsley
Colours: White, Navy, Red or White **Change:** Red, White, Red or White
Ground Capacity: 4,000 (142)   **Record:** 2,000 v Wolves, f.o. 2/81
Rail: Stroud.
Directions: Approx 4 miles from Stroud on A46 to Bath. On entering Nailsworth turn right into Spring Hill, ground is 1 mile at top of hill on left.

GRANTHAM TOWN

Ground: South Kestevan Sports Stadium, Trent Road, Grantham, Lincs
Phone: 0476-62011 **Nickname:** The Gingerbreads **Founded:** 1874
Manager: Bob Duncan **Secretary:** P.S. Nixon **Chairman:** A. Balfe
Colours: White, Black, Black   **Change:** Yellow, Blue, Blue
Ground Capacity: 4,000 (700) **Record:** 1,402 v Ilkeston Town, FAC, 8/91
Rail: Grantham.

GRESLEY ROVERS

Ground: Moat Street, Church Gresley, Burton on Trent
Phone: 0283-216315   **Nickname:** Rovers   **Founded:** 1882
Manager: Steve Doleby
Colours: White, Red, Red   **Change:** All Blue
Ground Capacity: 3,500 (250)   **Record:** 3,950 Birmingham Lg 1957/8
Rail: Burton on Trent (5 miles from ground).
Directions: Take A444 south from Burton on Trent. After approx four miles turn left onto A514. Ground just off A514.

HINCKLEY TOWN

Ground: Leicester Road, Hinckley, Leics
Phone: 0455-615062   **Nickname:** The Eagles   **Founded:** 1958
Manager: Dave Grundy   **Secretary:** Julie Barnes   **Chairman:** David Needham
Colours: White, Claret, Sky Blue   **Change:** Yellow, Navy, Yellow
Ground Capacity: 3,000 (250)   **Record:** 1,500 v Real Sociedad, f.o. 8/87
Rail: Hinckley.
Directions: M69 Junction 1. Take A447 then A47 towards Leicester. Ground is on A47 about 2 miles from town centre on left.

KING'S LYNN

Ground: The Walks Stadium, Tennyson Road, King's Lynn, Norfolk, PE30 5PB
Phone: 0553-760060   **Nickname:** The Linnets   **Founded:** 1876
Manager: Alan Day   **Secretary:** M. Saddleton   **Chairman:** M.Saddleton
Colours: Yellow, Blue, Blue   **Change:** All Red
Ground Capacity: 8,200 (1,200)   **Record:** 13,500 v Exeter C, FAC1 1951
Rail: King's Lynn.
Directions: A10-A47. At mini-roundabout take Vancouse Avenue. Follow Vancouse Avenue for about 400 yards, ground on left.

LEICESTER UNITED

Ground: United Park, Winchester Road, Blaby, Leicester, LE43 3HN
Phone: 0533-778998   **Nickname:** United   **Founded:** 1900
Manager: Andy Potter   **Secretary:** J. Goodman   **Chairman:** Gary Glover
Colours: Red and White Stripes, Black with Red and White Flash, Black with Two Red Hoops   **Change:** All White
Ground Capacity: 6,000 (450)   **Record:** not known
Rail: Narborough.
Directions: M69/M1 Junction. 2½ miles along the Blaby to Countesthorpe road.

NEWPORT AFC

Ground: Meadow Park, Sudmeadow Road, Hempsted, Gloucester, GL2 6HS
Phone: not known   **Nickname:** The Exiles   **Founded:** 1989
Manager: John Relish **Secretary:** Marc Williams **Chairman:** David Hando
Colours: Amber, Black, Black   **Change:** All White
Ground Capacity: 5,000 (600)   **Record:** 2,400
Directions: Take A40 into city centre towards the historic docks area, then
Severn Road, then right into Hempsted Lane and right into Sudmeadow Road.
Ground is on the left 50 yards up the road.

NUNEATON BOROUGH

Ground: Manor Park, Beaumont Road, Nuneaton, Warwickshire, CV10 0SY
Phone: 0203-342690   **Nickname:** Boro   **Founded:** 1937
Manager: Paul Sugrue **Secretary:** Keith Parker **Chairman:** Joe Shooter
Colours: Blue and White, White, Blue   **Change:** Yellow, Black, Black
Ground Capacity: 2,800 (600)   **Record:** 22,114 v Rotherham, FAC3 1967
Rail: Nuneaton.   **Directions:** M6 Junction 3. Take A444 to Nuneaton, take
first exit at first island, at second island turn left then second left into
Greenmoor Road. At end of road turn right, ground on left.

RACING CLUB WARWICK

Ground: Townsend Meadow, Hampton Road, Warwick
Phone: 0926-495786/493622 **Nickname:** Racing   **Founded:** 1919
Manager: Stuart Dixon **Secretary:** Patrick Murphy **Chairman:** Jim Wright
Colours: Red, White, Black   **Change:** Yellow, Black, Black
Ground Capacity: 1,000 (300)   **Record:** 1,000 v Halesowen, FAC 87/8
Rail: Warwick.   **Directions:** The ground is situated on the B4095 Warwick
to Redditch road (Henley in Arden) next to the Owners' and Trainers' Car
Park on Warwick Racecourse.

REDDITCH UNITED

Ground: Valley Stadium, Bromsgrove Road, Redditch, Worcs, B97 4RN
Phone: 0527-67450   **Nickname:** The Reds   **Founded:** 1900
Manager: Paul Hendrie **Secretary:** M. Langfield **Chairman:** R. Berry
Colours: All Red   **Change:** Yellow, Blue, Blue
Ground Capacity: 7,500 (200)   **Record:** 5,500 v Bromsgrove, Lge 1954/5
Rail: Redditch.   **Directions:** M42 to town centre take ring road and come
off on access 7. This takes you into Bromsgrove Road. Also first exit off dual
carriageway from Bromsgrove on the Batchley side of Redditch. Ground 400
yards from main line station and town centre.

RUSHDEN & DIAMONDS

Ground: Nene Park, Irthlingborough, Northants
Phone: 0933-650345 **Nickname:** not known **Founded:** 1992 (amalgamation)
Manager: Roger Ashby **Secretary:** David Joyce **Chairman:** Max Griggs
Ground Capacity: 3,500 (350) **Record:** (new club)
Rail: Wellingborough.
Directions: On A6 on outskirts of Irthlingborough.

STOURBRIDGE

Ground: War Memorial Athletic Ground, High Street, Amblecote,
Stourbridge, DY8 4EB
Phone: 0384-394040 **Nickname:** The Glassboys **Founded:** 1876
Manager: John Chambers **Secretary:** Hugh Clark **Chairman:** J.C. Driscoll
Colours: Red and White, White, Red **Change:** White, Black, White
Ground Capacity: 2,000 (320) **Record:** 10,000 v WBA, 1902
Rail: Stourbridge Town.
Directions: On left-hand side of road 250 yards from Stourbridge ring road
on A491 to Wolverhampton and opposite Royal Oak public house.

SUTTON COLDFIELD TOWN

Ground: Central Ground, Coles Lane, Sutton Coldfield, W. Midlands, B72 1NL
Phone: 021-354-2997 **Nickname:** The Royals **Founded:** 1897
Manager: Phil Sharpe **Secretary:** Gerry Shanahan **Chairman:** C. Holt
Colours: Royal Blue, White, Royal Blue **Change:** White, Royal Blue, White
Ground Capacity: 4,500 (250) **Record:** 2,029 v Doncaster, FAC1 10/80
Rail: Sutton Coldfield. **Directions:** A5127 into Sutton Coldfield, turn
right at Odeon Cinema (Holland Road) and then first right into Coles Lane
ground is 150 yards on the left.

TAMWORTH

Ground: The Lamb Ground, Kettlebrook, Tamworth, B77 1AA
Phone: 0827-65798 **Nickname:** The Lambs **Founded:** 1933
Manager: Sammy Chung **Secretary:** Rod Hadley **Chairman:** Malcolm Jones
Colours: Red, Black, Black or Red **Change:** All Yellow
Ground Capacity: 2,500 (400) **Record:** 4,920 v Atherstone, 4/48
Rail: Tamworth.
Directions: A5 Watling Street to Two Gates, turn into Tamworth Road;
ground 1½ miles on left-hand side at Kettlebrook.

WESTON-SUPER-MARE

Ground: Woodspring Park, Winterstoke Road, Weston-super-Mare, BS22 8JP
Phone: 0934-21618   **Nickname:** not known   **Founded:** 1948
Manager: John Ellenor   **Secretary:** GD Milson   **Chairman:** Paul Bliss
Colours: White, Blue, Blue   **Change:** Yellow, Black, Yellow
Ground Capacity: 4,000 (500)   **Record:** 692 v Cheltenham 1987
Rail: Weston-super-Mare (1 mile from ground).
Directions: M5 Junction 21. Follow Town Centre for three miles. Left at traffic lights (Herluin Way) opposite Mac's Garage. Follow to roundabout. Turn left, ground on right.

YATE TOWN

Ground: Lodge Road, Yate, Bristol, BS17 5LE
Phone: 0454-228103   **Nickname:** Bluebells   **Founded:** 1946
Manager: Peter Jackson   **Secretary:** Terry Tansley   **Chairman:** R. Hawkins
Colours: White, Navy, White   **Change:** All Red
Ground Capacity: 2,000 (200)   **Record:** 2,000 v Bristol Rvrs, Test. 1990
Rail: Parkway Bristol (5 miles from ground).
Directions: M4 Junction 18. Take A46 signposted Stroud, filter left on to A432 at first set of lights towards Yate. Ground is signposted from Yate Ring Road.

SOUTHERN DIVISION

Final Table 1991-92

	P	W	D	L	F	A	Pts
Hastings Town	42	28	7	7	80	37	91
Weymouth	42	22	12	8	64	35	78
Havant Town	42	21	12	9	67	46	75
Braintree Town	42	21	8	13	77	58	71
* Buckingham Town	42	19	15	8	57	26	69
Andover	42	18	10	14	73	68	64
Ashford Town	42	17	12	13	66	57	63
Sudbury Town	42	18	9	15	70	66	63
† Sittingbourne	42	19	10	13	63	41	61
Burnham	42	15	14	13	57	55	59
Baldock Town	42	16	10	16	62	67	58
Salisbury	42	13	16	13	67	51	55
Hythe Town	42	15	10	17	61	62	55
Margate	42	13	16	13	49	56	55
Newport IoW	42	13	10	19	58	63	49
Dunstable	42	12	12	18	55	67	48
Bury Town	42	14	4	24	52	94	46
Witney Town	42	11	12	19	55	76	45
Fareham Town	42	12	8	22	45	71	44
Erith & Belvedere	42	11	10	21	44	67	43
Canterbury City	42	8	14	20	43	69	38
Gosport Borough	42	6	9	27	32	65	27

* Three points deducted † six points deducted (ineligible players)

Leading Southern League Goalscorers
Odey, P. (Andover) 29; Clarke, K. (Witney Town) 22; Tate, S. (Havant Town) 21; Arter, D. (Sittingbourne) 19; Smith, J. (Salisbury) 19.

Promotions and Relegations

Club	Position	Movement
Hastings Town	Champions	Promoted to Premier Division
Weymouth	Runners-up	Promoted to Premier Division
Hythe Town	13th	Resigned
Gosport Borough	22nd	Relegated to Wessex League
Fisher Athletic		Relegated from Premier Division
Gravesend & Northfleet		Relegated from Premier Division
Poole Town		Relegated from Premier Division
Wealdstone		Relegated from Premier Division

Leading League Goalscorers by Club

Club	Top scorers
Andover	Odey 29; Bale 9; Cenci 8.
Ashford Town	McRobert 15; Stanton 15; Nohilly 10.
Baldock Town	Shrieves 8; Phillips 7; Williams 7.
Braintree Town	Grice 14; Jefferies 10; England 8.
Buckingham Town	Jenkins 13; Pearson 10; Blencowe 7.
Burnham	Chandler 11; Algrave 8; Lindo 7.
Bury Town	Lee 12; Collins 9; Lee 9.
Canterbury City	Harmer 7; Neate 6; Holmes 5; Scott 5.
Dunstable	Campbell 9; Revell 7; Wheeler 7.
Erith & Belvedere	Hoyte 11; Mehmet 10; Coupland 4; Docker 4.
Fareham Town	Green 11; Taylor 11; Iannone 5.
Gosport Borough	Goater 7; Benson 4; Tavener 3.
Hastings Town	Miles 14; Giles 13; Wynter 9.
Havant Town	Tate 20; Webb 11; Sherry 8.
Hythe Town	Arter 21; Carey 5; Myers 5.
Margate	Buglione 17; Brenton 6; Toms 4.
Newport IoW	Greening 17; Deacon 12; Ritchie 7.
Salisbury	Smith 13; Gommershall 11; Chalk 10.
Sittingbourne	Jordan 14; Bourne 9; Freeman 9.
Sudbury Town	Parnell 13; Barker 9; Smith 9.
Weymouth	Cooke 17; Clifford 14; Brown 5; Daiz 5.
Witney Town	Clarke 21; Mills 12; Flannery 5.

Sportique Manager of the Month Awards

Month	Manager	Club
August	Lee Drake	Weymouth
September	Keith Baker	Buckingham Town
October	Peter Sillett	Hastings Town
November	Mark Weatherley	Margate
December	Tony Mount	Havant Town
January	Peter Collins/	
	Brian Honeywood	Braintree Town
February	John Ryan	Sittingbourne
March	Tony Mount	Havant Town

SOUTHERN DIVISION RESULTS 1991-92

	Andover	Ashford Town	Baldock Town	Braintree Town	Buckingham T	Burnham	Bury Town	Canterbury C	Dunstable	Erith & Bel	Fareham Town
Andover	•	0-2	2-0	2-5	2-4	2-1	1-2	7-1	3-1	2-0	0-2
Ashford Town	2-2	•	2-2	3-1	0-0	1-1	0-3	1-1	1-1	2-1	1-0
Baldock Town	2-3	1-0	•	1-3	0-0	2-1	3-2	4-3	2-1	2-0	3-0
Braintree Town	1-0	2-0	5-0	•	0-2	4-3	1-3	1-2	7-0	2-1	2-2
Buckingham Town	3-0	0-3	2-0	0-0	•	2-2	5-1	3-0	2-1	1-0	1-0
Burnham	0-0	0-0	2-2	2-1	0-0	•	2-3	1-0	1-2	2-1	1-0
Bury Town	2-0	2-1	1-2	0-4	0-3	1-0	•	0-0	2-5	3-1	3-1
Canterbury City	3-3	0-2	1-6	3-4	1-1	0-1	1-1	•	1-1	1-0	1-1
Dunstable	1-1	1-2	1-1	1-3	0-0	3-1	2-0	1-0	•	1-0	2-1
Erith & Belvedere	0-2	1-1	0-2	2-0	0-0	1-1	0-0	1-0	0-0	•	3-3
Fareham Town	1-2	1-3	3-0	1-2	0-3	2-3	1-2	3-2	1-5	1-0	•
Gosport Borough	2-0	0-2	3-0	0-2	1-2	0-0	2-1	0-1	0-2	0-1	2-0
Hastings Town	2-1	1-0	1-0	1-0	0-0	0-1	2-1	0-0	3-0	1-1	2-0
Havant Town	1-1	1-0	0-0	3-0	0-3	1-1	5-0	3-1	4-2	1-2	1-0
Hythe Town	1-2	3-1	0-0	2-2	2-0	1-3	3-1	1-0	0-4	1-3	1-1
Margate	0-3	2-2	1-1	1-3	1-1	1-2	1-0	1-0	0-0	5-0	2-2
Newport IoW	0-0	3-2	3-1	0-2	0-0	2-2	4-1	2-2	2-1	0-1	3-0
Salisbury	1-2	1-3	2-3	2-1	0-0	0-0	5-0	3-1	1-2	4-2	0-1
Sittingbourne	3-1	3-2	1-0	4-0	0-3	0-1	3-0	2-0	2-2	2-3	1-0
Sudbury Town	1-3	6-1	4-3	1-2	1-0	1-1	4-0	3-3	0-2	1-1	0-1
Weymouth	1-3	2-1	0-0	0-1	1-0	2-2	5-0	2-0	3-0	4-1	3-0
Witney Town	2-2	0-2	2-0	0-1	1-1	0-2	3-6	1-1	2-2	1-0	2-1

	Gosport Boro	Hastings Town	Havant Town	Hythe Town	Margate	Newport IoW	Salisbury	Sittingbourne	Sudbury Town	Weymouth	Witney Town
Andover	0-0	3-1	3-1	2-7	1-3	2-2	1-1	3-2	1-2	3-0	2-1
Ashford Town	2-0	3-4	0-2	2-1	1-1	2-1	2-2	3-1	5-3	0-0	3-0
Baldock Town	1-4	2-1	1-1	2-3	2-1	2-0	1-1	2-3	0-3	2-1	4-1
Braintree Town	1-2	0-2	4-2	1-1	1-1	3-1	2-0	1-1	1-1	0-0	1-0
Buckingham Town	1-1	0-1	2-0	3-1	0-2	1-0	0-0	1-0	5-0	0-2	3-1
Burnham	3-2	1-2	0-0	3-1	1-0	1-3	3-2	3-2	0-2	1-2	2-3
Bury Town	0-3	1-3	4-1	0-3	1-2	1-0	0-3	1-3	1-0	1-2	1-4
Canterbury City	2-0	1-2	0-0	1-0	2-0	1-0	1-3	0-0	0-1	0-1	2-2
Dunstable	0-1	0-4	1-2	1-0	0-0	3-1	1-1	0-1	0-2	0-1	2-2
Erith & Belvedere	2-1	2-2	1-3	2-1	1-3	1-4	0-1	0-3	1-2	0-1	3-1
Fareham Town	2-4	0-2	1-0	0-0	1-1	1-0	0-4	2-1	3-2	1-1	2-1
Gosport Borough	•	0-1	1-1	2-1	4-0	2-2	0-3	0-3	0-2	0-1	1-1
Hastings Town	4-0	•	2-1	2-3	3-1	1-0	2-1	1-1	3-0	1-2	1-1
Havant Town	2-1	3-2	•	3-1	0-1	1-0	3-1	1-0	2-2	0-1	4-1
Hythe Town	2-0	2-1	3-3	•	2-0	2-2	3-1	0-2	1-3	1-1	3-1
Margate	0-1	1-1	0-0	2-0	•	3-1	1-0	0-0	0-2	1-1	4-4
Newport IoW	3-1	0-3	0-2	1-1	0-1	•	1-0	0-1	4-0	1-1	1-0
Salisbury	3-2	1-1	0-0	1-2	5-1	2-2	•	0-2	0-0	2-2	3-1
Sittingbourne	0-0	2-0	0-1	2-1	1-1	0-2	2-2	•	3-0	2-1	1-0
Sudbury Town	1-0	1-2	0-0	2-1	4-0	4-2	1-3	1-6	•	2-0	0-0
Weymouth	0-0	1-2	0-0	3-1	3-0	0-0	1-0	0-0	5-3	•	5-1
Witney Town	2-0	1-2	2-2	2-0	0-0	4-2	0-3	0-0	1-0	2-1	•

SOUTHERN DIVISION CLUBS

ANDOVER

Ground: The Portway Stadium, West Portway IE, Andover, Hants, SP10 3LF
Phone: 0264-333052   **Nickname:** The Lions   **Founded:** 1883
Manager: Steve Mellor   **Secretary:** David Macey   **Chairman:** A.F. Baker
Colours: Red and Black, Black, Red **Change:** Tangerine, White, Tangerine
Ground Capacity: 3,000 (250)   **Record:** 3,484 v Gillingham, FAC1 1962
Rail: Andover.
Directions: The ground is located on the western outskirts of the town, adjacent to the West Portway Industrial Estate. Follow any road signs to Portway Industrial.

ASHFORD TOWN

Ground: The Homelands, Ashford Road, Kingsnorth, Ashford, Kent, TN26 1NJ
Phone: 0233-61183   **Nickname:** Nuts & Bolts   **Founded:** 1930
Manager: Neil Cugley   **Secretary:** A. Lancaster   **Chairman:** K. Cunningham
Colours: White with Green Trim, Green, Green and White **Change:** All Yellow
Ground Capacity: 5,000 (500)   **Record:** not known
Rail: Ashford (3 miles from ground).
Directions: Off A2070 4 miles south of Ashford town centre. Approach Ashford A20 from Maidstone, at second roundabout take Tenterden A28 – after 1 mile turn left at Tesco roundabout into Brookfield Road (B2229) to traffic lights and turn right into Kingsnorth Road (A2070). Continue for 2 miles through Kingsnort; ground is on left at illuminated bollards.

BALDOCK TOWN

Ground: Norton Road, Baldock, Herts
Phone: 0462-89544   **Nickname:** Reds   **Founded:** 1889
Manager: Ian Allinson **Secretary:** Don Swain **Chairman:** Ray Childerstone
Colours: Red, White, Red   **Change:** All Yellow
Ground Capacity: 2,900 (200)   **Record:** 1,200 v Arsenal, f.o. 1983
Rail: Baldock.
Directions: On main A505 Hitchin to Baldock road. Turn left into Norton Road, left after Orange Tree public house, ground on right after railway bridge.

BRAINTREE TOWN

Ground: Cressing Road Stadium, Clockhouse Way, Braintree, Essex
Phone: 0376-345617   **Nickname:** The Iron   **Founded:** 1894
Manager: Peter Collins/Brian Honeywood   **Secretary:** T. Woodley
Chairman: G. Rosling
Colours: Yellow and Blue   **Change:** All Blue or All White
Ground Capacity: 4,000 (292)   **Record:** 4,000 v Spurs, Charity, 5/52
Rail: Braintree & Bocking (1 mile from ground).
Directions: A12 to Witham; follow B1018 to Braintree. Take first left after
The Sportsman Snooker Club, then left again. Entrance on left.

BUCKINGHAM TOWN

Ground: Ford Meadow, Ford Street, Buckingham, Bucks
Phone: 0280-816257   **Nickname:** The Robins   **Founded:** 1883
Manager: Keith Barber   **Secretary:** E.J. Seaton   **Chairman:** C.D. Lawrence
Colours: All Red   **Change:** All White
Ground Capacity: 2,000 (150)   **Record:** 2,500 v Orient, FAC1 1984
Rail: Milton Keynes.
Directions: From town centre take Aylesbury A413 out of town. Turn right at
Phillips garage (about 400 yards).

BURNHAM

Ground: Wymers Wood Road, Burnham, Slough, Bucks, SL1 8JG
Phone: 0628-602567   **Nickname:** The Blues   **Founded:** 1876
Manager: Colin Barnes   **Secretary:** David Eavis   **Chairman:** Malcolm Higton
Colours: Blue and White, Blue, White   **Change:** Red and White, Red, Red
Ground Capacity: 4,000 (100)   **Record:** 2,451 v Orient, FAC 1984/5
Rail: Burnham.
Directions: North-west of village centre, 2 miles from M4, Junction 7.

BURY TOWN

Ground: Ram Meadow, Cotton Lane, Bury St. Edmunds
Phone: 0284-754721/754820   **Nickname:** The Blues   **Founded:** 1872
Manager: Chris Symes   **Secretary:** Mike Parker   **Chairman:** Vic Clark
Colours: Blue and White   **Change:** Red, Black, Red
Ground Capacity: 3,500 (200)   **Record:** 2,500 v Enfield, FAC4Q 86
Rail: Bury St Edmunds.   **Directions:** Leave A45 by second exit towards
central Bury St Edmunds and take third exit at roundabout. Take first exit at
next roundabout into Northgate Street. At second set of traffic lights turn left
into Mustow Street and immediately left again into Cotton Lane. Ground is
300 yards on right through coach/car park.

CANTERBURY CITY

Ground: Kingsmead Stadium, Kingsmead Road, Canterbury, Kent, CT2 7PH
Phone: 0227-464732   **Nickname:** City   **Founded:** 1947
Manager: Les Hall   **Secretary:** Richard Tolson   **Chairman:** Derek Owen
Colours: Royal Blue and White, Royal Blue and two White Hoops.
Change: Green and White, Green, Green.
Ground Capacity: 5,000 (500)   **Record:** 3,001 v Torquay, FAC1 1964
Rail: Canterbury East or West.
Directions: From London just off M2 and A2, follow signs for A28 into Kingsmead Road. Ground opposite swimming pool.

DUNSTABLE

Ground: Creasey Park, Brewers Hill Road, Dunstable, Beds.
Phone: 0582-606691   **Nickname:** The Blues   **Founded:** 1895
Manager: John Wortley   **Secretary:** Doug Simpson   **Chairman:** A. Fieldhouse
Colours: Blue and White Quarters, Blue, White   **Change:** All Red
Ground Capacity: 5,000 (200)   **Record:** 6,000 v Man. Utd, 1974
Rail: Luton.
Directions: Brewers Hill Road runs west from A505 at the north end of Dunstable, at large traffic island turn right.

ERITH & BELVEDERE

Ground: Park View, Lower Road, Belvedere, Kent, DA17 6DF
Phone: 081-311-4444   **Nickname:** The Deres   **Founded:** 1922
Manager: Harry Richardson   **Secretary:** David Joy   **Chairman:** E. Powell
Colours: Blue and White, Blue, White   **Change:** All Red
Ground Capacity: 6,000 (250)   **Record:** 8,000 v Coventry City, FAC 1932
Rail: Belvedere.
Directions: Entrance in Station Road, off Lower Road, adjacent to Belvedere (BR) Station.

FAREHAM TOWN

Ground: Cams Allders, Highfield Avenue, Fareham, Hants, PO14 1JA
Phone: 0329-231151   **Nickname:** Town   **Founded:** 1947
Manager: Harry Miller   **Secretary:** K.F. Atkins   **Chairman:** R.A. Grant
Colours: Red, White, Red   **Change:** White, Black, White
Ground Capacity: 5,500 (300)
Record (Club): 6,035 v Kidderminster, FATsf 1987 (at The Dell, Soton)
Rail: Fareham.   **Directions:** From Fareham railway station take A27 towards Southampton. Second turning left into Redlands Lane, turn right at Redlands Inn into St Michaels Grove, and then first left into Highfield Avenue.

FISHER ATHLETIC

Ground: Surrey Docks Stadium, Salter Road, London, SE16 1LQ
Phone: 071-237-1432   **Nickname:** The Fish   **Founded:** 1908
Manager: Jimmy Quinn   **Secretary:** M. Vigus   **Chairman:** P. Woolf
Colours: Black and White Stripes, White, Black & White **Change:** All Red
Ground Capacity: 5,300 (400)   **Record:** 4,283 v Barnet, GMVC 5/91
Rail: 400yds from Rotherhithe Underground Station.
Directions: Near south-side entrance to Rotherhithe Tunnel.

GRAVESEND & NORTHFLEET

Ground: Stonebridge Road, Northfleet, Gravesend, Kent, DA11 9BA
Phone: 0474-533796   **Nickname:** The Fleet   **Founded:** 1946
Manager: Gary Aldous   **Secretary:** Stephen Jones   **Chairman:** L. Ball
Colours: Red, White, Red   **Change:** White, Black, White
Ground Capacity: 9,750 (4,000) **Record:** 12,036 v Sunderland, FAC4 1963
Rail: Northfleet.
Directions: From Dartford Tunnel follow A226 to Northfleet or A2
(Northfleet turn-off B262). Pick up B2175 to junction with A226, turn left,
ground about 1 mile on right-hand side at bottom of hill.

HAVANT TOWN

Ground: Westleigh Park, Martin Road, Havant, Hants
Phone: 0705-455465   **Nickname:** not known   **Founded:** 1958
Manager: Tony Mount   **Secretary:** T. Brock   **Chairman:** R. Jones
Colours: Yellow, Black, Yellow and Black   **Change:** Green, White, White
Ground Capacity: 3,000 (214)   **Record:** 3,000 v Wisbech, FA Vase 1985/6
Rail: Havant (1 mile from ground).
Directions: M27, A27 B2149 to Havant. Right into Bartons Road, then first
right into Martin Road.

MARGATE

Ground: Hartsdown Park, Hartsdown Road, Margate, Kent, CT9 5QZ
Phone: 0843-221769   **Nickname:** Gat   **Founded:** 1880
Manager: Mark Waetherley **Secretary:** K. Tomlinson   **Chairman:** G. Wallis
Colours: Royal Blue and White, Royal Blue, Royal Blue **Change:** All White
Ground Capacity: 8,500 (400)   **Record:** 8,500 v Spurs, FAC3 1/73
Rail: Margate.
Directions: Follow A28 to Margate, turn right opposite hospital at pedestrian
lights into Hartsdown Road, proceed over crossroads and the ground is on the
left.

NEWPORT IoW

Ground: St. Georges Pk, St. Georges Way, Newport, Isle of Wight, PO30 4BA
Phone: 0983-525027   **Nickname:** not known   **Founded:** 1888
Manager: J. Horne   **Secretary:** C.R. Cheverton   **Chairman:** K. Newbery
Colours: Gold, Royal Blue, Gold   **Change:** White, Red, White
Ground Capacity: 5,000 (300)   **Record:** 2,500 v Fulham, g.o. 1988
Rail: Ryde Esplanade.
Directions: Roads from all ferry ports lead to Coppins Bridge roundabout at eastern extremity of town. Take Sandown/Ventnor exit, continue to next roundabout and take first exit for St Georges Way.

POOLE TOWN

Ground: Poole Stadium, Wimborne Road, Poole, Dorset, BH15 2BP
Phone: 0202-674747   **Nickname:** The Dolphins   **Founded:** 1880
Manager: Brian Chambers **Secretary:** Barry Hughes **Chairman:** Derek Block
Colours: All Blue   **Change:** Yellow, Blue, Yellow
Ground Capacity: 6,000 (1,250)   **Record:** 11,155 v Watford, FAC 1962/3
Rail: Poole.
Directions: Close to the centre of Poole and near railway station

SALISBURY

Ground: Victoria Park, Castle Road, Salisbury, Wiltshire, SP1 3ER
Phone: 0722-336689   **Nickname:** The Whites   **Founded:** 1947
Manager: Geoff Butler   **Secretary:** S. Gallagher   **Chairman:** P. McEnhill
Colours: White, Black, Black   **Change:** All Blue
Ground Capacity: 4,600 (200)   **Record:** 8,900 v Weymouth, Western Lge 48
Rail: Salisbury.
Directions: From city centre take A345 towards Amesbury. Victoria Park is located on the left as you leave the city.

SITTINGBOURNE

Ground: Central Park, Eurolink, Sittingbourne, Kent.
Phone: 0795-475547   **Nickname:** Bourne   **Founded:** 1881
Manager: John Ryan   **Secretary:** I. Kingsnorth   **Chairman:** M. Fletcher
Colours: Red with Black Trim, White, Red   **Change:** White and Green
Ground Capacity: 2,800 (200)   **Record:** not known
Rail: Sittingbourne (½ mile from ground).
Directions: A2 to Sittingbourne. Well signposted from all directions.

SUDBURY TOWN

Ground: Priory Stadium, Priory Walk, Sudbury, Suffolk
Phone: 0787-79095   **Nickname:** not known   **Founded:** 1898
Managers: Richie Powling **Secretary:** David Webb **Chairman:** not known
Colours: All Yellow   **Change:** All Red
Ground Capacity: 5,000 (200)   **Record:** 4,700 v Ipswich, Test. 1978
Rail: Sudbury.   **Directions:** From town centre proceed along Friars Street, passing the cricket ground, until the Ship and Star public house. Turn left into Priory Walk and follow this road down to the ground.

WEALDSTONE

Ground: Vicarage Road, Watford, Herts, WD1 8ER
Phone: 0923-21296   **Nickname:** Stones **Founded:** 1906
Manager: Brian Hall **Secretary:** Peter Braxton **Chairman:** David Pollock
Colours: White / Blue Trim, White, Blue   **Change:** Yellow, Royal Blue, Yellow
Ground Capacity: 3,000 (496) **Record:** 13,504 v Leytonstone , FAAmC 1949
Rail: Harrow-on-the-Hill (Underground – Metropolitan line).
Directions: From M1 leave at Junction 5 and follow North Watford signs and then signs to football ground.

WITNEY TOWN

Ground: Marriot's Close, Welch Way, Witney, Oxon, OX8 7AE
Phone: 0993-702549/705930 **Nickname:** not known   **Founded:** 1885
Manager: Malcolm McIntosh **Secretary:** C. Miles **Chairman:** A. Oakey
Colours: Yellow, Royal Blue, Royal Blue   **Change:** Blue, White, White
Ground Capacity: 2,000 (200) **Record:** 800 v Billericay, 5/76
Rail: Oxford.
Directions: Situated off the A40 (12 miles west of Oxford), the ground is sited near the town centre and adjacent to a public car park.

HFS LOANS LEAGUE

Stalybridge's Mean Machine

Following the runaway successes of Witton Albion and Colne Dynamoes in the past two seasons, this 91-92 HFS Loans Premier Division title chase threatened to be a much closer-fought affair, with no fewer than four clubs, Frickley Athletic, Buxton, Leek Town and Goole Town, all having held top spot by the middle of October. When Stalybridge Celtic became the fifth team to head the Division on 29 October, their sheer consistency meant they were never to be headed again, eventually clinching the title in anti-climatic fashion on Easter Monday when they lost their unbeaten home record in a 1-2 defeat at the hands of local rivals Hyde United. They owed much of their success to a mean defence which conceded just 26 goals in the first 38 games; while up-front, Chris "Buffalo" Camden had netted 37 goals by the end of February. With the title in the bag, Stalybridge picked up only three points out of the last 12, otherwise their winning margin would have been even more than the 14 points they had to spare. Nevertheless, Celtic equalled the League record of only two defeats set by Wigan Athletic in 1970.

Celtic's nearest challengers, Marine, lost their chance of the Championship with a glorious run in the FA Trophy, where they just lost out to last season's HFS Loans Champions, Witton Albion, in the semi-final. Roly Howard's outfit also reached the final of the HFS Loans Challenge Cup and, for a long time, it looked as if they could finish a highly successful campaign with nothing to show for their efforts until Eddie Murray scored the only goal of the game against Frickley in the 86th minute. Pre-season favourites in many pundits' eyes were Southport and Morecambe, but both blew their chances early on, with Southport winning only one of their first ten matches and Morecambe faring only slightly better with five wins in their first 13 games. Morecambe, in my view as good as any team in the League, at least had the satisfaction of beating Stalybridge in the President's Cup final with two great goals from their two class strikers, Steve Holden and John Coleman. Strangely, this was Morecambe's first-ever success during their 24-year membership of the HFS Loans League.

In the First Division, the newly promoted clubs, Knowsley United, Guiseley and Colwyn Bay, all had successful seasons. Although they were eventually to finish the lowest of the three, Knowsley made surely the most telling start to the season of any club in the country, marking their debut in the HFS with a goal inside 30 seconds and another three in the next five minutes! Like Marine in the Premier, a backlog of fixtures, due to cup runs which saw them in the FA Cup first round and a return trip to Wembley in the FA Vase, cost Guiseley dearly in the League. Colwyn Bay took the First

Division Cup, defeating Worksop in the final despite a magnificent goal from Kenny Clark, and reached the semi-final of the Welsh Cup before finishing a remarkable season by taking the First Division title when Winsford United, whose manager Mike McKenzie became such a local hero he was invited to switch on the town's Christmas lights, slipped up in their final home match of the season.

On the minus side, over a third of the clubs changed managers in the ever-elusive search for success, the shadow of the League of Wales hung over the League's five Welsh clubs, and Irlam Town resigned immediately they had completed their fixtures due to mounting financial problems. Once again, however, many players left the HFS ranks to make an immediate impact in the Football League, demonstrating the strength there is in the League. Fleetwood Town pocketed nearly £50,000 from the sale of Phil Clarkson and Steve Macauley to Crewe Alexandra and Bridlington Town gained a similar amount from the sale of striker Mike Norbury to Cambridge United. *Phil Bradley.*

The Northern Premier League History

The Northern Premier League was formed in 1968 with 20 clubs drawn from the Cheshire County League (7), Lancashire Combination (5), Midland League (4), North Regional League (3) and the West Midlands (Regional) League (1). In 1970-71 the League comprised 22 clubs, later increasing to 24 but returning to 22 by the end of the 1970s. A second division of 19 clubs was added in 1987-88, which increased to 22 the following season.

Promotion to and relegation from the League has always been a feature of its structure, while, since the formation of the Alliance Premier League, a team is normally promoted to that League in exchange for a relegated club.

Once known as the Multipart League, it has been known as the HFS Loans League since 1988-89.

5-Year One, Two, Three Records

	1st	Pts	2nd	Pts	3rd	Pts
1986-87	Macclesfield T	88	Bangor City	87	Caernarfon Town	76

Premier Division

	1st	Pts	2nd	Pts	3rd	Pts
1987-88	Chorley	88	Hyde United	85	Caernarfon Town	76
1988-89	Barrow	87	Hyde United	80	Witton Albion	79
1989-90	Colne Dynamoes	102	Gateshead	76	Witton Albion	73
1990-91	Witton Albion	93	Stalybridge C	77	Morecambe	73

First Division

	1st	Pts	2nd	Pts	3rd	Pts
1987-88	Fleetwood Town	73	Stalybridge C.	72	Leek Town	70
1988-89	Colne Dynamoes	98	B. Auckland	89	Leek Town	85
1989-90	Leek Town	86	Droylsden	80	Accrington St	76
1990-91	Whitley Bay	85	Emley	84	Worksop Town	82

LEAGUE CUP

Preliminary Round
Alfreton Town v Netherfield.................1-2
Congleton Town v Workington 2-1

1st Round
Colwyn Bay v Rhyl.............................1-1
   Replay......................................7-0
Farsley Celtic v Bridlington Town........4-2
Guiseley v Congleton Town..................2-0
Knowsley United v Eastwood Town......3-1
Lancaster City v Harrogate Town.........0-3
Radcliffe Borough v Caernarfon Town..4-1
Rossendale United v Irlam Town...........3-0
Warrington Town v Curzon Ashton......0-0
   Replay......................................0-1
Winsford United v Newtown 4-1
Worksop Town v Netherfield................1-0

2nd Round
Accrington Stanley v Southport............1-2
Bishop Auckland v Hyde United 1-0
Chorley v Winsford United 2-0
Colwyn Bay v Matlock Town...............1-2
Curzon Ashton v Farsley Celtic 6-2
Fleetwood Town v Emley 1-0
Frickley Athletic v Worksop Town........2-1
Guiseley v Bangor City 6-2
Harrogate Town v Buxton....................1-2
Knowsley United v Horwich................2-1
Marine v Gainsborough Trinity 2-0
Morecambe v Shepshed Albion 3-1
Radcliffe Borough v Goole Town.........0-2
Rossendale United v Mossley 2-1
Stalybridge Celtic v Leek Town 4-1
Whitley Bay v Droylsden.....................1-0

3rd Round
Buxton v Knowsley United 3-2
Curzon Ashton v Bishop Auckland.......4-3
Frickley Athletic v Whitley Bay 2-1
Goole Town v Southport......................1-0
Morecambe v Guiseley 1-1
   Replay...................................† 3-3
   (Guiseley won 4-2 on penalties)
Rossendale United v Matlock Town 1-1

   Replay......................................0-1
Stalybridge Celtic v Fleetwood Town...5-0
Winsford United v Marine 1-3

4th Round
Buxton v Guiseley...............................1-2
Curzon Ashton v Marine 2-3
Matlock Town v Goole Town 3-2
Stalybridge Celtic v Frickley Athletic....0-2

Semi-Final 1st Leg
Guiseley v Marine 1-0
Matlock Town v Frickley Athletic.........3-2

Semi-Final 2nd Leg
Marine v Guiseley 2-0
   (Marine won 2-1 on aggregate)
Frickley Athletic v Matlock Town...... †1-0
   *(Aggregate score 3-3, Frickley won on
away goals rule)*

Final
at Manchester City FC
Marine...1
   Murray
Frickley Athletic.................................0
   Att: 864

† after extra time

PRESIDENT'S CUP

1st Round

Eastwood Town v Buxton.................2-1
Emley v Fleetwood Town...............0-0
   Replay.................................3-2
Marine v Warrington Town...........2-1
Morecambe v Lancaster City.........2-0
Rhyl v Leek Town.......................0-2
Southport v Worksop Town...........2-3
Stalybridge Celtic v Acc. Stanley......3-0
Whitley Bay v Bishop Auckland......0-0
   Replay.................................1-2

2nd Round

Bishop Auckland v Emley...........4-0
Eastwood Town v Stalybridge Celtic 0-2
Marine v Morecambe..................1-1
   Replay.............................†3-4
Worksop Town v Leek Town..........3-5

† after extra time

Semi-Final 1st Leg

Stalybridge Celtic v B. Auckland......3-2
Leek Town v Morecambe...............0-0

Semi-Final 2nd Leg

B. Auckland v Stalybridge Celtic......0-1
   (Stalybridge won 4-2 on aggregate)
Morecambe v Leek Town...............2-0
   (Morecambe won 2-0 on aggregate)

Final 1st Leg

Morecambe.....................................1
   Holden
Stalybridge Celtic..............................2
   Brown, Edwards   Att: 511

Final 2nd Leg

Stalybridge Celtic................................0
Morecambe..2
   Holden, Coleman   Att: 713
   (Morecambe won 3-2 on aggregate)

FIRST DIVISION CUP

1st Round

Caernarfon Town v Farsley Celtic...2-1
Curzon Ashton v Irlam Town.........2-1
Guiseley v Radcliffe Borough.........2-2
   Replay.................................1-2
Knowsley United v Bridlington Town 4-1
Rhyl v Winsford United................0-2
Rossendale United v Eastwood Town 4-1

2nd Round

Colwyn Bay v Caernarfon Town......2-0
Congleton Town v Worksop Town...2-4
Knowsley United v Curzon Ashton...3-4
Lancaster City v Workington.........0-2
Newton v Harrogate Town............4-0
Radcliffe Borough v Netherfield.....1-5
Rossendale United v Winsford United 4-2
Warrington Town v Alfreton Town...4-0

3rd Round

Colwyn Bay v Netherfield.............5-2

Curzon Ashton v Workington.........2-0
Rossendale United v Newton..........4-4
   Replay.............................† 2-2
   (Newton won 4-3 on penalties)
Worksop Town v Warrington Town...2-0

Semi-Final 1st Leg

Newton v Colwyn Bay..................0-2
Worksop Town v Curzon Ashton......2-1

Semi-Final 2nd Leg

Colwyn Bay v Newton..................5-0
   (Colwyn Bay won 7-0 on aggregate)
Curzon Ashton v Worksop Town......2-2
   (Worksop won 4-3 on aggregate)

Final

at Stalybridge Celtic FC
Colwyn Bay..3
   Cooke, Donnelly, Williscroft
Worksop Town.....................................1
   Clark   Att: 278   † after extra time

PREMIER DIVISION

Final Table 1991-92

	P	W	D	L	F	A	Pts
Stalybridge Celtic	42	26	14	2	84	33	92
Marine	42	23	9	10	64	32	78
Morecambe	42	21	13	8	70	44	76
Leek Town	42	21	10	11	62	49	73
Buxton	42	21	9	12	65	47	72
Emley	42	18	11	13	69	47	65
Southport	42	16	17	9	57	48	65
Accrington Stanley	42	17	12	13	78	62	63
Hyde United	42	17	9	16	69	67	60
Fleetwood Town	42	17	8	17	67	64	59
Bishop Auckland	42	16	9	17	48	58	57
Goole Town	42	15	9	18	60	72	54
Horwich RMI	42	13	14	15	44	52	53
Frickley Athletic	42	12	16	14	61	57	52
Droylsden	42	12	14	16	62	72	50
Mossley	42	15	4	23	51	73	49
Whitley Bay	42	13	9	20	53	79	48
Gainsborough Trinity	42	11	13	18	48	63	46
Matlock Town	42	12	9	21	59	87	45
Bangor City	42	11	10	21	46	57	43
Chorley	42	11	9	22	61	82	42
Shepshed Albion	42	6	8	28	46	79	26

Leading Premier Division Goalscorers

40	Chris Camden	Stalybridge Celtic
31	Steve Holden	Morecambe
28	Brian Ross	Marine
25	John Coleman	Morecambe
21	Paul Beck	Accrington Stanley
20	Craig Maden	Fleetwood Town
	Eric Priest	Stalybridge Celtic
19	Jimmy Clarke	Buxton
	Paul Kirkham	Hyde United
17	Steve Bunter	Buxton
	Ian Chandler	Goole Town
	Peter Collier	Goole Town (now Bridlington)

Annual Awards 1991-92
Premier Division
Manager of the Year	Roley Howard	Marine
Player of the Year	John Aspinall	Stalybridge Celtic
Goalscorer of the Year	Chris Campden	Stalybridge Celtic

First Division
Manager of the Year	Bryn Jones	Colwyn Bay
Player of the Year	Kenny Clark	Worksop Town
Goalscorer of the Year	Kenny Clark	Worksop Town

Premier Division Awards
Mail On Sunday Manager of the Month Awards
Month	Manager	Club
September	Phil Wilson	Stalybridge Celtic
October	Roly Howard	Marine
November	Harry Dunn	Bishop Auckland
December	Ken Wright	Horwich RMI
January	Phil Wilson	Stalybridge Celtic
February	Phil Stanley	Accrington Stanley
March	Phil Wilson	Stalybridge Celtic
April	Gerry Quinn	Emley

Mail On Sunday Player of the Month Awards
Month	Player	Club
September	Brendan Burke	Mossley
October	Ray Redshaw	Horwich RMI
November	Phil Chadwick	Hyde United
December	Peter Collier	Goole Town
January	Carl Dyson	Chorley
February	Nick Tilly	Matlock Town
March	Steve Haydock	Fleetwood
April	John Aspinall	Stalybridge Celtic

PREMIER DIVISION RESULTS 1991-92

	Accrington St	Bangor City	Bishop Auck	Buxton	Chorley	Droylsden	Emley	Fleetwood Tn	Frickley Ath	Gainsboro Tr	Goole Town
Accrington Stanley	•	1-0	2-2	1-1	3-2	2-2	2-1	3-0	2-1	1-1	4-0
Bangor City	4-3	•	1-1	0-1	1-1	4-0	2-0	0-2	1-2	1-3	2-0
Bishop Auckland	0-6	0-0	•	2-0	3-0	1-0	1-1	3-0	1-0	3-1	1-2
Buxton	0-1	2-0	2-1	•	4-2	2-0	1-3	1-0	3-0	2-1	1-1
Chorley	2-1	4-3	1-0	0-2	•	1-2	0-1	1-0	2-2	3-1	4-4
Droylsden	3-2	2-0	1-2	0-0	2-0	•	4-0	1-4	4-2	0-0	3-2
Emley	3-1	0-2	4-1	1-2	5-0	1-2	•	4-0	2-0	6-0	2-0
Fleetwood Town	2-1	2-1	2-1	1-1	5-0	2-1	1-1	•	3-2	0-1	2-3
Frickley Athletic	1-1	2-1	3-4	1-1	3-1	1-1	0-0	3-2	•	0-0	1-2
Gainsborough Trinity	0-4	1-1	2-0	0-0	3-1	0-0	1-0	1-1	2-2	•	0-2
Goole Town	2-4	2-1	0-1	2-2	3-1	2-2	0-1	2-1	1-3	4-1	•
Horwich RMI	1-1	0-1	1-2	0-0	1-2	1-0	3-0	0-1	1-1	3-0	2-1
Hyde United	2-1	2-2	2-0	2-1	2-0	3-1	5-3	7-0	2-1	2-1	1-3
Leek Town	1-0	0-0	4-0	4-1	2-1	2-0	1-1	0-3	1-0	0-1	1-1
Marine	0-1	1-0	1-1	2-0	2-2	3-1	2-0	5-0	1-0	2-1	2-0
Matlock Town	0-4	2-0	0-1	0-2	2-2	3-2	0-3	1-1	1-1	1-3	4-1
Morecambe	4-1	3-0	0-1	2-1	1-0	1-0	0-1	1-2	2-0	1-1	1-1
Mossley	0-1	1-3	0-2	1-3	2-3	3-0	0-3	4-1	1-1	1-1	3-1
Shepshed Albion	4-0	0-0	0-0	2-3	1-1	2-3	3-2	0-1	1-3	2-2	0-1
Southport	2-2	4-0	3-0	2-1	3-3	1-1	2-3	1-0	3-2	3-0	1-1
Stalybridge Celtic	2-1	1-1	0-0	2-2	3-3	2-0	1-0	2-0	2-2	3-0	7-0
Whitley Bay	2-2	0-1	0-2	0-2	0-6	3-1	0-0	0-0	2-2	3-3	2-0

	Horwich RMI	Hyde United	Leek Town	Marine	Matlock Town	Morecambe	Mossley	Shepshed Alb	Southport	Stalybridge C	Whitley Bay
Accrington Stanley ...	1-1	1-1	1-0	0-3	2-2	3-1	5-1	3-1	1-1	0-3	3-2
Bangor City	1-2	2-2	0-1	0-2	2-3	0-1	4-0	1-0	1-1	0-1	1-2
Bishop Auckland ...	1-3	0-1	0-2	3-0	1-1	3-0	1-2	4-1	0-1	1-4	1-1
Buxton	5-0	2-0	3-0	0-3	3-1	1-3	1-3	1-0	1-0	1-2	3-1
Chorley	0-0	2-0	0-2	3-1	2-1	1-2	1-2	1-2	2-2	2-3	1-3
Droylsden	5-1	3-2	2-2	1-1	2-2	0-1	1-4	3-2	1-1	2-2	1-1
Emley	0-0	0-0	0-0	0-1	4-0	3-3	3-1	0-0	3-2	2-2	3-1
Fleetwood Town ...	0-2	5-1	2-2	0-0	4-0	1-1	3-1	2-0	5-1	0-2	5-0
Frickley Athletic ...	0-2	3-0	0-1	0-4	2-2	1-1	3-0	6-1	2-0	1-1	4-0
Gainsborough Trinity	4-0	1-0	1-2	0-0	0-1	5-1	0-1	3-1	0-2	3-1	1-3
Goole Town	1-0	0-1	1-2	1-2	3-0	0-2	3-1	0-1	2-1	1-1	1-0
Horwich RMI	•	0-2	1-1	1-0	2-1	2-2	4-1	0-0	1-1	0-0	0-1
Hyde United	1-1	•	1-0	0-4	1-3	0-4	3-2	3-1	4-0	1-2	2-0
Leek Town	3-1	3-3	•	3-2	3-3	0-1	3-2	3-0	3-0	2-3	3-0
Marine	2-1	2-0	3-0	•	1-3	0-1	2-1	4-3	1-1	0-0	5-3
Matlock Town	1-0	2-1	3-0	0-1	•	1-2	1-0	0-2	3-3	0-3	0-1
Morecambe	1-1	3-0	2-2	2-1	3-3	•	1-0	2-1	0-1	0-1	3-2
Mossley	1-1	1-1	1-2	0-1	0-1	1-4	•	0-1	0-0	0-1	0-1
Shepshed Albion ...	1-3	1-2	1-0	0-0	4-1	2-4	0-1	•	0-1	3-3	3-2
Southport	1-1	2-0	1-0	3-1	2-0	1-1	1-0	3-0	•	0-0	0-1
Stalybridge Celtic ...	2-0	1-2	1-0	0-1	4-0	1-0	5-0	2-1	1-0	•	3-1
Whitley Bay	1-3	4-1	0-3	2-2	3-1	1-1	2-1	2-1	1-2	0-2	•

PREMIER ATTENDANCES 1991-92

	Accrington St	Bangor City	B. Auckland	Buxton	Chorley	Droylsden	Emley	Fleetwood Tn	Frickley Ath	Gainsborough	Goole Town
Accrington Stanley	•	462	709	485	281	832	352	385	358	195	392
Bangor City	305	•	215	303	275	192	279	214	211	192	209
Bishop Auckland	247	199	•	221	249	251	357	206	414	434	229
Buxton	402	257	298	•	351	301	389	206	320	148	387
Chorley	340	301	289	279	•	206	197	334	322	203	273
Droylsden	423	310	213	304	307	•	333	201	241	605	203
Emley	389	354	453	345	558	465	•	314	552	201	203
Fleetwood Town	130	163	196	184	180	207	187	•	155	242	272
Frickley Athletic	415	222	208	371	197	202	316	205	•	496	168
Gainsborough Trinity	343	335	336	335	315	278	363	219	494	•	307
Goole Town	195	415	275	278	335	365	390	195	418	345	•
Horwich RMI	252	263	206	258	566	236	220	269	249	237	169
Hyde United	489	325	325	352	537	418	427	369	404	405	402
Leek Town	415	455	246	678	604	502	565	354	549	427	456
Marine	507	405	314	339	510	403	451	280	409	305	317
Matlock Town	417	285	303	748	308	367	463	313	447	377	569
Morecambe	424	308	402	363	451	320	389	422	266	318	375
Mossley	288	257	278	353	266	405	402	241	243	202	252
Shepshed Albion	291	203	219	271	218	201	286	248	337	205	280
Southport	458	311	342	404	552	280	427	411	206	272	327
Stalybridge Celtic	687	471	405	587	717	726	679	606	544	577	338
Whitley Bay	423	233	123	179	353	166	252	221	222	440	460

204

	Horwich RMI	Hyde United	Leek Town	Marine	Matlock Town	Morecambe	Mossley	Shepshed Alb	Southport	Stalybridge C	Whitley Bay
Accrington Stanley ...	365	640	704	628	484	721	385	561	502	632	338
Bangor City	152	321	257	223	270	278	218	245	262	211	212
Bishop Auckland	202	269	315	217	208	207	216	239	230	225	439
Buxton	354	360	1153	384	611	343	507	351	359	735	255
Chorley	539	262	374	260	204	329	218	296	297	329	223
Droylsden	204	325	229	274	288	294	352	309	254	580	198
Emley	542	269	359	423	251	274	218	308	326	501	429
Fleetwood Town	215	241	220	224	105	349	234	119	179	251	194
Frickley Athletic	151	238	276	228	229	276	264	217	176	374	174
Gainsborough Trinity	258	321	308	261	386	230	320	252	204	369	319
Goole Town	215	505	235	285	225	285	216	355	210	325	405
Horwich RMI	•	254	227	259	208	210	198	277	410	243	214
Hyde United	438	•	297	307	301	503	887	319	425	1117	277
Leek Town	411	430	•	585	490	502	438	602	634	675	532
Marine	261	402	439	•	322	377	387	349	1029	433	451
Matlock Town	254	418	542	421	•	397	309	427	382	523	275
Morecambe	368	350	407	350	304	•	365	274	403	660	305
Mossley	296	571	322	238	230	334	•	224	436	605	317
Shepshed Albion	309	185	293	313	367	249	224	•	387	288	247
Southport	408	341	409	509	275	413	337	301	•	388	306
Stalybridge Celtic	628	1225	629	411	303	405	739	631	523	•	364
Whitley Bay	253	402	432	164	183	397	183	216	174	333	•

Attendance Summaries by Club

Club	Psn	Home		Away	
		Total	Ave	Total	Ave
Stalybridge Celtic	1	12,195	581	9,797	467
Accrington Stanley	8	10,601	505	7,840	373
Leek Town	4	10,550	502	8,427	401
Hyde United	9	9,324	444	8,329	397
Buxton	5	8,757	417	7,637	364
Marine	2	8,690	414	6,964	332
Matlock Town	19	8,545	407	6,244	297
Emley	6	8,207	391	7,724	368
Morecambe	3	7,824	373	7,373	351
Southport	7	7,677	366	7,802	372
Mossley	16	6,760	322	7,215	344
Gainsborough Trinity	18	6,553	312	6,715	320
Goole Town	12	6,472	308	6,881	328
Droylsden	15	6,045	288	7,323	349
Chorley	21	6,020	287	8,130	387
Whitley Bay	17	5,809	277	6,474	308
Shepshed Albion	22	5,621	268	6,872	327
Frickley Athletic	14	5,477	261	7,361	351
Horwich RMI	13	5,425	258	6,823	325
Bishop Auckland	11	5,332	254	6,355	303
Bangor City	20	5,047	240	6,534	311
Fleetwood Town	10	4,102	195	6,213	296

Total Attendances: 161,033   **Average Attendance: 349**

Full Records of all 1991-92 Premier Clubs 1968-1992

Club	P	W	D	L	F	A	Pts	Ave
Marine	544	263	146	150	844	611	890	1.64
Leek Town	82	38	20	24	124	105	134	1.63
Emley	42	18	11	13	69	47	65	1.55
Hyde United	494	217	116	161	877	710	767	1.55
Stalybridge C	166	69	47	50	222	201	257	1.55
Bangor City	858	363	217	278	1464	182	1306	1.52
Accrington St	42	17	12	13	78	62	63	1.50
Mossley	862	366	200	296	1372	1194	1294	1.50
B. Auckland	124	50	27	47	182	178	177	1.43
Southport	588	209	174	205	800	811	801	1.36
Frickley Ath	384	142	93	149	585	578	519	1.35
Matlock Town	988	365	239	384	1550	1586	1334	1.35

Chorley	460	162	123	175	670	667	609	1.32
Morecambe	1026	337	292	397	1397	1545	1303	1.27
Goole Town	1026	344	246	436	1429	1653	1278	1.25
Gainsboro T	1026	335	272	419	1503	1609	1276	1.24
Buxton	816	236	198	355	962	959	984	1.21
Droylsden	82	24	25	33	129	142	97	1.18
Horwich RMI	376	117	97	162	480	562	445	1.18
Fleetwood Tn	514	150	136	288	618	865	586	1.14
Whitley Bay	42	13	9	20	53	79	48	1.14
Shepshed Alb	124	23	22	79	139	244	91	0.73

Top League Goalscorers by Club

Club	Scorers and goals
Accrington Stanley	Beck 19; Bondswell 14; Hughes 13.
Bangor City	Lloyd 15; Powell 6; R. Jones 4; Nicholas 4.
Bishop Auckland	Glen Liddle 12; Wiggan 8.
Buxton	Bunter 15; Clarke 13; Dove 11.
Chorley	Dyson 11; Ross 9; Griffiths 7.
Droylsden	McCrory 11; Schofield 11; Wood 11.
Emley	Balmer 13; Bradshaw 8; Tunniclift 7.
Fleetwood Town	Madden 20; Walmsley 7; Thompson 6.
Frickley Athletic	Woodhead 9; Brook 7; Fuller 6.
Gainsborough Trinity	Logan 10; Snow 7; Dwyer 4; Lowe 4.
Goole Town	P. Collier 12; Banton 9; Travis 5.
Horwich RMI	Redshaw 12; McDonald 8; Gayle 4.
Hyde United	Chapman 13; Kirkham 13; O'Gorman 11.
Leek Town	Sutton 13; Lowe 10; Devaney 7.
Marine	Gautrey 11; Ross 11; Grant 9.
Matlock Town	Tilly 10; Hoyland 8; Sheppard 7.
Morecambe	Holden 23; Coleman 16; Brown 6.
Mossley	Burke 14; Bowler 10; Heywood 3.
Shepshed Albion	Dakin 12; Roderick 4; Meachin 3; Mathews 3.
Southport	Blackhurst 12; Jarvis 10; Gamble 5; McCormack 5.
Stalybridge Celtic	Camden 31; Brown 8; Aspinall 7.
Whitley Bay	Chandler 16; Johnson 9; Boagey 4; Teasdale 4.

PREMIER DIVISION CLUBS

ACCRINGTON STANLEY

Reformed in 1968 as successors to the Football League side, they joined the Lancashire Combination in 1970. Moved to the Cheshire County League in 1978 and then on to the North West Counties League in 1982. They were founder members of the Northern Premier League First Division in 1987.

Ground: Crown Ground, Livingstone Road, Accrington
Phone: 0254-383235   **Nickname:** Reds   **Founded:** 1968
Manager: Dave Thornley   **Secretary:** Joe Daly   **Chairman:** John Alty
Colours: All Red   **Change:** Yellow, Green, Green

5-Year Record		P	W	D	F	A	Pts	Psn	Cup	FAT
87-88	NPL1	36	21	6	71	39	69	4	Pr	2q
88-89	HFS1	42	21	10	81	60	73	6	2q	1q
89-90	HFS1	42	22	10	80	53	76	5	2q	1q
90-91	HFS1	42	21	13	83	57	76	4	4q	3q
91-92	HFSP	42	17	12	78	62	63	8	2q	3q

Capacity: 2,460 (150)   **Record:** 1,110 v Fleetwood, NPL 1988
Rail: Accrington (1½ miles from ground).
Directions: M6: A677 to Blackburn, A6119 Ring Road, take M65 and leave at first exit A678 to Clayton-le-Moors, then A680 to Accrington. Livingstone Road approx 50 yards past Crown Hotel on left.

BARROW

Formed in 1901 and Lancashire Combination members from 1903-1921 when they joined the Football League. The club lost their League place in 1972, dropping into the Northern Premier League and becoming founder members of the Alliance Premier League in 1979. Subsequently relegated from the Alliance three times and promoted twice.

Ground: Holker Street, Barrow in Furness, Cumbria
Phone: 0229-820346/823061   **Info Line:** 0898-888620
Manager: John King   **Secretary:** C.H. Whiteside   **Chairman:** S. Morgan
Colours: White, Navy, White   **Change:** All Red
Nickname: Bluebirds

5-Year Record		P	W	D	F	A	Pts	Psn	Cup	FAT
87-88	NPLP	42	21	8	70	41	71	5	4q	SF
88-89	HFSP	42	26	9	69	35	87	1	1	3
89-90	CONF	42	12	16	51	67	52	14	3q	W

| 90-91 | CONF | 42 | 15 | 12 | 59 | 65 | 57 | 10 | 3 | 2 |
| 91-92 | CONF | 42 | 8 | 14 | 52 | 72 | 38 | 22 | 4q | 2 |

Ground Capacity: 7,000 (1,500) **Record:** 16,840 v Swansea Tn, FAC 1/54

Non-Lg: 6,002 v Enfield, FAT 4/88

Rail: Barrow in Furness (½ miles from ground).

Directions: M6 Junction 36. Follow A590 to Barrow. Turn right at fourth set of lights, and continue for ½ mile.

BISHOP AUCKLAND

Formed as Auckland Town by theology undergraduates from Auckland Castle. Early Northern League and Northern Alliance members, after changing to their current name they rejoined the Northern League in 1893. In 1988 they joined Division One of the HFS Loans League and were promoted to the Premier Division in 1989.

Ground: Kingsway, Bishop Aukland, Co. Durham

Phone: 0388-603686 **Nickname:** Bishops **Founded:** 1886

Manager: Harry Dunn **Secretary:** A. Russell **Chairman:** C. Townsend

Colours: All Light and Dark Blue **Change:** Red and White

5-Year Record	P	W	D	F	A	Pts	Psn	Cup	FAT
87-88	NL1	38	19	7	70	48	64	6	1	1
88-89	HFS1	42	28	5	78	28	89	2	2q	3
89-90	HFSP	42	17	8	72	64	59	11	2	1
90-91	HFSP	40	17	10	62	56	61	7	1	1
91-92	HFSP	42	16	9	48	58	57	11	4q	1

Capacity: 4,500 (300) **Record:** 17,000 v Coventry C, FAC2 1952

Rail: Bishop Auckland (½ mile from ground).

Directions: A1 to Scotch Corner. Follow signs to Bishop Auckland; ground behind town centre.

BUXTON

Formed in 1877 and played in several leagues, including the Combination and the Manchester League before joining the Cheshire County League in 1932. In 1973 they joined the Northern Premier League.

Ground: The Silverlands, Buxton, Derbyshire

Phone: 0298-24733 **Nickname:** The Bucks **Founded:** 1877

Manager: Bob Murphy **Secretary:** David Belfield **Chairman:** David Mellor

Colours: All White **Change:** All Yellow

5-Year Record	P	W	D	F	A	Pts	Psn	Cup	FAT
87-88	NPLP	42	11	14	72	76	47	16	2q	1
88-89	HFSP	42	12	14	61	63	50	15	2q	1

89-90	HFSP	42	15	8	59	72	53	16	3q	3q
90-91	HFSP	40	17	11	66	61	59	8	2q	1q
91-92	HFSP	42	21	9	65	47	72	5	2q	2q

Capacity: 4,000 (654)   **Record:** 6,000 v Barrow, FAC1 11/62
Rail: Buxton (½ mile from ground).
Directions: 200 yards from Buxton Market Place, directly opposite County Police Headquarters.

CHORLEY

Formed in 1883 and joined the Lancashire League in 1894. Founder members of the Lancashire Combination Second Division from which they were promoted in 1907 and again in 1909. In 1968 they were founder members of the Northern Premier League, only to be relegated in 1969, then promoted back in 1970. In 1972 they were relegated to the Cheshire County League, but in 1982 they returned to the Northern Premier. They were promoted to the Conference in 1988 but relegated in 1990.
Ground: Victoria Park, Duke Street, Chorley, PR7 3DU
Phone: 02572-63406   **Nickname:** Magpies   **Founded:** 1883
Manager: Glen Buckley   **Secretary:** Jack Hayes   **Chairman:** David Murgatroyd
Colours: Black and White Stripes, White, Black   **Change:** All Yellow

5-Year Record		P	W	D	F	A	Pts	Psn	Cup	FAT
87-88	NPLP	42	26	10	78	35	88	1	1	2q
88-89	CONF	40	13	6	57	65	45	17	4q	1
89-90	CONF	42	13	6	42	67	45	20	4q	3q
90-91	HFSP	40	12	10	55	55	46	14	2	1
91-92	HFSP	42	11	9	61	82	42	21	4q	3q

Capacity: 9,900 (700) **Record:** 9,679 v Darwen 1931/2
Rail: Chorley (400 yards from ground).
Directions: M61 to Westhoughton, follow A6 to Chorley. M6 to Standish, follow signs to Chorley.

COLWYN BAY

Formed in 1886, they were a prominent North Wales side and members of, among others, the National League of 1921-30. Founder members of the reformed Welsh League (North) in 1945, they moved to the North West Counties League in 1984 and to the HFS last season.
Ground: The Drill Field, Drill Field Road, Northwich, Cheshire, CW9 5HN
Phone: 0606-41450   **Nickname:** Bay   **Founded:** 1886
Manager: Bryn Jones   **Secretary:** A.J. Banks   **Chairman:** G. Owens
Colours: Sky Blue, Maroon, Blue   **Change:** Maroon, Sky Blue, Maroon

5-Year Record		P	W	D	F	A	Pts	Psn	Cup	FAT
87-88	NWC1	34	20	7	60	42	45 †	4	1	1q
88-89	NWC1	34	19	9	77	45	47	4	1q	1
89-90	NWC1	34	16	12	79	50	60	3	3q	1q
90-91	NWC1	36	22	10	85	37	76	2	4q	3q
91-92	HFS1	42	30	4	99	49	94	1	4q	1q

† *Two points deducted*

Capacity: 16,000 (600)   **Record:** First season at ground

Rail: Northwich (1 mile).

Directions: M6 Junction 19. Take Chester road to roundabout and head for Bus Station (6 miles from M6). Ground adjacent to Bus Station.

DROYLSDEN

Formed in 1866. Lancashire Combination members in the 1930s, they joined the Cheshire County League in 1939, only to return to the Combination in 1949. In 1968 they re-entered the Cheshire County League and in 1982 were founder members of the North West Counties League Division Two. They became founder members of the Northern Premier League Division One in 1987 and were promoted to the Premier Division in 1990.

Ground: Butchers Arms, Market Street, Droylsden, Manchester

Phone: 061-370-1426   **Nickname:** The Bloods   **Founded:** 1866

Manager: John Cooke **Secretary:** Gordon Hargreaves **Chairman:** D. Sterling

Colours: All Red   **Change:** All Yellow

5-Year Record		P	W	D	F	A	Pts	Psn	Cup	FAT
87-88	NPL1	36	16	10	63	48	58	6	2q	(VPr)
88-89	HFS1	42	25	9	84	48	84	4	1q	(V2)
89-90	HFS1	42	27	6	81	46	80 *	2	2q	(V3†)
90-91	HFSP	40	12	11	67	70	47	13	2q	2
91-92	HFSP	42	12	14	62	72	50	15	3q	3q

*Seven points deducted †Tie awarded to opponents.

Capacity: 3,500 (200)   **Record:** 4,250 v Grimsby T, FAC1 11/76

Rail: Fairfield (1½ miles from ground).

Directions: Market Street off Ashton New Road.

EMLEY

Joined the Yorkshire League from the Huddersfield League in 1969. In 1982 became founder members of the Northern Counties East League and in 1989 were promoted to the First Division of the HFS Loans League. Promoted to Premier Division 1991.

Ground: Emley Welfare SG, Emley, Huddersfield, West Yorkshire

Phone: 0924-848398/840087   **Nickname:** not known   **Founded:** 1903

Manager: Steve Codd   **Secretary** Gordon Adamson   **Chairman:** Roy Shirley
Colours: Sky Blue, Maroon, Sky Blue   **Change:** Amber, Black, Amber

5 Year Record		P	W	D	F	A	Pts	Psn	Cup	FAT
87-88	NCEP	32	20	8	57	21	68	1	3q	(VF)
88-89	NCEP	32	25	5	80	18	80	1	3q	(V4)
89-90	HFS1	42	20	9	70	42	69	5	1q	(V5)
90-91	HFS1	42	24	12	78	37	84	2	2q	QF
91-92	HFSP	42	18	11	69	47	65	6	1	3q

Capacity: 2,600 (230)   **Record:** 5,134 v Barking, FAAC 2/69
Rail: Huddersfield (7 miles from ground).
Directions: M1 Junction 38. Follow signs to Huddersfield to roundabout, then left on Denby Dale Road A636 for approximately ¾ mile, then turn right for Emley.

FLEETWOOD TOWN

Formed in 1977, following the disbanding of former Northern Premier League team Fleetwood. Joined the Cheshire County League in 1978. Founder members of the North West Counties League Division Two in 1982, they were promoted to Division One after two seasons. Founder members of the Northern Premier League Division One in 1987 and promoted to the Premier Division in 1988.
Ground: Highbury Stadium, Park Avenue, Fleetwood, Lancs
Phone: 03917-6443   **Nickname:** Fishermen   **Founded:** 1977
Manager: Larry Milligan   **Secretary:** R. Atkinson   **Chairman:** J. Wilkinson
Colours: Red and White, White, Red   **Change:** Black and White, Black, Black

5-Year Record		P	W	D	F	A	Pts	Psn	Cup	FAT
87-88	NPL1	36	22	7	85	45	73	1	3q	(V4)
88-89	HFSP	42	19	16	58	44	73	7	4q	1
89-90	HFSP	42	17	12	73	66	63	8	1q	1q
90-91	HFSP	40	20	9	69	44	69	4	1	1
91-92	HFSP	42	17	8	67	64	59	10	2q	1

Capacity: 9,700 (200)   **Record:** 6,000 v Rochdale, FAC1 1965
Rail: Poulton le Fylde (7 miles from ground).
Directions: M55 Junction 3. A585 to Fleetwood – ground is behind fire station on left just before town centre. Turn back on yourself for 100 yards at the point where the tramtracks cross the road.

FRICKLEY ATHLETIC

Formed as Frickley Colliery. Joined the Midland League from the Yorkshire League in 1924. In 1960 joined the Cheshire County League, moving back to the Midland Counties League in 1970. In 1976 they joined the NPL and moved up to the Conference in 1980. Relegated in 1987.

Ground: Westfield Lane, South Elmsall, West Yorkshire

Phone: 0977-642460/644453   **Nickname:** The Blue   **Founded:** 1910

Manager: Ronnie Glavin **Secretary:** Bob Bates **Chairman:** Mike Twiby

Colours: Blue and White, Blue, Blue **Change:** All Yellow and Red

5-Year Record		P	W	D	F	A	Pts	Psn	Cup	FAT
87-88	NPLP	42	18	11	61	55	65	10	4q	1
88-89	HFSP	42	17	10	64	53	61	9	1	2
89-90	HFSP	42	16	8	56	61	56	12	2q	3q
90-91	HFSP	40	16	6	64	62	54	10	4q	2
91-92	HFSP	42	12	16	61	57	52	14	3q	1

Capacity: 8,000 (900)   **Record:** 7,000 v Rotherham U, FAC1 1971

Rail: South Elmsall (2 miles from ground).

Directions: M62 to A1 Junction 33. Follow A1 (South) towards Doncaster. Leave A1 at first exit after Trusthouse Forte. Follow signs for South Kirby, then South Elmsall. In town centre near Market Place, travel along Westfield Lane into Oxford Street; ground at bottom of Oxford Street on right.

GAINSBOROUGH TRINITY

One-time Football League Second Division Club, and founder members of the Midland League. They re-joined the Midland League in 1912 and, apart from the 1960-61 season which was spent in the Central Alliance, they stayed there until being founder members of the NPL in 1968.

Ground: The Northolme, North Street, Gainsborough

Phone: 0427-613295   **Nickname:** The Blues   **Founded:** 1873

Manager: Gary Simpson **Secretary:** Frank Nicholson **Chairman:** John Davis

Colours: Royal Blue with White Trim, White, Blue and White

Change: White, Black, Red

5-Year Record		P	W	D	F	A	Pts	Psn	Cup	FAT
87-88	NPLP	42	8	10	38	81	34	20	1q	3q
88-89	HFSP	42	12	11	56	73	47	17	1q	2q
89-90	HFSP	42	16	8	59	55	53*	15	1q	1q
90-91	HFSP	40	9	11	57	84	38	20	1q	2q
91-92	HFSP	42	11	13	48	63	46	18	1q	2q

Three points deducted

Capacity: 9,950 (350)   **Record:** 9,600 v Scunthorpe, 1948

Rail: Gainsborough (2 miles from ground).

Directions: Ground is situated near the town centre, 250 yards from the General Post Office and Magistrates' Court.

GOOLE TOWN

Played in the Midland League before the First World War. Yorkshire League members from 1924 until moving back to the Midland League in 1948. Apart from spending 1960-61 in the Central Alliance, they stayed with the Midland until becoming founder members of the NPL in 1968.

Ground: Victoria Pleasure Grounds, Carter St, Goole, North Humberside
Phone: 0405-762794   **Nickname:** Town   **Founded:** 1900
Manager: Dale Banton **Secretary:** Graeme Wilson **Chairman:** C. Raywood
Colours: Blue and Red, Blue, Red   **Change:** Red and White Stripes

5-Year Record		P	W	D	F	A	Pts	Psn	Cup	FAT
87-88	NPLP	42	17	9	71	61	60	12	2q	1q
88-89	HFSP	42	22	7	75	60	73	6	1q	3q
89-90	HFSP	42	12	5	54	77	41	19	4q	2q
90-91	HFSP	40	14	10	68	74	52	12	1q	1q
91-92	HFSP	42	15	9	60	72	54	12	1q	2q

Capacity: 4,500 (200)   **Record:** 8,700 v Scunthorpe, Mid. Lg 1950
Rail: Goole (400 yards from ground).
Directions: M62 Junction 36, Goole exit. A614 to Goole centre and turn right at second set of traffic lights. Carter Street is sixth turning on the right.

HORWICH RMI

Joined the Lancashire Combination during the First World War and stayed until 1968 when they moved to the Cheshire County League. Were founder members of the North West Counties League in 1982 and after one season moved to the Northern Premier League.

Ground: Grundy Hill, Victoria Road, Horwich
Phone: 0204-696908   **Nickname:** Railwaymen   **Founded:** 1896
Manager: Ken Wright **Secretary:** Les Hamer **Chairman:** Paul O'Berg
Colours: Blue and White Stripes, Blue, Blue   **Change:** not known

5-Year Record		P	W	D	F	A	Pts	Psn	Cup	FAT
87-88	NPLP	42	17	9	46	42	60	13	2q	1q
88-89	HFSP	42	7	14	42	70	35	20	2q	1q
89-90	HFSP	42	15	13	66	69	55 *	13	1q	1q
90-91	HFSP	40	13	6	62	81	45	16	3q	QF
91-92	HFSP	42	13	14	44	52	53	13	2q	3q

Three points deducted

Capacity: 5,000 (500)   **Record:** not known
Rail: Blackrod (3 miles from ground).
Directions: M61 Junction 6. Follow Horwich signs at roundabout, bear left, just prior to second zebra crossing turn right (Victoria Road). Ground along side-road on left.

214

HYDE UNITED

Joined the Cheshire County League in 1930. Founder members of the Northern Premier League in 1968, they returned to the Cheshire County in 1970 and to the Northern Premier in 1982.

Ground: Tameside Stadium, Walker Lane, Hyde, Cheshire, SK14 2SB

Phone: 061-368-1031 **Nickname:** Tigers **Founded:** 1919

Manager: Cliff Roberts **Secretary:** Alan Slater **Chairman:** Steve Hartley

Colours: Red White and Black, White, Black **Change:** White and Blue

5-Year Record		P	W	D	F	A	Pts	Psn	Cup	FAT
87-88	NPLP	42	25	10	91	52	85	2	2q	1
88-89	HFSP	42	24	8	77	44	80	2	3q	SF
89-90	HFSP	42	21	8	73	50	71	4	3q	2
90-91	HFSP	40	14	11	73	63	53	11	3q	2
91-92	HFSP	42	17	9	69	67	60	9	1q	1

Capacity: 4,000 (400) **Record:** 9,500 v Nelson, FAC 1952

Rail: Newton (400 yards from ground).

Directions: On entering Hyde follow signs for Tameside Leisure Park, and on Walker Lane take second car park entrance near Leisure Pool. Follow road round to Stadium.

LEEK TOWN

Formed in 1945 as Abbey Green Rovers and later known as Leek Lowe Hamil, the club played local football before joining the Staffs County League. They became Leek Town in 1951 on joining the Manchester League. Moved to the Birmingham League in 1954 but returned to the Manchester in 1957, later falling back into the Staffs County. Re-emerged to join the Cheshire County League in 1973 and become North West Counties League founder members in 1982. Founder members of the Northern Premier League Division One in 1987 and promoted to the top division in 1990.

Ground: Harrison Park, Macclesfield Road, Leek, Staffs, ST13 8LD

Phone: 0538-399278 **Nickname:** The Blues **Founded:** 1945

Manager: Neil Baker **Secretary:** Michael Rowley **Chairman:** Tony Rogers

Colours: Blue, White, Blue **Change:** Red, Yellow, Red

5-Year Record		P	W	D	F	A	Pts	Psn	Cup	FAT
87-88	NPL1	36	20	10	63	38	70	3	3q	3q
88-89	HFS1	42	25	11	74	41	85 *	3	4q	1q
89-90	HFS1	42	26	8	70	31	86	1	1q	F
90-91	HFSP	40	15	11	48	44	56	9	2	1
91-92	HFSP	42	21	10	62	49	73	4	4q	1

One point deducted

Capacity: 5,000 (200) **Record:** 3,500 v Macclesfield, FAC 1973/4
Rail: Stoke (13 miles from ground) or Macclesfield (13 miles from ground).
Directions: Situated on the A53 main Buxton to Macclesfield road about ½
mile outside Leek on north-west side of the town.

MARINE

Formed in 1894 as an off-shoot of Waterloo Melville, in 1935 they joined the
Lancashire Combination from the Liverpool County Combination. In 1969
they transferred to the Cheshire County League and, in 1979, joined the
Northern Premier League.
Ground: Rossett Park, College Road, Crosby, Liverpool
Phone: 051-924-1743 **Nickname:** Lilywhites **Founded:** 1894
Manager: Roly Howard **Secretary:** John Wildman **Chairman:** T. Culshaw
Colours: White, Black, Black **Change:** Yellow, Blue, Yellow

5-Year Record		P	W	D	F	A	Pts	Psn	Cup	FAT
87-88	NPLP	42	19	10	67	45	67	9	3q	2
88-89	HFSP	42	23	7	69	48	76	5	2q	1
89-90	HFSP	42	16	14	59	55	62	9	1	1
90-91	HFSP	40	18	11	56	39	65	6	4q	3q
91-92	HFSP	42	23	9	64	32	78	2	3q	SF

Capacity: 4,000 (400) **Record:** 4,000 v Nigeria 1947
Rail: Blundellsands (½ mile from ground).
Directions: From North: M6-M58 (end) then follow Crosby and Marine signs.
From South: M6-M62-M57 (end) then as before.

MATLOCK TOWN

Founder members of the new Central Alliance in 1947. In 1961 they were
founders of the revived Midland Counties League, and in 1969 they moved on
to the Northern Premier League.
Ground: Causeway Lane, Matlock, Derbyshire
Phone: 0629-55362 **Nickname:** The Gladiators **Founded:** 1886
Manager: Roy Reid **Secretary:** Keith Brown **Chairman:** Cliff Britland
Colours: Royal Blue, White, Royal Blue **Change:** All Yellow

5-Year Record		P	W	D	F	A	Pts	Psn	Cup	FAT
87-88	NPLP	42	10	8	58	89	38	19	3q	3q
88-89	HFSP	42	16	5	65	73	53	13	1q	1
89-90	HFSP	42	18	12	61	42	66	6	1	2q
90-91	HFSP	40	12	7	52	70	43	17	2q	2q
91-92	HFSP	42	12	9	59	87	45	19	3q	3q

Capacity: 7,500 (240) **Record:** 5,123 v Burton A, FAT 1975

Rail: Matlock (½ mile from ground).
Directions: On A615 – 500 yards from the town centre.

MORECAMBE

Joined the Lancashire Combination on their formation. Founder members of
the Northern Premier League in 1968.
Ground: Christie Park, Lancaster Road, Morecambe, LA4 5TJ
Phone: 0524-832230/411797   **Nickname:** Shrimps   **Founded:** 1920
Manager: Brian Griffiths   **Secretary:** B. Cowburn   **Chairman:** E. Weldrake
Colours: Red, White, Black   **Change:** All White

5-Year Record		P	W	D	F	A	Pts	Psn	Cup	FAT
87-88	NPLP	42	19	15	61	41	72	4	1q	3q
88-89	HFSP	42	13	9	55	50	47 *	16	3q	3q
89-90	HFSP	42	15	9	58	70	54	14	1q	1q
90-91	HFSP	40	19	16	72	44	73	3	1q	3q
91-92	HFSP	42	21	13	70	44	76	3	1	3

* One point deducted
Capacity: 2,500 (1,300) **Record:** 9,383 v Weymouth, FAC3 1/62
Rail: Morecambe Promenade (2 miles from ground).
Directions: From South: M6 Junction 34 to Lancaster A589 to Morecambe.
From North: M6 Junction 35 to Carnforth, A6 to Bolton-le-Sands, A5105 to
Morecambe. Ground on main town-centre road.

MOSSLEY

Founder members of the Cheshire County League in 1919, they moved from
there to the Northern Premier League in 1972.
Ground: Seel Park, Market Street, Mossley, nr Ashton-under-Lyne, Lancs
Phone: 0457-832369   **Nickname:** Lilywhites   **Founded:** 1909
Manager: Ged Coyne   **Secretary:** Les Fitton   **Chairman:** Roger Finn
Colours: White, Black, White   **Change:** Yellow and Red, Red, Red

5-Year Record		P	W	D	F	A	Pts	Psn	Cup	FAT
87-88	NPLP	42	11	11	54	75	44	17	1q	2q
88-89	HFSP	42	17	9	56	58	60	10	2q	1q
89-90	HFSP	42	11	10	61	82	43	18	4q	2q
90-91	HFSP	40	13	10	55	68	45	15	1q	2q
91-92	HFSP	42	15	4	51	73	49	16	2q	1q

Capacity: 3,000 (250) **Record:** 7,000 v Stalybridge, Ches. Lg 1950
Rail: Mossley (½ mile from ground).
Directions: From M62: Oldham, Lees, Grotton Mossley. From M1 or
Sheffield to Stalybridge, Mossley. From Manchester or Stockport to Ashton-
under-Lyne, Mossley.

SOUTHPORT

Founded as Southport Central and early Lancashire League members. Changed name, for a season, to Southport Wanderers and then joined the Lancashire Combination. From the Central League they became founder members, under their present name, of the Football League Division Three (North) in 1921. Lost their League place in 1978.

Ground: Haig Avenue, Southport, PR8 6JZ
Phone: 0704-533422 **Nickname:** The Sandgrounders **Founded:** 1881
Manager: Brian Kettle **Secretary:** Roy Morris **Chairman:** C. Clapham
Colours: Old Gold and Black, Black, Old Gold/Black **Change:** All White

5-Year Record		P	W	D	F	A	Pts	Psn	Cup	FAT
87-88	NPLP	42	15	12	43	48	57	14	1q	3q
88-89	HFSP	42	13	12	66	52	51	14	1	1q
89-90	HFSP	42	17	14	54	48	65	7	4q	1q
90-91	HFSP	40	18	14	66	48	68	5	2q	1q
91-92	HFSP	42	16	17	57	48	65	7	2q	2

Capacity: 6,500 (2,000) **Record:** 20,010 v Newcastle United, FAC4 1932
Rail: Southport (1½ miles from ground).
Directions: M6 to M58 to Ormskirk, then Southport. Haig Ave is on right ½ mile before town centre, ground signposted from all entrances to town.

WHITLEY BAY

Formed in 1958 as successors to Whitley Bay Athletic, a Northern Alliance and latterly North Eastern League Club. Joined the Northern League in 1958. Moved to the HFS Loans League Division One in 1988. Promoted to Premier Division as champions in 1991.

Ground: Hillheads Park, Hillheads Road, Whitley Bay, Tyne and Wear
Phone: 091-251-3680 **Nickname:** The Bay **Founded:** 1958
Manager: Bob Graham **Secretary:** Robert Harding **Chairman:** A. Lingwood
Colours: Blue and White Stripes, Blue, Blue **Change:** All Yellow

5-Year Record		P	W	D	F	A	Pts	Psn	Cup	FAT
87-88	NL1	38	22	9	60	27	75	4	1q	3q
88-89	HFS1	42	23	6	77	49	75	5	3q	3q
89-90	HFS1	42	21	11	93	59	74	4	3	2q
90-91	HFS1	42	25	10	95	38	85	1	2	1q
91-92	HFSP	42	13	9	53	79	48	17	4q	2q

Capacity: 4,500 (300) **Record:** 7,301 v Hendon, FAACqf 1965
Rail: Monkseaton (1 mile from ground). **Directions:** A1M or A19 through Tyne Tunnel, follow A1 Morpeth. Join A1059 to Tynemouth at first roundabout then A1058 Tynemouth. Pick up signs A192 Whitley Bay, then A191 Whitley Bay. Ground down Hillheads Road behind Ice Rink.

WINSFORD UNITED

Formed in 1883. Founder members of the Cheshire County League in 1919. On amalgamation of that League with the Lancashire Combination, were founder members of the North West Counties League in 1982. Were founder members of the First Division of the Northern Premier League in 1987.

Ground: Barton Stadium, Wharton, Winsford, Cheshire, CW7 3EU

Phone: 0606-593021   **Nickname:** Blues   **Founded:** 1883

Manager: Mike McKenzie   **Secretary:** Brian Redmond   **Chairman:** M. Gaskill

Colours: Royal Blue, White, Royal Blue   **Change:** Maroon, White, White

5-Year Record		P	W	D	F	A	Pts	Psn	Cup	FAT
87-88	NPL1	36	15	6	59	47	51	8	Pr	1q
88-89	HFS1	42	13	6	58	93	45	19	Pr	1q
89-90	HFS1	42	18	10	65	53	64	7	Pr	2q
90-91	HFS1	42	11	13	51	66	46	18	1q	1q
91-92	HFS1	42	29	6	96	41	93	2	1	1q

Capacity: 8,000 (300) **Record:** 7,000 v Witton Albion 1947

Rail: Winsford (1 mile from ground).

Directions: From North: M6 Junction 19; A556 towards Northwich to Davenham, then take A5018 to Winsford. From South: M6 Junction 18; A54 through Middlewich towards Chester.

FIRST DIVISION

Final Table 1991-92

	P	W	D	L	F	A	Pts
Colwyn Bay	42	30	4	8	99	49	94
Winsford United	42	29	6	7	96	41	93
Worksop Town	42	25	5	12	101	51	80
Guiseley	42	22	12	8	93	56	78
Caernarfon Town	42	23	9	10	78	47	78
Bridlington Town	42	22	9	11	86	46	75
Warrington Town	42	20	8	14	79	64	68
Knowsley United	42	18	10	14	69	52	64
Netherfield	42	18	7	17	54	61	61
Harrogate Town	42	14	16	12	73	69	58
Curzon Ashton	42	15	9	18	71	83	54
Farsley Celtic (1)	42	15	9	18	79	101	53
Radcliffe Borough (3)	42	15	9	18	67	72	51
Newtown	42	15	6	21	60	95	51
Eastwood Town	42	13	11	18	59	70	50
Lancaster City	42	10	19	13	55	62	49
Congleton Town	42	14	5	23	59	81	47
Rhyl	42	11	10	21	59	69	43
Rossendale United	42	9	11	22	61	90	38
Alfreton Town	42	12	2	28	63	98	38
Irlam Town (1)	42	9	7	26	45	95	33
Workington (1)	42	7	8	27	45	99	28

(-) – points deducted for breach of rule

Leading Premier Division Goalscorers

42	Kenny Clark	Worksop Town
34	Mark Williscroft	Colwyn Bay
32	Bevan Blackwood	Winsford United
	Peter Donnelly	Colwyn Bay
26	Gavin McDonald	Warrington Town
25	Steve French	Harrogate Town
24	Mark Tennison	Guiseley
21	Peter Coyne	Radcliffe Borough
	Alan Radford	Bridlington Town
20	Ian Howat	Rhyl

Attendance Summaries for HFS Loans First Division

Club	Psn	Total	Ave.
Guiseley	4	11,441	545
Colwyn Bay	1	10,180	485
Winsford United	2	8,409	400
Harrogate Town	10	5,089	242
Caernarfon Town	5	4,965	236
Rossendale United	19	4,300	205
Newtown	14	4,126	196
Warrington Town	7	3,891	185
Rhyl	18	3,674	175
Congleton Town	17	3,506	167
Bridlington Tovn	6	3,462	165
Netherfield	9	3,448	164
Farsley Celtic	12	3,225	154
Lancaster City	16	3,151	150
Curzon Ashton	11	3,089	147
Eastwood Town	15	2,730	130
Workington	22	2,654	126
Alfreton Town	20	2,489	119
Worksop Town	3	2,308	110
Radcliffe Borough	13	2,107	100
Knowsley United	8	2,059	98
Irlam Town	21	1,492	71

Mail On Sunday Manager of the Month Awards

Month	Manager	Club
September	Gordon Rayner	Guiseley
October	Mike McKenzie	Winsford United
November	Paul Orr	Knowsley United
December	Bryn Jones	Colwyn Bay
January	John Roberts	Caernarfon Town
February	Gordon Rayner	Guiseley
March	Tommy Spencer	Worksop Town
April	Gordon Rayner	Guiseley

Mail On Sunday Player of the Month Awards

Month	Player	Club
September	Paul Bottomley	Guiseley
October	Kenny Clark	Worksop Town
November	Neil Wilson	Caernarfon Town
December	Graham Millington	Alfreton Town
January	Richard Annan	Guiseley
February	Steve French	Harrogate Town
March	Kenny Clark	Worksop Town
April	Ced Edey	Winsford United

FIRST DIVISION RESULTS 1991-92

	Irlam Town	Harrogate Tn	Guiseley	Farsley Celtic	Eastwood Tn	Curzon Ashton	Congleton Tn	Colwyn Bay	Caernarfon Tn	Bridlington Tn	Alfreton Town
Alfreton Town	5-1	3-3	1-2	2-4	0-1	3-1	1-0	0-1	2-4	2-3	•
Bridlington Town	3-1	1-1	4-0	1-0	5-0	2-0	1-2	2-1	0-3	•	8-0
Caernarfon Town	3-0	3-0	3-0	0-1	4-1	2-1	2-2	3-2	•	0-2	5-2
Colwyn Bay	3-0	1-1	1-2	4-1	2-0	4-3	2-1	•	1-2	1-4	5-3
Congleton Town	2-1	0-1	0-2	4-2	1-2	2-4	•	2-5	0-2	0-3	3-1
Curzon Ashton	1-1	0-2	2-2	1-2	2-0	•	2-0	2-2	0-0	0-0	4-1
Eastwood Town	2-3	0-1	2-0	1-2	•	1-1	3-4	0-2	2-5	0-1	3-1
Farsley Celtic	2-1	2-3	2-0	•	2-3	4-3	1-1	0-2	2-1	2-1	2-3
Guiseley	5-0	2-4	•	5-0	1-1	3-2	3-1	2-0	6-1	1-1	3-1
Harrogate Town	4-2	•	0-1	1-1	3-2	1-2	3-5	2-3	3-1	1-1	0-2
Irlam Town	•	0-3	0-1	1-1	0-4	0-1	0-0	0-2	2-1	0-1	1-0
Knowsley United	2-2	2-3	1-6	2-4	1-1	3-1	5-2	0-2	1-0	0-4	0-1
Lancaster City	4-3	2-0	1-2	4-1	2-0	1-0	5-1	1-4	2-2	3-1	0-2
Netherfield	1-0	0-4	2-2	0-1	1-1	0-0	3-0	0-2	2-2	1-2	0-1
Newtown	1-2	0-5	2-2	1-2	2-1	3-1	1-2	0-1	0-2	0-0	3-0
Radcliffe Borough	1-0	1-1	1-2	2-4	1-1	1-0	1-2	1-4	1-2	1-2	3-3
Rhyl	1-0	2-0	2-2	1-4	0-1	3-4	1-2	0-2	0-0	1-0	1-2
Rossendale United	3-1	1-1	3-1	1-0	3-1	7-0	1-0	1-5	1-0	1-1	2-1
Warrington Town	4-0	1-5	2-2	1-4	3-1	4-1	1-2	3-3	1-0	2-1	1-0
Winsford United	4-1	1-5	2-2	2-4	3-1	1-1	4-1	1-2	2-3	0-3	1-0
Workington	0-0	5-2	2-2	2-2	0-1	2-4	0-2	1-2	0-0	0-3	3-2
Worksop Town	6-0	5-0	3-2	6-2	0-0	3-0	6-2	1-3	1-1	1-3	1-0

	Knowsley Utd	Lancaster City	Netherfield	Newtown	Radcliffe Boro	Rhyl	Rossendale Utd	Warrington Tn	Winsford Utd	Workington Tn	Worksop Towr
Alfreton Town	0-3	1-2	0-1	4-3	2-3	3-2	0-1	1-6	2-3	1-3	3-0
Bridlington Town	1-1	2-0	0-2	0-1	1-1	4-1	4-0	0-2	3-1	3-2	1-3
Caernarfon Town	1-3	3-2	2-1	2-1	2-1	2-1	2-0	0-1	1-0	5-0	1-3
Colwyn Bay	3-1	2-0	3-2	3-2	3-0	2-0	1-1	1-0	1-0	6-1	4-2
Congleton Town	0-2	0-0	1-2	1-2	3-0	2-1	2-0	2-3	0-2	3-0	2-1
Curzon Ashton	2-0	2-3	1-1	1-1	1-0	4-1	4-1	1-1	1-5	6-1	0-3
Eastwood Town	1-0	1-1	6-4	2-2	0-2	3-3	4-4	1-3	1-2	3-1	1-2
Farsley Celtic	0-5	1-1	3-2	3-2	2-2	5-2	2-4	2-5	4-5	2-2	2-1
Guiseley	2-0	0-1	1-0	1-1	3-1	2-2	2-2	2-1	1-4	6-0	1-1
Harrogate Town	3-1	1-1	2-2	2-2	3-3	1-1	4-2	2-1	1-4	0-2	1-1
Irlam Town	1-0	0-0	1-0	1-3	4-1	3-0	1-2	0-1	1-2	1-0	2-1
Knowsley United	•	0-0	0-0	5-0	2-2	1-1	2-3	2-1	0-2	5-1	0-2
Lancaster City	0-0	•	0-1	0-2	1-2	0-1	2-2	3-0	0-1	4-2	1-2
Netherfield	1-2	0-2	•	2-0	2-0	1-0	1-0	2-0	1-3	2-1	2-1
Newtown	1-4	5-1	0-1	•	2-1	2-3	0-0	2-2	1-1	1-1	4-1
Radcliffe Borough	4-2	2-3	3-1	3-1	•	1-3	3-2	3-1	1-2	1-0	1-4
Rhyl	1-1	0-0	4-0	2-3	1-3	•	5-1	3-3	3-5	1-1	0-2
Rossendale United	0-1	1-3	0-1	5-1	1-2	2-1	•	1-0	0-1	2-2	2-1
Warrington Town	3-3	2-1	2-1	1-1	1-0	0-0	4-0	•	1-0	3-0	5-0
Winsford United	0-2	2-2	0-1	7-0	1-0	1-3	5-0	1-0	•	1-0	0-1
Workington	0-2	5-1	1-3	0-2	1-0	1-0	1-1	0-2	0-3	•	
Worksop Town	4-0	1-1	5-0	9-0	1-0	1-0	5-1	3-0	1-2	4-0	•

DIVISION ONE CLUBS

ALFRETON TOWN

Ground: North Street, Alfreton, Derby
Phone: 0773-832819   **Nickname:** The Reds   **Founded:** 1959
Manager: Danny Hague **Secretary:** Tom McRoy **Chairman:** D. Bearder
Colours: Red and White Stripes, Black, Red   **Change:** All White
Capacity: 6,000 (120) **Record:** 5,200 v Matlock, Central All. 1961
Rail: Alfreton & Mansfield Parkway (½ mile from ground).
Directions: M1 Junction 28. A38 towards Derby, follow for 2 miles then take slip road on to B600, turn right at main road towards town centre ½ mile, turn left into North Street and ground is on the right-hand side.

ASHTON UNITED

Ground: Surrey Street, Hurst Cross, Ashton-under-Lyne, Tameside
Phone: 061-339-4158   **Nickname:**   **Founded:** 1878
Manager: Dave Denby **Secretary:** Ernie Jones **Chairman:** John Milne
Colours: Red, Black, Red   **Change:** Blue, White, Black
Capacity: 8,000 (300) **Record:** 11,000 v Halifax, FA Cup 1953
Rail: Ashton Charlstown (1 mile)
Directions: M62 Junction 20. A627(M) to Oldham/Ashton-under-Lyne. Leave at Ashton, follow Stalybridge (B6194) until Hurst Cross. Ground on right behind Royal Oak public house.

BRIDLINGTON TOWN

Ground: Queensgate, Bridlington, YO16 5LN
Phone: 0262-606879/670391   **Nickname:** Seasiders   **Founded:** 1926
Manager: Neil Brandon **Secretary:** Graham Proudlock **Chairman:** Charles Dunn
Colours: All Red   **Change:** All Blue
Capacity: 3,000 (750) **Record:** 3,000 v Scarborough
Rail: Bridlington (¾ mile from ground).
Directions: M62 Junction 37. Howden to Bridlington, A614 Spalding Moor, A613 Driffield, A166 Bridlington through lights – across roundabout signed town centre, through lights, left second lights, ground on right.

CAERNARFON TOWN

Ground: National Park, Katherine Street, Ashton-under-Lyne, Lancashire
Phone: 061-330-6033   **Nickname:** Canaries   **Founded:** 1876
Manager: J. T. Roberts **Secretary:** W.Gray-Thomas **Chairman:** J. F. Thomas
Colours: Yellow, Green, Yellow   **Change:** Red, White, Red
Capacity: 8,000 (350)   **Record:** First year at Curzon Ashton FC
Rail: Ashton-under-Lyne (1½ miles from ground).
Directions: Behind Ashton Police Station, off A635 Manchester Road.

CONGLETON TOWN

Ground: Booth Street Ground, Crescent Road, Congleton, Cheshire
Phone: 0260-274460   **Nickname:** The Bears   **Founded:** 1901
Manager: Billy Wright **Secretary:** Alan Smith **Chairman:** Peter Warren
Colours: White, Black, Black   **Change:** All Red
Capacity: 5,000 (300)   **Record:** 7,000 v Huddersfield, Ches. Lg
Rail: Congleton (2 miles from ground).
Directions: On approach to Congleton via Clayton by-pass, take second turning right after Fire Station into Booth Street; ground off Booth Street.

CURZON ASHTON

Ground: National Park, Katherine Street, Ashton-under-Lyne, Lancashire
Phone: 061-330-6033   **Nickname:** Curzon   **Founded:** 1963
Manager: Steve Waywell **Secretary:** Alun Jones **Chairman:** Harry Twamley
Colours: Blue, Blue, White   **Change:** All White
Capacity: 8,000 (350)   **Record:** 1,862 v Stamford, FAVsf2 1980
Rail: Ashton-under-Lyne (1½ miles from ground).
Directions: Behind Ashton Police Station, off A635 Manchester Road.

EASTWOOD TOWN

Ground: Coronation Park, Eastwood, Notts
Phone: 0773-2301/715823   **Nickname:** The Badgers   **Founded:** 1953
Manager: Bryan Chambers **Secretary:** Paddy Farrell **Chairman:** George Belshaw
Colours: Black and White Stripes, Black, Red   **Change:** Yellow
Capacity: 6,000 (200)   **Record:** 2,500 v Wealdstone, FAAC 2/68
Rail: Nottingham (10 miles).
Directions: From North: M1 Junction 27 – follow Heanor signs via Brinsley to traffic lights in Eastwood, here turn left then first right past Fire Station. From South: M1 Junction 26 – B6010 to first exit, left at traffic lights; take first left at the Man in Space public house.

FARSLEY CELTIC

Ground: Throstle Nest, Newlands, Farsley, Pudsey, Leeds, LS28 3TE
Phone: 0532-561517   **Nickname:** Celts   **Founded:** 1908
Manager: Denis Metcalf **Secretary:** Brian Falkingham **Chairman:** John Palmer
Colours: All Blue   **Change:** All White
Capacity: 5,000 (300)   **Record:** not known
Rail: New Pudsey (1 mile from ground).
Directions: M62 Junction 28. Follow the Leeds ring road to A647. Turn right at roundabout towards Leeds; after approx ½ mile turn left down New Street (Tradex warehouse on corner). After approx 400 yards turn right down Newlands, ground at bottom.

GREAT HARWOOD TOWN

Ground: The Showground, Wood Street, Great Harwood, Lancs
Phone: 0254-883913   **Nickname:** not known   **Founded:** 1978
Manager: Eric Whalley **Secretary:** Steve Brown **Chairman:** Chris Hickley
Colours: All Red   **Change:** not known
Capacity: 2,000 (200)   **Record:** 1,200 v Manchester United, 1987
Rail: Blackburn (6 miles from ground)
Directions: M66 Haslingden exit. A680 through Baxenden, Accrington, Clayton-le-Moors. Left at Hyndburn Bridge Hotel into Hyndburn Road, right into Wood Street.

GRETNA

Ground: Raydale Park, Domminion Road, Gretna, Carlisle
Phone: 0461-37602   **Nickname:** not known   **Founded:** 1946
Manager: Mick McCartney **Secretary:** Keith Rhodes **Chairman:** Ian Dalgliesh
Colours: Black and White Hoops, Black, Black and White   **Change:** All red
Capacity: 3,500 (200)   **Record:** 2,000 v Glasgow Rangers, 1989
Rail: Carlisle (8 miles from ground)
Directions: A74, north end of town, 8 miles north of Carlisle.

GUISELEY

Ground: Nethermoor Ground, Otley Road, Guiseley, Yorks
Phone: 0493-72872   **Nickname:** not known   **Founded:** 1909
Manager: Gordon Rayner **Secretary:** D. Martin **Chairman:** D. Brotherton
Colours: All Yellow with Blue Trim **Change:** All White
Capacity: 4,000 (400)   **Record:** 2,142 v Sudbury Town FAVsf 3/92
Rail: Guiseley (½ mile from ground)

Directions: M1, M62 Junction 26. Follow to Leeds, take Leeds Ring Road (A6110) to A65. On to A65 to Rawdon, then Guiseley. Ground 400 yards on right past traffic lights.

HARROGATE TOWN

Ground: Wetherby Road, Harrogate, North Yorkshire
Phone: 0423-883671   Nickname: not known   Founded: 1919
Manager: Alan Smith   Secretary: Roy Dalby   Chairman: C. Dunnington
Colours: Amber, Black, Amber   Change: All Blue
Capacity: 3,800 (370)   Record: 3,208 v Starbeck, Whitworth Cup Final 1948
Rail: Harrogate (¾ mile from ground).
Directions: From Leeds on A61 turn right at first traffic lights (Appleyards Garage) into Hook Stone Road, continue to Woodlands Hotel traffic lights then turn left into Wetherby Road – ground 300 yards on the right.

KNOWSLEY UNITED

Ground: Alt Park, Endmoor Road, Huyton, Merseyside
Phone: 051-480-2529   Nickname: The Reds   Founded: 1984
Manager: Max Thompson   Secretary: John Richards   Chairman: Paul G. Orr
Colours: All Red   Change: Grey, White
Capacity: 5,000 (300)   Record: not known
Rail: Huyton.
Directions: M62 Junction 6. M57 to Junction 3. Towards Huyton. At roundabout take Huyton Link Road. Ground on left-hand side.

LANCASTER CITY

Ground: Giant Axe, West Road, Lancaster, Lancs
Phone: 0524-382238   Nickname: The Blues   Founded: 1905
Manager: Keith Brindle   Secretary: B. Newsham   Chairman: J. Bagguley
Colours: All Blue   Change: Yellow, Black, Yellow
Capacity: 5,000 (500)   Record: 7,500 v Carlisle, FAC 1936
Rail: Lancaster Castle (400 yards from ground).
Directions: From South: M6 Junction 33. Follow into city, turn left at Waterstones Bookshop by traffic lights, following signs to railway station. Take second right and follow road down hill, ground on the right-hand side. From North: M6 Junction 34. Follow signs to railway station.

NETHERFIELD

Ground: Parkside Road, Kendal, Cumbria
Phone: 0539-722469   Nickname: Founded: 1920
Manager: Gary Pierce Secretary: Peter Savage Chairman: D. Willan
Colours: Black and White Stripes, Black, Red
Change: Yellow and Green, Green, Yellow and Green
Capacity: 6,000 (300)   Record: 5,184 v Grimsby, FAC1 11/55
Rail: Oxenholme (½ mile from ground).
Directions: M1 Junction 36. Follow Skipton sign for 200 yards, left at roundabout straight into Kendal, opposite K Shoes into Parkside Road, 400 yards on right.

NORTH SHIELDS

Ground: Hillheads Park, Hillheads Road, Whitley Bay, Tyne and Wear
Phone: 091-251-3680   Nickname: not known   Founded: not known
Manager: Colin Richardson Secretary: Bob Wilkinson
Chairman: Chris Wynne
Colours: Red   Change: Yellow
Capacity: 4,500 (300)   Record: First season at Whitley Bay FC
Rail: Monkseaton (1 mile from ground).
Directions: A1M or A19 through Tyne Tunnel, follow A1 Morpeth. Join A1059 to Tynemouth at first roundabout then A1058 Tynemouth. Pick up signs A192 Whitley Bay, then A191 Whitley Bay. Ground down Hillheads Road behind Ice Rink.

RADCLIFFE BOROUGH

Ground: Stainton Park, Pilkington Road, Radcliffe, Manchester, M26 0PE
Phone: 061-725-9197   Nickname: Boro   Founded: 1949
Manager: Kevin Glendon Secretary: Graham Fielding Chairman: Ian Wood
Colours: All Blue   Change: All Red
Capacity: 2,500 (270)   Record: 1,365 v Caernarfon, Bass Lg Div 2 1983
Rail: Radcliffe (½ mile from ground).
Directions: M62 Junction 17. Follow signs for Whitefield and Bury. Follow A665 to Radcliffe, through town centre to Bolton Road, turn right into Unsworth Street, ground on left, Colshaw Close.

ROSSENDALE UNITED

Ground: Dark Lane, Newchurch, Rossendale, Lancs, BB4 7UA
Phone: 0706-215119   Nickname: The Stags   Founded: 1898
Manager: Steve Conaghan Secretary: D. Cooke Chairman: Steve Conaghan

Colours: Blue and White Stripes, White, Blue   **Change:** All Yellow
Capacity: 4,000 (480)   **Record:** 3,400 v Shrewsbury, FAC1 11/75
Directions: M62 Junction 18 (M66). North following signs for Blackburn then Rawtenstall (motorway then dual carriageway). At large roundabout take second exit (Burnley A682). At first set of official traffic lights turn right into Newchurch Road (Rams Head PH), after approx 1½ miles turn right into Staghills Road, through council estate to ground ½ mile.

SHEPSHED ALBION

Ground: The Dovecote, Butt Hole Lane, Loughborough Rd, Shepshed, Leics
Phone: 0509-502684   **Nickname:** Raiders   **Founded:** 1891
Manager: Daren Heyes **Secretary:** Steve Pears **Chairman:** Bryan Edwards
Colours: Red and Blue Stripes, Red, Red   **Change:** Yellow, Black, Yellow
Capacity: 5,000 (200)   **Record:** 2,600 v Billericay, FAVsf2 2/79
Rail: Loughborough (5 miles from ground).
Directions: M1 Junction 23. A512 towards Ashby, right at first set of traffic lights, into Leicester Road. Tturn right at garage into Forest St, Loughborough Rd continues off – turn right into Butt Hole Ln at the Black Swan.

WARRINGTON TOWN

Ground: Common Lane, Latchford, Warrington, WA4 2RS
Phone: 0925-31932   **Nickname:** The Wires   **Founded:** 1961
Manager: Derek Brownbill **Secretary:** Graham Ost **Chairman:** Bob Smith
Colours: Yellow, Blue, Yellow   **Change:** Red and White
Capacity: 3,500 (200)   **Record:** 2,120 v Halesowen, FAVsf1 3/86
Rail: Bank Quay (2 miles from ground).
Directions: From town centre (Bridge Foot) via A49 South to Loushers Lane (1 mile) turn left at lights. From M6 via A50 to Latchford Swing Bridge, turn left into Station Road, ground ½ mile.

WORKINGTON

Ground: Borough Park, Workington, Cumbria, CA14 2DT
Phone: 0900-602871   **Nickname:** Reds   **Founded:** 1884
Manager: George Norrie **Secretary:** Tom Robson **Chairman:** Colin Doorbar
Colours: Red, White, Red   **Change:** Sky Blue, Navy, Sky Blue
Capacity: 5,000 (200)   **Record:** 21,000 v Man. Utd, FAC3 1958
Rail: Workington (400 yards from ground).
Directions: From Penrith A66 to town, down hill to T-Junction – right. Approx ½ mile under bridge, first right – ground 200 yards on left.

WORKSOP TOWN

Ground: The Northolme, Gainsborough, Lincs
Phone: 0427-613295 **Nickname:** The Tigers **Founded:** 1861
Manager: Tommy Spencer **Secretary:** Wally Peace **Chairman:** Mel Bradley
Colours: Amber and Black, Black, Amber **Change:** Blue and White
Capacity: not known **Record:** 8,171 v Chesterfield, FAC 1925
Rail: Worksop.
Directions: The ground is situated near town centre, 250 yards from the General Post Office and Magistrates' Court. Car park opposite ground.

OFFICIAL FEEDER
LEAGUES –
DIADORA LEAGUE

The Isthmian League Division Two was expanded and regionalised into a
North and South Division for the start of the 1984-85 season. For the 1991-92
season the division was altered again to create, without regionalisation, a
Second and Third Division. Since 1985 clubs have joined the League from
lower feeder leagues. Details of these, and their source leagues are listed
below.

Season	Club(s) Joining	Division	Source and Position	
1985-86	Chertsey Town	South	Combined Counties	2nd
	Collier Row	North	London Spartan	1st
	Wivenhoe Town	North	Essex Senior	1st
1986-87	Southwick	South	Combined Counties	2nd
	Vauxhall Motors	North	South Midland	2nd
1987-88	Witham Town	North	Essex Senior	2nd
	Yeading	South	Greene King Spartan	1st
1988-89	Purfleet	North	Essex Senior	1st
1989-90	Abingdon Town	South	Greene King Spartan	1st
	Malden Vale	South	Dan Air	2nd
1990-91	Cove	South	Dan Air	3rd
	Edgware Town	North	Greene King Spartan	1st
1991-92	Aldershot Town	Div 3	Football League †	
	East Thurrock Utd	Div 3	Essex Senior	3rd
	Farnham Town	Div 3	Dan Air League	1st
	Leighton Town	Div 3	South Midlands	1st
	Northwood	Div 3	Spartan	1st

† Reformed from Aldershot FC who resigned from the Football League
during the 1991-92 season.

Dan Air League

The Surrey Senior League was formed in 1922 by 11 clubs. It became the Home Counties League in 1978 and the Combined Counties League in 1979.

	P	W	D	L	F	A	Pts
Farnham Town	36	26	7	3	89	28	85
Malden Town	36	21	7	8	72	39	70
Chipstead	36	19	7	10	68	46	64
Cobham	36	17	10	9	81	56	61
Ditton	36	16	11	9	61	44	59
Ashford Town (Mx)	36	17	7	12	57	41	58
Cranleigh	36	18	3	15	68	62	57
Bedfont	36	16	8	12	56	40	56
Ash United..................	36	14	13	9	63	52	55
Steyning Town	36	16	6	14	67	65	54
Farleigh Rovers	36	14	9	13	53	59	51
Viking Sports	36	13	10	13	59	49	49
Frimley Green..............	36	13	9	14	64	61	48
Merstham	36	12	6	18	49	68	42
Hartley Wintney	36	12	5	19	50	70	41
Westfields...................	36	8	10	18	43	60	34
Godalming Town...........	36	6	8	22	35	76	26
Horley Town................	36	5	8	23	39	83	23
Sandhurst Town...........	36	6	2	28	34	109	20

5-Year One, Two, Three Records

Year	1st ....Pts	2nd.........Pts	3rd ....Pts
1986-87	Ash United............78	Farnham Town 72	Malden Vale 69
1987-88	BAe Weybridge....72	Merstham 69	Farnham Town 69
1988-89	BAe Weybridge....77	Malden Vale 70	Merstham 66
1989-90	Chipstead 79	Merstham 78	Cove 67
1990-91	Farnham Town 76	Chipstead 74	Malden Town 72

Essex Senior League

Formed by nine clubs in 1971, the inclusion of a reserve team inhibited its full participation in the Pyramid. Now, however, it is a feeder to the Isthmian arm of the Pyramid.

	P	W	D	L	F	A	Pts
Ford United	32	20	6	6	64	18	66
Brentwood	32	20	6	6	77	37	66
East Thurrock United...........	32	19	9	4	62	24	66
Sawbridgeworth Town.........	32	19	8	5	67	43	65

	P	W	D	L	F	A	Pts
Canvey Island 32	19	6	7	49	24	63
Basildon United 32	17	5	10	65	39	56
Bowers United 32	15	9	8	49	31	54
Southend Manor.................32	14	6	12	62	40	48
Stambridge.........................32	12	8	12	60	49	44
Woodford Town 32	12	7	13	46	44	43
Concord Rangers................32	10	10	12	39	52	40
Stansted.............................32	11	6	15	40	50	39
Burnham Ramblers 32	10	4	18	48	71	34
Hullbridge Sports...............32	7	7	18	25	63	28
East Ham United 32	7	5	20	35	72	26
Eton Manor........................32	5	3	24	24	71	18
Maldon Town......................32	1	3	28	20	104	6

5-Year, One, Two, Three

Year	1st ....Pts	2nd ....Pts	3rd ....Pts
1986-87	Canvey Island 70	Witham Town.......63	Purfleet...............61
1987-88	Purfleet................73	Brentwood 71	Halstead Town......63
1988-89	Brightlingsea 68	East Thurrock U...65	Ford United..........61
1989-90	Brightlingsea 68	Woodford Town...64	East Thurrock U ...56
1990-91	Southend Manor...64	Brentwood 60	Burnham Rams.....59

Spartan League

Formed in 1975 as the London Spartan League on the amalgamation of the Spartan League (1907) and the Metropolitan London League (itself a result of an amalgamation of leagues in 1971). The league originally comprised Divisions One and Two but in 1977 changed to a Premier Division and a Senior Division. Was known as the Greene King Spartan League for the period 1987-91.

Premier Division	P	W	D	L	F	A	Pts
Northwood 36	26	4	6	97	36	82
Brimsdown Rovers 36	23	7	6	76	28	76
Haringey Borough...............36	21	8	7	74	57	71
Brook House 36	21	6	9	68	51	69
Walthamstow Pennant 36	20	8	8	92	35	68
Barkingside 36	19	8	9	56	41	65
Hanwell Town......................36	18	7	11	78	41	61
Cheshunt 36	16	12	8	52	31	60
Corinthian Casuals..............36	17	3	16	75	44	54
Croydon Athletic.................36	16	5	15	66	63	53
Waltham Abbey 36	14	8	14	49	52	50
Cockfosters 36	12	10	14	47	52	46

Hillingdon Borough	36	13	6	17	52	65	45
Beaconsfield United	36	11	8	17	43	69	41
Southgate Athletic	36	11	5	20	41	61	38
Amersham Town	36	7	6	23	33	69	27
North Greenford United	36	5	10	21	36	81	25
Beckton United	36	4	8	24	33	100	20
Eltham Town	36	2	3	31	25	115	9

Division One	P	W	D	L	F	A	Pts
Willesden Hawkeye	26	21	3	2	75	28	63 *
Tower Hamlets Tipples	26	19	3	4	69	15	60
Elms	26	19	3	4	86	36	60
Craven	26	12	6	8	68	51	42
Metrogas	26	12	6	8	55	45	42
Walthamstow Trojans	26	11	9	6	55	48	42
Leyton County	26	12	4	10	52	44	40
Cray Valley	26	10	4	12	48	60	34
Metpol Chigwell	26	9	4	13	52	72	31
Royal George	26	8	4	14	46	50	28
Old Roan	26	6	6	14	39	69	24
Swanley Town	26	5	5	16	37	77	20
Phoenix Sports	26	4	4	18	31	73	16
Catford Wanderers	26	2	3	21	19	64	9

* Three points deducted

5-Year, One, Two, Three

Year	1st	Pts	2nd	Pts	3rd	Pts

Premier Division

1986-87	Yeading	84	Redhill	71	Brimsdown Rvrs	59
1987-88	Edgware Town	68	Southgate Ath	66	Southwark Spts	58
1988-89	Abingdon Town	84	Wandsworth N	84	Northwood	79
1989-90	Edgware Town	86	Northwood	84	Southgate Ath	70
1990-91	Walthamstow P	81	Barkingside	80	Northwood	78

Division One

1986-87	Southwark Spts	64	Swanley Town	58	Thamesmead T	54
1987-88	Catford Wands	53	Hackney D. Ath	50	Thamesmead T	48
1988-89	Newmont Travel	74	Metrogas	63	Catford Wands	62
1989-90	KPG Tipples	66	Royal George	64	Newmont Travel	60
1990-91	Sangley Sports	69	AFC Millwall	58	Royal George	57

Campri South Midlands League

Formed by eight clubs in 1922 as the Bedfordshire County League. It later became the Bedfordshire & District League and, in 1929, the South Midlands League. A second division was added in 1925. The League was reconstituted into three divisions (Premier, One and Two) in 1948 but in 1955 Division Two was discontinued. Former sponsors were Benskins, Key Consultants while Campri have been sponsors since 1990-91.

Premier Division	P	W	D	L	F	A	Pts
Leighton Town....................40	29	8	3	98	30	95
Milton Keynes Borough.......40	30	3	7	116	29	93
Biggleswade Town 40	26	6	8	96	38	84
Shillington.........................40	25	6	9	82	35	81
Wingate & Finchley.............40	22	10	8	87	51	76
Hoddesden Town 40	20	13	7	80	42	73
Brache Sparta.....................40	21	8	11	82	48	71
Leverstock Green.................40	21	6	13	63	38	69
Oxford City........................40	19	7	14	74	50	64
Langford.............................40	18	8	14	52	48	62
Potters Bar Town.................40	17	10	13	76	64	61
Harpenden Town..................40	14	11	15	70	63	53
Totternhoe.........................40	15	4	21	62	84	49
Letchworth Garden City 40	13	6	21	58	63	45
Pitstone & Ivinghoe 40	12	8	20	63	101	44
Pirton...............................40	10	11	19	36	61	41
Welwyn Garden City 40	10	10	20	62	87	40
Buckingham Athletic 40	10	6	24	60	77	36
New Bradwell St Peter.........40	5	8	27	34	93	23
61 FC Luton 40	4	5	31	39	114	17
Winslow United 40	2	0	38	20	194	6

5-Year, One, Two, Three
Premier Division

Year	1st	Pts	2nd	Pts	3rd	Pts
1986-87	Selby.....................67		Shillington..............63		Hoddesdon T 59
1987-88	Shillington..............70		Selby.....................69		Langford................66
1988-89	Langford.................82		Thame United.........75		Selby.....................66
1989-90	Pitstone & Iv.........74		Thame United.......68		Leighton Town......66
1990-91	Thame United......80		Wolverton AFC....80		Biggleswade T......75

First Division	P	W	D	L	F	A	Pts
Ashcroft 38	30	5	3	93	30	95
Luton Old Boys...................38	28	7	3	104	41	91

Bedford United 38	28	5	5	118	39	89	
Bedford Town 38	26	6	6	100	32	84	
Shenley & Loughton 38	20	5	13	85	42	65	
Toddington Rovers 38	17	13	8	76	53	64	
Delco Products.....................38	17	6	15	69	59	57	
Risborough Rangers..............38	14	11	13	61	65	53	
Ampthill Town.......................38	14	10	14	65	57	52	
Cranfield United 38	13	10	15	62	66	49	
Ickleford...............................38	12	12	14	54	60	48	
Tring Athletic........................38	12	11	15	57	58	44	*
Sandy Albion 38	11	8	19	61	87	41	
Potters Bar Crusaders...........38	12	4	22	86	99	40	
Walden Rangers....................38	9	13	16	65	82	40	
Flamstead.............................38	11	7	20	60	87	40	
Shefford Town 38	11	7	20	41	72	40	
Emberton..............................38	9	6	23	47	91	33	
Caddington...........................38	4	7	27	40	103	19	
Stony Stratford Town............38	2	7	29	41	162	13	

Three points deducted

First Division

1986-87	Electrolux...........63	Biggleswade T 48		Walden Rangers ...46	
1987-88	Pitstone & Iv.........59	Brache Sparta........44		Caddington............43	
1988-89	Welwyn G. City 50	Buckingham A. ...50		Caddington............42	
1989-90	Harpenden T 70	Wingate.................66		Caddington............59	
1990-91	Buckingham A. 82	Shenley & L...........78		Oxford City...........69	

ADDITIONAL REGIONAL LEAGUES

Charrington Chiltonian League

Premier Division	P	W	D	L	F	A	Pts
Peppard 26	22	4	0	74	15	70	
Binfield 26	19	3	4	90	38	60	
Holmer Green 26	15	7	4	54	32	52	
Letcombe 26	13	7	6	48	37	46	
Finchampstead 26	11	5	10	47	36	38	
Stocklake 26	11	4	11	40	37	37	
Martin Baker Sports...............26	10	3	11	38	57	33	
Mill End Sports.......................26	8	8	10	47	47	32	
Wraysbury Coopers 26	9	5	12	54	55	32	
Prestwood..............................26	7	7	12	36	58	28	

	P	W	D	L	F	A	Pts
Reading Town	26	8	3	15	35	65	27
Brill United	26	6	4	16	44	66	22
Chalfont Wasps	26	6	3	17	32	60	21
Penn & Tylers Green	26	4	3	19	25	61	15

Division One	P	W	D	L	F	A	Pts
Eton Wick	24	18	2	4	66	18	56
Molins Sports	24	17	2	5	57	32	53
Slough YC OB	24	14	3	7	60	39	45
Broomwade Sports	24	13	5	6	46	41	44
Hazells Aylesbury	24	13	1	10	50	39	40
Stokenchurch	24	11	3	10	48	45	36
Uxbridge Town	24	11	3	10	45	33	33 *
Wooburn Athletic	24	9	6	9	44	50	33
Denham United	24	7	6	11	33	49	27
Kodak Harrow	24	6	4	14	33	54	22
Henley Town	24	6	3	15	40	51	21
Wallingford United	24	4	5	15	24	63	17
Chinnor	24	4	3	17	27	58	15

* Three points deducted

5-Year, One, Two, Three

Year	1st	Pts	2nd	Pts	3rd	Pts

Division One

1986-87	Coopers Payen	43	Sandhurst Town	38	Prestwood	37
(Renamed as Premier Division)						
1987-88	Finchampstead	77	Coopers Payen	68	Sonnong CP	66
1988-89	Coopers Payen	73	Finchampstead	64	Sonning CP	60
1989-90	Coopers Payen	67	Sonning CP	61	ITS Reading	52
1990-91	Peppard	67	Stocklake	57	Penn & Tylers G	47

Division Two

1986-87	Seer Green	44	Molins Spts	42	Brill United	37
(Renamed as Division One)						
1987-88	Henley Town	57	Bromley Park R	56	Stokenchurch	45
1988-89	Mill End Sports	70	Loudwater	60	Chalfont Wasps	58
1989-90	Binfield	65	Stocklake	59	Kodak Sports	56
1990-91	Letcombe Sports	60	Brill United	56	Kodak (Harrow)	54

Herts Senior County League

Premier Division	P	W	D	L	F	A	Pts
Hatfield Town AFC	28	21	4	3	85	30	67
Kings Langley	28	16	6	6	65	35	54
London Colney	28	15	5	8	57	53	50
Elliott Star	28	14	5	9	62	47	47
Sun Sports	28	14	5	9	47	43	47
Bushey Rangers	28	12	6	10	60	48	42
St Margaretsbury	28	12	4	12	58	51	40
Chipperfield Corries	28	9	12	7	53	45	39
Bedmond Social	28	11	6	11	47	43	39
Sandridge Rovers	28	11	6	11	45	48	39
Cuffley	28	10	4	14	35	46	34
Park Street	28	9	5	14	29	55	32
Colney Heath	28	8	5	15	47	61	29
Oxhey Jets	28	4	5	19	28	59	17
J & M Sports	28	4	2	22	27	81	14

Division One	P	W	D	L	F	A	Pts
Wellcome	26	19	2	5	81	35	59
Wormley Rovers	26	17	6	3	63	27	57
Bovingdon	26	16	5	5	56	38	53
BAC Stevenage	26	15	5	6	63	35	50
Lucas Soorts	26	14	6	6	49	26	48
Allenburys Sports	26	12	5	9	50	40	41
Walkern	26	11	4	11	58	37	37
Croxley Guild	26	9	6	11	41	52	33
Kodak Hemel Hempstead	26	7	10	9	41	47	31
Knebworth	26	7	9	10	39	46	30
Dynamics Stevenage	26	7	8	11	41	47	29
ICL Letchworth	26	3	7	16	27	68	16
Welwyn	26	4	3	19	38	83	15
Sarratt	26	2	2	22	17	83	8

5-Year, One, Two, Three

Year	1st	Pts	2nd	Pts	3rd	Pts
Premier Division						
1986-87	London Colney	71	J & M Sports	58	Bedmond Social	57
1987-88	Sandridge Rvrs	55	Kings Langley	54	Sun Sports	53
1988-89	London Colney	71	Bedmond Soc.	64	Park Street	56
1989-90	London Colney	57	Bedmond Soc.	57	Sun Sports	57
1990-91	Mount Grace	62	Leverstock Green	61	Bedmond Social	60

Kent County League

Eastern Senior Division	P	W	D	L	F	A	Pts
Lydd Town	20	17	0	3	70	20	51
Phoenix Rovers	20	15	1	4	51	24	46
New Romney	20	13	2	5	51	28	41
Bromley Green	20	11	5	4	49	32	38
Wondnesborough	20	9	3	8	43	34	30
Rye United	20	7	3	10	29	32	24
Teynham & Lynstea	20	7	2	11	36	44	23
Kennington	20	6	4	10	35	52	22
Knatchbull	20	5	4	11	33	56	19
Univ. of Kent	20	5	3	12	33	62	18
Walmer Rovers	20	0	3	17	11	57	3

Surrey County League

	P	W	D	L	F	A	Pts
St Andrews	26	16	9	1	70	34	57
Chobham	26	17	4	5	75	23	55
Netherne	26	16	5	5	69	28	53
Burpham	26	14	3	9	54	45	45
Croydon MO	26	12	5	9	45	38	41
British Telecom	26	9	8	9	42	42	35
Vandyke	26	10	5	11	43	46	35
Surbiton Town	26	10	5	11	44	48	35
Frinton Rovers	26	8	7	11	46	49	31
Ashtead	26	8	5	13	39	53	29
Ottershaw	26	9	2	15	39	58	29
Hersham RBL	26	8	4	14	41	42	28
Springfield Hospital	26	7	7	12	36	54	28
Kingswood Wanderers	26	2	3	21	21	104	9

5-Year, One, Two, Three

Year	1st	Pts	2nd	Pts	3rd	Pts
1986-87	Bedfont	68	Frinton Rovers	65	Ditton F&SC	51
1987-88	Frinton Rovers	70	Ditton F&SC	60	British Telecom	50
1988-89	Ditton F&SC	47	Frinton Rovers	45	Springfield Hosp	44
1989-90	Frinton Rovers	51	Ashford Town	42	Springfield Hosp	42
1990-91	Ditton F & SC	52	Frinton Rovers	50	Surbiton Town	45

OFFICIAL FEEDER
LEAGUES –
BEAZER HOMES LEAGUE

The regionalised competition was reorganised for season 1982-83 with the return of the Premier Division and the establishment of a Division One (South) and a Division One (Midland). These leagues are generally referred to as the Southern and Midland Divisions. Several clubs have moved 'sideways' to and from the other arms of the Pyramid but the following clubs have joined from the Southern League's own 'feeders'.

Season	Club(s) Joining	Division	Source and Position	
1983-84	Bridgnorth Town	Midland	Midland Combination	1st
	Chatham Town	Southern	Kent	7th
	Coventry Sport	Midland	W. Midlands (Regional)	16th
	Moor Green	Midland	Midland Combination	2nd
	Rushden Town	Midland	United Counties	2nd
	VS Rugby	Midland	W. Midlands (Regional)	7th
1984-85	Hednesford Town	Midland	W. Midlands (Regional)	2nd
	Sheppey United	Southern	Kent	2nd
1985-86	Bilston	Midland	W. Midlands (Regional)	2nd
	Hastings Town	Southern	Sussex County	9th
	Mile Oak Rovers	Midland	Midland Combination	1st
	Ruislip	Southern	Middlesex County	11th
	Burnham & Hil.	Southern	Green King Spartan (as Burnham)	1st
1986-87	Buckingham Town	Midland	United Counties	1st
	Halesowen Town	Midland	W. Midlands (Regional)	1st
1987-88	Atherstone Utd	Midland	W. Midlands (Regional)	1st
	Baldock Town	Southern	United Counties	1st
	Bury Town	Southern	Jewson Eastern	3rd
	Paget Rovers	Midland	Midland Combination	3rd
1988-89	Ashtree Highfield	Midland	Midland Combination	3rd
	Spalding United	Midland	United Counties	1st
1989-90	Bashley	Southern	Wessex	1st
	Hythe Town	Southern	Kent	1st
	RC Warwick	Midland	Midland Combination	2nd
	Yate Town	Midland	Hellenic League	1st
1990-91	Hinckley Town	Midland	W. Midlands (Regional)	1st
	Newport IOW	Southern	Wessex	2nd
	Newport AFC	Midland	Hellenic	1st
	Sudbury Town	Southern	Jewson Eastern	1st

1991-92	Braintree Town	Eastern Counties	1st
	Havant Town	Wessex League	1st
	Sittingbourne Town	Kent League	1st
	Solihull Borough	Midland Combination	1st
1992-93	Evesham United	Midland Combination	1st
	Gresley Rovers	West Midlands (Regional)	1st
	Weston-super-Mare	Western League	1st

West Midlands (Regional) League

This League is a successor to the Birmingham and District League which was formed in 1889. It adopted the name of the West Midlands (Regional) League in 1962. In 1965 a second division was formed (Premier and First) and another division, Division Two, was added in 1977. Banks's Brewery were recent sponsors.

Premier Division	P	W	D	L	F	A	Pts
Gresley Rovers	36	24	7	5	83	37	79
Paget Rangers	36	20	5	11	81	44	65
Stourport Swifts	36	18	10	8	62	45	64
Blakenall	36	17	10	9	67	49	61
Chasetown	36	17	10	9	47	31	61
Rocester	36	17	8	11	64	52	59
Oldbury United	36	17	7	12	61	47	58
Rushall Olympic	36	16	9	11	61	38	57
Lye Town	36	14	11	11	51	34	53
Halesowen Harriers	36	13	11	12	63	52	50
Willenhall Town	36	14	6	16	56	63	48
Pelsall Villa	36	12	11	13	52	58	47
West Bromwich Town	36	11	11	14	41	60	44
Cradley Town	36	12	7	17	39	56	43
Hinckley Athletic	36	9	7	20	36	56	34
Malvern Town	36	8	9	19	39	79	33
Wednesfield	36	8	8	20	43	69	32
Westfields	36	6	12	18	48	74	30
Oldswinford	36	7	5	24	34	84	26

Division One	P	W	D	L	F	A	Pts
Ilkeston Town	38	31	6	1	121	30	99
Darlaston	38	22	11	5	83	34	77
Donnington Wood	38	21	12	5	77	43	75
Gornal Athletic	38	21	8	9	73	41	71

Knypersley Victoria	38	19	9	10	84	54	66
Ettingshall H T	38	15	15	8	60	47	60
Hill Top Rangers	38	17	5	16	75	76	56
Cannock Chase	38	16	7	15	68	71	55
Ludlow Town	38	16	5	17	72	71	53
Moxley Rangers	38	14	9	15	32	42	51
Wolverhampton Casuals	38	13	11	14	51	59	50
Lichfield	38	14	5	19	57	50	47
Tipton Town	38	11	12	15	51	62	45
Wem Town	38	10	10	18	63	73	40
Wolverhampton United	38	8	14	16	63	80	38
Tividale	38	10	6	22	46	72	36
Oldbury United Res	38	8	11	19	34	68	35
Great Wyrley	38	9	6	23	45	86	33
Clancey Dudley	38	8	8	22	49	90	32
Brosely Athletic	38	8	8	22	38	93	32

Division Two	P	W	D	L	F	A	Pts
K. Chell	38	28	4	6	128	39	88
Gornal Sports	38	26	8	4	86	32	86
Rushall Olympic Res	38	21	8	9	91	54	71
Park Rangers	38	22	5	11	91	68	71
Mitchells & Butlers	38	21	7	10	96	48	70
Manders	38	20	9	9	70	40	69
Lye Town Res	38	19	7	12	75	51	64
Albright & Wilson	38	18	6	14	74	56	60
Bloxwich Strollers	38	14	10	14	81	71	52
Oldswinford Res	38	16	4	18	79	85	52
Halesowen Harriers Res	38	14	6	18	63	65	48
Alvechurch Res	38	13	9	16	62	84	48
Chasetown Res	38	13	7	18	63	86	46
Cradley Town Res	38	12	9	17	74	102	45
Blackheath Motors	38	12	6	20	65	93	42
Malvern Town Res	38	10	9	19	63	68	39
Rocester Res	38	11	5	22	53	119	38
Wolverhampton Casuals Rs.	38	9	5	24	58	116	32
Cheslyn Hay	38	7	9	22	62	93	30
Nuneaton Borough Res	38	4	7	27	50	114	19

5-Year, One, Two, Three

Year	1st	Pts	2nd	Pts	3rd	Pts

Premier Division

1986-87	Atherstone Utd.	62	Oldbury United	61	Wednesfield Soc	57
1987-88	Tamworth	57	Oldbury United	56	Lye Town	52

1988-89	Blakenhall	.86	Gresley Rovers	85	Halesowen Har.	78
1989-90	Hinckley Town	82	Rochester	82	Gresley Rovers	80
1990-91	Gresley Rovers	...101	Chasetown	85	Oldbury United	83

Division One

1986-87	Westfields	..61	Wolver'ton Cas	...57	Brosley Ath.	52
1987-88	Rochester	...62	Stourport Swifts	...51	Millfields	51
1988-89	Newport Town	78	Donnington	72	Ettingshall HT	69
1989-90	Darlaston	...73	Springvale-T.	63	Pelsall Villa	63
1990-91	Cradley Town	66	Ludlow Town	57	Cannock Chase	52

Great Mills League

Formed by nine clubs in 1892, with a second division added in 1894. Many Southern League clubs, including some from London, participated in early competition, most games being played midweek. Division Two was disbanded in 1909 but the League emerged from the First War again with two divisions. Division Two was disbanded between 1922 and 1925 and again in 1960. In 1976 Division One was added with the top section becoming the Premier Division.

Premier Division	P	W	D	L	F	A	Pts
Weston-super-Mare	40	32	2	6	110	44	98
Clevedon Town	40	28	5	7	90	28	89
Tiverton Town	40	27	5	8	106	47	85 *
Bideford	40	25	9	6	102	49	84
Saltash United	40	24	5	11	89	51	77
Plymouth Argyle Res	40	24	4	12	89	52	76
Taunton Town	40	17	11	12	88	56	62
Mangotsfield United	40	16	13	11	53	39	61
Elmore	40	17	10	13	76	72	61
Paulton Rovers	40	16	11	13	71	60	59
Minehead	40	16	10	14	65	74	58
Liskeard Athletic	40	14	10	16	68	69	52
Dawlish Town	40	15	5	20	77	76	50
Chippenham Town	40	13	7	20	58	95	46
Torrington	40	11	10	19	48	62	43
Bristol Manor Farm	40	10	10	20	42	66	40
Exmouth Town	40	10	8	22	56	97	38
Chard Town	40	8	8	24	48	76	32
Frome Town	40	9	5	25	44	91	32
Welton Rovers	40	8	6	26	32	78	30
Ottery St Mary	40	2	2	36	26	156	8

* One point deducted

First Division	P	W	D	L	F	A	Pts
Westbury United	42	27	10	5	80	39	91
Torquay United	42	26	11	5	96	32	89
Crediton United	42	20	12	10	57	32	72
Bath City	42	22	6	14	91	68	72
Warminster Town	42	19	13	10	80	49	70
Keynsham Town	42	19	13	10	80	69	70
Calne Town	42	20	9	13	73	49	69
Brislington	42	21	6	15	70	51	69
Bridport	42	17	16	9	61	50	67
Ilfracombe Town	42	17	14	11	76	44	65
Odd Down	42	20	5	17	58	46	65
Backwell United	42	17	10	15	64	49	61
Bishop Sutton	42	17	10	15	58	50	61
Glastonbury	42	14	8	20	52	61	50
Larkhall Athletic	42	12	12	18	58	65	48
Radstock Town	42	11	14	17	65	68	47
Barnstaple Town	42	12	8	22	42	55	44
Clandown	42	10	13	19	56	72	43
Wellington	42	9	11	22	42	70	38
Devizes Town	42	8	13	21	57	84	37
Melksham Town	42	8	12	22	44	77	36
Heavitree United	42	2	2	38	26	206	8

5-Year, One, Two, Three

Year	1st	Pts	2nd	Pts	3rd	Pts
Premier Division						
1986-87	Saltash United	70	Exmouth Town	54	Bristol City Res	51
1987-88	Liskeard Athletic	68	Saltash United	60	Mangotsfield Utd	60
1988-89	Saltash United	62	Exmouth Town	62	Taunton Town	56
1989-90	Taunton Town	92	Liskeard Athletic	91	Mangotsfield Utd	88
1990-91	Mangotsfield Utd	92	Torrington	82	Plymouth A. Res	79
First Division						
1986-87	Swanage & H.	62	Portway Bristol	58	Bath City Res	56
1987-88	Welton Rovers	54	Chard Town	53	Tiverton Town	49
1988-89	Larkhall Ath.	61	Tiverton Town	60	Bridport	55
1989-90	Ottery St Mary	85	Backwell United	73	Ilfracombe Tn	71
1990-91	Minehead	93	Elmore	78	Calne Town	77

Hellenic League

Formed in 1953 by 16 clubs. A second division was added three years later and the divisions became the Premier and First Divisions. Despite being a feeder to the Beazer Homes League, few teams have moved up. Former sponsors have been Halls Brewery and Federated Homes.

Premier Division	P	W	D	L	F	A	Pts
Shortwood United	34	25	4	5	83	44	79
Cirencester Town	34	23	9	2	73	23	78
Almondsbury Picksons	34	19	7	8	63	38	64
Milton United	34	18	9	7	67	44	63
Cinderford Town	34	16	9	9	57	41	57
Abingdon United	34	17	5	12	54	40	56
Didcot Town	34	16	6	12	70	48	54
Swindon Athletic	34	15	9	10	61	44	54
Bicester Town	34	12	12	10	44	42	48
Banbury United	34	14	5	15	55	55	47
Fairford Town	34	12	9	13	72	55	45
Headington Amateurs	34	10	9	15	48	59	39
Pegasus Juniors	34	11	5	18	66	68	38
Kintbury Rangers	34	9	8	17	47	59	35
Rayners Lane	34	9	8	17	50	75	35
Moreton Town	34	7	4	23	38	100	25
Carterton Town	34	6	6	22	32	74	24
Bishops Cleeve	34	2	6	26	25	96	12

Division One	P	W	D	L	F	A	Pts
Wollen Sports	32	26	4	2	96	28	82
Wantage Town	32	23	6	3	83	32	75
Tuffley Rovers	32	20	8	4	95	34	68
North Leigh	32	20	4	8	84	38	64
Cheltenham Saracens	32	15	7	10	70	45	52
Purton	32	14	7	11	48	40	49
Chipping Norton Town	32	13	6	13	54	56	45
Highworth Town	32	11	7	14	53	54	40
Cirencester United	32	11	7	14	49	55	40
Lambourn Sports	32	11	7	14	52	74	40
Yarnton	32	11	6	15	42	60	39
Wootton Bassett Town	32	10	8	14	45	59	38
Easington Sports	32	12	0	20	42	80	36
Kidlington	32	7	9	16	48	70	30

Wallingford Town..............32	8	5	19	40	78	29
Clanfield........................32	5	10	17	35	66	25
Supermarine..................32	3	3	26	20	87	12

5-Year, One, Two, Three

Year	1st ....Pts	2nd.................Pts	3rd.................Pts

Premier Division

1986-87	Abingdon Town ...84	Hounslow...............77	Shortwood Utd 65
1987-88	Yate Town 82	Abingdon Town ...74	Shortwood Utd 68
1988-89	Yate Town 83	Sharpness.............71	Abingdon Town ...60
1989-90	Newport AFC 75	Shortwood Utd 67	Abingdon Utd.......67
1990-91	Milton United 71	Fairford Town.......71	Bicester Town......63

First Division

1986-87	Bishops Cleeve.....72	Chelt. Town Res....71	Didcot Town.........65
1987-88	Chelt.Town Res.....66	Wantage Town.......58	Kintbury Rangers .57
1988-89	Almondsbury P.....64	Headington A 62	Lanbourn Sports...49
1989-90	Carterton Town 76	Milton Utd 66	Chelt. Town Res...59
1990-91	Cinderford Town..75	Cirencester Tn 71	Purton...................60

Hereward Sports United Counties League

Formed in 1895 as the Northamptonshire League with a second division added in 1896 although it has not always operated. The competition became the United Counties League in 1934. In 1968 a third division was added and in 1972 the divisions became the Premier, First and Second. In 1980 Division Two became the Reserve Division. Former sponsors are Nene Group. Hereward Sports have been sponsors since 1990.

Premier Division	P	W	D	L	F	A	Pts
Northampton Spencer 46	31	8	7	101	44	101
Raunds Town 46	27	14	5	94	38	95
Rothwell Town 46	29	6	11	100	51	93
Bourne Town 46	27	8	11	113	57	89
Stotfold..............................46	26	8	12	93	52	86
Mirrlees Blackstone 46	23	12	11	77	60	81
Eynesbury Rovers 46	22	12	12	82	58	78
Boston 46	21	11	14	79	62	74
Hamlet S & L......................46	21	11	14	76	60	74
Arlesey Town 46	20	12	14	76	65	72
Peterborough City 46	22	5	19	81	66	71
Cogenhoe United 46	19	13	14	92	63	70
Potton United 46	20	9	17	76	61	69
Daventry Town 46	18	10	18	71	65	64

	P	W	D	L	F	A	Pts
Kempston Rovers	46	16	15	15	54	51	63
Long Buckby	46	18	9	19	66	67	63
Irthlingborough D	46	17	8	21	73	88	59
Desborough Town	46	13	10	23	57	85	49
Wootton Blue Cross	46	15	3	28	57	85	48
Stamford	46	11	8	27	60	85	41
Spalding United	46	10	11	25	59	104	41
Wellingborough Town	46	7	5	34	45	130	26
Holbeach United	46	4	9	33	44	133	21
Brackley Town	46	3	7	36	39	135	16

Division One	P	W	D	L	F	A	Pts
Harrowby United	34	25	5	4	92	30	80
Newport Pagnell Town	34	25	5	4	86	44	80
Ramsey Town	34	23	6	5	95	36	75
St Ives Town	34	22	6	6	78	32	72
Bugbrooke St Michael	34	21	5	8	78	42	68
Higham Town	34	19	7	8	73	45	64
Ford Sports	34	18	6	10	74	48	60
O N Chenecks	34	16	9	9	61	47	57
Cottingham	34	14	4	16	62	68	46
Thrapston	34	11	6	17	54	70	39
Blisworth	34	11	4	19	50	65	37
Olney Town	34	10	6	18	53	61	36
Wellingboro' Whitworths	34	10	6	18	41	70	36
British Timken	34	9	4	21	65	107	31
Sharnbrook	34	8	5	21	51	77	29
Burton Park Wanderers	34	6	10	18	38	58	28
Towcester Town	34	6	6	22	38	72	24
Irchester United	34	1	2	31	27	144	5

5-Year, One, Two, Three

Year	1st	Pts	2nd	Pts	3rd	Pts

Premier Division

Year	1st	Pts	2nd	Pts	3rd	Pts
1986-87	Potton United	69	Baldock Town	63	Stotfold	54
1987-88	Spalding United	90	Rothwell Town	76	Raunds Town	71
1988-89	Potton United	78	Brackley Town	68	Holbeach Utd	64
1989-90	Holbeach Utd	92	Rothwell Town	89	Raunds Town	70
1990-91	Bourne Town	93	Rothwell Town	85	Eynesbury Rvrs	81

First Division

Year	1st	Pts	2nd	Pts	3rd	Pts
1985-86	Kempston Rvrs	57	Towcester Town	55	Baker Perkins	53
1986-87	Baker Perkins	58	Cogenhoe Utd	55	Ramsey Town	52
1987-88	British TD	91	M. Blackstone	84	Blisworth	83

1988-89	Ramsey Town.....88	Burton Pk Wds ...76	Sharnbrook 75
1989-90	Daventry Town...81	Higham Town.....80	Ramsey Town.....72
1990-91	Bourne Town......93	Rothwell Town...85	Eynesbury Rvrs ..81

Jewson (Eastern) League

This League was formed in 1935 with 12 clubs. Membership was increased to 16 clubs in 1948, and for several seasons Football League 'A' teams and some reserve sides took part. A second division was added in 1988. The League is in the Beazer Homes League arm of the Pyramid.

Other sponsors of this League have been Magnet & Planet; Town & Country; and Building Scene. Jewson has been the sponsor since 1988.

Premier Division	P	W	D	L	F	A	Pts
Wroxham	42	31	6	5	113	41	99
Stowmarket Town...............	42	26	9	7	86	50	87
Cornard United	42	24	8	10	85	47	80
Norwich United..................	42	23	7	12	72	53	76
Wisbech Town..................	42	23	6	13	86	62	75
Harwich & Parkeston........	42	24	2	16	106	61	74
Newmarket Town	42	19	14	9	66	50	71
Haverhill Rovers	42	18	11	13	70	61	65
Halstead Town..................	42	18	6	18	79	72	60
March Town United...........	42	15	12	15	64	49	57
Lowestoft Town................	42	16	9	17	67	64	57
Gorleston......................	42	16	8	18	62	64	56
Felixstowe Town...............	42	14	11	17	55	61	53
Great Yarmouth Town........	42	15	6	21	60	71	51
Histon.........................	42	15	5	22	61	89	50
Tiptree United..................	42	11	16	15	54	70	49
Bantham Athletic	42	12	12	18	51	69	48
Watton United..................	42	12	9	21	57	70	45
Chatteris Town.................	42	12	7	23	49	72	43
Brightlingsea United	42	11	9	22	60	83	42
Clacton Town...................	42	11	9	22	50	90	42
Thetford Town	42	3	4	35	31	135	13

First Division	P	W	D	L	F	A	Pts
Diss Town.....................	38	28	6	4	105	28	90
Fakenham Town	38	25	7	6	80	35	82
Woodbridge Town	38	19	10	9	70	34	67
Ely City.......................	38	20	6	12	66	52	66

Downham Town 38	19	5	14	68	61	62
Long Sutton Athletic...........38	18	7	13	70	58	61
Sudbury Town Res..............38	17	8	13	72	58	59
Soham Town Rangers..........38	16	11	11	70	55	59
Cambridge City Res............38	17	7	14	84	74	58
Somersham Town 38	16	9	13	75	56	57
Hadleigh United 38	17	6	15	59	61	57
Sudbury Wanderers 38	16	6	16	63	62	54
King's Lynn Res................38	12	11	15	58	61	47
Warboys Town..................38	13	8	17	60	69	47
Ipswich Wanderers 38	10	9	19	47	70	39
Bury Town Res 38	10	9	19	45	74	39
Clarksteel Yaxley..............38	11	6	21	49	79	39
Swaffham Town 38	11	5	22	53	80	38
Huntingon United 38	7	7	24	34	90	28
Mildenhall Town................38	2	9	27	31	102	15

6-Year, One, Two, Three

Year	1st ....Pts	2nd...................Pts	3rd...................Pts
1985-86	Sudbury Town......66	Colch'ter U. Res...64	Great Yarmouth T 63
1986-87	Sudbury Town......67	Braintree Town......65	Bury Town............65
1987-88	March Town U 67	Braintree Town......64	Sudbury Town......63

Premier Division

1988-89	Sudbury Town......93	Braintree Town......85	Wisbech Town 84
1989-90	Sudbury Town......88	Thetford Town......76	Braintree Town.....75
1990-91	Wisbech Town 91	Braintree Town......85	Halstead Town......82

First Division

1988-89	Wroxham 62	Halstead Town......62	Diss Town............59
1989-90	Cornard United 71	Norwich United.....69	Soham Town R.....68
1990-91	Norwich United....84	Brightlingsea Utd .77	Fakenham Town...74

Jewson Wessex League

Formed for season 1984-85 for clubs in the Chiltern and Thames Valley region. A second division was added for season 1985-86.

First Division	P	W	D	L	F	A	Pts
Wimborne Town 36	25	5	6	82	37	80
AFC Lymington.................36	23	5	8	73	39	74
Thatcham Town 36	22	4	10	85	45	70
Romsey Town 36	21	6	9	72	42	69
Swanage Town & Herston....36	20	7	9	78	38	67

	P	W	D	L	F	A	Pts
Bournemouth 36	20	6	10	73	48	66
Ryde Sports.........................36	18	8	10	61	51	62
Bemerton Heath Harlequins.36	17	10	9	51	38	61
Aerostructures.....................36	18	5	13	59	40	59
Eastleigh.............................36	18	4	14	61	53	58
Fleet Town..........................36	13	10	13	59	55	49
Brockenhurst.......................36	12	9	15	47	52	45
Christchurch........................36	9	11	16	39	54	38
East Cowes Victoria............36	9	9	18	36	72	36
Sholing Sports.....................36	9	7	20	43	81	34
B. A. T...............................36	9	4	23	41	57	31
AFC Totton.........................36	7	8	21	43	71	29
Horndean............................36	5	3	28	33	109	18
Portsmouth Royal Navy FC.36	4	5	27	30	84	17

5-Year, One, Two, Three

Year	1st ....Pts	2nd....................Pts	3rd.......................Pts
1986-87	Bashley.................75	Road Sea 73	AFC Totton............67
1987-88	Bashley.................84	Havant Town........80	Romsey Town 69
1988-89	Bashley.................82	Havant ownT 71	Newport IoW.........66
1989-90	Romsey Town 81	Newport IoW.........79	B A T 70
1990-91	Havant Town.......80	Swanage & Her 78	Bournemouth....76

Influence (Midlands) Combination

Formed in 1927 as the Worcestershire Combination, the League became the Midland Combination in 1968. A second division was added in 1961 and a third in 1979. For season 1983-84 the divisions were renamed Premier, One and Two. Few teams have moved up to the Beazer Homes League.

Premier Division	P	W	D	L	F	A	Pts
Evesham United.................40	28	7	5	76	31	91
Armitage '90 AFC 40	27	7	6	84	28	88
West Midlands Police 40	24	8	8	86	44	80
Highgate United.................40	22	11	7	71	34	77
Sandwell Borough...............40	21	8	11	81	45	71
Pershore Town '88...............40	19	11	10	76	41	68
Walsall Wood 40	18	13	9	66	42	67
Stapenhill...........................40	18	9	13	83	67	63
Boldmere St Michaels.........40	17	9	14	69	52	60
Bolehall Swifts...................40	15	14	11	59	47	59
Northfield Town 40	14	15	11	48	54	57
Coleshill Town....................40	12	15	13	46	48	51

	P	W	D	L	F	A	Pts
Alcester Town	40	11	9	20	53	74	42
Stratford Town	40	11	8	21	47	64	41
Chelmsley Wood	40	12	5	23	61	111	41
Knowle	40	10	9	21	59	77	39
Barlestone St Giles	40	10	9	21	39	78	39
Kings Heath	40	10	8	22	45	68	38
Hinckley FC	40	10	8	22	49	79	38
Bloxwich Town	40	9	8	23	48	83	35
Mile Oak Rovers	40	3	7	30	35	114	16

Division One	P	W	D	L	F	A	Pts
Studley B K L	36	22	10	4	68	35	76
Badsey Rangers	36	22	7	7	78	37	73
Wellesbourne	36	21	8	7	76	41	71
West Heath United	36	21	7	8	77	37	70
Dudley Sports	36	18	8	10	57	46	62
Becketts Sporting	36	15	12	9	67	44	57
Southam United	36	13	12	11	52	50	51
Solihull Borough Res	36	14	7	15	65	66	49
Kings Norton Ex-Service	36	13	9	14	55	56	48
Handrahan Timbers	36	11	14	11	45	38	47
Wigston Fields	36	12	10	14	47	45	46
Polesworth N Warwick	36	13	6	17	54	65	45
Triplex	36	11	10	15	50	59	43
Upton Town	36	12	6	18	49	51	42
Wilmcote	36	11	4	21	53	64	37
West Mid Fire Service	36	8	12	16	44	61	36
Ledbury Town '84	36	10	5	21	41	91	35
Stapenhill Res	36	7	8	21	60	106	29
Kings Heath Res	36	5	11	20	34	80	26

Division Two	P	W	D	L	F	A	Pts
Marston Green	38	24	13	1	87	34	85
Hams Hall	38	24	7	7	96	42	79
Kenilworth Rangers	38	23	8	7	82	59	77
Sherwood Celtic	38	22	8	8	93	42	74

Top four positions only.

5-Year, One, Two, Three

Year	1st	Pts	2nd	Pts	3rd	Pts
Premier Division						
1986-87	Stratford Town	59	Paget Rangers	57	RC Warwick	56
1987-88	RC Warwick	56	Boldmere St M.	50	Ashtree High	50

1988-89	Boldmere St M. 55	RC Warwick.........52	Evesham United ...49
1989-90	Boldmere St M. 81	Northfield Town...74	Evesham United ...73
1990-91	W. Mid. Police......80	Solihull Borough ..78	Evesham United ...74

Division One

1986-87	Wilmcote...............44	Kings Norton E.....43	Wythall.................41
1987-88	Chelmsley Town ..39	Shirley Town 38	Bloxwich Strol......32
1988-89	Bloxwich AFC 40	Streetly Celtic 39	West Heath Utd 36
1989-90	Stapenhill Res......66	Kings Norton E.....61	Studley BKL.........60
1990-91	Alcester Town 64	Wilmcote..............60	Pershore Town......57

Division Two

1986-87	Bromsgrove Ath...43	College Celtic 43	West Mids FS 40
1987-88	West Mids FS 47	Streetly Celtic 46	Weston United......41
1988-89	Upton Town.........39	Wellesbourne.......38	Studley BKL.........34
1989-90	Pershore Town......70	Alcester Town 59	Becketts Sporting .58
1990-91	Badsey Rangers....81	Becketts Sporting .68	Monica Star..........62

Unijet Sussex County League

Formed in 1920 by 12 clubs. A second division was added in 1952 and a third in 1983. Unijet have been sponsors since 1990.

Division One	P	W	D	L	F	A	Pts
Peacehaven & Tels.............34	34	29	4	1	115	24	91
Langney Sports 34	34	22	10	2	96	36	76
Littlehampton Town 34	34	23	7	4	95	42	76
Pagham.............................34	34	18	9	7	85	52	63
Wick................................34	34	16	11	7	61	50	59
Burgess Hill Town 34	34	16	7	11	64	46	55
Three Bridges....................34	34	14	11	9	66	51	53
Hailsham Town 34	34	14	8	12	73	63	50
Ringmer 34	34	13	7	14	57	60	46
Newhaven 34	34	13	6	15	63	73	45
Arundel 34	34	10	10	14	43	49	40
Eastbourne Town 34	34	12	4	18	33	63	40
Whitehawk.........................34	34	9	7	18	36	56	34
Oakwood...........................34	34	7	9	18	50	70	30
Chichester City 34	34	7	5	22	37	96	26
Bexhill Town 34	34	5	10	19	33	71	25
Shoreham 34	34	5	9	20	34	71	24
Haywards Heath Town 34	34	2	8	24	29	96	17

Division Two	P	W	D	L	F	A	Pts
Portfield 32	32	22	8	2	73	27	74
Midhurst & Easebourne 32	32	21	3	8	88	53	66
Stamco 32	32	18	7	7	76	46	61
Redhill 32	32	18	6	8	70	40	60
Worthing United 32	32	18	5	9	73	49	59
Horsham YMCA...................32	32	17	7	8	72	44	58
Selsey 32	32	16	5	11	63	48	53
Seaford Town......................32	32	15	6	11	68	53	51
Crowborough Athletic 32	32	14	4	14	58	56	46
Sidley United 32	32	12	3	17	60	80	39
Broadbridge Heath...............32	32	10	5	17	50	63	35
Little Common Albion..........32	32	10	5	17	52	66	35
Saltdean United...................32	32	9	4	19	40	68	31
East Grinstead 32	32	7	7	18	43	69	28
Lancing 32	32	7	6	19	46	58	27
Bosham 32	32	7	5	20	41	106	26
East Preston.........................32	32	4	8	20	39	86	20

5-Year, One, Two, Three

Year	1st ....Pts	2nd.....................Pts	3rd ....Pts

First Division

1986-87	Arundel 65	Whitehawk.............63	Haywards Heath ...59
1987-88	Pagham..................67	Three Bridges 61	Wick 58
1988-89	Pagham..................81	Three Bridges 66	Whitehawk.............65
1989-90	Wick 79	Littlehampton T....76	Langney Sports.....66
1990-91	Littlehampton T....77	Peacehaven & T ...77	Langney Sports.....74

Second Division

1986-87	Pagham..................72	Selsey 65	Bexhill Town........52
1987-88	Langney Sports.....66	Bexhill Town........55	Oakwood...............52
1988-89	Seaford Town 52	Ringmer 51	Midhurst & E.......48
1989-90	Bexhill Town........69	Oakwood...............60	Chichester City 57
1990-91	Newhaven 64	Chichester City.....62	Horsham YMCA...58

Winstonlead Kent League

The Kent League was formed in 1894 with two divisions. The second division later regionalised and the competition was abandoned altogether in 1959. It was reformed in 1968 and a Second Division was added in 1978. Winstonlead have been sponsors since 1985.

Division One	P	W	D	L	F	A	Pts
Herne Bay	40	29	6	5	91	34	93
Faversham Town	40	25	11	4	78	33	86
Deal Town	40	26	6	8	119	43	84
Tonbridge AFC	40	26	6	8	93	44	84
Alma Swanley	40	24	11	5	92	49	83
Sheppey United	40	21	11	8	69	44	74
Whitstable Town	40	21	8	11	70	38	71
Slade Green	40	15	12	13	68	56	57
Greenwich Borough	40	15	10	15	77	62	55
Ramsgate	40	16	7	17	62	58	55
Kent Police	40	14	11	15	60	63	53
Tunbridge Wells	40	15	8	17	61	68	53
Corinthian	40	14	8	18	57	63	50
Beckenham Town	40	13	10	17	52	67	49
Thames Polytechnic	40	8	11	21	43	78	35
Crockenhill	40	7	13	20	48	83	34
Thamesmead Town	40	9	7	24	44	100	34
Cray Wanderers	40	8	7	25	38	84	31
Chatham Town	40	7	10	23	41	89	31
Danson Furness United	40	8	6	26	39	95	30
Darenth Heathside	40	6	7	27	42	96	25

5-Year, One, Two, Three

Year	1st	Pts	2nd	Pts	3rd	Pts
Division One						
1986-87	Greenwich Boro	78	Crockenhill	75	Alma Swanley	67
1987-88	Greenwich Boro	83	Faversham Town	76	Whitstable Town	68
1988-89	Hythe Town	90	Deal Town	76	Faversham Town	73
1989-90	Faversham Town	88	Sittingbourne T	86	Tonbridge AFC	84
1990-91	Sittingbourne T	104	Cray Wanderers	92	Herne Bay	83

OFFICIAL FEEDER LEAGUES – HFS LOANS LEAGUE

An additional division, the First Division, was added for season 1987-88. In 1988-89 three clubs plus one from a 'feeder' brought the new division up to strength and, thereafter, the two 'feeder' League champions were promoted. The Northern League champions now also gain automatic promotion along with those of the Bass North West Counties League and Northern Counties East League, while for 1992-93 an additional club was promoted in order to retain a full complement of clubs.

Season	Club(s) Joining	Source and Position	
1988-89	Bishop Auckland	Northern	6th
	Colne Dynamoes	North West Counties	1st
	Newtown	Central Wales	1st
	Whitley Bay	Northern	4th
1989-90	Emley	North West Counties	1st
	Rossendale Utd	Northern Counties East	1st
1990-91	Bridlington Town	Northern Counties East	1st
	Warrington Town	North West Counties	1st
1991-92	Guisley	Northern Counties East	1st
	Knowsley	North West Counties	1st
1992-93	Ashton United	North West Counties	1st
	Gt Harwood Town	North West Counties	2nd
	Gretna	Northern Counties East	1st
	North Shields	Northern League	1st

Bass North West Counties League

Formed in 1982 on the amalgamation of the Cheshire County League and Lancashire Combination clubs not moving into the Northern Premier League. Originally comprising three divisions, the League was reduced to two divisions in 1987.

The champions are normally promoted to the NPL (with a team relegated) while other regional leagues serve the bottom division. Bass have been the sponsors since 1986.

First Division	P	W	D	L	F	A	Pts
Ashton United	34	24	5	5	61	30	77
Great Harwood Town	34	22	8	4	68	38	74
Eastwood Hanley	34	18	9	7	54	35	63
Blackpool Rovers	34	16	7	11	73	57	55
Prescot	34	15	6	13	48	43	51
Penrith	34	15	5	14	57	58	50
Skelmersdale United	34	11	11	12	48	52	44
Flixton	34	11	9	14	46	50	42
Clitheroe	34	11	9	14	44	55	42
Darwen	34	10	11	13	56	55	41
Atherton L R	34	11	8	15	38	45	41
Nantwich Town	34	11	10	13	44	49	40 *
Vauxhall G M	34	10	10	14	42	51	40
Bacup Borough	34	9	11	14	41	45	38
St Helens Town	34	9	9	16	49	55	36
Maine Road	34	9	9	16	40	60	36
Bradford Park Avenue	34	10	5	19	57	68	35
Bootle	34	9	8	17	41	61	35

* Three points deducted

Second Division	P	W	D	L	F	A	Pts
Bamber Bridge	34	25	3	6	97	39	78
Newcastle Town	34	23	6	5	69	26	75
Blackpool Mechanics	34	20	9	5	75	34	69
Burscough	34	19	7	8	82	46	64
Formby	34	17	5	12	49	39	56
Glossop	34	15	9	10	61	44	54
Salford City	34	14	9	11	57	41	51
Castleton Gabriels	34	14	9	11	54	43	51
Cheadle Town	34	15	6	13	53	50	51
Kidsgrove Athletic	34	14	7	13	44	45	49
Chadderton	34	14	6	14	50	48	48

Oldham Town	34	11	8	15	49	62	41
Atherton Collieries	34	12	4	18	51	64	40
Squires Gate	34	11	5	18	45	60	38
Holker Old Boys	34	10	6	18	37	53	36
Maghull	34	7	2	25	38	90	23
Ashton Town	34	4	7	23	47	101	19
Westhoughton Town	34	5	4	25	33	106	19

5-Year, One, Two, Three

Year	1st	Pts	2nd	Pts	3rd	Pts

First Division

Year	1st		2nd		3rd	
1986-87	Stalybridge Cel.	58	Accrington St	53	Clitheroe	52
1987-88	Colne Dynamoes	55	Rossendale Utd	55	Clitheroe	46
1988-89	Rossendale Utd	56	Knowsley Utd	50	St Helens Town	48
1989-90	Warrington T	72	Knowsley Utd	69	Colwyn Bay	60
1990-91	Knowsley Utd	83	Colwyn Bay	76	Ashton United	67

Second Division

Year	1st		2nd		3rd	
1986-87	Droylsden	48	Warrington T	45	Ashton United	44
1987-88	Ashton United	70	Flixton	64	Wren Rovers	61
1988-89	Vauxhall GM	58	Maine Road	51	Chadderton	49
1989-90	Maine Road	70	Bacup Borough	68	Blackpool Mech.	57
1990-91	Great Harwood T	86	Blackpool Rovers	78	Bradford PA	69

Northern Counties East League

Formed in 1982 on the amalgamation of the Yorkshire and Midland Leagues. With a huge number of clubs involved, the League originally had a Premier Division and regionalised Divisions One and Two (each North and South). In 1984 Division Two disappeared and Division One was split into three leagues – North, Central and South. In 1985 the format was changed to a Premier and three (non-regionalised) divisions. In 1986 the size of the League was reduced and Division Three was disposed of.

The champions are now normally promoted to the Northern Premier League (with a team relegated) while additional leagues serve the bottom division.

Premier Division	P	W	D	L	F	A	Pts
North Shields	36	31	3	2	109	14	96
Sutton Town	36	21	9	6	79	41	72
Denaby United	36	22	3	11	78	47	68 *
North Ferriby United	36	19	8	9	63	45	65
Spennymoor United	36	17	8	11	61	45	59
Sheffield	36	16	9	11	71	48	57

	P	W	D	L	F	A	Pts
Maltby M W	36	16	8	12	61	61	56
Brigg Town	36	15	7	14	44	42	52
Thackley	36	14	9	13	45	45	51
Ossett Albion	36	14	8	14	40	51	50
Belper Town	36	12	11	13	48	50	47
Ossett Town	36	11	12	13	48	57	45
Armthorpe Welfare	36	12	9	15	57	67	45
Liversedge	36	11	8	17	54	72	41
Winterton Rangers	36	10	5	21	53	78	35
Pontefract Collieries	36	9	7	20	36	71	34
Eccleshill United	36	7	10	19	38	83	31
Harrogate Rail Athletic	36	5	8	23	31	60	23
Glasshoughton Welfare	36	5	8	23	35	74	23

* One point deducted

Division One	P	W	D	L	F	A	Pts
Stocksbridge Pk Steel	30	19	5	6	71	34	62
Pickering Town	30	19	4	7	84	46	61
Bradley Rangers	30	18	7	5	59	26	61
Yorkshire Amateurs	30	18	3	9	56	27	57
Hallam	30	17	6	7	57	36	57
Hall Road Rangers	30	17	5	8	68	36	56
Rossington Main	30	13	5	12	44	38	44
R E S Parkgate	30	12	5	13	41	59	41
Immingham Town	30	12	4	14	48	64	40
Worsbrough Bridge	30	11	6	13	44	43	39
Garforth Town	30	10	5	15	48	44	35
Tadcaster Albion	30	8	4	18	37	62	28
Selby Town	30	8	4	18	32	67	28
York Railway Inst.	30	6	7	17	32	77	25
Brodsworth M W	30	6	6	18	45	72	24
Hatfield Main	30	7	2	21	36	71	22 *

* One point deducted

5-Year, One, Two, Three

Year	1st	Pts	2nd	Pts	3rd	Pts
Premier Division						
1986-87	Alfreton Town	81	Farsley Celtic	78	North Ferriby	70
1987-88	Emley	68	Armthorpe Wel.	68	Denaby United	61
1988-89	Emley	80	Hatfield Main	72	Bridlington T	68
1989-90	Bridlington Town	75	North Shields	69	Denaby United	62
1990-91	Guiseley	76	North Shields	71	Spennymoor Utd	61

258

First Division

1986-87	Ossett	70	Rowntree Mac	64	Hatfield Main	64
1987-88	York Railway In	68	Rowntree Mac	65	Maltby MW	60
1988-89	Sheffield	68	Rowntree Mac	60	Woolley MW	59
1989-90	Rowntree Mack	61	Liversedge	54	Ossett	54
1990-91	Sheffield	64	Hallam	55	Liversedge	47

Second Division

1986-87	Frenchville CA	79	Eccleshill Utd	72	Immingham T	58
1987-88	Pickering Town	60	Collingham	57	Yorkshire Amats	57
1988-89	Ossett	60	Liversedge	52	Selby Town	50
1989-90	Winterton Rgrs	51	Selby Town	47	Bradley Rangers	45
1990-91	Hall Road Rgrs	50	Worsbrough Bdge	47	Rowntree Mack	44

Northern League

Formed by ten clubs in 1889 with a second division added in 1897. The second division lasted just three seasons. In this early period several Football League reserve teams participated in the competition. In 1982, however, the second division was reinstated. Several clubs in recent years have moved elsewhere in search of the advantages of the Pyramid and the League finally joined the Pyramid system itself for the 1991-92 season feeding into the HFS Loans League First Division. Past sponsors have included Skol and Dryboroughs.

Division One	P	W	D	L	F	A	Pts
Gretna	38	25	10	3	81	33	85
Murton	38	23	9	6	83	36	78
Whitby Town	38	23	9	6	74	41	78
Guisborough Town	38	22	10	6	81	36	76
Billingham Synthonia	38	21	6	11	70	44	69
Blyth Spartans	38	19	8	11	63	44	65
South Bank	38	18	9	11	68	50	63
Northallerton Town	38	18	8	12	63	53	62
Consett	38	15	5	18	59	59	50
Tow Law Town	38	13	11	14	60	73	50
Seaham Red Star	38	13	9	16	50	57	48
Peterlee	38	14	3	21	47	70	45
Newcastle Blue Star	38	14	5	19	49	52	44 *
West Auckland Town	38	11	8	19	45	68	41
Brandon United	38	10	10	18	61	75	40
Ferryhill Athletic	38	10	10	18	45	60	40
Easington Colliery	38	11	7	20	42	61	40
Shildon	38	11	7	20	47	83	40

Langley Park	38	7	7	24	51	89	28
Wickham	38	4	5	29	38	93	17

* Three points deducted

Division Two	P	W	D	L	F	A	Pts
Stockton	38	27	7	4	102	35	88
Durham City	38	26	9	3	82	24	87
Chester le Street Town	38	26	8	4	80	36	86
Hebburn	38	27	4	7	101	44	85
Dunston Fed Brewery	38	26	6	6	104	33	84
Prudhoe East End	38	22	4	12	61	36	70
Billingham Town	38	18	7	13	60	47	61
Crook Town	38	16	9	13	54	53	57
Alnwick Town	38	15	12	11	54	60	57
Ryhope C A	38	17	5	16	77	59	56
Esh Winning	38	13	9	16	76	74	48
Ashington	38	13	9	16	50	69	48
Norton & Stockton Anc	38	11	10	17	61	69	43
Shotton Comrades	38	11	6	21	52	66	39
Horden C W	38	10	6	22	52	76	33 *
Washington	38	8	9	21	36	63	33
Evenwood Town	38	8	7	23	42	105	31
D. Cleveland Bridge	38	7	4	27	47	97	25
Bedlington Terriers	38	7	2	29	38	97	20 *
Willington	38	4	3	31	33	119	15

* Three points deducted

5-Year, One, Two, Three

Year	1st	Pts	2nd	Pts	3rd	Pts

First Division

Year	1st	Pts	2nd	Pts	3rd	Pts
1986-87	Blyth Spartans	94	B. Auckland	80	Spennymoor Utd	73
1987-88	Blyth Spartans	92	Newcastle BS	87	Billingham Syn	77
1988-89	Billingham Syn	84	Tow Law Town	77	Gretna	73
1989-90	Billingham Syn	91	Gretna	75	Tow Law Town	73
1990-91	Gretna	95	Guisborough T	75	Blyth Spartans	68

Second Division

1986-87	Billingham Syn	87	Guisborough T	79	Shildon	65
1987-88	Stockton	73	Seaham RS	71	Durham City	63
1988-89	Consett	93	Alnwick Town	84	Whickham	84
1989-90	Murton	89	Northallerton T	87	Peterlee	82
1990-91	West Auckland T	79	Langley Park	76	Easington Collry	68

McEwan's Northern Alliance

Founded in 1890 with seven clubs and often included League club reserve or 'A' teams. It grew to just short of 20 members but in 1926 amalgamated with the North Eastern League. Reformed with 13 clubs in 1935. In 1964-65 there was no competition, but otherwise the Alliance continued with a one division format until major growth and the formation of Premier, First and Second divisions in 1988.

Premier Division	P	W	D	L	F	A	Pts
West Allotment Celtic	30	20	4	6	77	26	64
Walker	30	18	4	8	63	35	58
Gillford Park	30	17	5	8	77	35	56
Seaton Delaval Amateur	30	15	9	6	62	35	54
Spittal Rovers	30	16	4	10	56	32	52
SD Seaton Terrace	30	15	6	9	65	45	51
Westerhope Hillheads	30	13	6	11	48	46	45
Wark	30	12	7	11	62	58	43
Halwhistle C-P	30	13	5	12	39	38	41 *
Ponteland United	30	11	7	12	55	46	40
Blyth Kitty Brewster	30	11	7	12	48	54	40
Forest Hall	30	9	8	13	38	55	35
Morpeth Town	30	8	8	14	38	61	32
Heaton Stannington	30	7	10	13	42	39	31
Swalwell	30	3	7	20	33	72	16
Newbiggin C W	30	2	3	25	31	157	6 *

* Three points deducted

Division One	P	W	D	L	F	A	Pts
Carlisle City	30	24	3	3	121	32	75
Winlaton Hallgarth	30	19	8	3	75	38	65
Longbenton	30	18	7	5	69	49	61
Benfield Park	30	15	8	7	69	44	53
Percy Main Amateurs	30	14	5	11	60	53	47
NEI Reyrolle	30	12	7	11	61	56	43
Wylam H S	30	11	9	10	58	56	42
Ryton	30	11	9	10	56	57	42
Proctor & Gamble FC	30	12	5	13	71	71	41
Northern Electric	30	10	6	14	53	69	36
Northern Counties	30	9	8	13	51	66	35
New York United	30	8	9	13	48	63	33
Dudley Welfare	30	7	9	14	52	72	30
Hexham Swinton	30	10	2	18	46	68	29 *
Newcastle University	30	5	6	19	33	69	21

Wallsend Rising Sun	30	3	3	24	34	95	12

* Three points deducted

Division Two	P	W	D	L	F	A	Pts
St Columbas	28	22	4	2	64	25	70
Percy Rovers	28	20	4	4	76	32	64
C K Brinkburn	28	16	7	5	103	50	52 *
Shankhouse	28	14	9	5	82	42	51
Ashington H P	28	15	6	7	74	54	51
Amble Town	28	15	5	8	75	49	50
Marden Athletic	28	12	7	9	57	57	43
Gosforth Bohemians	28	11	6	11	63	54	39
Swalwell C C	28	9	8	11	69	70	35
Norgas United	28	9	4	15	62	65	31
Monkseaton KOSA	28	7	6	15	40	77	27
Highfields United	28	6	4	18	53	90	22
Stobswood Welfare	28	4	9	15	48	72	21
Heddon Institute	28	5	4	19	34	79	19
Spartan FC Blyth	28	3	1	24	48	132	10

*Three points deducted

5-Year, One, Two, Three

Year	1st	Pts	2nd	Pts	3rd	Pts
1986-87	W Allotment	40	Dunston T. S.	40	Morpeth Town	37
1987-88	SD Seaton Ter	43	Prudhoe East	39	Gosforth St N	39

Premier Division

1989-89	SD Seaton Ter	69	W Allotment	62	Seaton Delaval	58
1989-90	Seaton Delaval	59	W Allotment	58	Forest Hall	57
1990-91	W. Allotment C	62	Seaton Terrace	54	Heaton Stann	49

Division One

1988-89	Ashington HP.	63	Haltwhistle	61	Westerhope W	59
1989-90	Westerhope W	73	Walker	62	Hexham	62
1990-91	Blyth KB	64	Spittal Rovers	60	Heaton Corner H	56

Division Two

1988-89	Blyth KB	65	Stobswood Utd	65	Walker S	63
1989-90	Heaton CH	66	Longbenton	61	Spittal Rovers	58
1990-91	Proctor & Gmbl	58	Wylam Home S	57	Hebburn Reyrole	53

Vaux Wearside League

Founded in 1892 with 10 clubs and often included League club reserve or 'A' teams. There was a major increase of membership in the early 1970s but it was not until 1988-89 that a Second Division, comprising 12 clubs was introduced.

Division One	P	W	D	L	F	A	Pts	
Eppleton CW	30	22	3	5	79	34	69	
Hartlepool Town	30	20	7	3	60	30	67	
South Shields	30	21	3	6	90	34	66	
Marske United	30	20	4	6	85	37	58	*
Annfield Plain	30	17	3	10	57	48	54	
Boldon CA	30	12	9	9	48	41	45	
Wolviston	30	13	5	12	59	55	44	
Cleadon South Shields	30	12	7	11	45	43	43	
Newton Aycliffe	30	13	3	14	44	45	42	
Vaux Ryhope	30	11	8	11	56	65	41	
IFG Roker	30	12	4	14	43	46	40	
Cleator Moor Celtic	30	8	6	16	43	64	30	
Herrington CW	30	7	3	20	32	65	24	
Darlington Railway Ath	30	4	9	17	36	66	18	
Usworth Village	30	4	5	21	22	72	17	
Bohemians	30	3	3	24	27	81	12	

* Six points deducted

Division Two	P	W	D	L	F	A	Pts
Silksworth	22	15	3	4	70	35	48
Jarrow Roofing	22	15	3	4	53	29	48
Windscale	22	15	0	7	45	39	45
Hebburn Colliery	22	13	2	7	45	31	41
Hartlepool BWOB	22	12	1	9	46	29	37
Stanley United	22	9	3	10	29	37	30
Marchon	22	8	4	10	37	41	28
Nissan	22	7	7	8	32	43	28
Esh Albion	22	7	3	12	33	46	24
Wingate	22	6	5	11	28	32	23
Jarrow	22	5	1	16	32	53	16
Sunderland Flogas	22	3	2	17	26	61	11

HFS Loans Additional Regional Leagues

Central Midlands League

Supreme Division	P	W	D	L	F	A	Pts
Lincoln United	34	26	5	3	95	26	83
Hucknall Town	34	22	3	9	86	44	69
Louth United	34	20	6	8	72	41	66
Harworth Colliery	34	20	5	9	76	51	65
Sheffield Aurora	34	22	2	10	68	33	62 †
Mickleover RBL	34	19	3	12	77	54	60
Blidworth Welfare	34	16	5	13	46	46	53
Arnold Town	34	15	7	12	73	60	52
Priory Eastwood	34	14	7	13	50	56	49
Nettleham	34	13	8	13	49	52	47
Heanor Town	34	13	6	15	48	54	45
Oakham United	34	13	6	15	52	59	45
Borrowash Victoria	34	8	11	15	49	63	35
Shirebrook Colliery	34	10	5	19	51	68	35
Wombwell Town	34	10	4	20	52	71	31 *
Melton Town	34	7	5	22	42	93	26
Stanton Ilkeston	34	7	4	23	29	78	25
Glapwell	34	3	4	27	44	112	13

* Three points deducted   † Six points deducted

Premier Division	P	W	D	L	F	A	Pts
Fryston C W	26	20	2	4	75	33	62
Kiveton Park	26	17	4	5	63	29	55
Norton Woodseats	26	14	7	5	58	33	49
Mexborough Town	26	12	8	6	46	31	44
South Normanton Ath	26	13	5	8	42	32	44
Blackwell M W	26	11	6	9	38	44	39
Rossington	26	11	4	11	42	50	37
Lincoln Moorlands	26	9	6	11	44	40	33
Holbrook M W	26	8	9	9	35	42	33
Kilburn M W	26	8	6	12	56	60	30
Biwater	26	8	4	14	43	41	28
Selston	26	6	6	14	33	60	24
Retford Rail	26	3	6	17	33	70	15
Nuthall	26	4	3	19	34	77	15

Division One	P	W	D	L	F	A	Pts
Slack & Parr...........................30	30	24	3	3	81	23	75
Gedling Town 30	30	19	6	5	91	42	63
Kimberley Town..................30	30	17	6	7	66	40	57
Highfield Rangers...............30	30	15	8	7	48	28	53
Newhall United...................30	30	17	2	11	63	49	53
Shardlow St James.............30	30	15	4	11	49	38	49
Long Eaton United..............30	30	13	5	12	67	49	44
Derby C & W Reckitts........30	30	14	2	14	47	42	44
Alvaston & Boulton.............30	30	12	6	12	45	44	42
Derby Rolls Royce...............30	30	11	7	12	48	62	40
Radford 30	30	12	3	15	49	72	39
Leicester Nirvana 30	30	11	1	18	37	65	31 *
Brailsford 30	30	8	5	17	43	74	29
West Hallam 30	30	7	2	21	38	73	23
Bulwell United 30	30	6	4	20	46	85	22
Attenborough 30	30	5	4	21	37	69	19

* *Three points deducted*

5-Year, One, Two, Three

Year	1st ....Pts	2nd.......................Pts	3rd ....Pts

Supreme Division

1986-87	Hinckley Town.....54	Harworth Col........44	Lincoln Utd...........42
1987-88	Harworth Col........66	Hinckley Town.....64	Ilkeston Town.......58
1988-89	Boston.................65	Arnold.................60	Gainsborough T....57
1989-90	Hucknall Town.....93	Heanor Town.......81	Arnold 76
1990-91	Hucknall Town.....75	Heanor Town.......67	Lincoln United......66

Premier Division

1986-87	Stanton 72	Huthwaite.............69	Mickleover............58
1987-88	Huthwaite.............80	Derby Prims..........68	Melton Town.........61
1988-89	Priory...................83	Mickleover............80	Highfield Rangers 74
1989-90	Mickleover............91	Highfield Rangers 81	Nettleham..............74
1990-91	Mickleover 78	Highfield Rangers 76	Blackwell 72

First Division

1986-87	Shirebrook C.........65	Shirebrook Coll 56	Thorntons..............55
1987-88	Stanton 57	Priory...................54	Blackwell...............46
1988-89	Brailsford.............66	Swanwick PR.........65	West Hallam..........65
1989-90	Glapwell................68	Leicester Nirvana .67	Bulwell United 63
1990-91	Gedling Town........54	Derby C & W 49	Nuthall.................46

Liverpool County Combination

First Division	P	W	D	L	F	A	Pts
Yorkshire Copper Tubes......30	30	22	4	4	96	45	70
St Dominics.................30	30	21	6	3	93	32	69
Stanton Dale................30	30	18	7	5	76	42	61
Ayone......................30	30	18	5	7	68	47	59
Waterloo Dock...............30	30	16	9	5	73	58	57
Crawfords U B...............30	30	15	7	8	69	43	52
Littlewoods Athletic........30	30	15	5	10	63	47	50
Speke......................30	30	14	4	12	67	60	46
Earle......................30	30	14	2	14	61	62	44
Ford Motors................30	30	11	6	13	46	60	39
B. Rail Nth. End S C........30	30	11	4	15	47	55	37
Electric Supply.............30	30	9	5	16	41	53	32
Mossley Hill................30	30	7	6	17	41	69	27
Crystal Villa...............30	30	6	3	21	49	80	21
Cheshire Lines..............30	30	2	2	26	35	115	8
Bootle Res..................30	30	1	5	24	23	80	5 *

Second Division	P	W	D	L	F	A	Pts
Lucas Sports................28	28	24	0	4	97	30	72
B.R.N.E.S.C. Res............28	28	17	6	5	90	56	57
Eldonians..................28	28	17	3	8	59	38	54
Beesix.....................28	28	16	5	7	67	53	53
Ford Motors Res............28	28	14	4	10	77	50	46
Camadale...................28	28	12	3	13	53	52	39
Royal Seaforth.............28	28	12	3	13	54	60	39
Knowsley United Res 28	28	13	0	15	60	63	36 *
Halewood Town..............28	28	8	10	10	46	52	34
Merseybus FC...............28	28	9	7	12	52	67	34
Speke Res..................28	28	9	5	14	54	68	32
Mersey Docks H C 28	28	8	6	14	43	67	27 *
Mossley Hill Res............28	28	5	10	13	47	69	22 *
Plessey GPT................28	28	6	4	18	55	91	22
Electric Supply Res.........28	28	5	4	19	38	76	19

Three points deducted

4-Year, One, Two, Three

Year	1st	Pts	2nd	Pts	3rd	Pts
1987-88	Uniasco	53	Waterloo Dock	44	Earle	38
1988-89	Waterloo Dock	46	St. Dominics	43	Ayone	40
1989-90	Waterloo Dock	72	St. Dominics	64	Stanton Dale	57
1990-91	Stanton Dale	64	St. Dominics	63	Crawfords UB	63

John Smith's West Lancashire League

Division One	P	W	D	L	F	A	Pts
Burnley Bank Hall	34	28	4	2	107	37	88
Vickers Sports Club	34	26	3	5	110	35	81
BAC Preston	34	22	8	4	93	44	74
Feniscowles	34	21	9	4	62	30	72
Eagley	34	16	5	13	65	53	53
Poulton Town	34	14	10	10	66	53	52
Dalton United	34	15	6	13	61	53	51
Burnley United	34	15	5	14	61	51	50
Lytham St Annes	34	11	15	8	63	60	48
Royal Ordnance	34	13	4	17	53	54	43
Vernon Carus	34	12	7	15	54	61	43
Wigan College	34	12	4	18	58	58	40
Turton Bolton	34	10	9	15	66	81	39
Norcross & Warbreck	34	9	5	20	47	90	32
Blackpool Rangers	34	7	7	20	36	86	28
Freckleton	34	6	7	21	38	81	25
Springfields	34	6	6	22	30	82	24
Carnforth Rangers	34	4	4	26	26	87	16

Division Two	P	W	D	L	F	A	Pts
ICI Thornton	34	23	4	7	104	49	73
Colne British Legion	34	23	4	7	90	63	73
Claxo Ulverston	34	22	5	7	98	43	71
Blackrod Town	34	22	5	7	95	52	71
Multipart Chorley	34	20	7	7	75	43	67
Longridge United	34	19	5	10	120	64	62
Lansil Lancaster	34	18	5	11	79	53	59
Padiham	34	16	8	10	68	49	56
Blackpool Rovers Res	34	16	6	12	75	53	51 *
Kirkham & Wesham	34	13	9	12	61	67	48
Hesketh Bank	34	14	6	14	71	77	48
Barrow Wanderers	34	12	5	17	65	67	41
Haslingden	34	9	7	18	49	68	34
Wigan Rovers	34	9	4	21	57	81	31
Fleetwood Hesketh	34	6	8	20	51	81	26
Nelson	34	6	7	21	61	95	25
BAE Warton	34	7	5	22	62	93	23 *
Lucas SC Burnley	34	1	0	33	19	192	3

Three points deducted

5-Year, One, Two, Three

Year	1st	Pts	2nd	Pts	3rd	Pts
1986-87	Holker OB	49	Vickers SC	49	BAC Preston	46
1987-88	BAC Preston	72	Holker OB	63	Squires Gate	59
1988-89	BAC Preston	74	Vickers SC	67	Holker OB	67
1989-90	Colne Dy. Res	89	Wigan College	74	BAC Preston	69
1990-91	BAC Preston	79	Vickers SC	74	Burnley Bnk Hall	70

Manchester League

Premier Division	P	W	D	L	F	A	Pts
East Manchester	34	24	4	6	107	41	76
Wythenshaw Amateurs	34	21	9	4	71	18	72
Abbey Hey	34	20	8	6	94	49	68
Little Hulton	34	21	4	9	69	56	67
Greater Man. Police	34	17	8	9	67	42	59
Springhead	34	16	8	10	64	49	56
Mitchell Shackleton	34	15	9	10	58	46	54
Ramsbottom United	34	16	5	13	58	48	53
BT Cables Leigh	34	12	11	11	63	66	47
Highfield United	34	10	13	11	53	54	43
Silcoms Woodside	34	11	8	15	61	70	41
ICI Blackley	34	9	11	14	55	62	38
Dukinfield Town	34	8	12	14	45	52	36
Stockport Georgians	34	8	8	18	47	78	32
Wythenshawe Town	34	7	9	18	34	63	30
Prestwich Heys	34	6	11	17	39	78	29
Crompton Town	34	7	3	24	32	102	24
Avro	34	3	9	22	39	82	18

Division One	P	W	D	L	F	A	Pts
Woodley Sports	36	29	2	5	95	37	89
Whitworth Valley	36	27	6	3	119	46	87
Old Altrinchamians	36	22	2	12	82	51	68
Atherton Town	36	20	5	11	95	48	65
Monton Amateurs	36	19	8	9	79	51	65
Sacred Hearts	36	17	12	7	85	55	63
Waterloo	36	18	4	14	75	62	58
Urmston	36	18	4	14	72	63	58
Gorton	36	15	9	12	77	64	54
Pennington	36	15	8	13	69	67	53
Milton	36	12	11	13	59	66	47

New Mills	36	12	8	16	64	72	44
Whalley Range	36	12	7	17	67	69	43
Brightmet	36	10	10	16	64	80	40
Ashton Athletic	36	10	6	20	65	85	36
Hollinwood	36	8	7	21	55	90	31
Little Lever	36	4	12	20	53	96	24
Oldham Victoria	36	6	6	24	49	117	24
British Vita	36	4	1	31	39	144	13

5-Year, One, Two, Three

Year	1st	Pts	2nd	Pts	3rd	Pts
1986-87	Adswood Am.	59	Maine Road	57	Wythenshaw Am.	52
1987-88	Stockport Geo.	60	Little Hulton	55	E. Manchester	49
1988-89	Abbey Hey	54	Little Hulton	54	Prestwich H.	51
1989-90	Wythenshawe Am	57	E. Manchester	55	Springhead	50
1990-91	Abbey Hey	75	Springhead	65	E. Manchester	63

Roger Smith Insurance Notts Football Alliance

Senior Division	P	W	D	L	F	A	Pts
GPT Plessey	30	23	3	4	77	25	49
Notts Police	30	23	1	6	75	32	47
Rainworth M W	30	18	8	4	60	21	44
Clipstone M W	30	21	2	7	62	31	44
Worthington Simpsons	30	16	4	10	62	45	36
Radcliffe Olympic	30	12	10	8	49	43	34
Pelican	30	13	6	11	64	66	32
Hucknall Rolls Royce	30	12	6	12	49	51	30
Dunkirk	30	11	6	13	59	52	28
John Player	30	10	7	13	45	44	27
Greenwood Meadows	30	9	7	14	40	50	25
Cotgrave M W	30	9	6	15	39	58	24
Ruddington	30	9	4	17	45	63	22
Thoreseby C W	30	7	6	17	33	61	20
Basford United	30	2	6	22	31	95	10
Clifton All Whites	30	3	2	25	23	77	8

Division One	P	W	D	L	F	A	Pts
Boots Athletic	30	24	2	4	93	28	50
Bulwell Forest Villa	30	21	4	5	71	27	46
Sneinton	30	21	4	5	73	29	46
Awsworth Villa	30	15	5	10	71	44	35
Keyworth United	30	·14	7	9	50	37	35

Worthington Simpson Res	30	12	6	12	73	74	30
Gedling C W	30	10	8	12	49	48	28
Carlton Athletic	30	12	4	14	47	52	28
Southwell City	30	10	7	13	48	62	27
Clipstone M W Res	30	10	4	16	43	58	24
Rainworth M W Res	30	7	10	13	41	53	24
Bilsthorpe C W	30	10	5	15	44	50	23 *
Stapleford Villa	30	9	5	16	33	49	23
City & Sherwood Hospital	30	8	7	15	41	70	23
British Rail	30	9	4	17	39	77	22
GPT Plessey Res	30	4	6	20	42	100	14

* Two points deducted

Division Two	P	W	D	L	F	A	Pts
Wollaton	32	28	1	3	100	30	57
Hucknall Rolls Royce Res	32	21	7	4	83	28	49
Ollerton & Bevercotes	32	20	8	4	91	42	48
Bestwood M W	32	20	7	5	89	44	47
Retford United	32	18	5	9	83	48	41
Calverton C W	32	16	8	8	64	44	40
Teversal Grange	32	17	6	9	66	52	40
Linby C W	32	16	5	11	88	45	37
Dunkirk Res	32	12	8	12	82	77	32
Fairham	32	9	11	12	60	50	29
John Player Res	32	12	5	15	62	66	29
Basford United Res	32	10	6	16	62	69	26
Greenwood Meadows Res	32	9	8	16	45	69	26
Ruddington Res	32	3	6	23	43	106	12
Ryecroft	32	4	4	24	47	133	12
Carlton Athletic Res	32	4	3	25	30	93	11
Southwell City Res	32	3	2	27	40	139	8

5-Year, One, Two, Three

Year	1st	Pts	2nd	Pts	3rd	Pts
Senior Division						
1986-87	Notts Police	47	Rainworth MW	46	Hucknall CW	46
1987-88	Hucknall Town	48	Rainworth MW	43	Notts Police	41
1988-89	Hucknall Town	47	Dunkirk	43	Worthington S	40
1989-90	John Player	43	Dunkirk	41	Notts Police	37
1990-91	Rainworth Mines	51	Dunkirk	44	Worthington S	38

Tetley Walker West Cheshire AF League

Division One	P	W	D	L	F	A	Pts
Cammell Laird	30	20	5	5	72	32	45
Shell	30	18	5	7	54	34	41
Heswall	30	15	10	5	70	36	40
Christleton	30	14	10	6	60	36	38
Bromborough Pool	30	14	9	7	59	37	37
Merseyside Police	30	16	4	10	69	45	36
Poulton Victoria	30	14	7	9	56	44	35
Mersey Royal	30	13	4	13	45	44	30
General Chemicals	30	12	6	12	37	49	30
Ashville	30	11	5	14	47	52	27
Stork	30	9	7	14	44	47	25
Vauxhall Motors	30	7	9	14	38	48	23
Newton	30	8	7	15	40	62	23
Upton Athletic Assoc.	30	8	3	19	34	82	19
Capenhurst	30	4	8	18	34	68	16
Moreton	30	4	7	19	24	67	15

Division Two	P	W	D	L	F	A	Pts
Poulton Victoria Res	34	23	7	4	74	35	53
Cammell Laird Res	34	23	6	5	106	42	52
Heswall Res	34	20	10	4	85	58	50
Bromborough Pool Res	34	18	10	6	75	50	46
Blacon Youth Club	34	18	7	9	86	63	43
Mond Rangers	34	14	8	12	67	61	36
Mersey Royal Res	34	10	15	9	72	61	35
Ashville Res	34	13	9	12	52	52	35
Manor Athletic	34	13	5	16	61	65	31
Willaston	34	10	9	15	52	62	29
Vauxhall Motors Res	34	11	6	17	57	68	28
Rivacre Sports Club	34	11	6	17	71	87	28
Christleton Res	34	10	8	16	52	72	28
St Werburghs	34	8	11	15	58	59	27
Merseyside Police Res	34	8	9	17	45	76	25
West Kirby	34	7	10	17	55	73	24
Stork Res	34	7	10	17	57	86	24
Shell Res	34	4	10	20	47	102	18

5-Year, One, Two, Three

Year	1st	Pts	2nd	Pts	3rd	Pts
1986-87	Cammell Laird	45	Heswall	43	Poulton Victoria	42
1987-88	Heswall Res	41	Gen. Chemicals	40	Cammell Laird	38

1988-89	Cammell Laird......46	Mersey Police 42	Gen. Chemicals 40
1989-90	Cammell Laird......42	Mersey Royal 42	Heswall Res..........38
1990-91	Cammell Laird......49	Mersey Royal 39	Mersey Police.......37

Whitbread County Senior League

Premier Division	P	W	D	L	F	A	Pts
Phoenix 26	26	20	3	3	50	18	63
Ash House..............................26	26	17	6	3	67	30	57
Mexborough Main St. 26	26	13	7	6	63	32	46
Goldthorpe Colliery 26	26	11	7	8	34	32	40
Oughtibridge MW SC 26	26	10	7	9	46	37	37
A B M 26	26	11	3	12	39	47	36
Hallam...................................26	26	10	5	11	51	43	35
Denaby & Cadeby MW 26	26	8	11	7	51	43	35
Wath Saracens Athletic.........26	26	9	6	11	44	45	33
Parramore Sports...................26	26	9	4	13	41	56	31
White Rose Throstles.............26	26	8	6	12	41	43	30
Wath St James.......................26	26	7	7	12	32	48	28
Ecclesfield Red Rose 26	26	7	3	16	36	53	24
Caribbean Sports...................26	26	3	3	20	18	86	12

5-Year, One, Two, Three

Year	1st ....Pts	2nd.....................Pts	3rd ....Pts
1986-87	Mexboro' Main ...39	Ash House.............40	Windsor.................36
1987-88	Ash House.............37	Davy McKee 31	Windsor.................30
1988-89	Ash House.............40	Aurora United........38	Mexboro' Main 36
1989-90	Ash House.............42	Aurora United........36	Mexboro' Main 30
1990-91	Ash House.............60	Denaby-Cadeby....54	Parramore Sports..46

MISCELLANEOUS LEAGUES

The Abacus Welsh League

National Division	P	W	D	L	F	A	Pts
Abergavenny Thursdays	30	23	5	2	64	24	74
Britton Ferry	30	23	1	6	76	43	70
Aberystwyth Town	30	18	6	6	65	35	60
Haverfordwest County	30	16	7	7	61	41	55
Ton Pentre	30	16	6	8	51	43	54
Maesteg Park	30	15	6	9	57	37	51
Cwmbran Town	30	11	12	7	50	42	45
Afan Lido	30	12	7	11	54	47	43
Pembroke Boro	30	10	7	13	50	48	37
Llanelli	30	9	6	15	43	61	33
Ebbw Vale	30	8	8	14	38	61	32
Inter Cardiff	30	7	8	15	32	45	29
Caldicot	30	6	6	18	32	59	24
Brecon Corries	30	6	5	19	36	61	23
Bridgend Town	30	4	8	18	25	58	20
Ferndale Athletic	30	4	6	20	31	63	18

Division One	P	W	D	L	F	A	Pts
Blaenrhondda	32	18	8	6	76	47	62
Morriston Town	32	18	3	11	58	37	57
Ammanford Town	32	16	9	7	55	35	57
Port Talbot	32	15	9	8	57	41	54
Caerleon	32	15	8	9	58	34	53
Pontypridd-Ynysybwl	32	15	4	13	57	53	49
Aberaman Athletic	32	14	6	12	52	48	48
Cardiff Civil Service	32	13	9	10	51	48	48
Taffs Well	32	13	7	12	42	41	46
Risca United	32	12	6	14	51	52	42
Llanwern	32	10	9	13	40	44	39
B P	32	11	5	16	47	54	38
Newport YMCA	32	11	5	16	41	54	38
Cardiff Corinthians	32	9	9	14	50	60	36
Pontllanfraith	32	8	10	14	38	57	34

	P	W	D	L	F	A	Pts
Seven Sisters	32	8	7	17	37	62	31
Garw	32	5	8	19	30	73	23

Division Two	P	W	D	L	F	A	Pts
AFC Porth	32	28	3	1	79	20	87
Carmarthen Town	32	22	6	4	71	19	72
Skewen Athletic	32	18	7	7	51	33	61
Tonyrefail Welfare	32	16	8	8	54	36	56
Caerau	32	16	8	8	52	39	56
South Wales Police	32	15	8	9	50	39	53
Pontyclun	32	13	9	10	51	39	48
Treharris Athletic	32	12	7	13	51	54	43
Pontardawe	32	12	5	15	43	52	41
Pontlottyn	32	10	9	13	42	42	39
Goytre United	32	10	8	14	40	47	38
Milford United	32	11	5	16	48	68	38
Panteg	32	8	5	19	37	63	29
Cardiff Inst. of HE	32	7	7	18	41	67	28
AFC Tondu	32	5	9	18	40	62	24
Abercynon Athletic	32	6	6	20	38	69	24
Trelewis	32	4	8	20	26	65	20

5-Year, One, Two, Three
National Division

Year	1st	Pts	2nd	Pts	3rd	Pts
1986-87	Barry Town	83	Ton Pentre	83	Cwmbran Town	62
1987-88	Ebbw Vale	82	Barry Town	80	Ton Pentre	76
1988-89	Barry Town	88	Aberystwyth T	76	Haverfordwest	63
1989-90	Haverfordwest	62	Aberystwyth T	61	Abergavenny	61
1990-91	Abergavenny	69	Aberystwyth T	59	Haverfordwest	54

Cymru Alliance

	P	W	D	L	F	A	Pts
Caersws	30	15	10	5	65	27	55
Llansantffraid	30	15	8	7	58	34	53
Porthmadog	30	14	10	6	63	43	52
Flint Town United	30	14	9	7	58	37	51
Conwy United	30	15	5	10	62	45	50
Connah's Quay Nomads	30	11	12	7	41	33	45
Mostyn	30	13	6	11	52	56	45
Lex XI	30	11	10	9	43	50	43
Penrhyncoch	30	11	7	12	53	51	40

	P						
Mold Alexandra	30	12	3	15	40	46	36 *
Holywell Town	30	7	10	13	48	49	31
Llandloes Town	30	8	7	15	37	57	31
Gresford Athletic	30	8	6	16	33	54	30
Carno	30	5	2	23	28	69	17
Brymbo	30	4	2	24	29	108	14
Welshpool Town	30	20	7	3	74	23	1 †

three points deducted † 66 points deducted

1-Year, One, Two, Three

Year	1st	Pts	2nd	Pts	3rd	Pts
1990-91	Flint Town U	67	Caersws	60	Connah's Quay	51

(League formed in 1990)

Dorset Football Combination League

	P	W	D	L	F	A	Pts
Blandford United	36	22	10	4	54	29	76
Westland Sports	36	21	8	7	74	47	71
Parley Sports	36	20	10	6	60	37	70
Dorchester Town Res.	36	18	9	9	78	48	63
Shaftsbury	36	18	9	9	81	56	63
Sturminster Newton	36	18	8	10	48	42	62
Hamworthy United	36	17	10	9	92	55	61
Bournemouth Sports	36	16	9	11	69	49	57
Flight Refuelling	36	15	12	9	59	42	57
Sherborne Town	36	16	8	12	63	47	56
Weymouth Res.	36	16	5	15	66	52	53
Bridport Res.	36	13	7	16	53	59	46
Portland United	36	11	8	17	59	72	41
Gillingham Town	36	8	11	17	55	62	35
Wareham Rangers	36	8	9	19	46	64	33
Swanage T & Herston Res	36	9	5	22	37	69	32
Cranborne	36	8	6	22	46	102	30
Poole Town Res	36	4	12	20	34	69	24
Holt United	36	2	8	26	26	99	14

5-Year, One, Two, Three

Year	1st	Pts	2nd	Pts	3rd	Pts
1986-87	Bridport	58	Parley Sports	53	Westland Sports	51
1987-88	Bridport	60	Flight Refuelling	52	Westland Sports	51
1988-89	Shaftesbury	53	Westland Sports	48	Parley Sports	44
1989-90	Weymouth Res	56	Flight Refuelling	46	Westland Sports	41
1990-91	Dorchester T. Res	54	Flight Refuelling	51	Westland Sports	47

Everards Brewery Leicestershire Senior League

Premier Division	P	W	D	L	F	A	Pts
Holwell Sports	30	21	6	3	97	30	69
St Andrews S C	30	19	4	7	65	49	61
Birstall United	30	15	8	7	57	44	53
Anstey Nomads	30	15	6	9	64	38	51
Barwell Athletic	30	12	11	7	56	48	47
Houghton Rangers	30	14	4	12	65	51	46
Lutterworth Town	30	12	10	8	46	39	46
Ibstock Welfare	30	9	15	6	45	39	42
Friar Lane Old Boys	30	10	8	12	63	62	38
Newfoundpool WMC	30	10	8	12	48	50	38
Leics Constabulary	30	9	9	12	48	52	36
Oadby Town	30	9	8	13	47	60	35
Pedigree Petfoods	30	7	7	16	43	61	28
Syston St Peters	30	8	4	18	49	78	28
Narboro' & Littlethorpe	30	5	7	18	38	86	22
Hillcroft	30	3	9	18	30	74	18

5-Year, One, Two, Three
Senior Division

Year	1st	Pts	2nd	Pts	3rd	Pts
1986-87	Stapenhill	48	Wigston Fields	44	Kirby Muxlow	41
1987-88	Holwell Works	46	Stapenhill	42	St. Andrews SC	41
1988-89	Stapenhill	53	Wigston Town	38	Birstall United	38
1989-90	St Andrews SC	67	Syston St Peters	64	Lutterworth Tn	55
1990-91	Lutterworth Tn	57	Anstey Nomads	57	Oadby Town	56

Jewson South Western League

First Division	P	W	D	L	F	A	Pts
Falmouth Town	34	26	5	3	91	20	57
Newquay	34	23	5	6	88	31	51
Bugle	34	16	9	9	65	46	41
Truro City	34	14	11	9	74	49	39
Bodmin Town	34	15	9	10	53	51	39
Clyst Rovers	34	15	8	11	59	60	38
Appledore-Bideford AAC	34	16	5	13	78	56	37
Porthleven	34	14	8	12	77	69	36
St. Blazey	34	15	6	13	72	67	36
Torpoint Athletic	34	14	7	13	49	50	35
Holsworthy	34	9	16	9	37	46	34
Wadebridge Town	34	12	7	15	45	52	31

St Austell	34	10	8	16	45	63	28
Millbrook	34	9	9	16	45	70	27
Launceston	34	8	6	20	45	73	22
Devon-Cornwall Police	34	7	8	19	43	78	22
Tavistock	34	8	5	21	53	79	21
Penzance	34	7	4	23	35	94	18

5-Year, One, Two, Three

Year	1st	Pts	2nd	Pts	3rd	Pts
1986-87	Falmouth Town	62	St Blazey	60	Millbrook	57
1987-88	Newquay	65	Falmouth Town	62	St Blazey	56
1988-89	Falmouth Town	55	St Blazey	53	Bodmin Town	53
1989-90	Falmouth Town	54	St Blazey	50	Bodmin Town	44
1990-91	Bodmin Town	55	St. Blazey	52	Falmouth Town	45

Leading Agencies Hampshire League

Division One	P	W	D	L	F	A	Pts
Coldon Common	34	20	10	4	56	33	70
Blackfield & Langley	34	20	8	6	70	32	68
Whitchurch United	34	18	10	6	71	39	64
Pirelli General	34	18	9	7	54	30	63
Malshanger	34	16	8	10	52	41	56
DCA Basingstoke	34	15	9	10	55	41	54
Arton Town Bass	34	15	8	11	48	41	53
A C Delco	34	15	6	13	50	42	51
Fleetlands	34	15	6	13	58	54	51
Locksheath	34	13	9	12	44	41	45
Downton	34	13	5	16	44	41	44
Bishops Waltham Town	34	12	6	16	51	61	42
Cowes Sports	34	9	12	13	40	51	39
ISL Midanbury	34	10	6	18	58	76	36
Alresford Town	34	8	5	21	46	74	29
Awbridge	34	7	8	19	38	70	29
Brading Town	34	8	4	22	37	73	28
West Wight	34	6	7	21	27	59	25

Division Two (top 6)	P	W	D	L	F	A	Pts
Winchester City	28	18	8	2	53	24	62
Overton United	28	17	7	4	56	21	58
New Milton	28	16	4	8	53	36	52
Paulsgrove	28	14	6	8	46	31	48
Verwood Town	28	14	5	9	48	38	47
Otterbourne	28	13	7	8	62	44	46

5-Year, One, Two, Three
Division One

Year	1st	Pts	2nd	Pts	3rd	Pts
1986-87	East Cowes Vic	62	Locksheath	51	Folland Spts	47
1987-88	BAT	55	Basing Rovers	49	Blackfield & L.	47
1988-89	BAT	53	Blackfield & L.	47	Pirelli Gen	46
1989-90	Ryde Sports	70	Arton Town	63	Netley CS	61
1990-91	Locksheath	81	DCA Basingstoke	74	Blackfield & L.	69

Mid-Cheshire League

Division One	P	W	D	L	F	A	Pts
Grove United	30	23	2	5	74	21	71
Knutsford	30	18	6	6	47	29	60
Linotype	30	18	5	7	67	40	59
North Trafford	30	16	7	7	56	37	55
Barnton	30	15	4	11	60	48	49
Hanley Town	30	14	6	10	42	36	48
Garswood United	30	14	4	12	48	42	46
Poynton	30	14	4	12	57	55	46
Bramhall	30	13	6	11	62	56	45
Rylands Rec	30	11	6	13	50	43	39
Whitchurch Alport	30	10	5	15	38	57	35
Newcastle Town	30	9	5	16	41	48	32
Chorlton Town	30	8	8	14	41	52	32
Wilmslow Albion	30	6	7	17	41	66	25
Winnington Park	30	5	7	18	40	67	22
Styal	30	4	2	24	33	100	14

Division Two	P	W	D	L	F	A	Pts
Broadheath Central	32	24	4	4	85	31	76
Beechams	32	23	4	5	78	24	73
ICI Pharmaceuticals	32	20	5	7	93	43	65
Pilkington	32	17	7	8	69	46	58
Alsager	32	16	5	11	48	42	53
Middlewich Athletic	32	14	8	10	54	46	50
Malpas	32	14	5	13	68	60	47
Bramhall Res	32	13	8	11	55	58	47
Linotype Res	32	13	5	14	60	71	44
Rylands Rec Res	32	13	5	14	59	74	44
Garswood United Res	32	11	7	14	60	47	40
Knutsford Res	32	10	9	13	40	42	39
Poynton Res	32	11	6	15	40	62	39

Poynton Res	32	11	6	15	40	62	39
Chorlton Town Res	32	9	3	20	45	77	30
Bollington Athletic	32	7	7	18	36	78	28
Wilmslow Albion Res	32	4	7	21	38	77	19
Grove United Res	32	3	5	24	38	87	14

5-Year, One, Two, Three

Year	1st	Pts	2nd	Pts	3rd	Pts

Divsion One

1986-87	Kidsgrove Ath	52	Newcastle Town	48	Hanley Town	47
1987-88	Kidsgrove Ath	53	Alsager United	47	Hanley Town	46
1988-89	Barnton	44	Grove United	40	Linotype	39
1989-90	Grove United	65	Linotype	63	Bramhall	62
1990-91	Linotype	57	Bramhall	54	Knutsford	50

Sportscene International Senior League

First Division	P	W	D	L	F	A	Pts
Redgate Clayton	34	24	6	4	94	33	78
Stafford MSHD	34	23	9	2	71	27	78
Meir K.A	34	23	6	5	72	32	75
Milton United	34	19	7	8	53	38	64
Leek CSOB	34	12	10	12	47	46	46
Staffordshire Police	34	13	7	14	37	43	46
Norton United	34	13	6	15	53	51	45
Rists United	34	12	9	13	47	62	45
Eccleshall	34	11	11	12	44	49	44
Heath Hayes	34	11	9	14	64	60	42
Brocton	34	12	6	16	48	50	42
Audley	34	11	8	15	53	63	41
Eastwood Hanley Res	34	10	8	16	38	52	38
Stafford Rangers Res	34	11	5	18	39	58	38
Goldenhill Wanderers	34	11	3	20	47	63	36
Congleton Hornets	34	10	5	19	43	58	35
Ball Haye Green	34	10	4	20	36	61	34
Hanford	34	8	5	21	30	70	29

5-Year, One, Two, Three

Year	1st	Pts	2nd	Pts	3rd	Pts
1986-87	Rochester	46	Redgate United	44	Stafford Town	41
1987-88	Redgate Clayton	45	Knypersley Vic	42	Meir Kings Arms	38
1988-89	Meir Kings A	46	Redgate Clayton	42	Hanford	40
1989-90	Eccleshall	58	Hanford	50	Knypersley Vic	49
1990-91	Meir Kings A	54	Staffs. Police	50	Eccleshall	47

GMVC FIXTURES 1992-93

	Altrincham	Bath City	Boston United	Bromsgrove R	Dagenham & R	Farborough T	Gateshead	Kettering Town	Kidderminster	Macclesfield	Merthyr Tydfil
Altrincham	•	6/2	19/9	24/4	14/11	17/10	25/8	26/12	17/11	12/4	29/8
Bath City	21/11	•	13/2	20/3	27/3	7/11	30/1	8/12	26/12	6/3	8/9
Boston United	13/3	3/10	•	30/1	2/1	23/1	3/4	14/4	29/8	14/11	1/5
Bromsgrove Rovers	12/12	2/1	25/8	•	6/2	26/12	20/2	23/1	12/4	15/9	28/11
Dagenham & Red	27/2	17/4	17/11	29/8	•	25/8	16/1	1/5	13/3	17/10	30/1
Farnborough Town	1/5	16/1	21/11	10/4	5/12	•	22/8	10/10	5/9	24/4	6/10
Gateshead	16/9	31/10	12/1	7/11	5/9	5/12	•	27/3	12/12	26/9	17/4
Kettering Town	10/4	20/2	28/12	21/11	29/9	8/9	28/11	•	24/4	29/8	17/10
Kidderminster Har	22/8	10/4	16/1	28/12	19/9	27/2	14/11	31/8	•	30/1	16/1
Macclesfield Town	28/12	5/9	29/9	17/4	10/10	17/4	19/12	31/10	10/11	•	•
Merthyr Tydfil	5/12	31/8	7/11	19/1	22/8	19/9	13/2	23/2	2/1	3/10	•
Northwich Victoria	6/10	3/4	6/3	1/12	24/4	3/4	26/12	19/9	25/8	13/10	31/10
Runcorn	2/1	1/5	27/3	27/2	23/1	29/8	6/10	7/11	26/9	25/8	20/3
Slough Town	5/9	2/2	31/10	3/10	31/8	14/11	20/3	22/8	23/1	12/12	26/12
Stafford Rangers	10/11	19/9	23/3	5/12	21/11	3/10	10/10	19/12	15/9	6/2	20/2
Stalybridge Celtic	27/3	22/8	10/10	17/10	12/12	13/3	12/4	15/9	13/2	26/12	19/9
Telford United	31/10	27/2	5/12	9/2	20/3	12/9	6/3	6/2	10/10	7/11	12/4
Welling United	23/1	12/12	10/4	27/3	28/12	17/4	24/4	3/10	28/11	28/11	21/11
Witton Albion	31/8	13/3	5/9	22/8	7/11	20/2	27/10	20/3	3/4	2/1	6/3
Woking	3/10	5/12	19/12	31/10	1/12	12/4	21/11	5/12	20/3	20/2	27/12
Wycombe Wanderers	17/4	17/10	9/3	19/9	15/2	20/3	29/8	5/9	6/2	1/5	19/12
Yeovil Town	13/2	28/12	24/4	19/12	10/4	30/1	19/9	5/9	6/3	3/4	25/8

	Northwich V	Runcorn	Slough Town	Stafford R	Stalybridge C	Telford Utd	Welling Utd	Witton Albion	Woking	Wycombe W	Yeovil Town
Altrincham	7/11	10/10	16/1	26/9	30/1	20/2	19/12	3/4	6/3	28/11	20/3
Bath City	10/12	28/11	25/8	24/4	19/12	23/1	13/10	29/8	15/9	29/9	12/4
Boston United	12/12	22/8	26/9	2/9	10/2	17/10	26/12	20/3	28/11	9/9	27/2
Bromsgrove Rovers	5/9	3/4	13/2	14/11	6/3	3/11	12/9	16/1	6/10	10/10	26/9
Dagenham & Red.	3/10	31/10	9/2	13/2	20/2	28/11	12/4	19/12	28/12	3/4	26/12
Farnborough Town	28/11	6/2	23/2	27/3	31/10	12/12	3/11	26/9	31/8	31/8	2/1
Gateshead	10/4	31/8	27/2	2/1	28/12	3/10	17/10	17/11	23/1	13/3	1/5
Kettering Town	13/2	30/1	3/11	6/10	3/4	2/1	13/3	27/2	25/8	26/9	12/12
Kidderminster Har	1/5	19/12	5/12	20/3	21/11	17/4	3/10	17/10	12/9	31/10	20/2
Macclesfield Town	31/8	13/3	21/11	17/11	10/4	13/2	27/2	5/12	27/3	22/8	23/1
Merthyr Tydfil	13/3	24/4	10/4	5/9	14/11	26/9	26/9	23/1	10/10	12/9	2/2
Northwich Victoria	•	5/12	29/8	23/1	13/10	21/11	14/11	12/4	6/2	27/2	27/3
Runcorn	20/2	•	17/10	3/4	6/2	29/8	13/2	26/12	2/1	20/2	3/10
Slough Town	17/4	6/3	•	27/2	25/8	10/4	27/2	13/2	26/9	28/12	17/4
Stafford Rangers	2/1	28/12	27/2	•	25/8	31/8	14/11	24/10	22/8	7/11	17/10
Stalybridge Celtic	31/8	17/11	1/12	25/8	•	1/5	11/12	8/12	2/1	24/4	13/3
Telford United	30/1	16/1	7/11	31/8	31/8	•	3/4	25/8	26/9	24/4	13/3
Welling United	20/3	19/9	10/10	14/11	22/8	3/4	•	31/10	8/12	2/1	5/12
Witton Albion	28/12	10/4	31/10	24/10	15/9	25/8	31/10	•	13/2	12/12	21/11
Woking	17/10	5/9	30/1	22/8	26/9	26/9	30/1	13/2	•	26/12	7/11
Wycombe Wanderers	16/1	20/2	28/12	7/11	24/4	24/4	25/8	24/10	10/4	•	9/2
Yeovil Town	22/8	3/10	17/4	17/10	16/1	13/3	5/12	21/11	7/11	9/2	•

	Aylesbury Utd	Basingstoke T	Bognor Regis T	Bromley	Carshalton Ath	Chesham Utd	Dulwich Ham	Enfield	Grays Athletic	Harrow Boro	Hayes
Aylesbury United	•	27/10	20/3	3/10	22/8	24/4	21/11	26/9	6/2	6/3	5/1
Basingstoke Town	13/3	•	26/12	17/10	26/9	5/12	10/10	25/8	9/1	3/10	23/1
Bognor Regis Town	17/10	12/4	•	28/12	27/3	13/3	16/1	17/4	10/10	31/8	31/10
Bromley	27/2	20/3	5/9	•	23/1	21/11	26/12	6/2	22/8	13/2	26/9
Carshalton Athletic	2/1	30/1	7/11	29/8	•	10/4	31/8	28/9	13/2	16/1	17/10
Chesham United	2/12	2/9	24/10	17/4	14/11	•	1/5	20/2	12/12	28/12	27/3
Dulwich Hamlet	17/4	20/2	25/8	12/4	28/12	9/1	•	14/11	5/9	27/3	12/12
Enfield	10/10	16/1	21/11	19/9	6/3	17/10	10/4	•	20/10	1/5	13/3
Grays Athletic	19/9	1/5	20/2	2/1	13/10	3/4	5/12	20/3	•	29/8	3/10
Harrow Borough	29/9	27/2	5/12	13/10	25/8	5/9	7/11	5/1	23/1	•	6/2
Hayes	1/5	29/8	19/12	30/1	20/3	7/11	3/4	12/9	27/2	15/9	•
Hendon	14/11	31/10	26/9	27/3	9/1	7/11	27/2	28/12	28/11	12/4	6/2
Kingstonian	29/8	15/9	3/4	16/1	24/10	19/12	24/4	27/2	29/9	2/1	13/10
Marlow	16/1	2/1	10/4	1/5	3/10	26/12	15/9	13/10	13/3	30/1	6/3
St Albans City	12/4	28/12	29/9	1/12	12/12	13/2	2/1	27/3	31/10	13/3	14/11
Staines Town	1/9	28/11	13/10	6/3	31/10	27/10	29/8	12/12	14/11	17/4	20/2
Stevenage Borough	27/3	17/4	22/8	31/10	5/9	6/2	28/9	12/4	17/4	10/10	28/11
Sutton United	31/10	27/3	23/1	12/12	12/4	26/9	20/3	1/12	26/9	14/11	22/8
Windsor & Eton	13/2	29/9	24/4	13/3	6/2	27/2	19/12	22/8	12/4	17/10	25/8
Wivenhoe Town	12/12	14/11	6/2	20/2	17/4	26/8	24/10	23/1	25/8	19/9	28/12
Wokingham Town	20/10	12/12	9/1	14/11	26/8	23/1	13/2	5/9	25/8	31/10	17/4
Yeading	28/12	13/10	27/2	1/9	23/1	29/9	30/1	31/10	27/3	12/12	12/4

FIXTURES 1992-93

	Hendon	Kingstonian	Marlow	St Albans City	Staines Town	Stevenage Boro	Sutton United	Windsor & E	Wivenhoe T	Wokingham T	Yeading
Aylesbury United	10/4	23/1	12/9	26/12	5/12	7/11	19/12	13/10	3/4	20/2	5/9
Basingstoke Town	19/12	6/2	22/8	5/9	24/4	21/11	7/11	6/3	10/4	3/4	13/2
Bognor Regis Town	30/1	12/12	14/11	6/3	13/2	2/1	29/8	14/9	28/11	1/5	3/10
Bromley	7/11	25/8	9/1	24/4	29/9	19/12	3/4	24/10	10/10	10/4	5/12
Carshalton Athletic	1/5	13/3	27/2	3/4	19/12	5/12	26/12	8/9	10/10	24/4	10/10
Chesham United	2/1	31/10	12/4	16/9	20/3	21/10	30/1	3/10	21/11	29/8	6/3
Dulwich Hamlet	3/10	1/12	6/2	22/8	23/1	6/3	17/10	31/10	16/1	13/10	26/9
Enfield	1/9	3/10	13/2	7/11	3/4	26/12	24/4	2/1	13/3	16/1	19/12
Grays Athletic	24/4	6/3	27/10	19/12	10/4	15/9	21/11	30/1	29/8	2/1	7/11
Harrow Borough	26/12	22/8	26/9	24/10	21/11	20/2	10/4	20/3	26/12	19/12	3/4
Hayes	5/12	13/2	10/10	10/4	20/10	24/4	2/1	16/1	24/4	21/11	26/12
Hendon	•	17/4	6/10	25/8	6/2	24/10	29/9	12/12	13/2	20/3	10/4
Kingstonian	21/11	•	20/3	20/2	26/12	30/1	19/9	1/5	13/2	7/11	10/4
Marlow	20/2	17/10	•	21/11	7/11	3/4	5/12	29/8	19/12	1/9	24/4
St Albans City	16/1	10/10	17/4	•	27/2	29/8	1/5	1/9	30/1	19/9	20/10
Staines Town	15/9	12/4	27/3	23/1	•	1/5	16/1	28/12	2/1	30/1	13/3
Stevenage Borough	13/3	26/9	12/12	23/1	25/8	•	13/2	14/11	26/10	27/2	24/8
Sutton United	6/3	28/12	5/9	9/1	5/9	10/4	•	20/2	3/10	27/10	6/2
Windsor & Eton	3/4	9/1	23/1	5/12	5/9	20/3	10/10	•	7/11	26/12	21/11
Wivenhoe Town	17/10	5/9	31/10	26/9	22/8	3/10	27/2	27/3	•	30/9	6/1
Wokingham Town	10/10	27/3	28/12	6/2	26/9	3/10	13/3	12/4	6/3	•	22/8
Yeading	29/8	14/11	28/11	20/3	24/10	16/1	15/9	17/4	1/5	2/1	•

	Atherstone Utd	Bashley	Burton Albion	Cambridge C	Chelmsford C	Cheltenham T	Corby Town	Crawley Town	Dartford	Dorchester T	Dover Athletic
Atherstone United	•	20/3	1/1	16/1	31/10	3/4	26/12	12/9	10/10	9/1	24/4
Bashley	22/8	•	23/1	5/9	14/11	6/2	10/10	27/3	20/1	31/8	13/3
Burton Albion	7/11	29/8	•	13/3	30/1	17/10	12/4	31/10	19/9	27/3	13/2
Cambridge City	12/12	2/1	20/3	•	10/4	30/1	18/11	12/4	28/12	24/4	26/8
Chelmsford City	20/2	3/4	24/4	26/12	•	22/8	19/12	23/1	26/10	28/11	16/11
Cheltenham Town	19/1	13/2	20/2	19/12	5/12	•	29/8	14/11	24/10	7/11	10/10
Corby Town	10/4	12/12	28/12	31/8	6/3	3/10	•	16/1	28/11	5/9	19/1
Crawley Town	17/4	21/11	6/2	27/2	28/12	28/11	22/8	•	7/11	27/10	26/12
Dartford	1/5	8/9	14/11	12/4	25/8	13/3	3/4	5/1	•	19/12	2/1
Dorchester Town	30/1	17/11	12/12	3/4	13/2	27/2	5/12	25/8	16/1	•	26/12
Dover Athletic	5/9	17/10	22/8	27/10	5/1	17/4	20/2	8/9	10/4	6/2	•
Gloucester City	19/9	6/3	21/11	22/8	17/4	12/4	16/1	20/2	12/12	5/1	14/11
Halesowen Town	31/8	16/1	19/1	14/11	3/10	26/12	20/3	1/5	6/3	20/2	30/1
Hastings Town	3/10	30/1	24/10	19/1	13/10	16/1	13/2	26/12	31/8	21/11	12/4
Hednesford Town	13/2	24/10	6/3	5/12	9/1	14/11	24/4	29/8	2/1	23/1	31/10
Moor Green	2/1	6/3	27/10	28/11	12/12	31/8	13/3	3/4	5/9	22/8	16/1
Solihull Borough	14/11	1/5	5/9	10/2	23/1	20/3	9/9	3/10	17/4	6/3	19/12
Trowbridge Town	5/12	31/10	30/1	3/10	20/2	31/10	21/11	19/12	20/2	19/1	6/3
VS Rugby	28/12	25/8	10/4	1/1	24/10	12/12	27/10	30/1	6/2	20/3	5/12
Waterlooville	17/10	19/9	17/4	31/10	1/5	1/5	2/1	17/11	27/3	28/12	29/8
Weymouth	6/3	28/12	3/10	6/2	8/9	28/10	7/11	17/10	24/4	10/4	27/3
Worcester City	26/10	10/4	31/8	1/5	21/11	2/1	30/1	5/12	22/8	3/10	19/9

PREMIER FIXTURES 1992-93

	Gloucester City	Halesowen T	Hastings Town	Hednesford T	Moor Green	Solihull Boro	Trowbridge T	VS Rugby	Waterlooville	Weymouth	Worcester City
Atherstone United	19/12	17/11	23/1	21/11	8/9	6/2	13/3	12/4	26/9	29/8	25/8
Bashley	5/12	24/4	5/1	20/2	3/10	27/2	28/10	19/12	26/12	12/4	7/11
Burton Albion	2/1	8/9	19/12	16/1	25/8	3/4	27/2	26/12	5/12	1/5	17/11
Cambridge City	23/1	27/3	9/9	7/11	29/8	24/10	17/4	13/2	6/3	10/10	21/11
Chelmsford City	29/8	13/3	7/11	5/9	10/10	2/1	16/1	13/2	18/1	27/2	6/2
Cheltenham Town	28/12	10/4	6/3	19/9	17/11	21/11	27/3	24/4	5/9	25/8	5/1
Corby Town	27/3	9/1	31/10	1/1	23/1	18/1	1/5	24/8	6/2	17/4	27/2
Crawley Town	10/10	26/9	10/4	12/12	6/3	5/9	13/2	2/1	31/8	16/1	24/4
Dartford	3/10	29/8	1/12	27/2	5/12	13/2	30/1	17/10	21/11	31/10	23/1
Dorchester Town	24/10	10/10	13/3	17/4	14/11	1/5	8/9	29/8	12/4	26/12	31/10
Dover Athletic	27/2	21/11	28/12	1/5	20/3	7/11	28/11	3/10	23/1	12/12	3/4
Gloucester City	•	28/11	1/5	31/8	30/1	27/10	26/12	31/10	20/3	8/9	17/10
Halesowen Town	5/9	•	17/4	27/10	27/10	31/10	2/1	2/1	22/8	5/9	12/4
Hastings Town	16/11	24/8	•	22/8	27/3	24/4	14/11	27/2	3/11	2/1	12/12
Hednesford Town	24/4	27/2	3/4	•	12/4	22/2	10/10	7/9	19/12	13/3	26/12
Moor Green	26/8	5/1	6/2	30/1	•	10/4	7/11	21/11	24/10	3/2	19/1
Solihull Borough	10/4	23/1	29/8	30/1	26/12	•	12/4	18/11	9/1	5/12	27/3
Trowbridge Town	13/3	7/11	9/1	20/3	5/1	28/12	•	3/4	24/4	5/12	13/10
VS Rugby	10/4	23/1	20/2	19/1	17/4	31/8	22/8	•	10/10	17/11	13/10
Waterlooville	10/4	7/11	25/8	3/10	20/2	28/11	12/12	16/1	•	30/1	5/9
Weymouth	20/1	19/12	13/2	9/1	3/10	22/8	31/8	23/1	1/1	•	13/3
Worcester City	13/2	28/12	19/12	20/1	7/11	10/4	26/8	24/4	14/11	20/2	•

HFS LOANS LEAGUE PREMIER

	Accrington St	Barrow	Bishop Auck	Buxton	Chorley	Colwyn Bay	Droylsden	Emley	Fleetwood Tn	Frickley Ath	Gainsboro Tr
Accrington Stanley	•	7/10	6/3	9/1	16/9	14/10	14/11	26/12	6/2	23/1	13/2
Barrow	25/8	•	20/10	5/9	13/3	6/2	22/9	3/10	26/12	5/12	16/1
Bishop Auckland	23/9	17/4	•	24/10	5/9	27/3	5/12	14/10	16/1	12/4	9/9
Buxton	17/4	20/3	20/2	•	13/10	25/8	10/4	16/1	19/12	30/1	3/4
Chorley	21/11	29/9	1/5	27/2	•	24/10	8/9	20/3	27/3	2/1	30/1
Colwyn Bay	28/12	7/11	22/8	13/3	17/4	•	2/10	30/1	10/4	3/10	28/11
Droylsden	20/2	23/1	3/4	31/8	6/2	2/1	•	5/9	22/8	13/3	21/11
Emley	10/4	1/5	31/8	27/3	19/12	21/11	6/3	•	19/9	24/8	2/1
Fleetwood Town	21/10	9/9	31/10	1/5	23/9	29/8	30/1	13/3	•	13/2	20/2
Frickley Athletic	7/11	6/3	15/9	6/10	22/8	19/12	16/1	3/11	17/10	•	31/8
Gainsborough Trinity	29/8	27/3	24/4	15/9	3/10	27/2	9/1	20/10	14/11	22/9	•
Goole Town	3/10	20/2	2/1	12/4	3/4	14/11	20/3	15/9	24/10	28/12	27/10
Horwich RMI	19/12	28/12	30/9	23/1	10/4	7/10	1/5	6/2	31/8	27/2	22/8
Hyde United	7/9	19/9	10/4	9/11	6/3	24/4	31/10	5/12	5/10	29/8	1/5
Leek Town	30/1	17/10	20/3	22/9	23/1	12/4	25/8	24/4	27/2	31/10	26/12
Marine	20/3	28/11	29/8	6/2	28/12	8/9	3/10	20/2	6/3	27/3	7/11
Matlock Town	24/10	22/8	14/11	26/12	27/10	16/1	13/2	12/4	17/4	13/10	29/9
Morecambe	16/1	31/8	30/1	3/10	20/2	6/3	24/10	14/11	3/11	19/9	20/3
Mossley	24/4	13/2	7/10	5/12	14/11	23/1	26/12	3/4	30/9	21/10	10/4
Southport	3/11	10/4	17/10	14/11	31/8	5/12	27/3	22/8	15/9	24/4	6/3
Whitley Bay	27/2	12/9	28/12	22/8	9/1	31/10	29/8	22/9	5/12	9/10	6/10
Winsford United	5/12	2/1	6/2	4/11	28/11	26/12	7/10	29/8	5/9	14/11	24/10

DIVISION FIXTURES 1992-93

	Goole Town	Horwich RMI	Hyde United	Leek Town	Marine	Matlock Town	Morecambe	Mossley	Southport	Whitley Bay	Winsford U
Accrington Stanley	13/3	27/3	12/4	5/9	31/8	1/5	2/1	28/10	3/4	28/11	22/8
Barrow	19/12	24/4	27/2	3/4	15/9	31/10	12/4	29/8	13/10	10/10	21/11
Bishop Auckland	26/12	13/2	21/11	19/9	27/2	23/1	7/11	19/12	13/3	26/8	3/10
Buxton	20/10	8/9	13/2	28/12	19/9	1/1	21/11	7/11	29/8	6/3	31/10
Chorley	31/10	16/12	7/11	5/12	6/10	29/8	25/8	16/1	20/10	13/2	12/4
Colwyn Bay	9/1	20/3	4/11	16/9	18/11	20/2	5/9	23/9	13/2	1/5	31/8
Droylsden	7/11	13/10	28/11	17/4	27/10	19/12	15/9	12/4	28/12	29/9	27/2
Emley	5/10	7/11	23/1	24/10	17/10	7/9	27/2	28/12	17/4	26/10	13/2
Fleetwood Town	23/1	12/4	3/4	3/10	2/1	7/11	28/12	21/11	26/8	20/3	14/10
Frickley Athletic	29/9	21/11	17/4	6/2	5/9	10/4	1/5	20/2	24/10	26/12	20/3
Gainsborough Trinity ..	25/8	31/10	5/9	13/10	5/12	28/12	19/12	6/2	23/1	12/4	13/3
Goole Town	•	5/12	22/8	6/3	13/2	22/9	24/4	13/10	30/1	31/8	16/1
Horwich RMI	19/9	•	24/10	14/11	4/11	3/4	13/3	16/9	1/1	5/9	21/10
Hyde United	6/2	16/1	•	19/10	14/11	24/8	17/10	1/1	20/3	20/2	28/12
Leek Town	21/11	29/8	19/12	•	13/3	6/10	13/2	1/5	7/11	2/1	8/9
Marine	1/5	25/8	16/1	16/1	•	21/11	20/10	24/10	12/4	19/12	22/9
Matlock Town	27/2	3/10	13/3	31/8	24/4	•	27/3	5/9	19/9	15/9	30/1
Morecambe	29/8	22/9	26/12	22/8	10/4	5/12	•	17/4	8/9	13/10	3/4
Mossley	9/9	6/3	31/8	4/11	22/8	20/3	31/10	•	27/2	30/1	9/1
Southport	5/9	27/10	22/9	20/2	26/12	6/2	6/10	3/10	•	16/1	9/1
Whitley Bay	10/4	17/4	3/10	27/3	23/1	20/10	6/2	13/3	21/11	•	1/5
Winsford United	27/3	20/2	16/9	10/4	17/4	6/3	23/1	26/8	19/12	24/4	•

Fixture Diary 1992-93

Month	Date	Competition	Round
August	29	FA Cup	Preliminary Round
September	5	FA Vase	Extra Preliminary Round
	12	FA Cup	1st Qualifying Round
	19	FA Trophy	1st Qualifying Round
	26	FA Cup	2nd Qualifying Round
October	3	FA Vase	Preliminary Round
	10	FA Cup	3rd Qualifying Round
	11	FA Sunday Cup	1st Round
	17	FA Trophy	2nd Qualifying Round
	24	FA Cup	4th Qualifying Round
	31	FA Vase	1st Round
November	8	FA Sunday Cup	2nd Round
	14	FA Cup	1st Round
	21	FA Vase	2nd Round
	28	FA Trophy	3rd Qualifying Round
December	5	FA Cup	2nd Round
	6	FA Sunday Cup	3rd Round
	12	FA Vase	3rd Round
January	2	FA Cup	3rd Round
	9	FA Trophy	1st Round
	16	FA Vase	4th Round
	17	FA Sunday Cup	4th Round
	23	FA Cup	4th Round
	30	FA Trophy	2nd Round
February	6	FA Vase	5th Round
	13	FA Cup	5th Round
	14	FA Sunday Cup	5th Round
	20	FA Trophy	3rd Round
	27	FA Vase	6th Round
March	6	FA Cup	6th Round
	13	FA Trophy	4th Round
	20	FA Vase	Semi-Final 1st leg
	21	FA Sunday Cup	Semi-Final
	27	FA Vase	Semi-Final 2nd Leg
April	3	FA Trophy	Semi-Final 1st Leg
	4	FA Cup	Semi-Final
	10	FA Trophy	Semi-Final 2nd Leg
May	2	FA Sunday Cup	Final
	8	FA Vase	Final
	9	FA Trophy	Final
	15	FA Cup	Final